LANGUAGE AND LEWIS CARROLL

JANUA LINGUARUM

STUDIA MEMORIAE
NICOLAI VAN WIJK DEDICATA

edenda curat

C. H. VAN SCHOONEVELD
INDIANA UNIVERSITY

SERIES MAIOR
26

1970
MOUTON
THE HAGUE · PARIS

LANGUAGE
AND
LEWIS CARROLL

by

ROBERT D. SUTHERLAND

ILLINOIS STATE UNIVERSITY

1970

MOUTON

THE HAGUE · PARIS

LIBRARY OF CONGRESS CATALOG CARD NUMBER: 73-101966

Printed in The Netherlands by Mouton & Co., Printers, The Hague.

PREFACE

The aim of this book is to analyze the nature and scope of the linguistic interests of Charles Lutwidge Dodgson (Lewis Carroll) and to determine, insofar as possible, his basic assumptions regarding the nature and functions of language. There is need for a study which attempts to be exhaustive; for although Carroll's literary works are permeated with evidence of his interest in language, and although some aspects of this interest have been commented upon by twentieth-century students of language, the true range, depth, and ultimate seriousness of his concern (as well as the sophistication and perceptivity of his linguistic insights) have not been generally recognized. The reason for this is that Carroll did not state his linguistic notions in a formal fashion, but rather preferred to illustrate them by depicting their operational manifestations in the situational contexts of language use provided by his literary works. As this study demonstrates, Carroll's illustrations of linguistic phenomena imply specific theoretical principles regarding the nature and functions of language which can provide a means for determining his unstated linguistic assumptions. But to do so, these linguistic principles must first be inferred from their illustrative situational manifestations. Through his oblique mode of presentation, Carroll obscured the nature and scope of his interest in language; the principles implicit in his depiction of language phenomena are so submerged beneath a dazzling surface of whimsicality that, for the most part, their presence has not previously been suspected.

Since the study is incremental and cumulative in its development, I would advise the reader not to skip about on a first reading, but to 'begin at the beginning' and proceed sequentially through the topics as they are presented. Chapter 3, which gives an account of Carroll's linguistic biography, outlining the possible influences on his linguistic concerns, may be read separately, as may Chapter 2, which briefly treats Carroll's concept of language as a vehicle for play, and Chapter 10, "Word Magic". But Chapters 4-9, which present a detailed analysis of language as an instrument of thought and of communication, should be read in consecutive order.

I wish gratefully to acknowledge the permissions given me by various publishers to quote from previously published works. The extracts from *The Diaries of Lewis*

Carroll are reproduced by permission of the Executors of the late Lewis Carroll, Mr. Roger Lancelyn Green, and Cassell & Co., Ltd. I am indebted to Macmillan & Co., Ltd. for permission to quote from *A Selection from the Letters of Lewis Carroll to his Child-friends*, edited by Evelyn M. Hatch (1933), and to The Bodley Head for permission to quote from *Lewis Carroll*, A Bodley Head Monograph by Roger Lancelyn Green (The Bodley Head [London, 1960], published in the United States by Henry Z. Walck, Inc. [New York, 1962]). I also wish to thank H. Rolf Gardiner and Oxford University Press for permission to quote from Sir Alan Gardiner's *The Theory of Proper Names*, 2nd ed. (1954); John Williams and Oxford University Press for permission to use material from *A Handbook of the Literature of the Rev. C. L. Dodgson* by Sidney H. Williams and Falconer Madan (1931); and W. H. Freeman and Company and Scientific American, Inc. for permission to quote from the article, "Lewis Carroll: Mathematician" by Warren Weaver, *Scientific American*, CXCIV (1956). *The Complete Works of Lewis Carroll* (New York, Random House, Inc. [The Modern Library], 1939) – cited as *Works* in this study – is the reference text from which most of the passages from Carroll's literary works are quoted.

I also wish to express my thanks to the following persons for the direct and indirect contributions they made to this study: Professor Roger A. Hornsby of the University of Iowa for his critique of the sample of Dodgson's schoolboy Latin; John C. McGalliard, William R. Irwin, D. Ellen Devlin, and Joseph Kolupke for the helpful criticisms and encouragement they provided at various stages of the study's composition. Finally, I wish to express my gratitude to my wife, Marilyn Sutherland, for her patience and cheerful perseverance.

TABLE OF CONTENTS

Preface 5

1. Introduction 13
   1.1 Lewis Carroll's Interest in Language; Scope of this Study . . 13
   1.2 Investigative Procedure: Thimbles and Care 14
   1.3 External Sources of Data: Biographies, Diaries, Letters . . 16
   1.4 Internal Sources of Data: Carroll's Literary Works 17
   1.5 Organization of the Study 19

2. Carroll's Use of Language as a Vehicle for Play 21
   2.1 Manipulatory Play: Language as Game 21
   2.2 Functional Play: Language as a Source of Humor in Situational
      Contexts 26

3. Professional and Amateur: Lewis Carroll and the Study of Language 29
   3.1 Prefatory Statement 29
   3.2 Formal Education and Attempts at Self-Improvement . . . 29
      3.2.1 Biographical Sketch; Early Formal Study of Latin and
           Greek 29
      3.2.2 Competence in Latin and Greek; Projected Informal Study
           of Foreign Languages and Philology 32
      3.2.3 Old English: Interest in Anglo-Saxon Language and
           Culture 34
      3.2.4 Study of French, German, Russian, Italian 38
   3.3 Interest in the Antiquarian and Philological Activity of His Time 41
      3.3.1 Association with Linguistic Scholars 41
      3.3.2 The Linguistic Climate of Nineteenth-Century England . 46
      3.3.3 Interest in British Antiquity: Its Literary Reflections . . 48
      3.3.4 Interest in Etymology: Its Literary Expression . . . 50
      3.3.5 Interest in, and Depictions of, Regional and Social Dialects 53
      3.3.6 Carroll's Reading in Books Concerned with Language . 56

3.4 Professional Study of Language as an Instrument of Thought and of Communication 58
    3.4.1 Carroll as Mathematician 58
    3.4.2 Carroll as Logician 61
3.5 Summary 66

4. Signs 68
4.1 Carroll and the Problem of Meaning 68
    4.1.1 Prefatory Statement; Carroll's Understanding of the Difference Between Ordinary and Logical Discourse . . 68
    4.1.2 Carroll's Interest in Signs; His Lack of Formal System in His Semiotic Speculations 69
4.2 Of Signs in General 71
4.3 Carroll's Illustrations of Non-Linguistic Sign Situations; Their Implications for this Study 73
4.4 Of Linguistic Signs 83
    4.4.1 The Nature of the Linguistic Sign 83
    4.4.2 Differential Meaning 85
    4.4.3 Referential Meaning 89
    4.4.4 Structural Meaning 90
    4.4.5 Contextual Meaning 91
    4.4.6 Summary 95
4.5 Carroll's Explicit Statements on Language: Forks and Hope . . 96

5. The Process of Classification 100
5.1 Carroll's Definition of 'Classification' 100
5.2 Causes of Error in Classification 102
    5.2.1 A Thing's Possessing Misleading Attributes 102
    5.2.2 Errors Which Lie with the Classifier 102
5.3 Causes of Difficulty in Classifying 106
    5.3.1 Difficulties Caused by the Lack of Available Class-Names 106
    5.3.2 Difficulties Caused by Equivocal Attributes 107
5.4 Summary 111

6. Names 113
6.1 Carroll's Definition of 'Name' 113
6.2 The Function of Names: J. S. Mill and Lewis Carroll . . . 115
6.3 Carroll's Conception of Names in General 117
    6.3.1 Terminology: 'Denotation', 'Designation', 'Connotation' . 117
    6.3.2 Designation: the 'Labeling' Function of Names . . . 118
    6.3.3 Informative Connotation: The ability of Names to Convey Information About the Thing Designated 121

6.3.4 Labels Inaccurate in Designation and False in Connotations   122

6.3.5 Names Without Designative Signification; Their Defeat of
       Communication Attempts Through Non-Understanding   .   123

6.3.6 The Ability of Names to be Inaccurate in their Designa-
       tions   126

6.4 The Identifying Function of Names   128

6.4.1 General Names as Indexical Signs; the Usefulness of Names   128

6.4.2 Personal Names as Indexical Signs   130

6.5 The Informative Function of Names   132

6.5.1 The Relationship of the Name to the Thing Named   .   .   132

6.5.2 The Kind of Meaning Conveyed by Personal Names .   .   136

6.5.3 The Kind of Meaning Conveyed by General Names .   .   142

7. Nominal Definition   145

7.1 Lexical and Stipulative Definition   145

7.2 Carroll and Lexical Definition   146

7.2.1 Humpty Dumpty's Definitions of the "Jabberwocky"
       Neologisms   148

7.2.2 Carroll's Neologisms; "Portmanteau" Words, or Blends   .   149

7.3 Carroll and Stipulative Definition   152

7.4 The Arbitrary Nature of Word-Meanings; The Need for Observing
       Conventions of Usage   155

7.5 Stipulative Definition a Safeguard Against Non-Understanding .   159

7.6 Summary   163

8. Ambiguity   164

8.1 Prefatory Statement   164

8.2 Lexical Ambiguity   164

8.2.1 The Nature and Functional Cause of Lexical Ambiguity .   164

8.2.2 Multiple Definition   166

8.2.3 The Effects of Lexical Ambiguity on Communication At-
       tempts: Non-Understanding or Misunderstanding   .   .   174

8.2.4 Homophonic Ambiguity   175

8.2.5 The Inherent Ambiguity of Comparative Terms .   .   .   176

8.3 Syntactic Ambiguity   179

8.4 Contextual Ambiguity; Conscious Equivocation With the Intention
       of Deceiving   179

8.5 Safeguards Against Ambiguity in Communication Attempts .   .   182

9. Sound and Sense   185

9.1 The Import of Statements   185

      9.1.1 Introductory: Ways of Viewing Import   185

      9.1.2 The Responsibility of Speakers to Make Their Intended Import Clear   187

      9.1.3 Equivalence of Import in Verbally Dissimilar Statements   189

  9.2 Divergence of Intended and Literal Import   191

      9.2.1 The Literal Import of Statements   191

      9.2.2 Literal Interpretation as an Obstacle to Communication: Divergence Between Literal and Idiomatic Import   .   .   194

      9.2.3 The Existential Treatment of the Null Class   .   .   198

      9.2.4 Summary   201

  9.3 Carroll's Concern With Precision and Clarity of Expression   .   202

      9.3.1 Carroll's Interest in Standards of Usage   202

      9.3.2 Bruno's Deviations from Standard Usage: Errors by Analogy   203

  9.4 Obstacles to Communication Presented by the Utterance Itself   .   204

      9.4.1 Obstacles Presented by Pronunciation .   .   .   204

      9.4.2 Obstacles Presented by Unfamiliar Idiom or by the Speaker's Operating in a Frame of Reference Not Recognized by the Interpreter   207

  9.5 Carroll's Awareness of the Respective Roles of Referential and Structural Meaning   208

  9.6 Summary: The Success of Communication Attempts Dependent Upon Speaker, Interpreter, Utterance: Failures Viewed as Non-Understanding or Misunderstanding   210

10. Word Magic   213

  10.1 Introductory Comments   213

  10.2 Affective Connotations   214

  10.3 Euphemism   216

  10.4 The Sovereignty of the Word   218

      10.4.1 The Power of Language to Influence Events; Ritual and Charm   218

      10.4.2 Therapeutic Powers of Words   .   .   .   220

      10.4.3 The Affectiveness of Long, Unfamiliar, or Foreign Words   222

      10.4.4 The Tendency of Men to Grant Autonomy to Words   .   224

11. Postscript   226

Appendix A: Chronological List of Carroll's Major Works   .   .   229

Appendix B: Critique of a Fragment of Schoolboy Latin   .   .   232

Appendix C: Anglo-Saxon Letters: Tooke and Carroll 235

Bibliography of Works Cited 236

Index 239

INTRODUCTION

"I never put things into people's hands – that
would never do – you must get it for yourself."
The Sheep, *Through the Looking-Glass*
"Everything's got a moral, if only you can find it."
The Duchess, *Alice's Adventures in Wonderland*

1.1 LEWIS CARROLL'S INTEREST IN LANGUAGE; SCOPE OF THIS STUDY

Lewis Carroll's interest in language has frequently been noticed by commentators
on his work, but usually from the standpoint of its functioning to produce his own
peculiar brand of humor, or as it aids them to define the general character of
'nonsense' as a literary genre. There have also been many writers not primarily
concerned with literary criticism who have been sufficiently struck by Carroll's
linguistic insights to mention his practices and to quote him illustratively in their
own works. These non-literary commentators in many cases have themselves been
professional students of language – linguists, logicians, psychologists, and General
Semanticists. Typically, four aspects of Carroll's linguistic interest are cited: his
ingenuity in coining '*portmanteau*' words, or blends; his extensive use of puns and
syllogisms to exploit the frequent illogicality of conventional usage; his pronouncements, through the mouth of Humpty Dumpty, on the arbitrary nature of word-
meanings; and his realization, exemplified in "Jabberwocky", that the presence of
familiar signals of syntactic structures may impart to lexical gibberish an illusion
of sense. Although these four aspects of Carroll's linguistic interest have received
the bulk of students' attention, they are merely parts of a larger whole. This study
will demonstrate that Lewis Carroll's interest in language was far more extensive
in scope, and his linguistic insights far more sophisticated, than has commonly
been supposed. In addition to his delight in using language as a vehicle for play,
there is throughout his work a serious concern with the nature and functions of
linguistic signs, and with the language phenomena that create obstacles to communication.

To the best of my knowledge, there has been no previous attempt to define comprehensively the theoretical nature of Carroll's interest in language. In recent years two books have been published which deal with Carroll's linguistic interest and his use of language. The first is Elizabeth Sewell's *The Field of Nonsense* (1952) which, though analyzing Carroll's neologisms and wordplay, his diction and dialectic, does so for the purpose of defining the linguistic rules which must be observed if literary 'nonsense' is to preserve its generic integrity and avoid lapsing into poetry and dream on one hand, and into prosaic 'sense' on the other. Sewell is concerned with determining the characteristics of Nonsense; and as a consequence, she is more interested in Carroll's use of language than in his theoretical views regarding it. The second book, Daniel F. Kirk's *Charles Dodgson, Semeiotician* (1963) is a valuable first step in the direction taken by the present study. Kirk asserts that Carroll was interested in language in nearly all of its aspects; that a concern with language systems of various kinds – mathematical, logical, and 'ordinary' – is 'ubiquitous' in his works. Although his assertion is valid, Kirk limits the value of his study by confining himself to a descriptive survey of Carroll's writings, choosing merely to demonstrate the pervasiveness of Carroll's linguistic interest rather than to analyze its nature. With the exception of his chapter "Word Ways in Wonderland", in which he discusses selected examples of Carroll's "semeiotic interest", Kirk's study remains on the level of rather superficial description. His survey of Dodgson's technical works is quite valuable, for it describes a group of publications with which most readers of Lewis Carroll are unfamiliar.

With the additional exception of a few scattered articles, notably Patricia Meyer Spacks' "Logic and Language in 'Through the Looking Glass'" (1961), Peter Alexander's "Logic and the Humour of Lewis Carroll" (1951), and the relevant sections of Richard Robinson's *Definition* (1950), little has been done to analyze the nature of Carroll's linguistic insights. This study will attempt such an analysis in an effort to determine what Carroll's theoretical assumptions about language actually were.

1.2 INVESTIGATIVE PROCEDURE: THIMBLES AND CARE

Determining his notions about the nature of language is not an easy task. Charles Lutwidge Dodgson, the man called "Lewis Carroll", was an exceptionally complex personality. He possessed an active and wide-ranging mind, was receptive to new ideas and technological advances, and was profoundly influenced by books and men. Yet he balanced this radical spirit of inquiry with a stubborn inflexibility of mind, a resistance to change, an indifference to new concepts in his profession of mathematics, and a staunch conservatism with regard to religious doctrine and academic tradition. A paradoxical nature, eager to try new things, yet reluctant to let old things go. As a result of both the variety of his interests and the paradoxical strains of his intellectual makeup, there is a Protean quality about Lewis Carroll which is soon discovered by anyone who attempts a serious study of his ideas. With regard to his ideas about language, he proves to be a very slippery customer indeed, hard to grasp and harder to hold; for by perpetually changing his form and keeping his true features hidden, he is able to elude the man who would question him. He is much like Alice's hedgehog at the Queen of Hearts' croquet game: whenever Alice had the creature lined up for a sure shot through the wicket, it would unroll itself and casually walk away.

The main difficulty is simply stated. Carroll rarely made explicit statements of theoretical problems which intrigued him. Instead, he preferred to illustrate them obliquely through humorous dramatization in his fiction. It is this tendency to illustrate the operation of linguistic principles rather than to state the principles outright that has caused the true scope and seriousness of his concern with language to remain unrecognized. By choosing to present theoretical principles only in terms of their practical manifestations, he concealed his basic assumptions in such a way that readers may perceive them only through inference from particular illustrations. Moreover, since these practical manifestations of theoretical principles are typically presented as brief dramatic interchanges between striking characters in the context of a whimsical and swiftly-moving narrative, each illustration becomes a self-contained unit, and the reader tends to see it individually rather than as an integral part of a larger concern.

Carroll's explicit statements on language are few in number. When these are given in a serious context and seem to represent his views in a straightforward manner, I think they may be assumed to be 'in earnest' and capable of being used as premises upon which to base sound deductive inferences. For the most part, however, since his views are stated indirectly through illustration, an inductive method will have to be employed. Examination of specific examples will reveal the operative linguistic principles; from these, with the exercise of due caution, his views about the nature of language can be inferred.

The hazards of an inductive method are obvious. There is always the danger of leaping to unwarranted conclusions through faulty sampling and overgeneralization, and thought the temptation of extracting more from an illustration than is actually implied by it. In the majority of instances that we shall examine, I think it unlikely that Carroll was consciously embodying theoretical principles in his illustrations with the expectation that his readers would try to work them out. As a literary man, Carroll was primarily a humorist and writer of children's books. His concern with language found expression in his works as it provided the possibility for entertaining incident, for stimulation of his readers' thought, and – above all – for comic effect. In the majority of instances, he seems to have been merely exploiting linguistic phenomena for humorous effect without being self-consciously aware that he was objectifying theoretical principles. However, there are many instances where he seems to have been very much aware of the underlying principles, and was deliberately setting linguistic 'brain-teasers' for his readers to puzzle over. In these instances he is quite literally playing games with his readers, and is using his oblique statement to beguile and bewilder. In so doing, he is much like the Sheep in *Through the Looking-Glass* who never put things into people's hands: "that would never do – you must get it for yourself."

1.3 EXTERNAL SOURCES OF DATA: BIOGRAPHIES, DIARIES, LETTERS

When a scholar delves into the biographies of Dodgson and into his voluminous diaries and letters, he encounters another of those paradoxes which characterize the man. A wealth of external material is available, but there is little in it relevant to Dodgson's interest in language. Unlike many authors, who do leave detailed records of their intellectual development, Dodgson is reticent about the experiences which influenced his thinking. Since the information provided by his biographies and personal records is meager, the scholar must rely on inference to determine the possible influences which may have stimulated his linguistic interest.

The life of Lewis Carroll has been well documented by a variety of hands. His nephew, Stuart Dodgson Collingwood, wrote an 'official' biography in 1898, the year of Dodgson's death. This work drew much of its information from Dodgson's living relatives and friends, from his diaries (some of which have subsequently disappeared), and from miscellaneous papers which have since been lost or destroyed. This book has served as the basis for all subsequent biographies. One of the best of these is Derek Hudson's *Lewis Carroll* (1954), which brings together the best of what had been said before and adds much new material. Roger Lancelyn Green's *The Story of Lewis Carroll* (1951) is brief but sound.[1]

A large body of primary material has been published also. In 1933, Evelyn M. Hatch edited 170 of Lewis Carroll's letters to his child-friends; and in 1935, John Francis McDermott published the journal of Carroll's trip to Russia in 1867. Both of these books reveal much about Dodgson's characteristic attitudes and habits of expression. The most valuable publication relating to Dodgson's life to appear recently is the two-volume edition of his *Diaries* (1954), the closest thing to an autobiography that we possess. The diaries originally consisted of thirteen manuscript volumes, all of which Collingwood used in his *Life and Letters of Lewis Carroll* (1898). After Dodgson's death the diaries remained in the family's possession, and

---

[1] Some of these biographies, such as those by Langford Reed (1932), Alexander L. Taylor (1952), Florence Becker Lennon (1962), and Phyllis Greenacre (1955), attempt to prove specific theses on the subject of Dodgson's psychological makeup. Reed advances the view, now discredited, that Dodgson and Carroll represented the two halves of a split personality. Postmortem psychoanalysis is a treacherous business; both Lennon and Greenacre are too willing to support their cases with unwarranted conjecture. Mrs. Lennon's book may be recommended for its collection of miscellaneous information (though there are some inaccuracies) and especially for its success in defining Dodgson's cultural milieu. It should be used with caution. A. L. Taylor's *The White Knight* contains brilliant critical analyses of the *Alice* books.

when Roger Lancelyn Green was given permission to edit them for publication, he found that four of the thirteen volumes had been lost, probably through neglect. Of the lost diaries, Volume One probably covered the period of Dodgson's undergraduate years at Oxford (1851-54); [2] Volume Three, the period from September 27, 1855 to December 31, 1855; Volumes Six and Seven, April 18, 1858 to May 8, 1862. It is unfortunate for the purposes of this study that these records have been lost. An account of Dodgson's undergraduate years – providing information on his studies, his interests, the books he read, and the men with whom he came into contact – would in all probability have thrown needed light on the development of his interest in language.

Probably, but not certainly: for in the diaries that do remain, Dodgson is strangely silent on those topics which would seem to be the very matters on which an intelligent, diversified, and sensitive artist could not fail to register his feelings. He records the books that he reads (mostly history, mathematics, poetry, and popular novels) and occasionally criticizes them, but he says almost nothing about the creative processes involved in the writing of his own books. Time and again he merely mentions in passing that he has begun a poem, finished a poem, or sent off a pamphlet or chapter of a book to the printer. Mundane matters of book production are occasionally listed: some of his dealings with Macmillan, conferences with Sir John Tenniel, the need to call back the first printing of *Wonderland* because of faulty reproduction of the illustrations – but very little else. Unlike the journals and notebooks of such writers as Emerson and Henry James, the *Diaries* of Lewis Carroll, notwithstanding their 550 printed pages, shed very little light on the author's intellectual and artistic development. It is therefore not surprising that they contain little information about the genesis and true scope of Dodgson's interest in the nature and functions of language. For evidence of this interest, one must turn to his literary works; and there one sees only the fruits of his speculation, not the process of speculation itself.

1.4 INTERNAL SOURCES OF DATA: CARROLL'S LITERARY WORKS

As Daniel F. Kirk has demonstrated in his monograph, *Charles Dodgson, Semeiotician* (1963), an interest in language "in almost all of its aspects" is "ubiquitous" in Dodgson's writing. This interest encompasses the technical language of mathematics and symbolic logic as well as the ordinary language of everyday use. The works of Dodgson's maturity, published between 1855 and 1898, are astonishing in quantity and in variety of subject matter. He published without ceasing – books, articles, pamphlets, poems, and letters-to-the-editor. Roger Lancelyn Green's *The Lewis Carroll Handbook* (1962) lists over three hundred separate publications which

---

[2] Roger Lancelyn Green, ed., *The Diaries of Lewis Carroll*, Vol. I (Oxford, 1954), p. 34.

appeared during Dodgson's lifetime: formal mathematical treatises, study aids for undergraduates, editions of Euclid, and papers on logic; essays on systems of proportional representation, vivisection, and the working conditions of theatrical children; many volumes of poetry and fiction; mathematical recreations, satires on Oxford affairs, and original word-games. Much of his writing was educational or had some other utilitarian purpose; much was written merely to be enjoyed. This study will be concerned primarily with the latter group, since it is in Carroll's purely literary works that most of his illustrations of linguistic principles occur. The utilitarian works are, for the most part, seriously conceived and soberly written. They contain little Carrollian humor (and, as a consequence, little of his sophisticated play with language); but almost without exception they do reveal his intense concern with precise definition, strict logicality of argument, and economical use of mathematical and verbal symbols. The purely technical works imply an awareness of the abuses which language is prey to, and exhibit a realization on Dodgson's part of the disadvantages which may result from the wholesale introduction of new mathematical symbols into established systems. Discussion of the technical works will be deferred until the general treatment of Dodgson as mathematician and logician in the third chapter. However, it will be useful at this point to survey briefly the major literary works which will provide most of the material for this study.

In his earliest writings, the stories and poems which he composed in the 1840's and 1850's and collected in various 'family magazines' for the enjoyment of his brothers and sisters, an interest in linguistic matters is apparent in his frequent use of puns, archaic diction and spelling, regional dialects, and ambiguity resulting from unclear syntax. *Alice's Adventures under Ground* (written, 1862; published in facsimile, 1886) contains some matter of linguistic interest, but only a small portion of that which is found in the expanded version, *Alice's Adventures in Wonderland* (1865). *Wonderland* and *Through the Looking-Glass* (1871), written during the period of his most intensive mathematical publication, are filled with linguistic matter, and will provide most of the illustrations dealt with in this study. The strictly literary works which followed the publication of *Alice* (both books are to be understood by this term) – the numerous poems, puzzles, and bagatelles which continued to appear until his death – reveal, though to a lesser degree, a continuing interest in linguistic phenomena. In these minor pieces, however – with the exception of *The Hunting of the Snark* (1876) – the linguistic matter does not have the theoretical significance of that found in *Alice*. Instead, these works tend to reflect Dodgson's interest in manipulating language for purposes of play. As the years progressed, he devoted himself more and more to devising ingenious trifles – acrostics, word-games, anagrams, and quibbles. In *Sylvie and Bruno,* published in two parts after sixteen years of gestation (1889; 1893), there is much of this triviality. But there is also much linguistic matter of the *Alice* variety, in a considerably diluted form. The numerous puns are trite, predictable, and silly; and

Dodgson too often calls attention to them by italicizing the equivocal words. In these last works, as in his earliest, there is an interest in the representation of regional and social speech dialects, and a concern with problems of communication.

Several works seem to bridge the gap between his purely technical and purely literary publications. Some of the satires on Oxford affairs during the period 1864-74 are of this type. Though humorously conceived, they have a polemical aim. In "The Elections to the Hebdomadal Council", "The Offer of the Clarendon Trustees", "The Deserted Parks", "The New Belfry of Christ Church", "The Vision of the Three T's", and "The Blank Cheque", he vents his indignation at certain policies adopted by Oxford's officials which he felt to be detrimental to the welfare of the university and the students. Although they are brilliantly conceived and employ such tactics as puns, parodies, and allegorical fabling, these pamphlets leave a bitter aftertaste. This is not true of "The New Method of Evaluation as Applied to π" and "The Dynamics of a Parti-cle" which, though satirical, are more *jeux d'esprit* than angry broadsides. These last-mentioned pamphlets are two of Dodgson's wittiest pieces; they deal with persons and events in a quasi-mathematical fashion, and embody parodies of mathematical operations and of Euclid's definitions, postulates, and axioms.

A Tangled Tale (1885), originally published serially in *The Monthly Packet* between April, 1880 and March, 1885, consists of ten chapters called "knots", each of which contains at least one mathematical problem to be solved by the reader. The narrative, intended to be humorous, exists for the sake of the problems embedded within it. The amusing illustrations of "word magic" and communication-failure contained in this work provide some insight into Dodgson's views regarding the nature of language. In letters to his child-friends written throughout his adult life, Dodgson reveals a constant preoccupation with his correspondents' grammar, with verbal jokes, puns, and consciously ambiguous statement. In the pamphlet *Eight or Nine Wise Words about Letter-Writing* (1890), he makes several explicit comments about the ease with which misunderstanding can occur in personal letters, and stresses always the need for clarity and precision of expression.

1.5 ORGANIZATION OF THE STUDY

Although it is in Carroll's works that most of the data for this study is found, I have not dealt with the works individually, either chronologically or according to their respective classifications as 'utilitarian' or 'literary'. Rather, I have formulated a series of topics which represent his major linguistic concerns – a method which is more economical and of much greater value for providing an overall view of Carroll's linguistic theory and practice.

A word of caution is necessary. Although a theoretical concern with linguistic principles does permeate his works, Carroll should not be regarded as a scientific or even systematic philosopher of language. Since, as will be seen in the third chapter, he arrived at his linguistic insights in a largely intuitive fashion (as a result of his professional work and his being a member of an intellectual community in an age of philological ferment), it would be an error to try to derive a coherent and consistent system of linguistic theory from the data that Carroll has left us. His statements are neither sufficiently comprehensive nor sufficiently explicit to be generalized into a scheme. His notions about language were not systematically ordered, and I have not attempted to force them into a system of my own devising. The topical organization used here is merely a convenient way of treating those aspects of language which intrigued him; the categories are merely a grouping together, for purposes of discussion of those illustrations which embody similar theoretical concerns. When an illustration contains elements that would allow it to be assigned to more than one category, I treat it in only one place, giving cross-references when the circumstances seem to warrant it. The various aspects of Carroll's linguistic interests are closely interwoven, and my classification of them into topics is purely arbitrary.

Before taking up the general topics which comprise the bulk of this study, two matters remain to be examined: (1) Carroll's conception of language as a vehicle for play, and (2) the influences in Carroll's personal life which engendered his interest in language and determined the directions it was to take.

2

CARROLL'S USE OF LANGUAGE AS A VEHICLE FOR PLAY

2.1 MANIPULATORY PLAY: LANGUAGE AS GAME

The use of language as a vehicle for play is undoubtedly as old as language itself. Certainly in English it is found in the oldest literary writings. From the time of the Anglo-Saxon riddles to that of the nonsense-writers and parodists of the nineteenth century, play with language has been an ever-present and characteristic feature of English literature. Carroll had many distinguished predecessors who indulged in linguistic play – among them Shakespeare, Donne, Swift, Fielding, Sterne, Lamb, and Thomas Hood. And many of his immediate contemporaries expended at least some of their literary energies in the same way: Thackeray, Gilbert, Edward Lear, Calverley, Swinburne, and Oscar Wilde. Carroll surpassed his contemporaries, however – with the possible exception of Edward Lear – both in the frequency of his indulgence and in the range of his virtuosity.

Two separate aspects of Carroll's play must be distinguished: first, his use of linguistic symbols as mere counters to be conjured with, or manipulated, without particular regard for their potential or established conventional significance; second, his exploitation of linguistic phenomena (and of the underlying theoretical principles) to create situational humor in his fiction and to provide a commentary on the nature of language itself.

Carroll's manipulatory play with language employed the linguistic units of both speech and writing. Trained in the manipulation of mathematical symbols, and fascinated by their ability to be combined in various ways to represent the performance of significant operations, Carroll took delight in exploiting the ability of graphic and phonic forms (which, in language situations, constitute linguistic symbols) to be altered and rearranged to suit the manipulator's fancy. As forms, the letters of the alphabet, the physical appearance of individual words, and the syntactic patterns of sentence-types lend themselves to arbitrary permutation and shuffling. In one sense, Carroll regarded letters, written words, whole phrases, and sound-sequences simply as objects to be played with in almost the same manner as tokens in a game. In *The Field of Nonsense,* Elizabeth Sewell treats this aspect of

Carroll's linguistic play in detail, comparing it to the wordplay of Edward Lear. She defines literary "nonsense" as a game played with words and with their component parts.

> Words are themselves units made up of collections of smaller units, the twenty-six letters of the alphabet, and play with these lesser units is possible as well. The individual letters can be disordered and rearranged, as in anagrams or word-building games played with letter cards. . . . games of this type . . . do not depend merely upon the possibility of arranging series of letters in various ways. They turn upon the fact that certain combinations of letters bear reference, i.e. form a *word*, and the object of the game is always directed towards such a group. The result of the building or reshuffling has to be a word and not gibberish which is a group of letters to which no unit of reference is attached.
>
> (Sewell, p. 33)

In Carroll's work, graphic symbols manipulated as counters do, of course, have reference of the sort described by Sewell; if they did not, there would be no wit discernible, and hence no humor to be derived from the play. However, this reference is pertinent only to the context of play; it has no relevance to anything outside the game. An example of this type of linguistic play may be seen in a letter which Carroll wrote to Gertrude Chataway in 1878:

> There mustn't be a smile in your pen, or a wink in your ink (perhaps you'll say, "There can't be a *wink* in *ink*: but there *may* be *ink* in a *wink*" . . .)
>
> (*A Selection from the Letters of Lewis Carroll to his Child-Friends*, ed. Evelyn M. Hatch [1933], p. 105)

Another is this riddle sent to Agnes Hull in the same year:

> "Why is Agnes more learned in insects than most people?"
>
>   "Because *she* is so deep in entomology." Of course you know that 'she' is 'elle'? . . . "Well!" you will say, "And why is 'elle' deep in entomology?" Oh, Agnes, Agnes! Can't you spell? Don't you know that "L" is the 7th letter of "entomology"? Almost exactly in the middle of the word: it couldn't be well deeper (unless it happened to be a *deeper well*, you know).
>
> (*Letters to Child-Friends*, pp. 139-140)

This kind of manipulation also occurs on the phonic level, as in the "geography lesson" in *Sylvie and Bruno*. The play in this passage stems from the homophony of lexical items and place names, the puns being revealed in the spelling of the key words:

> "When a King-fisher sees a Lady-bird flying away, he says '*Ceylon*, if you *Candia*!' And when he catches it, he says 'Come to *Media*! And if you're *Hungary* or thirsty, I'll give you some *Nubia*!' When he takes it in his claws, he says '*Europe*!' When he puts it into his beak, he says '*India*!' When he's swallowed it, he says '*Eton*!' That's all."
>
> (*The Complete Works of Lewis Carroll*, Random House, The Modern Library, p. 530. [Hereafter referred to as *Works*.])

Since this manipulatory type of linguistic play is not the focus of this study, I shall merely indicate its prevalence and scope in Carroll's writing before taking up the second and major aspect of his play with language.

The alphabet fascinated Carroll. He published three word-games which involve the manipulation of letters: *Doublets* (1879), *Mischmasch* (1882), and *Syzygies* (1891). *Doublets*, the only one to become popular, requires its players to convert one word into another by serial alteration of only one letter, as in "HEAD, heal, teal, tell, tall, TAIL". The player who uses the fewest links wins the game. Carroll also records in his diary for December 19, 1880, that the idea has occurred to him "that a game might be made of letters, to be moved about on a chess-board till they form words" (*Diaries*, II, p. 392); but the game seems not to have been published.

Anagrams intrigued him. In 1856, when Edmund Yates, editor of *The Train,* wished him to adopt a pseudonym, Dodgson submitted the following for him to choose from: 'Edgar Cuthwellis' and 'Edgar U. C. Westhill', both anagrams on 'Charles Lutwidge'; 'Louis Carroll' and 'Lewis Carroll', both derived from 'Lutwidge = Ludovic = Louis' and 'Charles [Carolus]' (*Diaries*, I, p. 77). Yates chose the fourth. 'William Ewart Gladstone' becomes in Carroll's anagrams 'Wilt tear down all images?', 'Wild agitator! Means well.', and 'A wild man will go at trees.' To an anagram on Gladstone's name not by himself, 'I, wise Mr. G, want to lead all', Carroll answers, 'Disraeli: "I lead, Sir!"'. 'Edward Vaughan Kenealy' becomes 'Ah! We dread an ugly knave'; and 'Florence Nightingale', 'Flit on, cheering angel.' There are others.

In 1868, Carroll invented "The Alphabet Cipher" and "The Telegraph Cipher" (the former is reprinted in *Works*, pp. 1283-84), and was writing cryptograms to his child-friends (see *Letters to Child-Friends*, pp. 52-56). He wrote many acrostic verses on the names of children, allowing some of them to preface his books as dedications (for a selection, see *Works*, pp. 922-945). Occasionally these were complex double acrostics, or had the second instead of the first letter of each line spell out the person's name. Often his ingenuity expended itself in triviality. In a letter of 1892 to Olive, Ruth, and Violet Butler, he conceals the name of the eldest daughter in that of the youngest. "To find the eldest of the pets,/ Go search among the Violets!"

        VIOLET
        VIOLET
         VIOLET
          VIOLET
       VIOLET

                    (*Letters to Child-Friends*, p. 229)

He tried his hand at many different types of symbolic manipulation, which ranged in complexity from the satirical alphabet of "Examination Statute" (1864), based on the familiar nursery rhyme

A is for [Acland], who'd physic the Masses,
B is for [Brodie], who swears by the gases,
C is for [Conington], constant to Horace,
D is for [Donkin], who integrates for us.

   . . . . . .

I am the Author, a rhymer erratic –
J is for [Jowett], who lectures in Attic:
K is for [Kitchen], than attic much warmer.
L is for [Liddell], relentless reformer!

                (*Works*, p. 920)

to the elaborate "Four Riddles" printed in *Phantasmagoria* (1869), which consist of two double acrostics and two charades (*Works*, pp. 893-898). Alliteration is employed in his parody of Swinburne's "By the North Sea" in *Sylvie and Bruno Concluded* (1893), where the other poet's meter and stanza are used to re-tell the nursery rhyme "The little man that had a little gun". An excerpt shows Carroll's alliterative skill:

The music of Midsummer-madness
   Shall sting him with many a bite,
Till, in rapture of rollicking sadness,
   He shall groan with a gloomy delight:
He shall swathe him, like mists of the morning,
   In platitudes luscious and limp,
Such as deck, with a deathless adorning,
      The Song of the Shrimp!

                (*Works*, p. 672)

This echoes the sense, as well as the sound, of much of Swinburne's poetry. The Cockney habit of adding and dropping initial *h*'s provides some humor (not much) in the short story "Wilhelm Von Schmitz" (1854) and in "Knot X" of *A Tangled Tale* (1884). [See § 9.4.1 of this study.]

Simple reversals of letters interested Carroll; Bruno, for example, sees by just "twiddling his eyes" that 'EVIL' is 'LIVE' spelled backwards. As with letters, so with word order. In the Dormouse's story in *Wonderland*, three little girls, Elsie, Lacie, and Tillie, lived in a well: "well in", according to the Dormouse. The names of the three girls represent those of the three Liddell sisters for whom the story was told: 'Elsie' = 'L. C.' = 'Lorina Charlotte'; 'Lacie' = an anagram on 'Alice'; 'Tillie' = diminutive of Edith's pet name, 'Matilda'. Also in *Wonderland*, Alice at one point asks "Do cats eat bats?" and drowsily reverses it: "Do bats eat cats?" She later incurs the censure of the creatures at the Mad Tea Party by equating the sense of 'I say what I mean' with that of 'I mean what I say'.

Play with words as whole units finds its most characteristic expression in Carroll's neologisms and puns. Some of the former are pure gibberish, such as the Gryphon's unpronounceable ejaculation in *Wonderland*: "Hjckrrh!" – a lipogram omitting vowels. Many, however, such as those in the poem "Jabberwocky", have a strangely evocative quality, suggesting meanings where none are actually present. In *Here,*

There and Everywhere (1950), Eric Partridge analyzes and compares the nonsense words of Edward Lear and Lewis Carroll in a cogent and entertaining fashion, concluding that together the two men were the most fertile inventors of words in the nineteenth century. Sewell (1952) also gives detailed analyses of their coinages and puns. I will discuss Carroll's neologisms in Chapter Seven, his puns in Chapter Eight.

Carroll's letters to child-friends are filled with riddles, puns, puzzles, and alphabetical whimsies (we have already seen that a 'wink' may have 'ink' in it; in a letter of 1893, we find that " 'gloves' have got 'love' *inside* them – there's none *outside*" [*Letters to Child-Friends*, p. 218]). They display such peculiarities of the written word as mirror-image writing (also used in *Through the Looking-Glass* in the first stanza of "Jabberwocky"); reversed sequence of words ("For it made you that *him* been have *must* it see you so: *grandfather* my was, *then* alive was that, 'Dodgson Uncle' only the. Born was *I* before long was that, see you, then" [p. 215]); verse disguised as prose (Letters XXI and CXLIII), a device also used in the foreword to the poem "Hiawatha's Photographing" (1857): "In an age of imitation, I can claim no special merit for this slight attempt at doing what is known to be so easy. Any fairly practised writer, with the slightest ear for rhythm, could compose, for hours together, in the easy running metre of 'The Song of Hiawatha' " (*Works*, p. 856); and picture-writing in the form of the rebus (*Letters to Child-Friends*, pp. 113-116).

Carroll employs emblematic verse in "The Mouse's Tale" in *Wonderland*, having used the same verse-form, but different words, in *Alice's Adventures under Ground* (1862). In the Gryphon and Mock Turtle sequence in *Wonderland* there is a high concentration of puns: their "lessons", for example – so-called because they lessened from day to day – consisted of Ambition, Distraction, Uglification, and Derision; Reeling and Writhing; Laughing and Grief; Drawling, Stretching, and Fainting in Coils. Perhaps the richest lode of verbal wit in all of Carroll's canon is that found in the Oxford satires published between 1865 and 1874, collected in the latter year as *Notes by an Oxford Chiel*. These are so filled with verbal play of the manipulatory sort, so densely packed with *tours-de-force*, that little justice can be done them by random quotation. I can do no better than refer the reader to them for a first-hand examination. They may be found in *Works*, pp. 1121-76, and in *The Lewis Carroll Picture Book* (1899), pp. 41-159 [reprinted by Dover Publications as *Diversions and Digressions of Lewis Carroll* (1961)]. "The New Method of Evaluation as Applied to π" (1865), "The Dynamics of a Parti-cle" (1865), "The New Belfry" (1872), and "The Vision of the Three T's" (1873) show Carroll's verbal ingenuity at its finest.

I have only been able to give a faint indication of the scope of Carroll's manipulatory play with language. Although this type of play will be seen frequently in the illustrations to be discussed, I shall not comment upon it further. The second aspect of Carroll's linguistic play – that which I call 'functional' – is of more relevance to this study. In this type of play, Carroll's humor is derived from his pushing to the logical extreme the implications of linguistic phenomena observable in particular situational contexts.

2.2 FUNCTIONAL PLAY: LANGUAGE AS A SOURCE
OF HUMOR IN SITUATIONAL CONTEXTS

As a literary man, Carroll was primarily a humorist and writer of children's books. The family magazines composed for his brothers and sisters in the period 1845-1855 were humorous in nature, filled with whimsical verse and quasi-learned treatises. Although he later achieved fame as a writer of children's books, he first met the public as a humorist in the periodical press. In the period 1854-1863, he published in magazines many humorous poems and several short stories, using the pseudonyms 'B.B.', 'R.W.G.' (the middle letters of each of the names in 'Charles Lutwidge Dodgson'), and after 1856, 'Lewis Carroll'. In 1862, when he wrote the manuscript book *Alice's Adventures under Ground* for Alice Liddell, he had no way of knowing that he would become known as a children's author. It is probable that he foresaw his literary career as one of humorous publication under a genteel pseudonym, a hobby to be pursued in conjunction with his academic career. The immediate success of *Wonderland* (1865) encouraged him to write a sequel and thus determined the course of his literary endeavor.

It was primarily as a humorist that he approached the linguistic matter which he put into his literary works. Having been led by the philological ferment of his time and by his professional work in mathematics and logic to study language in its theoretical and practical aspects, he saw that linguistic phenomena presented many opportunities for humorous exploitation. While investigating these phenomena and having, perhaps, not all of the answers to the many questions that they raised, he turned them to humorous account in his writings.

I do not wish to imply that he cold-bloodedly tried to find humorous applications for the insights that he developed. This would be assuming too great a degree of self-consciousness with regard to his tendency to give operational illustrations of theoretical principles. Sometimes, it is true, he did consciously work linguistic matter into his fiction to enhance a scene or to give a striking twist to dialogue. The results are occasionally satisfying, especially in his early work; but more often, as in *Sylvie and Bruno*, they are labored and flat.

Rather than assume a self-consciousness on his part, I wish to suggest that, by and large, the linguistically-derived humor in his works is a spontaneous outgrowth of the situations and events depicted in the narrative action. It was a product of his peculiar cast of mind which, inclining toward linguistic speculation, saw in the operations of language a rich field for humorous cultivation, and which typically expressed itself in linguistic play. The following passage from a letter written by

Carroll at the age of twenty-three to a younger brother and sister will serve as an example of what I mean by 'functional play'. The linguistically-derived humor is not of the merely manipulatory sort which has just been discussed, but arises from the situational context in which the linguistic phenomena occur. The passage reveals Carroll's interest in communication-failure; it is, incidentally, the only illustration I have found in his writing of failure brought about by external interference – in this instance, the distortion of sounds through distance and muffling. Carroll is describing how his mathematical lectures are conducted for the benefit of a single student:

"It is the most important point, you know, that the tutor should be *dignified* and at a distance from the pupil, and that the pupil should be as much as possible *degraded*.

Otherwise, you know, they are not humble enough.

So I sit at the further end of the room; outside the door (*which is shut*) sits the scout; outside the outer door (*also shut*) sits the sub-scout; half-way downstairs sits the sub-sub-scout; and down in the yard sits the *pupil*.

The questions are shouted from one to the other, and the answers come back in the same way – it is rather confusing till you are well used to it. The lecture goes on something like this:

> *Tutor.* What is twice three?
> *Scout.* What's a rice-tree?
> *Sub-Scout.* When is ice free?
> *Sub-sub-Scout.* What's a nice fee?
> *Pupil (timidly).* Half a guinea!
> *Sub-sub-Scout.* Can't forge any!
> *Sub-Scout.* Ho for Jinny!
> *Scout.* Don't be a ninny!
> *Tutor (looks offended, but tries another question).*
> Divide a hundred by twelve!
> *Scout.* Provide wonderful bells!
> *Sub-Scout.* Go ride under it yourself.
> *Sub-sub-Scout.* Deride the dunderheaded elf!
> *Pupil (surprised).* Who do you mean?
> *Sub-sub-Scout.* Doings between!
> *Sub-Scout.* Blue is the screen!
> *Scout.* Soup-tureen!
> And so the lecture proceeds.
>   Such is Life."
>   (*Letters to Child-Friends*, pp. 17-18)

There is much in the narrative matrix of Carroll's writing which spontaneously gives rise to linguistic humor. The bulk of his fiction is comprised of dialogues, each of which may be conceived as a series of communication-attempts which alternate sequentially between the speakers; and the difficulties inherent in establishing communication lend themselves to humorous treatment. Moreover, the purely narrative passages are frequently devoted to his characters' involvement in linguistic processes: reasoning and solving problems, classifying and giving names to objects, testing the validity of propositions, and worrying about the nature of language.

Since this functional play with language arises spontaneously from a situational context, it goes far deeper in its theoretical implications than does the mere manipulation of linguistic symbols: furthermore, it is an integral part of the literary work as a whole, indivisibly fused with the non-linguistic matrix in which it is embedded. Without greatly concerning himself about underlying theoretical principles, Carroll simply capitalized upon the functional characteristics of language which, as revealed in general usage, offered inherent possibilities for absurdity. He saw that, at least part of the time, most people are careless in their use of language, that they often confuse the symbols with the things symbolized, invest words with a 'magical' autonomy, and fall prey, through their carelessness, to lexical and structural ambiguity. He saw that much in conventional usage is quite illogical when viewed from a vantage point outside the conventions, and realized that humor could be derived from treating these usages in a strictly logical and non-conventional manner.

In using these insights in his writing, he expressed his serious concerns through whimsical illustrations that could be enjoyed in their own right. Language thus became a vehicle for play in a more comprehensive sense than the merely manipulatory. Questions into the nature of meaning, into the character and functions of names, and into the formal structures of language which aid or thwart attempts at communication are exploited for humorous effect simply because they are capable of being so exploited, and because Carroll saw them as such. The whimsical use of language phenomena enabled Carroll to indulge his own delight in playing with language, to puzzle his readers, and – although this was not his paramount intention – to comment indirectly upon the nature of language itself.

It is this last point that concerns us most. Although such commentary was not his primary aim, the linguistically-derived humor in his works does provide it. Thus, in its larger literary aspect, the functional, Carroll's play with language provides a means for determining his linguistic assumptions: his characteristic use of linguistic phenomena in situational contexts reveals indirectly what he conceived the theoretical nature of these phenomena to be.

Before turning to a detailed examination of the topics which interested him, I shall take up the possible reasons for Carroll's interest in language and the environmental influences which may have strengthened and molded it.

PROFESSIONAL AND AMATEUR:
LEWIS CARROLL AND THE STUDY OF LANGUAGE

3.1 PREFATORY STATEMENT

In attempting to trace the genesis and development of Lewis Carroll's interest in language, we are hampered by a lack of specific information. There is little biographical material and almost no statements of his own to act as guides. The purpose of this chapter is to examine the available information and, insofar as possible, to reconstruct the development of his interest and define the environmental influences which may have fed it. The most fruitful method is to approach Carroll as a student of language, distinguishing three separate aspects of his linguistic study. The first is that entailed by his formal education and attempts at self-improvement, the study of classical and modern foreign languages; the second, his amateur interest in the antiquarian and philological activity of his time; and third, the rigorous scrutiny of language as an instrument of thought and communication which was demanded by his professional work in mathematics and logic. These aspects of his study of language are discussed in the following sections.

3.2 FORMAL EDUCATION AND ATTEMPTS AT SELF-IMPROVEMENT

3.2.1 *Biographical Sketch; Early Formal Study of Latin and Greek*

Charles Lutwidge Dodgson was born in Daresbury, Cheshire, on January 27, 1832. His father, a High Church parson conscientious in his duties and demanding of excellence in his son, had distinguished himself at Oxford with a double first in Mathematics and Classics, and had translated Tertullian for Dr. Pusey's "Library of the Fathers". He supervised Charles's education at home until the boy was sent at twelve years of age to Richmond Grammar School (1843). At Richmond, Charles was a diligent scholar and showed such promise that Mr. Tate, the headmaster, was moved to write in his first report to the boy's father:

Sufficient opportunities having been allowed me to draw from actual observation an estimate of your son's character and abilities, I do not hesitate to express my opinion that he possesses, along with other and excellent natural endowments, a very uncommon share of genius. Gentle and cheerful in his intercourse with others, playful and ready in conversation, he is capable of acquirements and knowledge far beyond his years, while his reason is so clear and so jealous of error, that he will not rest satisfied without a most exact solution of whatever appears to him obscure. He has passed an excellent examination just now in mathematics, exhibiting at times an illustration of that love of precise argument, which seems to him natural.

High praise indeed for a boy of twelve. Already apparent are those traits of mind which were to characterize Dodgson throughout his life, and the "love of precise argument" which was to bear fruit in his literary play with logic and language. Mr. Tate's praise is diluted, however, by the following, which – in view of Dodgson's later development – is particularly significant for this study:

I must not omit to set off against these great advantages one or two faults, of which the removal as soon as possible is desirable, tho' I am prepared to find it a work of time. As you are well aware, our young friend, while jealous of error, as I said above, where important faith or principles are concerned, is exceedingly lenient towards lesser frailties – and, whether in reading aloud or metrical composition, frequently sets at nought the notions of Virgil and Ovid as to syllabic quantity. He is moreover marvellously ingenious in replacing the ordinary inflexions of nouns and verbs, as detailed in our grammars, by more exact analogies, or convenient forms of his own devising.

(Quoted in Stuart Dodgson Collingwood,
The Life and Letters of Lewis Caroll
[1898], pp. 24-25)

Is what Mr. Tate calls marvelous ingenuity merely schoolboy fumbling, or is it a possible foretaste of that understanding of "structural signals" which enables "Jabberwocky" to preserve an illusion of sense despite its lack of referential meaning? There is one example of Dodgson's schoolboy Latin recorded; it bears the date November 25, 1844, and is almost contemporaneous with the above letter. The exercise is filled with errors in grammar and usage. (Professor Roger A. Hornsby of Iowa University has kindly supplied me with a critique of the exercise which analyzes the nature of the errors [see Appendix B].)

Charles entered Rugby in February, 1846. He mentions at a later time that while at Rugby he "spent an incalculable time in writing out impositions" (Collingwood, *Life*, p. 30), penalties for which his difficulties and freedoms with Latin verse may have been responsible. In the spring of his second year, he won first prize for Latin composition. At the end of 1848, he was awarded a first class in Mathematics, a first class in History and Divinity, and a second class in Classics.[1] Dodgson matriculated at Oxford in May, 1850; on January 24, 1851, he came into residence at Christ Church, his father's college. He remained in residence for forty-seven years.

---

[1] Roger Lancelyn Green, ed., *The Diaries of Lewis Carroll*, Vol. I (New York, Oxford University Press, 1954), p. 14. [Henceforward, *Diaries*.]

Only the barest outline remains of Dodgson's undergraduate years. In Moderations at the end of 1852, he obtained First Class Honors in Mathematics and Second Class Honors in Classics. The measure of his linguistic achievement may be inferred from Florence Becker Lennon's summary of the requirements for Moderations (*The Life of Lewis Carroll* [1962], p. 76):

The Honors Schools in Greek and Latin, established in 1852, gave a preliminary examination in the poets and orators, and a final one ("greats") in the historians and philosophers. Philology, ancient literature, and logic, with composition and sight translations in both languages, made up the rest of the examination. The four compulsory books were Homer, Virgil, Demosthenes, and Cicero's *Orations*; then a choice of three books from four optional groups. It was no doubt this part of the examination Charles referred to when he wrote [his sister] Elizabeth he had to cover "the Acts of the Apostles, 2 Greek plays, & the Satires of Horace." This was when he felt "almost totally unable to read at all: I am beginning to suffer from the reaction of reading for Moderations." For that examination covered, besides two-way translations and grammar, the contents, style, literary history, criticism, and antiquities of these books. It was supposed to take a year and a half of college work to prepare for "greats", but Charles, after taking a second class in Moderations (1852), gave up classics.

This final statement of Mrs. Lennon's needs qualification. It would seem from Collingwood's account that Dodgson continued his classical studies through "Greats" in the spring of 1854. Moreover, it seems that he had some difficulty in preparing for this final examination and may have felt insecure going into the test: "For the last three weeks before the examination he worked thirteen hours a day, spending the whole night before the *viva voce* over his books. But philosophy and history were not very congenial subjects to him, and when the list was published his name was only in the third class" (Collingwood, *Life*, p. 57). Whether, as Collingwood suggests, it was an uncongenial subject matter that enabled him to achieve only Third Class distinction, or whether it was the difficulties presented to him by the classical languages themselves, is impossible to say. From the available evidence, it would seem that Dodgson had always encountered some difficulty with Classics. Though unable to duplicate his father's achievement of a double first, Charles redeemed himself in part by being at the head of the list for First Class Honors in the Final Mathematical School in October, 1854.

Two years before this final triumph, he had been granted a Christ Church Studentship on Dr. Pusey's nomination after performing well in Moderations. The conditions for keeping this lifetime sinecure were that he remain unmarried and proceed to Holy Orders. Charles fulfilled both conditions, becoming ordained as deacon (his highest office) in 1861. After taking his Bachelor of Arts in 1854, he was made Sub-Librarian at Christ Church in 1855 (a post he relinquished in 1857, upon receiving his Master of Arts degree), and Mathematical Lecturer (October, 1855). After twenty-six years of teaching mathematics to undergraduates, he resigned his Lectureship in 1881.

In 1867 he traveled to Russia with H. P. Liddon and recorded in a journal his

impressions of the Continent and some of the amusing difficulties he experienced
with foreign languages. With the exception of this trip, he remained in England for
the rest of his life, making only infrequent excursions to other parts of the British
Isles. His life was placid and largely a matter of routine. He taught, wrote mathematical treatises, became one of the first (and one of the best) photographers in
Victorian England; he amused himself by writing and publishing articles and poems,
satires on local affairs, and books for children; he went frequently to plays, maintained a voluminous correspondence, followed the doings of his numerous relatives,
and cultivated relationships with a multitude of female child-friends. As he grew
older, he became increasingly obsessed with the passing of time and began to fear
that he would die before completing the literary and mathematical projects he had
planned. His diaries reflect the sense of urgency and increasing activity (as well as
a growing rigidity of mind). The entries become less frequent, less detailed, more
perfunctory. They rely more and more upon his memory for "bringing them up to
date", and in many cases consist of mere summaries of his activities for the days
skipped. The early diaries, dating from the years immediately following his receiving
the Bachelor of Arts, and continuing into the mid-eighteen-seventies, contain the
fullest entries and most clearly reveal his varied intellectual pursuits. It is to these
early diaries that we must turn for whatever information there may be concerning
Lewis Carroll's interest in language.

3.2.2 Competence in Latin and Greek; Projected Informal Study of Foreign Languages and Philology

Dodgson's performance as a student justified the expectations of his early teachers.
He distinguished himself in mathematics and did himself credit in classics, though
Latin and Greek seem to have been somewhat difficult for him. His interest in
classics did continue in later years, if only mildly. On March 3, 1855, he records
that he "spent most of the morning over a Latin Theme to be read out in Hall"
(*Diaries*, I, 42); on March 13, he admonishes himself to "Review methodically all
the books I have read, and perhaps add a new one – Aeschylus?" and to "Keep
up Gospels and Acts in Greek, and go on to Epistles" (*Diaries*, I, 43). He evidently
made some progress on this plan of reading, for twelve years later on May 21,
1867, he mentions that he has begun reading the "Epistle to the Galatians" in
Greek (*Diaries*, I, 260). During his stay in Russia the following August, he was
able to follow the religious service of the Greek Church "With the help of books,
in spite of the pronunciation".[2] And, in the last year of his life, he reveals that
his knowledge of New Testament Greek was rather extensive: forced to endure a

---

[2] From the book *A Russian Journal and Other Writings of Lewis Carroll* edited by John
Francis McDermott. Copyright, 1935, renewal, ©, 1963 by John Francis McDermott. Reprinted
by permission of E. P. Dutton & Co., Inc. [Henceforward, *Russian Journal*.] Quotation, p. 114.

dull sermon, he resorted to his evidently habitual remedy "of saying by heart passages from the Greek Testament" (*Diaries*, II, 537).

Dodgson was addicted to plans of systematic reading and frequently listed such schemes in his journal. One entry in particular, dated February 5, 1856, reveals both his compulsion to work and his need for a precise and orderly system:

I am resolved once more to make an attempt at something like a system of reading. I shall not try for regular quantities of hours: it must fit in as well as it can with the paramount work of the lecture. The plan I have resolved on is:

1st. *Mon: and Thurs: Greek.* Beginning with Thucydides – right through.

2nd. *Tu: and Fri: Latin.* Beginning with Horace – right through. In both books I shall take the rule 'at the end of a chapter review the chapter: at the end of a book review the book,' etc.

3rd. *History.* At present English. I shall no longer try to master whole periods, a feat I have long despaired of. I believe the best way is to take one single point (I shall begin with the Reformation) and get it up thoroughly, and so on. Thoroughness must be the rule of all this reading.

(*Diaries*, I, 75-76)

The entry is followed by this melancholy note of one week later:

My reading scheme is failing: it is in fact nearly impossible to do more in the day than the work of the lecture.

(*Diaries*, I, 77)

There is barely any further reference to reading in Greek and Latin. In his works after 1865, occasional phrases appear, as in "The Dynamics of a Parti-cle" and "The Vision of the Three T's" – but he seems not greatly interested in pursuing the classical languages. His reading does not appear to have been extensive; and although it is obvious that he had a moderate degree of competence in classical Greek and Latin (as well as in New Testament Greek), it appears from the available evidence that his proficiency was that of a bright undergraduate, that he lacked both inclination and will to pursue the study, that he was content (after some amount of struggle) to let classics slide in favor of more congenial pursuits.

Dodgson's youthful interest in 'foreign' languages embraced more than Greek and Latin, however. In the diary entry of March 13, 1855 already quoted, he lists in his program immediately after his intention to continue with the Greek Gospels:

Languages. Read something French – begin Italian – (I think German had better be postponed).

. . . . . .

Miscellaneous Studies. I should like to go on with *Etymology* and read White – and all Trench's books – and Horne Tooke – 2nd *Logic*, finish Mill and dip into Dugald Stewart.

. . . . .

Other Subjects. Scripture History – Church Architecture – Anglo-Saxon – Gothic.

(*Diaries*, I, 43-44)

A highly suggestive passage, coming as it does near the beginning of the first extant volume of Carroll's diaries. It reveals that linguistic matters such as etymology had occupied Dodgson for some time, in hints at the antiquarian interest that he possessed throughout his life, and it indicates the direction which his study of languages would take. It is a pity, in view of the suggestiveness of this passage, that the first volume of the diaries, covering his undergraduate years, is missing. However, this entry does provide some material to work with. I shall take up the linguistic matters in reverse order of their listing, beginning with the ancient languages and concluding with the modern.

3.2.3   *Old English: Interest in Anglo-Saxon Language and Culture*

The desire to study Gothic and Anglo-Saxon probably derives in part from Dodgson's reading of John Horne Tooke, a politician and etymologist of the late eighteenth century. On January 5, 1855, two months before the entry under discussion, Dodgson had commented casually: "Read some of *Diversions of Purley*" (*Diaries*, I, 38). This book, first published in 1786 and revised in 1798, was a pioneer work of English etymology which was influential upon two generations of British philologists who were required to give it a hearing whether or not they agreed with the notions Tooke was advancing. Horne Tooke felt that "the perfections of language, not properly understood, have been one of the chief causes of the imperfections of our philosophy"; [3] that in the search after truth and the inquiry into human understanding, into the nature of good and evil, right and wrong, it was impossible to progress very far without "well considering the nature of language", which seemed "inseparably connected with them". [4] According to Tooke, if philologists are to understand the basic signification of linguistic signs and comprehend their essential import, they must employ scientific etymology and trace them back to their origins in metaphor and allusion to natural events. Hence, Tooke stressed the importance of studying ancient languages, particularly – for speakers of English – Anglo-Saxon and Gothic.

Although Charles Dodgson acknowledges an interest in both languages two months after reading in Tooke's volume, there is no further mention of Gothic in his writings. Anglo-Saxon, however, seems to have held a special interest for him, for there are recurrent allusions to the Old English language and Anglo-Saxon culture throughout his life.

This interest stems from his being fascinated by British antiquities. As early as

---

[3]   John Horne Tooke, *The Diversions of Purley*, 3rd ed. (London, Thomas Tegg, 1840), p. 19. The book is framed as a dialogue in which the author expounds his views, answers the questions and objections of his companion, criticizes the works of previous writers on language, and gives lengthy lists of etymologies. Humor is occasionally present in Tooke's analogies and illustrations, and in some of the footnotes where he alludes to his political misfortunes and sufferings at the hands of "justice". Both in form and in method of argument (not to mention the subtle use of humor in discussing a serious subject) *The Diversions of Purley* is quite similar to Lewis Carroll's *Euclid and His Modern Rivals* (1879). I think it highly probable that Tooke's work influenced the style of argument and the dramatic form of Carroll's book.
[4]   Tooke, p. 7.

1849-50, when Dodgson was seventeen or eighteen years of age, the antiquarian bent appears in a humorous footnote to a poem written for "The Rectory Umbrella", one of the family magazines. The note refers to the great age of Croft Rectory, where the Dodgson family was living at the time.

This Rectory has been supposed to have been built in the time of Edward VI., but recent discoveries clearly assign its origin to a much earlier period. A stone has been found in an island formed by the river Tees on which is inscribed the letter "A", which is justly conjectured to stand for the name of the great King Alfred, in whose reign this house was probably built.

(Quoted in Collingwood, *Life*, p. 37)

On July 10, 1855, four months after the entry stating his intention to study Anglo-Saxon, Dodgson records in his diary:

I have an idea for a new drama for the Marionette Theatre – *Alfred the Great*, but have not yet begun to write it. His adventures in disguise in the neatherd's hut, and in the Danish Camp, will furnish two very effective scenes.

(*Diaries*, I, 55)

If he wrote this play, it does not survive. In 1862, the Mouse in *Alice's Adventures under Ground* recites history, the "driest" thing he knows; he chooses for his recitation the coming of William the Conqueror, the event that terminated the Anglo-Saxon hegemony in England.

Antiquarian interest in Anglo-Saxon culture is further revealed in the "Stanza of Anglo-Saxon Poetry" dated 1855, which Dodgson included in "Mischmasch", another of the family magazines. This fourline stanza, beginning "Twas bryllyg, and ye slythy toves", ultimately became the first and concluding stanzas of the poem "Jabberwocky" in *Through the Looking-Glass* (1871). In its original form, as found in "Mischmasch", the quatrain was carefully written in archaic characters purporting to be the work of an Anglo-Saxon scribe.[5] When he incorporated the poem into *Through the Looking-Glass*, he had added the five stanzas which recount the slaying of the Jabberwock. He also dropped the original title of the quatrain and merely called the composite poem "Jabberwocky".

The original title is somewhat misleading, for by no stretch of the imagination could the fragment be called "Stanza of Anglo-Saxon Poetry". The form, a quatrain rhyming *abab*, is not one that an Anglo-Saxon poet would have used; the word order is that of Modern English; the inflectional endings are not those of Old English; and the words, whose unfamiliarity produces their strange effect, far from being Old English nouns, adjectives, and verbs, are merely Dodgson's coinages. That he would call such a creation "Stanza of Anglo-Saxon Poetry" indicates merely that his interest in English antiquity had been sparked by his reading and that his first-hand knowledge of Anglo-Saxon language and literature was almost nil.

Although the composite poem was always known as "Jabberwocky", it seems,

[5] *Diaries*, I, 68-69.

from an incident that occurred around 1883, that some vestige of the "Anglo-Saxon" origin of the first stanza remained in his mind. The Fourth-class of the Girls' Latin School in Boston asked Dodgson if they might use *The Jabberwock* as the title of their school magazine. He graciously replied:

Mr. Lewis Carroll has much pleasure in giving to the editors of the proposed magazine permission to use the title they wish for. He finds that the Anglo-Saxon word "wocer" or "wocor" signifies "offspring" or "fruit". Taking "jabber" in its ordinary acceptation of "excited and voluble discussion", this would give the meaning of "the result of much excited discussion." Whether this phrase will have any application to the projected periodical, it will be for the future historian of American literature to determine. Mr. Carroll wishes all success to the forthcoming magazine.

(Quoted in Collingwood, *Life*, p. 274)

Though his etymological definition of *Jabberwock* is sheer fudge, his definition of *wocor* is entirely correct. But rather than assume that Dodgson knew this from a detailed or systematic training in Old English, I think we may take him at his word and assume that he FOUND the definition in a dictionary of the Anglo-Saxon language. *Wocor* is a far cry from 'wock', and the attempt to give an etymological derivation of *Jabberwock* savors of post-factum fabrication.

The most intriguing manifestation of Dodgson's interest in Anglo-Saxon language and culture – intriguing because it has never been satisfactorily explained – is found in Chapter VII of *Through the Looking-Glass*. Two of the chief characters in this chapter are Haigha and Hatta, the White King's "Anglo-Saxon Messengers". As may be seen from Sir John Tenniel's illustrations (it is not apparent from the text), these messengers are the March Hare and the Hatter from *Alice's Adventures in Wonderland*. They are dressed in the loose-fitting tunics, crossed garters, and shoes which characterize the figures depicted in the illustrations of the Junius Manuscript of "Caedmonian" Anglo-Saxon poems. Since the Junius Manuscript is in the Bodleian Library, it would have been easily accessible to Dodgson and Tenniel; these medieval drawings had also been reproduced in an engraved facsimile by Henry Ellis in his *Account of Caedmon's Metrical Paraphrase* published in 1833.[6] The reason for Tenniel's scrupulous reproduction of Anglo-Saxon costumes for Dodgson's characters has not been explained; nor, for that matter, has the reason for Dodgson's creation of the "Anglo-Saxon Messengers". In the context of Alice's dream they come like ghosts to trouble scholars' joy.

When Haigha makes his appearance, he is "skipping up and down, and wriggling like an eel ... with his great hands spread out like fans on each side". These antics are called by the White King "Anglo-Saxon attitudes", and the extended fanlike hands once again recall the figures depicted in the Junius Manuscript. Harry Morgan Ayres has attempted to explain the passage by regarding it as Carroll's playful ridicule of the Anglo-Saxon scholarship of his day. The name *Haigha* Ayres conjectures to be a pun on the word *hare* (Carroll tells us that *Haigha*

[6] Harry Morgan Ayres, *Carroll's Alice* (Columbia University Press, 1936), pp. 72-73.

is to be pronounced to rhyme with *mayor*) and on the surname of Daniel Henry Haigh (1819-1879),

who, through his Anglo-Saxon studies, was led to the Roman Catholic priesthood, and who published a number of works on English antiquities, notably *The Anglo-Saxon Sagas* and *The Conquest of Britain by the Saxons*, both in 1861. Apparently a most estimable person and stuffed with lore, he was beset by a kind of etymological madness which is still fascinating in its extravagance. One of his leading ideas is that the proper names of Old English heroic poetry are all English and have nothing to do with the Continent at all, and that this can be proved by English place names. The acrobatics in which he engages to establish this remarkable thesis might well amaze even an uncritical reader, but especially one with Carroll's love of doing strange things with strange words.

(Harry Morgan Ayres, *Carroll's Alice*
[Columbia University Press, 1936], pp. 67-68)

If this interpretation be correct – and I am inclined to agree with Ayres that *Haigh* may be incorporated in Haigha's name – a further pun on 'attitudes' becomes apparent: the physical attitudes indulged in by the messenger, and the mental acrobatics and posturings of a dogmatic scholar.

Ayres's explanation of *Hatta*, the name of the second messenger, is less satisfying. He feels that while reading Sharon Turner's *History of the Anglo-Saxons* (1799-1805), Dodgson chanced upon the statement that *Hatte* (an Old English verb meaning 'was called') was the only Anglo-Saxon surname pre-dating the Norman Conquest; that Dodgson, taking *Hatte* for a surname, used it for the name of his second messenger, spelling it with an *a* instead of an *e* to insure the reader's giving it "the full measure of two syllables". For, says Ayres, "with what joy would it dawn upon him that his Mad Hatter bore the unique authentic (as it seemed) Anglo-Saxon surname!" (p. 72).

I think that Mr. Ayres is stretching a little in considering *Hatta* to be Dodgson's distortion of what he felt to be an Anglo-Saxon surname, and not only because we have no proof that Dodgson ever read Turner's history. Since each name is, in its punning sense, a common noun (*hatter, hare*), would it not be simpler to assume that Dodgson was merely creating two nouns on the pattern of the Old English masculine nouns of the *n*-stem declension, whose forms in the nominative singular end in *a*- [*hunta*, 'hunter'; *guma*, 'man']? We have only to assume a rudimentary knowledge on Dodgson's part of Old English inflectional noun-endings; and it is possible that he acquired this knowledge – that many Old English nouns end with an *a* – through random reading, and not through formal study. What is particularly puzzling is how the Anglo-Saxon Messengers come to be in the book at all. The presence in Alice's dream of the chess-men, the characters from nursery rhymes, the talking animals, the various more bizarre creatures is easily explained. They either have their counterparts in Alice's waking experience or are the fantastic creations of a little girl's dreaming mind. But the Anglo-Saxon Messengers! They are not mentioned in the first chapter, where various aspects of the dream are foreshadowed in Alice's drawing-room. Are we to assume on Alice's part a reading of Anglo-Saxon history in her schoolbooks? Or is the presence of the Anglo-Saxon Messengers a gratuitous addition of Carroll's, constituting a minor flaw in the otherwise consistently-conceived structure of the book? Is their presence an intrusion of a private joke at the expense of contemporary Anglo-Saxon scholarship, and a reflection of his own interest in British antiquity? The question of Dodgson's intentions in creating the Anglo-Saxon Messengers is a vexed problem which will remain obscure until further information comes to light.

In spite of Dodgson's avowed intention to study Old English, in spite of the acquaintance with it that his etymological derivation of *Jabberwock* (and my interpretation of *Haigha* and *Hatta*) seems to imply, I think it highly unlikely that he at any time studied Old English in a systematic fashion, or that he ever acquired any proficiency in it. There is no mention of such a study in his diaries or letters. I think, therefore, that we may safely infer that he did not follow up his intention recorded in 1855. Of the Gothic language, mentioned in conjunction with Anglo-Saxon, there is no trace after the entry of March 13, 1855. Hebrew is the only other ancient language which Dodgson desired to learn. On February 3, 1866, he records that he asked Liddon's advice "as to getting books for learning Hebrew" (*Diaries*, I, 240); but since there is no further mention of his plan, it would seem that Dodgson never began his study of that language either.

3.2.4 *Study of French, German, Russian, Italian*

Although Dodgson seems to have studied seriously none of the ancient languages except Greek and Latin, the same may not be said of the modern languages. With regard to French and German in particular, his effort may be said to have matched the earnestness of his intention. In the program of study already quoted, he stated his desire to learn French and Italian, and German at some later time. Slightly over a month later, on April 18, 1855, he records: "This evening I began reading Tasso instead of Dante; I think I shall like it much better. Though I have only been learning Italian for three days, I can already make out the author tolerably well. I intend reading Italian, French and German at Oxford" (*Diaries*, I, 46). Italian is mentioned only once more, on July 24, 1856, when he casually says that he is "taking up" Italian and Natural Botany in a capacity subordinate to his regular work (*Diaries*, I, 88). He probably did not continue with it.

In French, he evidently did not make much progress from 1855 to 1867. Or, if we assume that he had a limited competence in reading or speaking French at the time of the earlier diary entries, it would seem that by 1867 he had become rusty. On June 24 of that year, shortly before leaving for the Continent with Liddon, he mentions that he "went to [Jules?] Bue for my fourth lesson in French which I am getting up in the hope of visiting the Paris Exhibition" (*Diaries*, I, 260). The reference is probably to spoken French. While he was in Russia, this knowledge of French proved serviceable, for since neither he nor Liddon could understand more than a few words of Russian, they had to rely upon this third language (and occasionally a fourth, German) to communicate with the natives. Dodgson's proficiency in spoken French was not very great, however; for in Paris, on their return journey, he records that while he was visiting the Convent of S. Thomas, one of the Sisters spoke to him in very fluent French – "much of which was lost on me" (*The Russian Journal*, ed. John Francis McDermott [New York, 1935], p. 120).

Dodgson evidently did not progress very far in his study of German after his postponing it in 1855. His knowledge of spoken German during the Continental tour of 1867 was limited (though it is possible that his reading ability was greater than his proficiency in speaking it). For example, in Berlin,

I also met ... a very pleasant German gentleman, & had a sort of conversation with him: he was most good-natured in guessing at my meaning, & helping me out with my sentences of what would have been very bad German, if it had deserved the name of German at all. Nevertheless, the German I talk is about as good as the English I hear – at breakfast this morning, for which I had ordered some cold ham, the waiter, when he had brought the other things, leant across the table, & said to me in a confidential under-tone "I bring in minutes ze cold ham."

(*Russian Journal*, pp. 81-82)

Shortly before he began his trip, Antoine Zimmermann offered to make a German translation of *Alice's Adventures in Wonderland*. Before giving his consent, Dodgson asked her to submit specimen translations of two passages: the page preceding the Mouse's Tale and the poem "Alice's Evidence" (*Diaries*, I, 257). The selections reveal that Dodgson was aware of the difficulty of translating poetry, puns, and intricate wordplay from the idiom of one language into that of another; for the first passage involves a pun on the words *tale* and *tail*, and the second contains much juggling with the cases of pronouns:

> They told me you had been to her,
>   And mentioned me to him:
> She gave me a good character,
>   But said I could not swim.
>
> . . . . . .
>
> I gave her one, they gave him two,
>   You gave us three or more;
> They all returned from him to you,
>   Though they were mine before.
>
> . . . . . .
>
> My notion was that you had been
>   (Before she had this fit)
> An obstacle that came between
>   Him, and ourselves, and it.
>
> (*Works*, p. 126)

But monitoring a translator's rendering of English into German does not necessarily mean that his own competence was very great.[7] That it was in fact not, is borne out by three diary entries for 1881 which throw further light on his attainments in both French and German:

July 24: Learn Prendergast's German hand-book and go through the French one again. Also do some double translation from [George Sand's] *La Petite Fadette*.

Aug. 11: Arranged with M. Talon to have two lessons a week in French. I want, if possible, to learn *talking* it.

Oct. 6:   [summing up his progress since July 24] *German:* – a little. *French:* – have made considerable progress, I hope.

(*Diaries*, II, 398-399)

No further mention of either language is found in the diaries. That he earnestly desired to achieve competence in French and German is apparent from his dogged perseverance in studying them intermittently for the better part of thirty years. But it is obvious from the record that he made little progress in learning these relatively simple Continental languages between 1855 and 1881. And although he still had seventeen years of life before him, by 1881 his greatest books – and those which most clearly reveal his fascination with language – had been written.

Russian seems to have interested him, but he never studied it. During his trip with Liddon he reveals a tourist's concern with Russian words, making lists of them with their English equivalents in his journal. In a letter written to Maud Standen in 1890, apparently when she was making a trip to Russia, Dodgson asks her to write him girls' names

in Russ – (in printed capitals, please: the *written* Russ bothers me) with the pronunciation. I used to know the alphabet pretty well, but that was when I went to Russia in 1867, and I'm beginning to forget now.

(Quoted in Florence Becker Lennon,
The Life of Lewis Carroll [1962], p. 184)

Although there is ample evidence that Dodgson was quite interested in modern European languages, it is apparent that his reading and speaking proficiency in French, German, Italian, and Russian was slight. Whether, in view of this interest, his failure to master all or any of these foreign languages should be ascribed to lack of time, motivation, or facility is open to question: probably to a combination of all three.

---

[7] For an interesting account of Dodgson's supervision of the early translations, see Warren Weaver, *Alice in Many Tongues* (University of Wisconsin Press, 1964), pp. 31-52. Dodgson's statements regarding the French and German translations, drawn from his correspondence with Macmillan's, his publisher, support my contention that his competence in these languages was slight.

3.3 INTEREST IN THE ANTIQUARIAN AND PHILOLOGICAL ACTIVITY OF HIS TIME

3.3.1 *Association with Linguistic Scholars*

Dodgson's postgraduate contact with philologists and other professional students of language such as grammarians and translators was fairly limited, and probably not such that he would have extensively discussed linguistic matters with them. Once again we must rely upon his biographies and diaries; and these sources, being highly selective and sketchy, do not provide much information about the subjects he discussed on walks with friends, or in the context of after-dinner conversation and chats with colleagues in the common room.

Dodgson did know many professors of foreign languages, both ancient and modern, and was acquainted with students of Sanskrit and Anglo-Saxon. But in most cases it would seem that his relationships with them were brief and casual, and largely a function of Oxford social life. He frequently sallied forth from Christ Church to dine with men from other colleges, and in so doing met a wide variety of people. Many of these are mentioned in his diaries: once, twice, several times – but rarely is anything said about what was discussed on the occasion. For example, he dined with Thomas H. Tristram, Boden Sanskrit Scholar at Lincoln College, on more than one occasion. At one of these parties there were also present Mark Pattison and "a Mr. Walesby" – probably Francis Pearson Walesby, formerly Professor of Anglo-Saxon, but at the time of the recorded meeting (February 10, 1856), a "coach" in law (*Diaries*, I, 77). On August 3, 1869, Dodgson records that he attended a dinner at which Ingram Bywater was present, a man later famous for his translation of Aristotle's *Poetics*; at that time Bywater was a Fellow of Exeter, but he later became Student of Christ Church and Regius Professor of Greek. A meeting with W. E. Jelf, author of a Greek grammar used widely in the schools, is recorded on June 5, 1871; Jelf on this occasion "started, and maintained a long theological talk on Rome, etc." (*Diaries*, II, 299). There were undoubtedly many other men of this type with whom Dodgson associated during his residence at Oxford; but it is impossible, from the scanty information that Dodgson has provided, to know how much he may have discussed linguistic matters with them. It should be remembered that in a social context with relatively casual acquaintances there always would have been other topics to discuss as well: photography, politics, Oxford reforms, teaching, boating, mathematics, logic, the theater, vivisection, and – inevitably – colleagues.

Not all of Dodgson's contacts with students of language were of the casual sort just described. He knew several classical scholars at rather close range, such men, for example, as Thomas Gaisford, Regius Professor of Greek and Dean of Christ Church, who died in 1855, the year following Dodgson's graduation. But, judging from his diary entry recording the dean's death, Dodgson seems not to have known him particularly well.[8] Gaisford's successor as Dean of Christ Church was Henry George Liddell, co-author with Dr. Robert Scott of the famous *Greek Lexicon* (1843) and father of Alice, for whom Carroll wrote his two finest books. In the 1860's, Dodgson was a frequent visitor at Liddell's house; not, however, to cultivate the dean, who must have seemed rather cold and aloof to the young mathematics lecturer, but to photograph his beautiful children, and to arrange diversions for them. Dodgson's continual presence at the Deanery became something of a nuisance; as he came to be more and more underfoot (and Mrs. Liddell began to question the propriety of his attentions to her daughters), his relations with Alice's parents became strained. The dean was an ambitious man with radical ideas for reforming Oxford's medievalisms; his liberal tendencies clashed noisily with Dodgson's fundamental conservatism, and after Dodgson's satirical attacks on his reforms at Christ Church in the late 1860's and 1870's, their relationship became quite distant and formal.

Dodgson was acquainted with Benjamin Jowett, successor to Gaisford as Regius Professor of Greek, translator of Plato, and Master of Balliol College; but it is extremely unlikely that they were on close enough terms to have had much conversation. For one thing, Jowett's unorthodox religious views would have alienated Dodgson; for another, Dodgson was a declared member of the Christ Church opposition to the endowment of the Regius Professorship held by Jowett after 1855. In the long controversy that raged over the raising of Jowett's salary, Dodgson did not keep silent. On November 20, 1861, he records:

Promulgation, in Congregation, of the new statute to endow Jowett. The speaking took up the whole afternoon, and the two points at issue, the endowing of a *Regius* Professorship, and the countenancing of Jowett's theological opinions, got so inextricably mixed up that I rose to beg that they might be kept separate. Once on my feet, I said more than I at first meant, and defied them ever to tire out the opposition by perpetually bringing the question on. . . . This was my first speech in Congregation.

(*Diaries*, I, 165-166)

In 1865, the year that saw Jowett's salary as Regius Professor finally raised from the £40 per annum established in the reign of Henry VIII to a more realistic sum of £500, Dodgson published his satire on the proceedings and on the personalities involved – "The New Method of Evaluation as Applied to π". Though little bitterness is to be found in the pamphlet, and the controversy is treated "mathematically" with brilliant wit, the satire undoubtedly grated on the nerves of the long-suffering Jowett, who had put up with a good deal of "nonsense" for more than ten years. The last entry in Dodgson's diary referring to Jowett dates from 1883, when the Greek Professor had become Vice-Chancellor of Oxford:

March 1. Called on the Vice-Chancellor (Jowett) at his request, to speak about the backs I wish to give to the seats in the gallery at St. Mary's.

(*Diaries*, II, 414-415)

[8]   *Diaries*, I, 51 (June 2, 1855).

Thus it seems unlikely that Dodgson and Jowett were at all close or had much to say to each other – particularly on the subject of philology.

Dr. Robert Scott, Dean of Rochester and co-author with Liddell of the *Greek Lexicon*, published a fine German translation of "Jabberwocky" in 1872, claiming that the German version was the original of Dodgson's poem. Delighted with this "German Ballad", Dodgson presented Scott with a copy of *The Hunting of the Snark* in 1876. In an undated letter (perhaps of 1872), Scott writes to Dodgson:

Are we to suppose, after all, that the Saga of Jabberwocky is one of the universal heirlooms which the Aryan race at its dispersion carried with it from the great cradle of the family? You must really consult Max Müller about this. It begins to be probable that the *origo originalissima* may be discovered in Sanscrit, and that we shall by and by have a *Iabrivokaveda*. The hero will turn out to be the Sun-god in one of his *Avatars*; and the Tumtum tree the great ash *Ygdrasil* of the Scandinavian mythology.

(Quoted in Collingwood, *Life*, p. 143)

Scott is thus able to joke with Dodgson about Indo-European linguistics and comparative mythology, a fact which suggests that the two men were known and kindly disposed to each other, and that Dodgson was familiar with some of the general climate in comparative philology.

Four men deserve special mention since Dodgson's association with them extended over a period of years. The first, Robert Gandell, was Professor of Arabic and Chaplain of Corpus Christi College. On November 30, 1866, Dodgson lunched with the Gandells in order to show Mrs. Gandell how to mount photographs (*Diaries*, I, 248). Nearly twelve years later (March 12, 1878) he records that he dined with the Gandells and taught the party his game of "Word-Links", which was later to be published as *Doublets* (*Diaries*, II, 369).

John Earle, whose election to the Anglo-Saxon Professorship Dodgson records on October 17, 1876 (*Diaries*, II, 356), was a friend long before his daughter Beatrice became one of the more favored child-friends. Earle dined with Dodgson on May 17, 1877, the year that the first edition of his Anglo-Saxon primer was published (*Diaries*, II, 363). After meeting Beatrice in 1884, Dodgson frequently mentions her in his diaries, but not her father. She remained a close friend into the 1890's. How close Dodgson's relations were with Earle, and to what degree the professor may have stimulated his interest and satisfied his curiosity with regard to etymology and Anglo-Saxon language and culture, remains obscure.

Another of Dodgson's relationships that continued for a number of years was that with Sir Monier Monier-Williams, who was elected Boden Professor of Sanskrit in 1860 to the exclusion of the more famous (and to some minds more qualified) Friedrich Max Müller. The first meeting of Dodgson with Monier-Williams occurred on May 1, 1866. The true reason for his desire to meet the Sanskrit scholar may be inferred from the diary entry for that day:

Dined at Professor Monier Williams's. We had each called on the other twice, but never met before. I thought him pleasant and Mrs. Williams particularly so. Also I saw the little

Ella whom I had noticed before and wished to photograph. There was a large party.

(Diaries, I, 242)

On May 24, Dodgson succeeded in photographing Ella Monier-Williams, and she became established as one of his child-friends. The final mention of Monier-Williams occurs on May 5, 1879:

Dined with the Monier Williams. The party occupied themselves, most of the evening, with working 'Doublets'.

(Diaries, II, 379)

Did Dodgson's association with a noted Sanskrit scholar provide him with specific information regarding Indo-European philology? Once again, as in the case of Gandell (Arabic) and Earle (Anglo-Saxon), there is no recorded proof that it did. But we may conjecture that linguistic scholars who would submit to playing Dodgson's word-games might easily have discussed philological matters with him. Monier-Williams was in the process of publishing many scholarly studies during the years that Dodgson was in personal contact with him. His reputation had long been established when Dodgson met him. He had made translations of classical Sanskrit, had published a Sanskrit grammar in 1846 (which reached its fourth edition in 1876), a Sanskrit manual of composition (1862), and a Sanskrit-English Dictionary (1872). It is most probable that Dodgson would have learned something – if only very little – about Sanskrit and about comparative philology in general during his association with Monier-Williams.

It is even more probable that such was the case during Dodgson's association with Max Müller, the noted German philologist and orientalist. The first mention of Max Müller occurs on February 16, 1863 (Diaries, I, 192), when Dodgson records meeting him at dinner. Four years later, on May 30, 1867, he records that Müller brought his wife and two daughters to be photographed (Diaries, I, 260). Dodgson dined with the Müllers on April 30, 1873 (Diaries, II, 321) and met them while dining at the Symonds' on February 6, 1874 (Diaries, II, 327). However friendly their relations may have been between 1863 and 1874, it would seem that Dodgson and Müller drifted apart as a result of one of those internal disputes that characterized Oxford in the mid-nineteenth century.

Müller had been appointed to the new Chair of Comparative Philology in 1868. In 1876, he retired from active duty to pursue his oriental studies, and a deputy was appointed to take over the duties of the professorship at half of Müller's salary. Dodgson felt that the deputy was being treated unfairly, and – as might be expected – said so in print. The relevant diary entries are quite interesting:

Feb: 3   [1876] I wrote, and took to the University Press to be printed, a paper on a subject which I first heard of last night, the Decree which is to be proposed to Convocation on the 15th in order to allow Professor Max Müller to pursue Indian study without interruption, to appoint a Deputy on half the salary. (The other half will be virtually a pension, and the Deputy will be virtually a new Professor).

Feb: 5   The paper on *The Professorship of Comparative Philology* came out in the middle of the day.

Feb: 12   Wrote a second paper about the Decree.

Feb: 15   Sent the [third] paper to all Common Rooms, and had copies also distributed at the door of the Convocation-house. I had not meant to speak, but the advocates of the Decree persisted so much in praising Max Muller, and ignoring the half-pay of the Deputy that I rose to ask them to keep more to the point. The Decree was carried by 94 to 35.

(Diaries, II, 349-350)

It is perhaps significant with regard to their subsequent relations that this entry contains the last mention of Müller to be found in Dodgson's *Diaries*. Both men continued to live at Oxford until the end of the century, and Müller's massive editorial project of publishing the "Sacred Books of the East" was still before him. The diary entry of February 15 is strangely reminiscent of the one, fifteen years earlier, which records Dodgson's speech in Congregation opposing the Christ Church endowment of Jowett's salary.

Yet the diaries indicate that Dodgson's relations with Müller were congenial between 1863 and 1876. There is every probability that Dodgson knew the German scholar before the first diary entry which mentions his name, for Müller had been made a member of Christ Church in 1851, shortly after his arrival in England. Moreover, since Dodgson in the 1850's was very much interested in celebrities, he would probably have sought Müller out. Müller's scholarly reputation in England was considerable by mid-century. As A. A. Macdonell says in his article on Müller in the *Dictionary of National Biography, Supplement*, III (London, 1901), p. 155:

When he began his career, Vedic studies were in their infancy, and he had the good fortune to become the first editor of the 'Rigveda', the most important product of ancient Indian literature. Again, nothing was known about comparative philology in England when he came over to this country [1846]; being the first in the field, he introduced and popularised the new science, and was soon regarded as its chief exponent.

There is no doubt that prolonged association with such a man as Müller – even on a purely social level – would have proved stimulating to a man of Dodgson's catholic interests. Dodgson's awareness of the nature and importance of Müller's studies is implied in the letter he received from Dr. Robert Scott on the subject of the Jabberwock's Indo-European origin.

Before Max Müller's coming to England there had been only tentative efforts on the part of English scholars to study the Indo-European languages in a systematic manner. In the eighteenth century an increasing interest in the scientific study of language had produced such books as Lord Monboddo's *Of the Origin and Progress of Language*, James Harris' *Hermes*, and John Horne Tooke's *Diversions of Purley*. Tooke was one of the first to realize the importance of a study of Gothic and Anglo-Saxon for students of English, and his book stimulated interest in developing a scientific study of etymology. Sir William Jones was one of the first to see the grammatical similarities of Sanskrit to Greek and Latin, and his investigations in the eighteenth century prepared the ground for the comparative study of languages during the nineteenth. Max Müller, having studied under Franz Bopp in Germany, was of the second generation of comparative philologists. A specialist in Sanskrit, he concentrated on Vedic studies and produced his monumental edition of the "Rigveda" (a labor which occupied him from 1859 to 1873). He came to Oxford in 1848, was made full Taylorian Professor of Modern European Languages in 1854 (the year in which Charles Dodgson received the Bachelor of Arts degree), unsuccessfully opposed Monier-Williams for the appointment to the Boden Professorship of Sanskrit in 1860, and became the first Professor of Comparative Philology in 1868. Müller brought with him to England the knowledge and analytic methods of Continental scholars. Once he was established at Oxford, he began to publish and lecture widely, popularizing linguistic science and stimulating considerable interest in ancient Indian culture.[9] Thus Müller was instrumental in bringing to fruition the seeds of a popular interest in the history of language which had been planted in English soil by earlier, less scientific investigators such as Hobbes, Locke, Wilkins, Samuel Johnson, Lord Monboddo, Sir William Jones, James Harris, John Horne Tooke, and the numerous antiquarians who had concerned themselves with Anglo-Saxon and Anglo-Norman culture. It was through the research of such men as Liddell and Scott, Daniel Henry Haigh, John Earle, Monier-Williams, and Max Müller that a favorable climate was established in England for the scientific study of language, and a channel opened for the influx of Continental linguistic scholarship.

3.3.2 The Linguistic Climate of Nineteenth-Century England

Charles Dodgson's association with Max Müller – casual though it may have been – certainly gave him an exposure to current developments in comparative philology. But there was a general interest in language prevalent in England before Müller's arrival which developed independently of whatever influence he may have exerted in making the public aware of the historical study of languages.

---

[9] Max Müller's publications are extraordinary both in quantity and scope. During the period of Dodgson's probable association with him, he published, in addition to the volumes of the "Rigveda", a history of Vedic literature (1859) and two series of lectures on "The Science of Language" (1861 and 1863), which aroused a great deal of interest in England in the "new" science of comparative philology. Besides these works he published translations of Sanskrit writings, Sanskrit grammars, books on comparative mythology and religion, miscellaneous literary essays, and – after Dodgson's break with him – a group of lectures on "The Science of Thought" (1887) which stress the inseparability of thought and language. Much of Müller's work is outdated by modern estimate; but his influence upon the development of modern comparative mythology, comparative religion, and general anthropology is extensive. There is no evidence that Dodgson ever read any of Müller's general works on language, but this of course doesn't prove that he didn't. It is likely that Dodgson did obtain some information of a general linguistic nature through his personal association with Müller.

As Arthur G. Kennedy has pointed out in his article "Odium Philologicum, or, A Century of Progress in English Philology", in the *Stanford Studies in Language and Literature*, ed. Hardin Craig (Stanford, 1941), pp. 11-27, the period 1834-1900 was one of ferment in English linguistic science. In 1834, two years after Dodgson's birth, a furor arose between the Anglo-Saxonists of Oxford and Cambridge on the subject of the proper method of studying Anglo-Saxon. The battle was joined between "the patriotic philological Tories and those radical scholarly Whigs, who had become contaminated by the 'upstart' philological science of Denmark and Germany" (p. 12). John Mitchell Kemble, who had studied with the brothers Grimm in Göttingen in 1831, made caustic remarks about English Anglo-Saxon scholarship in his laudatory review of Benjamin Thorpe's *Analecta Anglo-Saxonica,* "a first book for students" (1834), and touched off a controversy which must have been remembered twenty years after, when Dodgson was taking his degree. Kemble praised Danish and German philological scholarship and denounced that which was prevalent in England; James Ingram, former Rawlinson Professor of Anglo-Saxon at Oxford, wrote a letter to *The Gentleman's Magazine* denouncing Kemble. Thomas Wright, siding with Ingram, patriotically blasted German scholarship in his own letter to the magazine and denounced Kemble and Kemble's edition of *Beowulf* (published 1833). A correspondent who signed himself "M. N." defended Kemble and Thorpe and admonished their detractors to study the German methods of research to test their merits. From this point the controversy spread, involving more and more people; and thus the numerous readers of *The Gentleman's Magazine,* at least, were made aware in the 1830's of the current state of English Anglo-Saxon studies.

In the 1850's and 1860's there was another pitched battle, this time on the question of standards of English usage. As always in disputes concerned with grammar and usage, the opposing forces were manned by the conservative purists and the "permissive" students of style. The major combatants in this controversy were Henry Alford, Dean of Canterbury, who attempted to defend "the Queen's English" and George Washington Moon, who adopted a less prescriptive attitude. From an exchange of letters in the magazine *Good Words*, the antagonists advanced to the publication of books in 1864. According to Arthur Kennedy, after the books began to attract attention, "reviewers began to take sides in the controversy, so that gradually the discussion assumed a national character, and ultimately became almost international" (p. 21). Alford's book reached a fifth edition in 1880; Moon's book an eleventh edition in 1878. Charles Dodgson was undoubtedly aware of the controversy; but he nowhere mentions it, and it is useless to speculate as to which of the two positions he would have espoused. He was conservative with regard to usage (as may be seen in his frequent admonitions to his child-friends to be "correct" in their grammar), but he also shows in his own writing a certain freedom in handling conventional syntax: loosely-structured periodic sentences, for example, with independent clauses joined by colons. His frequent use of neologisms and his putting substandard English into the mouths of certain of his fictional characters is the result of his striving for humor and his attempt to give a realistic portrayal of the lower social classes. Probably he would have sided with Alford and condemned Moon as being too permissive. It is impossible to say. Certainly Dodgson took a keen interest in the history of English and its standards of current usage: his own writing, with the exception of the idiosyncratic punctuation mentioned above and the dismal baby talk of Bruno in his last major work of fiction, is invariably "correct" and in the best possible taste.

In nineteenth-century England there was, in addition to a growing awareness of comparative Indo-European philology, an increasing interest in etymology, in the historical development of languages, in the shift of word-meanings, and in the theoretical study of the nature and functions of language in general. Understandably, Englishmen were primarily concerned with their native tongue. As a result of the etymological research of such men as Tooke, and of the eighteenth-century study of English antiquities, Englishmen turned increasingly to a study of their nation's past. Reflections of this may be seen in the growing importance of Anglo-Saxon studies, in Sir Walter Scott's re-creation of historical settings, in the collecting of medieval ballads (and in the conscious imitation of them practiced by nineteenth-century poets), in the founding of the Early English Text Society (1864), in the compilation of the *New English Dictionary on Historical Principles* at Oxford (1858 and following), in agitation for spelling reform, and in the increased attention given to the indigenous Celtic languages and to the varieties of English dialects.

Charles Dodgson's life spanned the period of greatest linguistic ferment (1832-1898), and evidence appears throughout his work that he was aware of, and influenced by, the currents and cross-currents in the air about him.

3.3.3 *Interest in British Antiquity: Its Literary Reflections*

Dodgson had a keen, though dilettantish, interest in British antiquities. He was a subscriber to *Notes and Queries* and read many books on English history. His interest in the Anglo-Saxon period has already been discussed (§ 3.2.3); but other aspects of British antiquity intrigued him as well, particularly the literary styles and modes of earlier centuries. Much of his own literary work reflects this antiquarian interest.

He took delight in loosely imitating archaic styles of writing. In 1858, using the pseudonym "Edgar Cuthwellis", he wrote for the daughters of Archbishop Longley *The Legend of Scotland*, a prose work in "late Middle English" purporting to have been written in 1325 (much too early a date for the style of writing he employs). "The Vision of the Three T's" (1873) imitates the style of Isaak Walton's seventeenth-century English. Many of the early poems he wrote for the "family magazines" and for humorous periodicals such as *The Train* and *The Comic Times* are cast into ballad form, and many make use of archaic diction and spelling. Particularly good examples of this quasi-antiquarian experimentation are the "Stanza of Anglo-Saxon Poetry" (1855) already discussed; "The Two Brothers" (1853), a ballad employing Northern dialect; "Ye Fatalle Cheyse" (about 1850), a ballad in "medieval Scots" beginning

> Ytte wes a mirke an dreiry cave,
>   Weet scroggis owr ytte creepe
> Gurgles withyn ye flowan wave
>   Throw channel braid an deip
>
> Never withyn that dreir recesse
>   Wes sene ye lyghte of daye,
> Quhat bode azont yt's mirkinesse
>   Nane kend an nane mote saye . . .[10]

and finally, "Ye Carpette Knyghte" (1855), an imitation of "late Middle English" which begins:

> I have a horse – a ryghte goode horse –
>   Ne doe Y envye those
> Who scoure ye playne yn heady course
>   Tyll soddayne on theyre nose
> They lyghte wyth unexpected force –
>   Yt ys – a horse of clothes. . . .
>   (Works, pp. 855-856)

I say "quasi-antiquarian" because Dodgson in these early works is not attempting to produce accurate imitations of medieval verse. As Daniel F. Kirk has suggested, Dodgson is abstracting certain qualities from archaic verse and exploiting them for purposes of whimsy.[11] In the two poems quoted, he is exploiting the external features of archaic spelling and diction to create poems which in themselves are hardly "medieval". Rather than assume that his stimulus for writing "medieval" poetry stemmed from his historical studies or his acquaintance with original texts, I think it would be closer to the mark to assume that it arose from reading other poets of his time who were engaged in imitating archaic verse.

As a young man Dodgson was influenced by poetic practice around him – this is evident when a list is compiled of recent and contemporary poets whom he parodied: Wordsworth, Longfellow, Isaac Watts, Macaulay, Tennyson, Swinburne, Scott, Hood, and Thomas Moore. Most of his antiquarian information and much of his inspiration came at second hand. In this connection, I think it is significant that in his plan of reading recorded in the diary for March 13, 1855, he lists under the heading *Novels*: "Scott's over again to begin with (?)" (*Diaries*, I, 44).

---

[10] Stuart Dodgson Collingwood, *The Lewis Carroll Picture Book* (1899), p. 10. Also found in Carroll's *Works* (New York, Random House, The Modern Library), p. 789.
[11] Daniel F. Kirk, *Charles Dodgson, Semeiotician* (University of Florida, 1963), p. 44.

3.3.4 *Interest in Etymology: Its Literary Expression*

If his interest in British antiquity was sincere but superficial, and largely a product
of the age in which he lived, I think the same may be said of his interest in philology.
On the same day that he records his intention of re-reading Scott, he says that he
would "like to go on with *Etymology*" and read "all Trench's books – and Horne
Tooke". We know from his entry of January 5, 1855, that he read at least some
of Tooke's *Diversions of Purley*. "Trench" is presumably Richard Chenevix
Trench, churchman, philologist, and guiding spirit at the inception of the *New
[Oxford] English Dictionary*. The books relevant to this study that Dodgson had in
mind were probably the two sets of lectures, *On the Study of Words* (1851) and
English Past and Present (1855). Although we have no proof that Dodgson read
Trench, it is quite likely that he did; for these two books were immensely popular,
highly readable, and available for the asking. If he did read them, he received a
course in the growth and development of the English language, and in nineteenth-
century semantic theory. Trench discusses the ways in which the word-stock of a
language changes from generation to generation, a continuous process of accretion
and loss for the most part unnoticed by speakers of the language. He discusses
shifts in word-meanings, explaining how, in the course of time, the meanings of
individual words can become generalized or specialized, their connotations elevated
or degraded. He treats the importance of verbalization to the formation of concepts,
comments upon the capability of words for sustaining multiple definitions, and
stresses that in given contexts words can be made to mean whatever the users wish.

When Dodgson records that he would like to "go on with etymology", it would
seem that he had made some previous study of it, if only on a personal basis without
the benefit of formal instruction. Etymology occasionally provides him with a
source of humor in his writings. I have already mentioned the mock etymology of
Jabberwock which he composed around 1883 (Cf. § 3.2.3). In 1855, he invented
etymological definitions for many words in his "Stanza of Anglo-Saxon Poetry"
(definitions that underwent almost total revision when Humpty Dumpty gave his
exegesis of the stanza in *Through the Looking-Glass*). Here is the complete gloss
of 1855:

BRYLLYG. (derived from the verb to BRYL or BROIL). "the time of broiling dinner, i.e.
the close of the afternoon."

SLYTHY. (compounded of SLIMY and LITHE). "smooth and active."

TOVE. a species of Badger. They had smooth white hair, long hind legs, and short horns
like a stag: lived chiefly on cheese

GYRE. verb (derived from GYAOUR or GIAOUR, "a dog."). "to scratch like a dog"

GYMBLE (whence GIMBLET). "to screw out holes in anything"

WABE (derived from the verb to SWAB or SOAK). "the side of a hill." (from it's [sic] being
soaked by the rain.)

MIMSY (whence MIMSERABLE and MISERABLE) "unhappy"

BOROGOVE An extinct kind of Parrot The [sic] had no wings, beaks turned up, and made their nests under sun-dials: lived on veal

MOME. (hence SOLEMOME, SOLEMONE, and SOLEMN). "grave."

RATH. A species of land turtle. Head erect: mouth like a shark – the front [canceled] fore legs curved out so that the animal walked on it's [sic] knees: smooth green body. lived on swallows and oysters.

OUTGRABE. past tense of the verb to OUTGRIBE. (it is connected with the old verb to GRIKE or SHRIKE, from which are derived "shriek" and "creak." —) "squeaked."

Hence the literal English of the passage is: "It was evening, and the smooth active badgers were scratching and boring holes in the hill-side: all unhappy were the parrots; and the grave turtles squeaked out."

There were probably sun-dials on the top of the hill, and the "borogoves" were afraid that their nests would be undermined. The hill was probably full of the nests of "raths," which ran out, squeaking with fear, on hearing the "toves" scratching outside. This is an obscure, but yet deeply affecting, relic of ancient Poetry.

Croft – 1855 Ed:[12]

This imitation of "learned" etymology attests Dodgson's interest in the subject and reveals that he had at least a superficial acquaintance with etymologists' methods. He was not attempting serious etymologies. The stanza of poetry and the gloss were written for the entertainment of his brothers and sisters; the exercise was intended to be humorous, and he may have conceived it as a satire on the etymological fervor then current in England.

In "The New Belfry" (1872), one of Dodgson's wittiest pamphlets, mock etymology serves as an instrument of satire. During the architectural renovation of Christ Church in 1872, the cathedral bells were removed from the tower which had grown too weak to support them and were temporarily housed in a wooden belfry above the staircase of the Hall. Dodgson regarded this plain wooden box as "the ugliest and most conspicuous monstrosity" ever inflicted upon Oxford (*Diaries*, II, 333). He attacked the belfry in a variety of ways, framing his satire as a learned monograph; the first section is entitled "On the etymological significance of the New Belfry, Ch. Ch." and runs as follows:

The word "Belfry" is derived from the French *bel*, "beautiful, becoming, meet," and from the German *frei*, "free, unfettered, secure, safe." Thus the word is strictly equivalent to "meatsafe," to which the new belfry bears a resemblance so perfect as almost to amount to coincidence.

(*Works*, p. 1139)

In each of these three examples, Dodgson is merely indulging in linguistic play with no attempt to be serious. One can hope that the girls of the Boston Latin

[12] From the manuscript facsimile printed by Harry Morgan Ayres in *Carroll's Alice* (Columbia University Press, 1936), pp. [16-17].

School were not fooled by his derivation of *Jabberwock*; one can be sure that Dean Liddell was not by the etymological definition of *belfry*.[13]

There is an instance of etymology applied to a serious end in Dodgson's essay "Eternal Punishment" printed in galley-proof in 1897 but not published in his life-time.[14] In this work he clearly sets forth the difficulties faced by the devout Christian who must reconcile the concept of a perfectly good and just God with that of His inflicting eternal punishment for sins committed in a finite period of time. Dodgson analyzes the dilemma, sets up the logical alternatives for belief, and (without actually committing himself to the position) offers a solution subscribed to by many theologians: the hypothesis that the word *eternal* found in English Bibles is a mistranslation of the Greek 'αἰὼν', which does not necessarily mean 'endless', but 'of indefinite duration'.[15]

These instances, together with the use of pedantic footnotes to define archaic and dialectal words in such early poems as "Ye Fatalle Cheyse", represent the fruits of Dodgson's interest in etymology. If the harvest is small, we do know that the ground was seeded. In 1855, the field was promising, having been prepared by the Oxford plow and harrow, and subjected to constant cultivation. Did something blight the crop, or was the soil less fertile than it appeared? It is impossible to say for certain, but my own opinion is that Dodgson had little inclination for formal linguistic study. In spite of his avowed desire to study ancient and modern languages, he seems – on the basis of the evidence available – to have made little progress in doing so. After thirty years of intermittent study he had acquired only a reading proficiency in French and a rudimentary knowledge of German. Outside of pos-sessing a college graduate's competence in Greek and Latin, he was untrained in the ancient languages. In view of these limitations, it is not surprising that he did not pursue etymology in a serious fashion. But although unskilled in the practice of etymology himself, he was acquainted with its methods and with the pitfalls it provided for the unwary. He was in all probability highly amused at the errors committed by other unskilled amateurs, the half-baked scholars and parlor-etymo-logists who published voluminously in the first half of the nineteenth century. As is attested by his works, nearly everything he experienced was potential material for humorous exploitation. Mock etymology provided him with a toy for his own amusement, a diversion for the amusement of others, and a means for poking sly fun at the fervent etymologists of his time. His handling of *Jabberwock* and 'belfry' shows a high degree of dexterity.

[13]   There is another use of "etymology" in "The Dynamics of a Parti-cle" (1865) which hinges upon quibbles in Greek, and upon bilingual puns (*Works*, pp. 1138-39). Because an elaborate context would have to be set up to explain the punning references, I refer the reader to the text itself. This device of Carroll's in harking back to "the original Greek" is, of course, once again his using etymological procedure for purposes of play.

[14]   "Eternal Punishment" is reprinted in Collingwood, *Picture Book*, pp. 345-355; and in the reprint of this volume by Dover Publications, *Diversions and Digressions of Lewis Carroll* (1961).

[15]   Collingwood, *Picture Book*, p. 354.

3.3.5 *Interest in, and Depictions of, Regional and Social Dialects*

As was the case with antiquarianism and etymology, the spirit of the age aroused in Dodgson an interest in regional and social speech dialects. The nineteenth century gave rise in both England and America to "local color writing", and to an increased concern with varieties of English speech among people of different social classes, geographical locales, and national origins. According to Roger Lancelyn Green in his Walck Monograph, *Lewis Carroll* (1962), pp. 72-73:

'Dialect' was an extraordinary disease which ran riot through later Victorian literature, the greatest impetus coming from America with such popular works as Leland's *Breitmann Ballads* and pidgin-English poems supposed to be the work of a Chinaman, with *Uncle Remus* and the 'slang' of Mark Twain's *Huckleberry Finn*; and more indigenously with Kipling's *Barrack Room Ballads* and F. Anstey's *Baboo Jabberjee*. In the literature of childhood it reached the dimensions of an orgy in the immensely popular *Helen's Babies* (1876). Even the greatest writers about children felt constrained to use it to some extent, as Mrs Molesworth showed in *Carrots* (1876) and *Herr Baby* (1881), and it was only eradicated by the new approach to childhood exemplified by Kenneth Grahame and E. Nesbit.

Dodgson showed himself a typical man of his period by using the accepted medium of speech for Bruno, and by spreading the sentiment a little too thick whenever he got the chance.

The dialect variety called "baby talk" had, by the 1880's, "become an accepted, even an expected convention" in books dealing with childhood (p. 72). Dodgson succumbed to the convention and gave to the fairy-hero of *Sylvie and Bruno* (1889 and 1893) a particularly offensive brand of baby talk. We unfortunately shall have ample occasion to observe Bruno's dialect in the course of this study; here is a sample, drawn almost at random:

"First oo must sit up as straight as pokers. ... Then oo must clasp oor hands – *so*. Then – 'Why hasn't oo brushed oor hair? Go and brush it *toreckly*!' Then – 'Oh, Bruno, oo mustn't dog's-ear the daisies!' Did oo learn *oor* spelling wiz daisies, Mister Sir?"

(*Works*, p. 645)

In a book almost twice as long as both volumes of *Alice* put together, the cumulative effect of this is overwhelming. Had Dodgson used baby talk in *Alice*, he would not be remembered today.

Although as Green suggests, it was not till the 1880's that baby talk became an expected convention in literature about children, it was a cultivated practice long before this in the Victorian nursery. In the earliest preserved letter of Dodgson's, written to his nurse while he was away from home, there is a rather grim antecedent for Bruno's baby talk:

My dear Bun,

    I love you very much, & tend you a kitt from little Charlie with the horn of hair. I'd

like to give you a kitt, but I tan't, betause I'm at Marke. What a long letter I've written.
I'm twite tired.

(Quoted from Derek Hudson, *Lewis Carroll*
[London, 1954], p. 27)

Hudson comments, "How old he was at the time is a matter of guess-work, but
clearly he had been helped in the writing and had his hand guided. The note is
addressed on the back, in the hand of the guider, 'For dear kind Bun, from little
Charly.' ... The writing cannot, of course, be accepted as a fully authentic autograph
– still less the language, foisted on to him by some well-meaning grown-up" (pp. 26-
27). It is interesting to recall the passage in *Through the Looking-Glass* where Alice,
invisible to the chess-men, takes hold of the end of the White King's pencil and
begins writing for him in his memorandum book:

The poor King looked puzzled and unhappy, and struggled with the pencil for some
time without saying anything; but Alice was too strong for him, and at last he panted
out "My dear! I really *must* get a thinner pencil. I can't manage this one a bit: it writes
all manner of things that I don't intend –"
  "What manner of things?" said the Queen, looking over the book (in which Alice had
put '*The White Knight is sliding down the poker. He balances very badly*'). "That's not
a memorandum of *your* feelings!"

(*Works*, pp. 152-153)

As Hudson says, it was not only Charlie's hand that was being guided in the
composition of his letter, but his language too. The person "helping" him was
forcing his spelling to simulate on paper the SOUND of baby talk. If Charles were
old enough to write a letter, he was certainly old enough to know how *kiss, can't,
send, because,* and *quite* are normally spelled. Dodgson, in adult life a precisionist
in matters of grammar, spelling, and usage, undoubtedly remembered his own
experience with baby talk; and whether or not as a child he rebelled against being
forced to write it, by the time he came to write *Sylvie and Bruno,* he himself was
willing to submit to sentimental convention and 'guide' Bruno's pronunciation. As
will be seen, however, though Dodgson was following literary convention in making
use of baby talk, he was also exploiting its possibilities for humor – its perversion
of standard pronunciation and its tendency to produce grammatical errors through
analogy (a reflection of the struggles of very young minds to cope with the rules of
adult usage).

  Dodgson's interest in dialect encompassed more than baby talk; as a young man
he was caught up in the surge of literary 'realism' which attempted to represent the
speech habits of various social and economic classes in their regional varieties. As
a humorist trying to publish in the popular press, he was willing to fall in with the
prevailing mode and turn out poems and stories employing non-standard dialects.
His use of dialect in his literary work is more widespread than is generally realized.

  For example, he imitates Scottish dialect in two poems, "The Lang Coortin'"
(1862) and "The Wandering Burgess" (included in "The Vision of the Three T's"

[1873]; it begins: "Our Willie had been sae lang awa'/ Frae bonnie Oxford toon"); Irish, in the short story *A Photographer's Day Out* (1860; Captain Flanaghan speaking: "Faix! an' I hope she'll give you a decoisive one! ... won't you, Mely Darlint?" [*Works*, p. 1093]) and in the speech of Pat, the White Rabbit's gardener in *Alice's Adventures under Ground* (1862), deleted when Carroll revised the book for publication as *Wonderland* (Pat, answering the Rabbit as to his whereabouts: " 'Shure then I'm here! digging for apples, anyway, yer honour!' " Again, identifying the object in the window [note Carroll's parenthetical comment]: " 'Shure it's an arm, yer honour!' (He pronounced it "arrum".)"); Cockney, in the short story *Wilhelm Von Schmitz* (1854), where the humor stems from the hero's misunderstanding of the waiter's speech; and Northern, in the peasant scenes of *Sylvie and Bruno* [see in particular the conversation of the fishermen's wives, Chapter XXIII (*Works*, p. 475), and Chapter VI ("Willie's Wife") of *Sylvie and Bruno Concluded* (*Works*, pp. 568-571)]. The Mad Gardener in *Sylvie and Bruno*, the Gryphon in *Wonderland*, the old Frog in Chapter IX ("Queen Alice") of *Through the Looking-Glass*, the landladies in "Knot II" of *A Tangled Tale*, and the mechanic in *Novelty and Romancement* (1856; see *Works*, p. 1084) all speak substandard English in accord with the convention that produced the dialects of the Sam Wellers, Jerry Crunchers, and Mrs. Gummidges of the popular novels – the assumption that simple, uneducated country folk and town-dwelling servants and laborers would necessarily speak a less than standard form of English. Dodgson was undoubtedly working within this literary tradition; but, as is apparent from his *Russian Journal* and various letters to child-friends, he also was keenly observant of the speech habits he encountered in everyday life. For proof that he had a good ear for nuances of dialect and rhythms of speech, one need only read his fictional conversations aloud.

His literary use of speech dialects, like his use of etymology, served the cause of humor. He did not possess the modern linguist's interest in them as objects of scientific study, but merely observed the speech habits of those around him, read the dialect representations of many English and American authors, and reproduced in his own work the conventional representations of "Irish", "Cockney", "Scottish", "Northern", and non-localized uneducated "substandard".

Aware that difficulties in communication can and do arise because of differences in speech habits and conventions, he often used the peculiarities of specific dialects to provide instances of misunderstanding and non-understanding in his fiction. An example of this may be seen in *Novelty and Romancement*; in this instance, the crucial dialectal divergence is in the area of vocabulary, not pronunciation or grammar. The narrator of the story, a romantic young man with a "thirst and passion for poetry", misinterprets a signboard reading "ROMAN CEMENT" as an advertisement for "ROMANCEMENT". Thinking that he has been presented with an opportunity to fulfill his heart's desire, he questions a mechanic, or laborer, who works at the establishment about the properties of the supposed commodity. The mechanic's dialect, taciturn substandard, cannot cope with the narrator's pompous and exotic vocabulary:

What was the article employed for? (I brought this question out with a gasp, excitement almost choking my utterance.)
　　It would piece a most anything together, mechanic believed, and make it solider nor stone.
　　This was a sentence difficult of interpretation. I thought it over a little, and then said, doubtfully, "you mean, I presume, that it serves to connect the broken threads of human destiny? to invest with a – with a sort of vital reality the chimerical products of a fertile imagination?"
　　Mechanic's answer was short, and anything but encouraging: "mought be –, I's no scollard, bless you."
　　At this point conversation certainly began to flag. . . .

(Works, pp. 1083-84)

Although Dodgson often used the characteristics of divergent dialects as a basis for communication difficulties, his works testify his awareness that English is spoken legitimately in many geographical and functional varieties, and on many cultural levels; that within the English-speaking community, the possibility of communication does exist for speakers of dissimilar dialects.

3.3.6 *Carroll's Reading in Books Concerned with Language*

In the diary entry for March 13, 1855, which states Dodgson's intention to pursue Anglo-Saxon and to read Horne Tooke, Richard Trench, and Scott's novels "over again", he also mentions his desire to study logic: to "finish Mill and dip into Dugald Stewart".

He is undoubtedly referring to John Stuart Mill's *A System of Logic* (1843); and since he admonishes himself to "finish Mill", it is apparent that he at least read part of the book. In view of the facts that formal logic was one of his main interests in later life, that he regarded himself a logician as well as a mathematician, and that Mill's *Logic* was a standard work in the field, it is probable that he made good his intention and read it all. Even if he did not finish the book, he certainly would have read the extremely important chapters on "Names" which come near the beginning. Since in his fictional works Dodgson reveals an intense interest in the nature and function of names, it will be fruitful to examine some of Mill's statements in conjunction with a discussion of Dodgson's oblique speculations. I should say at this point that although Tooke, Mill, and Trench allude to Hobbes and Locke, there is no recorded evidence that Dodgson read these older authors.

　　If he did dip into Dugald Stewart, he may have come upon Stewart's criticisms of Horne Tooke. In 1855, the fifth volume of Sir William Hamilton's collected edition of Stewart's works was published; forty pages of this volume are devoted to an essay discussing the merits and limitations of "Tooke's Philological Speculations". Here, in addition to touching upon such important topics as the role of contexts in establishing word-meanings, the possibility of words having multiple definitions, the functions of signs in the process of communication, the nature of communication itself, the elevation and degradation of word-meanings over long periods of time, and the obstacles presented to an understanding of the nature of language by men's failure to vary the metaphors habitually used to characterize it, he comments upon the abuses of Tooke's etymological dogmatism. Stewart finds ridiculous Tooke's assumption that a philosopher is justified in using a word only in its primitive or etymological sense. He decries his notion that "in order to understand, with precision, the import of any English word, it is necessary to trace its progress historically through all the successive meanings which it has been employed to convey, from the moment it was first introduced into our language; or, if the word be of foreign growth, and transmitted to us from some dialect of our Continental ancestors, that we should prosecute the etymological research, till we ascertain the literal and primitive sense of the root from whence it sprung".[16] For Stewart, proper understanding of a word's meaning in current usage does not depend upon a knowledge of either its primitive sense or its historical shifts of meaning.

There is no recorded proof that Dodgson did read Dugald Stewart; if he did, I think there is no doubt that he found much to interest him in the Scottish philosopher's discussions of language. It is difficult to know how much reading Dodgson did do in books dealing with etymology, semasiology, and scientific philology. We learn only indirectly, for example, that he probably read George Boole's *An Investigation of the Laws of Thought* (1854), a book containing in its second chapter certain statements on the arbitrary nature of signs which seem to foreshadow some of Dodgson's own statements on meaning. But we don't know when he may have read it. The book was in his personal library.[17] He mentions Boole specifically, however, only in a diary entry of 1884 (*Diaries*, II, 430) – and then with reference to his system for representing logical propositions in algebraic notation.

I have presented here all that is recorded of his linguistic study: he read at least some of Tooke, Mill, and Boole, and intended to read Trench and Stewart. Beyond this the evidence will not take us. It is unfortunate that Volume Three of his *Diaries*, covering the period from September 27 to December 31, 1855, is missing, for it might provide further information on the extent of his reading at a time when he was actively pursuing linguistic study. His academic work during this period was probably quite heavy, for he undertook the duties of his Mathematical Lectureship (tutorial work, for the most part) in October. As a consequence, he may not have had much time for desultory reading – but, according to Roger Lancelyn Green, the "Stanza of Anglo-Saxon Poetry" (which reflects his reading of Tooke)

[16] Dugald Stewart, *Collected Works*, Vol. V, ed. Sir William Hamilton (Edinburgh, 1855), p. 178. The entire essay on Horne Tooke is found in this volume, pp. 149-188.
[17] Florence Becker Lennon, *The Life of Lewis Carroll* (1962), p. 406.

was probably written in the last three weeks of December (see *Diaries*, I, 68-69).

Though the record of serious linguistic reading is quite sparse, Dodgson undoubtedly was acquainted with many works which he did not mention in his diaries (or which were recorded in the volumes now lost). While he was Sub-Librarian at Christ Church (1855-57) he carried out a systematic plan of "looking over all the Library regularly, to acquaint myself generally with its contents, and to note such books as seem worth studying" (*Diaries*, I, 43). Undoubtedly, too, he was exposed through hearsay to many ideas on language which had been held by previous thinkers. In this connection the loss of the first volume of his diaries, covering his undergraduate years, is to be regretted. It is perhaps significant that the references to linguistic study which we do have come early in his life, immediately after his graduation from college, and that there is virtually no mention of them later. His literary works do reveal a continuing interest in linguistic matters; but the interest is manifest only in practical applications of theoretical principles, and is expressed in a whimsical manner. Whether Dodgson's formal study of philology was of as brief duration and as limited in scope as it seems to have been, there was another area of study of great importance to his linguistic awareness which he pursued throughout his adult life: mathematics and logic.

3.4 PROFESSIONAL STUDY OF LANGUAGE AS AN INSTRUMENT OF THOUGHT AND OF COMMUNICATION

3.4.1 *Carroll as Mathematician*

Dodgson's philological interest, though sincere and abiding, was essentially that of an amateur: his study of language as a cultural phenomenon was an avocation, and he did not commit the time and energy to it that he did to his professional work. As mathematician and, more particularly, as logician, he was of necessity a professional student of language as it fulfilled its roles as an instrument of thought and an instrument of communication. It is this aspect of his general interest which constitutes the bulk of the linguistic matter contained in his literary writings. The remainder of this study will focus upon this interest in language which grew out of Dodgson's professional work.

Dodgson, it will be recalled, took a First Class in Mathematics in 1854 and held the Mathematical Lectureship at Christ Church from 1855 to 1881. In this twenty-six-year period, in addition to teaching undergraduates elementary topics (below calculus), he published the *Alice* books, *The Hunting of the Snark*, satirical pamphlets on Oxford affairs, numerous minor poems, and a large group of mathematical works on various subjects [a brief chronological listing of his works will be found in Appendix A; for a detailed catalog of his publications, see Roger Lancelyn Green's *The Lewis Carroll Handbook* (Oxford, 1962)].

The majority of his mathematical works were designed as study aids for under-graduates, and did not venture very far into unexplored territory. His most ambi-tious publications were *A Syllabus of Plane Algebraical Geometry* (1860), *The Formulae of Plane Trigonometry* (1861), *An Elementary Treatise on Determinants* (1867), and *Euclid and His Modern Rivals* (1879) – none of which made any lasting contribution to the field of mathematics. There are many minor publications. One of the best discussions of Dodgson's mathematical career is that of D. B. Eperson, "Lewis Carroll – Mathematician", *Mathematical Gazette*, XVII (May, 1933), 92-100.[18] Of the first item in the above list, Eperson says,

The title is self-explanatory: the book is an attempt to arrange in logical sequence the processes of analytical geometry. Evidently he felt that the usual methods of teaching the subject lacked the logical cohesion of Euclid's pure geometry, and his passion for strict accuracy, shown even whilst at school, led him to attempt to give definitions to the concepts of algebraic geometry and to outline the axioms on which the subject is based.
(Eperson, p. 93)

In *The Formulae of Plane Trigonometry* Dodgson expresses the trigonometrical ratios by means of symbols rather than words, hoping to persuade other mathema-ticians to do away with the "cumbrous expressions" *sin, tan, cosec*, and so on. Eperson comments,

Dodgson apparently was doubtful whether this proposed reform would prove acceptable to the mathematical world and asked for opinions and suggestions. It is not recorded whether any favourable replies were received, but as the symbolism has not been gener-ally adopted, we must conclude that the mathematicians of 1861 failed to see its ad-vantages.
(Eperson, p. 94)

An Elementary Treatise on Determinants, which, says Eperson, "exhibits those same qualities of originality and logical consistency as his former books", is a treatise for the specialist, but has little significance as a mathematical study.

Euclid and His Modern Rivals is one of Dodgson's most interesting books. Its purpose is polemical. It systematically attacks on logical and stylistic grounds the books of Dodgson's contemporaries who claimed to have written geometry texts capable of supplanting Euclid's *Elements* in the schools. Over a dozen authors come under Dodgson's guns; and he disposes of them in a series of keen and closely reasoned arguments, challenging them on the basis of their suitability for beginners, on their clarity, economy, and principles of organization, on their accuracy of definition, validity of proofs, and precision of verbal style.

Although Dodgson is systematic and methodical in his destruction of the modern

[18] See also Warren Weaver, "Lewis Carroll: Mathematician", *Scientific American*, CXCIV (April, 1956), 116-128; Daniel F. Kirk, *Charles Dodgson, Semeiotician* (1963), pp. 7-40; Martin Gardner, "The Games and Puzzles of Lewis Carroll", *Scientific American*, CCII (March, 1960), 172-176; Florence Becker Lennon, *The Life of Lewis Carroll* (1962), pp. 321-346; and Theodore Maynard, "Lewis Carroll: Mathematician and Magician", *Catholic World*, CXXXV (1932), 193-201.

rivals' claims, his own book is cast into a highly unorthodox form. The text is a drama in four acts. Minos, a geometer exasperated by the inconsistencies and faulty logic of Euclid's modern rivals, undertakes to defend the Greek's book against all of those who would remove it from the schools. The ghost of Euclid suggests that Minos examine each of the rivals' books in turn; and Herr Niemand, the Phantasm of a German Professor who "has read all books, and is ready to defend any thesis, true or untrue" becomes the rivals' advocate. In the course of their debate, Minos leads Herr Niemand into a series of logical traps and thus disqualifies, one by one, each of the modern books. The tedious similarity of the arguments is relieved in some measure by Dodgson's ironic humor and witty wordplay; but the infusion of humor does not entirely conceal his own exasperation with the rivals' illogical thought and ambiguous writing. Although the book presents an interesting blend of mathematical and literary matter, the dominant impression one receives from it is an insistence on verbal precision and soundness of logic. It reveals Dodgson's almost obsessive concern for strict definition of terms; and although geometry is a realm where strict definition is necessary, Dodgson's rigor occasionally seems excessive and petty. While precariously preserving a humorous tone, the book often reveals a pedantic nastiness just beneath the surface. Dodgson's attack on the modern rivals is not essentially playful. Eperson says that it would be unjust to call Dodgson's effort a failure simply because Euclid was subsequently replaced in the schools by modern text-books: "Dodgson certainly showed the superiority of Euclid's Geometry as a logical treatise, whilst the Modern Rivals have succeeded in providing us with less formal and less formidable text-books which are better suited to the interests and abilities of the adolescent mind" (p. 96).

After resigning his Lectureship, Dodgson turned increasingly to recreational mathematics. He devoted himself to devising puzzles, intricate games, and methods of "simplifying" long multiplication and division, and to inventing systems for memorization, determining postage rates, and conducting elections on the basis of proportional representation. In 1888, he published *Curiosa Mathematica, Part I: A new Theory of Parallels,* a work for theoretical mathematicians in which he tried to improve upon Euclid's 12th Axiom. In 1893, he brought out *Curiosa Mathematica, Part II: Pillow-Problems*, a set of seventy-two problems involving operations in algebra, geometry, and trigonometry, each of which he had worked out in his head before committing the question and solution to paper. The third part of *Curiosa Mathematica* was never published (though much of the material may be found in Collingwood's *The Lewis Carroll Picture Book* [1899], p. 239 ff., itself reprinted by Dover Publications as *Diversions and Digressions of Lewis Carroll* [1961]).

Dodgson's stature as mathematician is summed up by Eperson as follows:

It would be idle to pretend that he was a great mathematical discoverer or genius. His life was spent in a busy round of tutorials and lectures at Christ Church, and judging by the pamphlets of simple formulae and notes on Euclid, it appears that he seldom had to do any advanced mathematical teaching. . . . As a lecturer he was considered rather dull, and one may reasonably suspect that this was partly due to his meticulous care in being precise and logical at all costs, not only when dealing with his beloved Euclid, but also in algebra and arithmetic. . . . Undoubtedly his greatest claim to be considered a genius was his ability to take pains. No one could have been more devoted to his work, and his conscientiousness and thoroughness, as well as his gifts of humour and his charm of manner, entitle him to a place amongst the Immortals. The world will always remember him as the author of *Alice in Wonderland*, yet we also may acclaim him as one of the illustrious English mathematicians of whom we are rightly proud.

(Eperson, pp. 99-100)

A rather genial estimate which – although taking into account the essential triviality of much of Dodgson's mathematical endeavor – really amounts to qualified praise of his industry and earnestness. A more uncompromising view of Dodgson's deficiencies as mathematician is that of Eric Temple Bell, whose estimate is recorded in Florence Becker Lennon's *The Life of Lewis Carroll* (1962), Chapter 15. Bell feels that Dodgson was hopelessly out of touch with the mainstream at a time when mathematics was undergoing revolutionary changes; that, although he was surrounded by the men and books that were producing these creative modifications, Dodgson preferred to avoid the main channel and explore the shallows: "His range was about that of a freshman today in a good technical school, though the freshman would have clearer ideas about elementary things than C.L.D., and would not be so far behind his own times mathematically as C.L.D. was behind his all through his mathematical life" (Lennon, p. 322). Dodgson seems not to have read the works of Riemann and H. J. S. Smith, nor those of William K. Clifford, who, in Bell's opinion, was "probably the most brilliant geometer Britain produced in the 19th century. . . . His translation of Riemann's paper 'On the Hypotheses which lie at the Bases of Geometry,' appeared in *Nature* in 1873. Dodgson, if he ever read this masterpiece . . . never gave any evidence of having understood what it was all about" (Lennon, p. 326). Warren Weaver, in "Lewis Carroll: Mathematician", *Scientific American*, CXCIV (April, 1956), 116-128, concurs in this general estimate of Dodgson's mathematical stature: "He was first of all a teacher, earnestly concerned with methods of instruction in elementary subjects" (p. 117). . . . "In all of Dodgson's mathematical writing it is evident that he was not an important mathematician. . . . in geometry his ideas were old-fashioned even for his time" (p. 120).[19]

3.4.2 *Carroll as Logician*

As his interest in theoretical mathematics decreased and his attention turned more and more to recreational mathematics and to practical means for problem-solving, Dodgson's interest in formal logic, nascent in the 1850's, grew to dominate his

---

[19] From "Lewis Carroll: Mathematician", by Warren Weaver. Copyright © 1956 by *Scientific American, Inc.* All rights reserved.

professional life. He had, of course, been using the principles of formal logic in his mathematical writings since the beginning of his career. But following his retirement, he began to focus his attention upon logic as a study in its own right. During the 1880's and 1890's, he devoted his energies to engaging in more-or-less friendly controversy over disputed points in logic, to the formulation and publication of paradoxes involving hypotheticals (such as "What the Tortoise Said to Achilles" [1895]), to preparing his two books on logic for the press, to teaching the principles of formal logic to numerous children and to young women in a series of lectures at Oxford High School, and to the working out of his own system of symbolic notation.

The first hint of his serious study of logic, outside of the reference to John Stuart Mill's book in 1855, is his laconic remark on May 25, 1876: "Have been writing a good deal today about Logic in algebraical notation" (*Diaries*, II, 353). On November 20, 1884, he records: "In these last few days I have been working at a Logical Algebra and seem to be getting to a simpler notation than Boole's" (*Diaries*, II, 430). This activity resulted in the publication of *The Game of Logic* (1886; 1887) and its greatly expanded version, *Symbolic Logic, Part I. Elementary* (1896). He says in the preface to the fourth edition of this latter work:

This is, I believe, the very first attempt (with the exception of my own little book, *The Game of Logic*, published in 1886, a very incomplete performance) that has been made to *popularise* this fascinating subject. It has cost me *years* of hard work: but if it should prove, as I hope it may, to be of *real* service to the young, and to be taken up, in High Schools and in private families, as a valuable addition to their stock of healthful mental recreations, such a result would more than repay ten times the labour that I have expended on it.[20]

In his introduction to the same volume he states the value to be gained from knowing the principles of symbolic logic:

Mental recreation is a thing that we all of us need for our mental health; . . . Once master the machinery of Symbolic Logic, and you have a mental occupation always at hand, of absorbing interest, and one that will be of *real* use to you in any subject you may take up. It will give you clearness of thought – the ability to *see your way* through a puzzle – the habit of arranging your ideas in an orderly and get-at-able form – and, more valuable than all, the power to detect *fallacies*, and to tear to pieces the flimsy illogical arguments, which you will so continually encounter in books, in newspapers, in speeches, and even in sermons, and which so easily delude those who have never taken the trouble to master this fascinating Art.[21]

Dodgson intended to publish *Symbolic Logic* in three parts: elementary, advanced, and transcendental; but only the first section was completed. The second would have dealt with such topics as the "Existential Import" of propositions, the use of a negative copula, and the theory that "two negative Premisses prove nothing";

---

[20]   Lewis Carroll, *Symbolic Logic*, 4th ed. (London, 1897), p. x; in the reprint by Dover Publications entitled *Symbolic Logic and The Game of Logic* (1958), p. xiv.
[21]   *Symbolic Logic*, 4th ed., p. xiii; Dover reprint, p. xvii.

with "Propositions containing ALTERNATIVES (such as 'Not-all x are y')"; with hypotheticals, dilemmas, propositions containing three or more terms, and sorites containing entities. His intention was "to go over all ground usually traversed in the text-books used in our Schools and Universities, and to enable my Readers to solve Problems of the same kind as, and far harder than, those that are at present set in their Examinations". Part Three would have dealt with "many curious and out-of-the-way subjects, some of which are not even alluded to in any of the treatises I have met with" – and with such specific topics as "the Analysis of Propositions into their Elements (let the Reader, who has never gone into this branch of the subject, try to make out for himself what ADDITIONAL Proposition would be needed to convert 'Some a are b' into 'Some a are bc'), the treatment of Numerical and Geometrical Problems, the construction of Problems, and the solution of Syllogisms and Sorites containing Propositions more complex than any that I have used in Part II" (*Symbolic Logic*, 4th ed. [1897], p. 185).

It would have been interesting if Dodgson had lived to complete his project. In the one extant volume, he introduces the student to the rudiments of propositional analysis and the solution of simple sorites. He has his readers interpret all propositions in terms of the existence or non-existence of classes, and then represent these data graphically by placing colored counters in square compartments of rectilinear diagrams representing the given universe of discourse. Dodgson claims that his method of diagrams, showing the inter-relation of propositions, is an improvement on Euler's circle notation and Venn's system of intersecting ellipses (see *Symbolic Logic*, 4th ed., pp. 173-183). With regard to the value of Dodgson's method, R. B. Braithwaite expresses the opinion that

The symbolic language which he uses for the translation of his diagrams has the virtue of showing clearly that the propositions are being interpreted in terms of class-relationships, but otherwise it is no improvement on more ordinary statements. It does not show in itself why the conclusion of a syllogism follows from the premisses, but only states that it does. . . . Carroll did not accept the doctrine that has done so much to simplify traditional formal logic – the interpretation of a universal proposition as not involving the existence of its subject-term. 'Canaries, that do not sing loud, are unhappy' involves, according to Carroll, the existence of some non-loud-singing canaries: without this assumption in this case no syllogistic conclusion can be drawn. . . . Carroll's lack of subtlety makes his system appear more satisfactory superficially than it is fundamentally.[22]

Thomas Banks Strong, writing on "Lewis Carroll" in *The Cornhill Magazine* (March, 1898), 303-310, comments as follows:

In the Logic Mr. Dodgson carried to the most violent excesses his habit of developing unexpected results and unnoticed inferences. He tried to give words a sharply defined meaning, as if they were mathematical symbols, and strove to systematise the various inferences which could be drawn from them. A word to him not only had its direct positive meaning, but also conveyed negative information in various directions. And all

[22] R. B. Braithwaite, "Lewis Carroll as Logician", *Mathematical Gazette*, XVI (July, 1932), 174-175.

this had to be drawn out and taken into account in his system. Besides this principle of analysis, Mr. Dodgson was ruled by a great belief in formulae in which letters (as in algebra) took the place of words. This confidence naturally led him to think of sentences as mere forms, of which the concrete meaning was insignificant. . . . Mr. Dodgson's great originality of mind was his chief danger. He read comparatively little of the works of other logicians or of mathematicians who had dealt with the same subjects as himself. He preferred to evolve the whole out of his own mind without being influenced by others. There was gain in this, but there was also loss. If he saved himself from being misled by others, he also deprived himself of the value of their work, which would both have saved him trouble and warned him of mistakes. He dealt with these scientific matters as he had dealt with the ordinary language of conversation, in his own way and from his own point of view. The one process produced 'Alice,' the other the 'Symbolic Logic.' And if the latter is a failure as a Logic, it is surely because a gift like his of eccentric originality lends itself but poorly to rigid analysis and systematic exposition. (pp. 309-310)

Warren Weaver says bluntly in his article "Lewis Carroll: Mathematician", *Scientific American*, CXCIV (April 1956), 116-128: "Amusing as Carroll's games of logic were, they were neither technically original nor profound" (p. 122); and in summary, "The Reverend Dodgson was a dull, conscientious and capable teacher of elementary mathematics. Lewis Carroll was, in a tantalizingly elusive way, an excellent and unconsciously deep logician. But when he tried to approach logic head on, in a proper professional way, he was only moderately successful. It was when he let logic run loose that he demonstrated his true subtlety and depth" (p. 124).

Being neither a mathematician nor a logician myself, I must rely upon the statements of those who are for an assessment of Dodgson's professional stature. The consensus is that in both mathematics and logic Dodgson was not a particularly profound or significant thinker, and that his technical writings have little importance in their respective fields. Gilbert Ryle, in discussing John Stuart Mill's contributions to the theory of meaning, does, however, give Carroll a place in the historical development of modern logic: "Mill's contributions to Formal or Symbolic Logic were negligible. It was not he but his exact contemporaries, Boole and de Morgan, and his immediate successors, Jevons, Venn, Carroll, McColl and Peirce who, in the English-speaking world, paved the way for Russell." [23] Bertrand Russell himself, discussing *Alice's Adventures in Wonderland* with Mark Van Doren and Katherine Anne Porter in a radio broadcast, has said of Dodgson, "I think he was very good at inventing puzzles in pure logic. When he was quite an old man, he invented two puzzles which he published in a learned periodical, *Mind*, to which he didn't provide answers. And the providing of answers was a job, at least so I found it" (*The New Invitation to Learning*, ed. Mark Van Doren [New York: Random House, 1942], p. 214). Further,

His works were just what you would expect: comparatively good at producing puzzles and very ingenious and rather pleasant, but not important. . . . None of his work was

[23] Gilbert Ryle, "The Theory of Meaning", in *Philosophy and Ordinary Language*, ed. Charles E. Caton (University of Illinois Press, 1963), p. 130.

important. The best work he ever did in that line was the two puzzles that I spoke of.
. . . there is nothing in *Alice in Wonderland* or *Through the Looking-Glass* that could
conceivably be thought a contribution. They offer only pleasant illustrations for those
who don't want to be thought too heavy.

(Van Doren, p. 218)

The logical matter in the *Alice* books has attracted the attention of many readers,
logicians and laymen alike; and the notion that Dodgson could not have written
them as they now stand if he had not been a professional logician has become a
cliche. I think this view is substantially correct; but critics who look no farther than
Alice generally do not realize that Dodgson's interest in logic is expressed (ad-
mittedly in a less concentrated form) in his other literary writings as well. This
interest appears in various guises: as syllogisms embedded in the text, as illustrations of valid and invalid inference on the part of characters, as puzzles to be
solved by the reader, as situational absurdities produced by the literal interpretation
of metaphorical statements, and as close attention paid to the form of utterances.
Formal logic, which establishes criteria for valid inference, is largely a linguistic
science. As John Stuart Mill phrases it, "Since Reasoning, or Inference, the principal
subject of logic, is an operation which usually takes place by means of words, and
in all complicated cases can take place in no other way, those who have not a
thorough insight into the signification and purposes of words, will be under almost
a necessity of reasoning or inferring incorrectly." [24]

As a student of formal logic, Dodgson was required to examine the resources
and limitations of English as an instrument of thought and of communication. As
is the case with most theoretical students of language, he was forced to deal with
the problem of meaning. He was led to speculate upon signs and their modes of
signifying, upon words and their relationship both to the things they symbolize,
and to other words in the contexts of specific utterances. Since logic, as Mill points
out, "includes . . . the operation of Naming; for language is an instrument of thought,
as well as a means of communicating our thoughts", and "includes also, Definition,
and Classification",[25] Dodgson, as logician, was required to devote much thought
to the means by which objects are classified and given names, and to the nature
and use of names themselves. Since he realized that English offered many possibilities for the creation of lexical, syntactic, and contextual ambiguity – a trait of
the language which often produces errors in reasoning and misunderstanding in
attempts at communication – he was much concerned with the establishment of
precise canons of usage through the definition of words. He was fascinated by
the frequent illogicality of statements in conventional usage and saw that the
habitual vagueness and metaphorical expression of ordinary language could be
humorously exploited by subjecting it to the rules of logical usage.

[24]   John Stuart Mill, *A System of Logic* (New York, 1852), p. 11.
[25]   Mill, p. 7.

Concerned in his professional work with the import of propositions, he was intrigued by the discrepancy which often exists in ordinary language between the literal import of utterances and their meanings as intended by speakers and understood by interpreters. Conscious of the need in formal logic for words to possess precision and clarity of reference, he was both amused and disturbed by the power which words have to produce emotional effects in people (and thus cause a given utterance to be variously interpreted) for reasons other than the words' designative signification. He was thus led to speculate on the tendency of people to endow words with an autonomous existence and sovereign potency – in effect, to make words their masters.

3.5 SUMMARY

Dodgson's speculations led him to certain conclusions about the nature and functions of language which the remainder of this study will attempt to define. He arrived at these linguistic insights largely through his professional work in mathematics and logic, but also through his amateur study of philology. His study of etymology and the development of English, for example, though basically superficial, did enable him to see that words often undergo historical shifts of meaning, that they can have – at any given point in their history – a potential multiplicity of reference, that they can take on new meanings through being arbitrarily applied to things in specific contexts with which they previously had no connection.

His study in scientific philology was quite limited, partly because he lacked time and inclination to pursue it diligently, but more importantly, because his lack of proficiency in reading modern European languages made many recent scholarly works inaccessible to him. Since it was on the Continent that most of the significant work was being done in comparative philology, and since English translations of these studies were not prevalent in the mid-nineteenth century, Dodgson's inability to read French and German easily prevented him from gaining a firsthand acquaintance with the work of Continental linguists. Whatever knowledge he had of comparative philology probably came at second hand through his association with linguistic scholars at Oxford.

His reading of works on logic and semasiology was probably quite limited also. The consensus of professional men is that Dodgson's work in mathematics and logic was not particularly significant, that his conservatism and ignorance of new developments in mathematics made his views old-fashioned for his time, and that, preferring to go his own way, he did not read the technical publications of his contemporaries. There is little recorded evidence that he read much in semasiology beyond Horne Tooke, Mill, and Boole (though we do know that he intended to read all of Richard Trench's works and "dip into Dugald Stewart"). In view of both his professional insularity and independence of mind, and the lack of evidence of extensive reading in the field, I think it may be conjectured that the insights he reached regarding the nature of language were arrived at for the most part independently – largely through intuition and as a result of the study of language imposed upon him by his pursuit of formal logic.

4

SIGNS

It is a very inconvenient habit of kittens (Alice had once
made the remark) that, whatever you say to them, they
always purr. "If they would only purr for 'yes,' and mew
for 'no,' or any rule of that sort," she had said, "so that
one could keep up a conversation! But how *can* you talk
with a person if they *always* say the same thing?"

Through the Looking-Glass, Chapter XII

4.1 CARROLL AND THE PROBLEM OF MEANING

4.1.1 *Prefatory Statement; Carroll's Understanding of the Difference Between Ordinary and Logical Discourse*

I have shown in the preceding chapter that Lewis Carroll (as Dodgson shall be
called hereafter) was drawn to a study of language by the nature of his professional
work and by the philological ferment of his time. The latter influence produced
his interest in the English language as a cultural phenomenon, directing his attention to its historical development, etymology, social and regional dialects, and
characteristic levels of usage. His work in mathematics and logic required him to
examine English as it functions as an instrument of thought and of communication.
One of the results of this professional concern was his realization of the marked
difference between the linguistic conventions of logical and ordinary discourse.

Although both types of discourse employ the same vocabulary and basic sentence structure, a subject and predicate form, their respective conventions for using
these elements are, in a sense, quite dissimilar. The discourse of formal logic,
employing stylized and rigidly structured types of statement, is governed by strict
rules of usage whose aim is to eliminate the possibility of vagueness and ambiguity.
Ordinary discourse, on the other hand, is less stylized in its statements, less tightly
structured syntactically, more vague and approximate, and susceptible in much
greater degree to ambiguity of import. It too, of necessity, is governed by rules of
usage; but these, instead of being a relatively fixed and uniform set of conventions

arbitrarily designed to insure precise statement, are a relatively loose and flexible set of ever-changing conventions, often happenstance in origin, which have been selectively adopted by the speech community at large for carrying on everyday affairs. Certain of these conventions, such as the accepted use of elliptic, hyperbolic, ironic, and metaphoric statement, cause ordinary discourse to be quite illogical when judged by the rules of logical discourse. Since both forms of discourse do employ the same word stock and basic syntactic structure, Carroll saw that humor could be derived from treating ordinary discourse as though it were amenable to the rules of logical discourse. For example, in his works he often causes metaphorical statements to be interpreted according to their literal import, or uses them as premises for arguments which lead inevitably to absurd conclusions.

4.1.2 *Carroll's Interest in Signs; His Lack of Formal System in His Semiotic Speculations*

Carroll's study of logic, however, gave him more than an awareness of language's ability to be exploited for humorous purposes. He saw that in order to understand the operation of language both as an instrument of thought and as a vehicle for communication, it is necessary to understand how the elements which comprise the linguistic code actually serve to convey meanings. This particular aspect of his language study necessarily involved him in studying the nature of signs, for the meaningful elements of the linguistic code are particular kinds of signs which, within a speech community, are interpreted in conventionalized ways. Carroll's concern with and speculations about the nature and functions of signs is the subject of the present chapter.

I wish to emphasize that neither in this nor in subsequent chapters have I attempted to derive a general system of semiotic theory from Carroll's illustrations of sign-processes. It is highly unlikely that he ever developed a coherent and consistent scheme of linguistic theory; at best, a general tendency or suggestive pattern is discernible in his thought. The principles to be inferred from his illustrations should not be regarded as scattered parts of a fossil skeleton, only requiring our articulation to form a reconstructed whole. One cannot hope to assemble a complete skeleton, for none is present. Over a period of years Carroll deposited these bones at random in a sedimentary matrix from which they must be extracted, and he did this without self-conscious plan or any expectation that a paleontologist would come seeking a complete skeleton. He was not a systematizer of linguistic theory. He was not a trained linguist. He was a logician and humorist who used his largely intuitive insights into the nature of language as a vehicle for a sophisticated kind of play. This, however, does not detract from the validity of his insights, many of which are shared by twentieth-century semioticians. Some of the theoretical principles embedded in his illustrations lie near the surface and are easily extracted; others are deeply buried, and much chipping is needed to free them from the matrix. With care in the use

of the tools, and patience in the process of removal, enough bones can be extracted
to provide – if not a complete skeleton – at least a possibility for seeing a certain
tendency in their configuration, for guessing at the general nature which the beast
would have possessed if it had ever come into being. At the risk of sounding
nonsensical (it is a statement worthy of the land behind the looking-glass), it may
be said that Carroll has left us a great many bones of an animal that in all probability was never entirely formed.

Before turning to Carroll's works to determine the semiotic principles implicit
in his illustrations of sign situations, it is necessary to establish a conceptual framework and working terminology which will serve as a background for the matters to
be treated in the chapter and in the remainder of the study. Choosing not to write
on the nature of signs, Carroll left no terminology to guide us. Moreover, many of
the principles which may legitimately be inferred from his illustrations can be
discussed only by employing the concepts and terminology of a body of semiotic
theory which has evolved since his time. Respectively in § 4.2 and § 4.4, I have
presented brief discussions of the nature of signs in general, and of linguistic signs.
Both discussions are overly schematized accounts of sign-processes, reduced to bare
skeletal outlines for the sake of brevity and clarity. Sign situations encountered in
everyday life are usually much more complex than these discussions reveal. But I
think my presentation compensates in clarity and suggestiveness for what it distorts
through oversimplification.

It is not my purpose to present an exhaustive analysis of sign-processes from a
twentieth-century point of view or to make a definitive statement on the nature of
the linguistic sign. Such attempts would be inappropriate to the aims of this study,
for not only would they inject a great deal of irrelevant material, they would be
misleading in that they would tend to ascribe to Carroll notions that probably never
occurred to him. My discussion goes only far enough to limn for the reader the
processes which we shall see at work in Carroll's illustrations (whether or not he
consciously formulated them to himself), and to establish the necessary theoretical
background and terminology. I have purposely avoided technical jargon whenever
possible.

The following account is not to be taken as a summary of Carroll's notions
regarding the nature of signs, but as an outline of my own views, which are based
on introspection, my reading of twentieth-century semioticians, and my study of
Lewis Carroll's illustrations of linguistic sign situations. Although the notions here
advanced are essentially my own and are not to be understood as being Carroll's
necessarily, many of my statements are substantiated – as will be seen later – by
the operative linguistic principles implicit in the sign situations depicted in his
works. Moreover, nothing that is presented in the background discussions is in-
compatible either with his few overt statements on the nature of signs or with the
theoretical principles which – in my analysis – seem to underlie his practices. Since
most of Carroll's illustrations of linguistic sign-processes occur in the context of

spoken discourse, my discussion of linguistic signs will focus on those which operate through the medium of speech. Those which operate through the medium of writing will receive much briefer treatment, though some of the conclusions pertaining to speech may be applicable to writing. Finally, my discussion will be confined to the English language, since it was in English that Carroll wrote, and to English that he confined his own semiotic speculations.

4.2 OF SIGNS IN GENERAL

For our purposes a sign may be defined in general terms as that which results when a stimulus to our nervous systems is responded to as having some specific meaning or meanings not inherent in the stimulus, and in addition to our knowledge that the stimulus has occurred. More simply, a sign is a stimulus which, once perceived and identified, is INTERPRETED.

By this definition, for a given interpreter and in a particular environment, any sort of stimulus may function as a sign: sensory stimuli such as light, odor, various types of pain, a single sound or a sequence of sounds conceived as having unitary significance; a perceived object such as a tree (conceptualized from a variety of diverse visual stimuli); or an 'idea' such as a pictorial image, an abstract formulation of sequentially-observed phenomena conceived as a process (such as a day-to-day drop in the stock market which we interpret as a sign that a financial recession is imminent), or a 'message' (statement, question, command) imparted propositionally through the medium of our linguistic code. For any of these types of stimuli to function as signs, they must have some meaning for us beyond our realization that they have occurred. Thus, an odor which we identify as the smell of smoke does not become a sign to us until we interpret the odor as indicating that there is a fire somewhere; an observed day-to-day drop in the stock market does not become a sign unless we take it to indicate something not intrinsic to the stimulus, such as the coming of a recession.

For a sign situation to exist (of any type, linguistic or non-linguistic), the following must be present:

(1) Something capable of providing a stimulus to an interpreter's perception: I shall call it the STIMULUS-OBJECT. In some cases, as in a perceived flash of light, it may be identical with (2).
(2) A stimulus capable of interpretation: SIGN-VEHICLE.
(3) An INTERPRETER who (a) perceives the stimulus, and who – on the basis of prior conditioning – (b) identifies the stimulus, (c) makes an association between the identified stimulus and something else (a conceptualized 'association-object') which is not intrinsic to the stimulus, and (d) conceptualizes the relationship of association.

(4) An ACT OF INTERPRETATION [comprised of (3c) and (3d)].

(5) A conceptualized object, not that of (1), which is associated by the interpreter with the sign-vehicle: ASSOCIATION-OBJECT. (The association-object is the 'signification' of the sign which is called into being by the interpretation of the sign-vehicle.)

(6) A SIGN, which may be conceived as an interpreted sign-vehicle. It is the act of interpretation operating on the sign-vehicle which creates the sign, or calls it into being; and it is this act of interpretation, creating a sign, that establishes a sign situation.

(7) A CONTEXT OF ASSOCIATION, the field encompassing and limiting the sign situation; it is this which determines how the sign-vehicle is to be interpreted (i.e., what specific association-object is to be associated with the sign-vehicle). The context of association is comprised of (a) the physical environment in which the sign-vehicle is perceived, (b) the interpreter's past experiences with similar stimuli in similar environments, (c) the set of predispositions which the interpreter holds regarding potential association-objects for specific kinds of sign-vehicles in given environments, and (d) the set of predispositions which the interpreter holds, at the moment of perception, regarding the potential association-objects capable of being linked with the given sign-vehicle in the current physical environment.

By definition, a sign will have a signification for the interpreter. This signification includes the body of additional personal associations which the association-object habitually evokes in the interpreter, their nature, number, and patterning being largely a function of the context of association. These personal associations embodied in the signification of a sign may be called the sign's 'connotations'. Those which are comprised of the interpreter's personal KNOWLEDGE of the nature, attributes, and present condition of the association-object may be called 'informative connotations' (while personal to the interpreter in that they have come to be linked with the association-object through his past experience, many of these may also be general in the sense that they are potentially available to any knowledgeable interpreter). Those which are comprised of the interpreter's set of ATTITUDES toward the association-object are 'affective connotations' (these are emotionally based and stem from the interpreter's past experience with occurrences of the association-object; and though they may possibly be shared in part with other interpreters, they will not necessarily be shared with them, and may not even be available to others). If affective connotations are sufficiently strong, the sign itself – as interpreted sign-vehicle – may acquire the chain of associations otherwise accruing to the association-object. In such a case, the interpreter may come to respond to the sign itself as he would normally to the conceptualized association-object alone. Put another way, in such a case the emotional response engendered by the association-object would be transferred to the interpreted sign-vehicle.

While a sign will have a signification that includes personal connotations, it may or may not have 'denotation'.[1] If we take the smell of smoke to be a sign of fire somewhere in the vicinity, our conceptualization of the presence of fire is the signification of smoke conceived as a sign. The connotations of the sign will be a set of concepts we typically associate with fire, informational or attitudinal. If there is actually a fire in the vicinity, the smoke acting as a sign will, in indicating its presence, have denotation; by actually existing, the association-object provides the sign's denotation. If, however, there is no fire (let us say that it has just been extinguished when we first smell the smoke), the sign which we create by interpreting the sign-vehicle smoke to signify the presence of fire has no denotation. It is true that the sign we have created purports to denote fire, or to testify its existence. But if the fire which it 'denotes' according to our interpretation does not in fact exist, the sign's purported denotation is false.[2]

4.3 CARROLL'S ILLUSTRATIONS OF NON-LINGUISTIC SIGN SITUATIONS; THEIR IMPLICATIONS FOR THIS STUDY

Although Carroll's interest in sign-processes was predominantly focused on those involving linguistic signs, his works contain numerous illustrations of non-linguistic sign-processes as well. Besides attesting Carroll's general interest in semiotic and providing a source of amusement in his writings, these illustrations are quite useful for this study; for the semiotic principles which may be inferred from them are generic counterparts of those principles which are embodied in his illustrations of linguistic sign-processes. In his depiction of non-linguistic sign situations we have both an implied commentary on the nature and functions of signs in general (and thus of the subset, linguistic signs) and a standard by which we may judge our interpretations of the semiotic principles implied in his depictions of linguistic sign situations. In view of Carroll's reticence in making overt statements about his linguistic notions, it is good to have a generalized point of reference against which we can test our inferences in the linguistic realm.

---

[1] Charles Morris has made a useful distinction between a sign's signification and its denotation (*Signs, Language, and Behavior* [1955], pp. 106-107; 258, note E). Although I do not adopt Morris's system of terminology in its entirety, I think that in this particular matter, his distinction seems to be a reasonable way to analyze the problem.

[2] Let us try a more general statement of the sign-process. When, in a context of association R we interpret the sign-vehicle X by linking the association-object Y with its perceived occurrence, we create a sign Z, whose signification is Y. We may express this relationship by saying that for us, Z has the signification Y in the context R, or Z signifies Y. If Y actually exists at the time of Z's creation, Z denotes Y; if it does not exist, Z merely purports to denote Y. In common usage, however, X (the sign-vehicle) is conceived to be the sign; and we have expressions such as "X is a sign of Y" ("Smoke is a sign of fire") or, equivalently, "X signifies Y". We may say this in most situations without dangerously misrepresenting the sign-process. But actually it is the INTERPRETATION of X to signify Y (i.e., the association of Y with the occurrence of X) that constitutes the sign (Z) in the situation. And to be rigorous, it is only Z, as sign, that may properly be said to have the signification Y.

In Wonderland, for example, the Queen of Hearts' gardeners, having planted a white rose-tree by mistake when they had been ordered to plant a red one, try to conceal their blunder by painting the white roses red. Had they not been interrupted and discovered in the act, their altering of the tree's external appearance might have effectively deluded the Queen as to the tree's true nature for (1) she would have interpreted the red color of the roses (an attribute which, by virtue of her previous experience with roses, she is capable of interpreting as signifying the flowers' nature) to signify that the flowers were red-roses and not some other kind of rose; and (2) she would have interpreted this knowledge (on the basis of her previous experience with rose-trees) to signify that the tree which had produced them was a red rose-tree. In the first sign situation, the red color of the roses – as a stimulus capable of her interpretation – is the sign-vehicle; in the second, the presence of red-roses on the tree is the sign-vehicle. The interpreted sign-vehicles are thus signs to her, having respectively the significations "(Those are) red-roses" and "(That is a) red rose-tree".

But the Queen is not deluded by the gardeners' attempt at deceit. She interprets the white color of the unpainted roses to signify "white-roses", and the presence of white-roses on the tree to signify that the tree is a white rose-tree. Moreover, she interprets the observable evidence of the gardeners' incomplete paint job to signify an attempt on their part to deceive.

The general semiotic principle implied by this passage concerns the relationship of the stimulus-object to the other elements of the sign-process. Let us first take the flower itself as stimulus-object (i.e., that which provides to an interpreter a stimulus capable of interpretation). Since the flower's observed color X (sign-vehicle) is associated by the interpreter with his concept of X-ROSE (association-object) to produce a sign whose signification is "X-rose", the observed attributes of whiteness or redness will, respectively, cause the interpreter to identify the flower in question as "white-rose" or "red-rose". In this particular instance, the white roses ARE white-roses, but the red roses are NOT red-roses. They too are white-roses. In the second sign situation, the stimulus-object is the tree itself, having as attributive features either white or red roses. The presence on the tree of white or red roses is the sign-vehicle with which the interpreter associates his concept WHITE (or RED) ROSE-TREE (association-object) to produce a sign whose signification is either "white rose-tree" or "red rose-tree". His previous experience will have taught him that only white rose-trees can produce white roses, only red rose-trees red. But in this particular instance, though the white rose-tree IS a white rose-tree, the tree possessing red roses is NOT a red rose-tree: it too is a white rose-tree.

The question which seems to be implied is this: Is there any inherent correspondence between the nature of the stimulus-object and the signification of the sign which its attributes, upon interpretation, give rise to? In this instance, does painting white-roses red, so that they are responded to as red-roses, in any way alter their essential nature? Does changing the apparent character of the tree, so that it is responded to as a red rose-tree, in any way affect the tree's ability to produce white-roses? Certainly the paint job obscures and apparently denies the attribute 'whiteness' of the roses and the tree's ability to produce white-roses. Had the job been completed, the Queen might indeed have been deceived as to the nature of the flowers and the tree. But regardless of the possibility of the gardeners' attempt at deception actually succeeding, the roses are still white under their coat of paint; and the tree is still a white rose-tree, as the next blossoming will prove.

Carroll's illustration of the gardeners' paint job embodies a general principle which could be stated thus: a sign-vehicle may or may not accurately characterize the true nature of the stimulus-object of which it purports to be an attribute; if it does not, the sign to which it gives rise upon interpretation will have a signification bearing no correspondence to the true nature of the object. Thus, falsely characterizing the roses and the tree with attributes contrary to those which they would intrinsically possess makes possible the interpreter's creation of signs whose significations are simply inaccurate with regard to the true natures of the objects. If an attribute, upon interpretation, gives rise to a sign of inaccurate signification, the interpreter may respond to the inaccurate signification as though it WERE accurate; but the interpreter's response in no way alters the essential nature of the object. Only white-roses accurately characterize a white rose-tree; painting white-roses red may make them red roses, but not red-roses. However, for evidence that the gardeners' paint job might have achieved their immediate aim, we have only to look to the realms of advertising and politics to see how manipulators of sign situations do successfully foster delusion in the public through willful misrepresentation of fact.

Functionally, of course, after such a paint job the tree is, insofar as the interpreter responds to the color, a red rose-tree; so the Queen would think and so believe until the paint washed off or a new crop of flowers appeared. In like manner, Mrs. Middleage might be naively convinced by advertising copy that she can truly "wash the gray right out of her hair" with a black rinse; but if she does believe this (and is confirmed in her belief by the immediate success of the experiment), she will be puzzled when the gray has unaccountably returned. In the realm of politics, the metaphor "whitewashing" is often used to refer to the covering up of scandal: though the results and implications of the scandal are still present, the public may be mollified into accepting fraud as "an unfortunate misunderstanding". Further, "Honest" John may indeed be elected governor on the basis of his campaign image (created by men who know him to be other than honest), and functionally the electorate is convinced of his honesty until the black day that he is caught with his hand in the public till.

When a sign-vehicle is so interpreted as to create a sign whose signification is inaccurate with reference to the true nature of the stimulus-object, that which the sign purports to denote (i.e., purports to testify the existence of) does not actually exist. Such a sign, properly speaking, has no denotation – for that which it purports to denote is a bogus entity: in the case of the gardeners' paint job, red-roses and a red rose-tree; in the other examples, respectively, the possibility of washing grayness from one's hair with a superficial dye, "an unfortunate misunderstanding" involving the public trust, and "Honest" John's honesty. Whether a sign does or does not denote, it will by definition have signification (though this signification may or may not be accurate with reference to the nature of the stimulus-object); and this signification will, by virtue of its attendant connotations, condition the interpreter's further behavior. For the Queen of Hearts, for example, as for most other knowledgeable interpreters, the signification "(That is a) red rose-tree" would have as informative connotations simply that a red rose-tree was present, and that the tree could be expected to produce red-roses at the next blossoming. But for the Queen, who had ordered a red rose-tree to be planted at that spot, there would be the additional informative connotation that the gardeners had followed her orders. The affective connotations provided by this signification would be different for the Queen and for a neutral observer such as Alice; the Queen would have a sense of pleased gratification at knowing that her orders had been followed, and that the tree was present, while the neutral interpreter would have no emotional response to the signification at all.

In the same chapter of *Wonderland*, there is another example of Carroll's interest in non-linguistic sign-processes. The three gardeners, hoping to escape the Queen's wrath after her discovery of their trick, throw themselves face-downward on the ground so that she cannot identify them. "For you see", explains Carroll, "as they were lying on their faces, and the pattern on their backs was the same as the rest of the pack, she could not tell whether they were gardeners, or soldiers, or courtiers, or three of her own children." The absence of a stimulus-object providing a sign-vehicle which, upon interpretation, could give rise to a sign whose signification would be the culprits' occupation – in this case "spades", as opposed to "clubs", "diamonds", and "hearts", respectively – prevents the Queen from identifying her gardeners as to occupation and social class. An analogous problem would be encountered by someone who tried to determine the occupations of a group of naked men. Unless, like Sherlock Holmes, he could infer their occupations from such physical characteristics as spatulated finger-ends and calloused knees, he would probably find himself baffled in the absence of stimulus-objects providing him with interpretable sign-vehicles. But let the men put on their respective clothing – policeman's uniform, sailor suit, priest's habit, and painter's overalls – and the problem is solved (provided of course that the men are not in masquerade). In *Through the Looking-Glass* Humpty Dumpty makes a further comment on the difficulty of identifying things in the absence of interpretable sign-vehicles which would serve to distinguish objects superficially similar:

"I shouldn't know you again if we *did* meet," Humpty Dumpty replied in a discontented tone, giving her one of his fingers to shake: "you're so exactly like other people."

"The face is what one goes by, generally," Alice remarked in a thoughtful tone.

"That's just what I complain of," said Humpty Dumpty. "Your face is the same as everybody has — the two eyes, so —" (marking their places in the air with his thumb) "nose in the middle, mouth under. It's always the same. Now if you had the two eyes on the same side of the nose, for instance – or the mouth at the top – that would be *some* help."

(*Works*, pp. 220-221)

The semiotic principle to be inferred from the Queen's difficulty in identifying the gardeners and from Humpty Dumpty's difficulty in distinguishing between individual human faces might be stated thus: In the absence of an interpretable sign-vehicle, no sign can be formed. There is simply nothing to interpret; hence no act of interpretation is possible.

Somewhat related to these illustrations in principle is the Bellman's sailing off to hunt the Snark using a map that is "a perfect and absolute blank":

He had bought a large map representing the sea,
    Without the least vestige of land:
And the crew were much pleased when they found it to be
    A map they could all understand.

"What's the good of Mercator's North Poles and Equators,
    Tropics, Zones, and Meridian Lines?"
So the Bellman would cry: and the crew would reply
    "They are merely conventional signs!

"Other maps are such shapes, with their islands and capes!
    But we've got our brave Captain to thank"
(So the crew would protest) "that he's bought *us* the best –
    A perfect and absolute blank!"

(*Works*, pp. 760-761)

Carroll is merely joking here, indulging in the same sort of nonsense as in his description of the Bellman's navigation: "and the bowsprit got mixed with the rudder sometimes". But the question does rise unbidden in the reader's mind, Can a blank piece of paper be a map? The answer is no, for a map is by definition an approximate iconic representation, scaled small, of an existent physical thing – all or a portion of the earth's surface. Once interpreted, the markings on a map are signs which signify and denote concrete objects existing in the phenomenal world: land-masses, islands, reefs, and coast-lines. If a map is to be an accurate representation of reality (and only if it is can it be an aid in navigation), it must accurately depict the objects which it purports to signify. The crew is quite correct in regarding Mercator's projection lines and the division markings representing zones as "merely conventional signs", for these lines are arbitrarily conceived and, when taken as signs, denote no physical objects existing on the earth's surface. But although to knowledgeable interpreters these marks are signs which denote no physical reality, they do function usefully in the act of navigation since their significations are agreed upon by convention; they do aid in determining a ship's location at sea (and, incidentally, in the drawing of accurate maps). The markings on a map, both those that signify and denote physical things and those that signify functionally convenient fictions, are sign-vehicles which CAN be interpreted and which should be, if the map is to be used for the purpose for which it was intended. It is highly imperceptive of the crew to assume that a blank piece of paper is the 'best' kind of map; but, unlike the Queen of Hearts who was angered at her inability to identify her prostrate gardeners, the Bellman's crew is pleased at having a 'map' with no sign-vehicles requiring interpretation. It was a map they could all 'understand': that is to say, they had no difficulty in grasping the significations of its markings. No sign-vehicles, no signs; no signs, no significations.

The Queen of Hearts' inability to identify her gardeners was brought about by the absence of interpretable sign-vehicles. In *Wonderland* there are two excellent examples of situations in which the process of classification and naming is facilitated by the presence of non-linguistic sign-vehicles.

In the first of these, Alice, having arrived at the Knave of Hearts' trial, looks about the courtroom and identifies the chief legalistic fixtures:

"That's the judge," she said to herself, "because of his great wig."

(Works, p. 114)

In the second, she is standing before the Duchess' house wondering what to do next, when suddenly

a footman in livery came running out the wood – (she considered him to be a footman because he was in livery: otherwise, judging by his face only, she would have called him a fish) . . .

(Works, p. 63)

In both of these examples Alice is able to affix a name to the objects of her scrutiny because of the interpretable sign-vehicles provided by their apparel: upon interpretation, the wig becomes a sign having the signification that the wearer is a judge; the livery becomes a sign signifying that the wearer is a footman (in spite of the fact that he is also a fish).

Both of these acts of classification are inferences on Alice's part, based upon her knowledge of the conventional significance of such apparel, and her experience with wigs and livery in the past. She may have seen livery similar to that worn by the fish on footmen in her own world; her experience with wigs worn by judges was limited to pictures she had seen, for she had never been in a court of justice before. When she makes her respective classifications, she has no empirical proof that these figures ARE what their characterizing attributes, conceived as signs, signify them to be. It is true that apparel oft proclaims the man – but not always. It would have been possible for the fish, though dressed in livery, not to have been a footman at all; and for the man wearing the wig (in spite of his being the King) to have been a mere court clerk. It so happens that in these instances Alice's inferences are correct. But they could have been erroneous, since the significations of signs MAY not correspond to the nature of the objects whose attributes give rise to the signs. A rose beneath its coat of paint would still be white.

As a process of inference, the act of classifying and naming an object on the basis of attributes interpreted as characterizing signs is subject to error if (1) the attributes are misinterpreted through ignorance of their conventional significance, or if (2) they fail to conform to the interpreter's expectations (based on his past experience) regarding their conventional significance, and thus come to have for him a signification which does not correspond to the nature of the object possessing those attributes. But Carroll is also illustrating the principle that non-linguistic characterizing signs often can be relied upon to convey accurate information about the objects whose attributes give rise to them. Indeed, it is on the basis of interpreting a thing's attributes as signifying something about the thing's nature that classification is possible.

A final example of Carroll's interest in non-linguistic signs: Alice, at the end of Chapter III of *Through the Looking-Glass,* having just left the wood where things have no names, comes upon two finger-posts pointing down the path in the same direction. She ponders a moment wondering which of the two indicators to follow.

It was not a very difficult question to answer, as there was only one road through the wood, and the two finger-posts both pointed along it. "I'll settle it,'" Alice said to herself. "when the road divides and they point different ways."

But this did not seem likely to happen. She went on and on, a long way, but wherever the road divided, there were sure to be two finger-posts pointing the same way, one marked "TO TWEEDLEDUM'S HOUSE," and the other "TO THE HOUSE OF TWEEDLEDEE."

"I do believe," said Alice at last, "that they live in the *same* house! ..."

(*Works*, p. 179)

One could not ask for a more explicit schematization of the sign-process. The two finger-posts are literally 'pointers' or indexical signs, having as their significations the information contained in the legends printed upon them, and purporting to denote, respectively, the house of Tweedledum and the house of Tweedledee, neither of these objects as yet visible. Alice's inference that the pointers designate the same object is not strictly warranted by her evidence. She has interpreted the fact of the two finger-posts' invariably pointing the same way whenever the road divides as signifying that both pointers designate the same specific location; as a sign, in other words, that both Tweedles live in the same house. But this signification may not be accurate as regards the true state of things. The road might divide at some further point with a corresponding divergence of the direction-pointers; or, if they do not diverge, she might reach one house long before she reached the other; or, if the same location is designated by the pointers, she might find two houses side by side; or she might find only one house down the road, and that occupied by only one of the Tweedles; or she might find that there aren't any houses at all. She is never able to verify her inference, for she does not reach either Tweedledum's house or the house of Tweedledee: she encounters the brothers in the wood, and their respective dwellings (whether the same or different) are never mentioned again. Still, it is possible that Alice's inference is correct, that both pointers designate the same building.

The finger-posts are able to be interpreted as indexical signs by virtue of two correlated features: first, the pointed board itself, minus the inscription, is interpreted as signifying that something down the road is being pointed at; second, the legend printed on the board, "TO X", signifies that X is that which is being designated. These two features of the finger-posts – the quality of pointing and the statement that X lies in the direction indicated – act in combination to produce a sign whose signification is "X lies down the road in this direction." This signification, as a proposition having conceptual import, itself becomes a sign having the signification "There is an X such that X lies down the road in the indicated direction." This second sign ("X lies down the road in this direction") purports to denote X, to testify X's existence. If there is no X to be found down the road, the sign has no denotation, but merely possesses signification. If there is an X, the sign may be said to denote X.

If both Tweedle brothers do live in one and the same house as Alice assumes, then both finger-posts (note that Carroll does not call them 'signs') designate a single thing in the same manner that two men may simultaneously point to a third and say, "That object which I am pointing at is located there." If we consider the boards only, minus their inscriptions, and assume that they do indeed designate a single object down the road, we have a principle implied in this illustration that can be stated thus: Two or more discrete signs may have identical significations, and (as a corollary) may denote the same thing. In a linguistic sign situation, this principle is analogously illustrated by the fact that to a knowledgeable interpreter, both 'Lewis Carroll' and 'Charles Dodgson' (conceived as identifying labels, a kind of indexical sign) designate and purport to denote a single man.

If the Tweedle brothers do not live in the same house, Alice's inference – based upon a series of situations in which both finger-posts seem to have identical significations – is of course wrong. (I am inclined to think that if she had ever reached the brothers' respective dwellings, she would have found two houses side by side, each the mirror-image of the other; but this, too, is an inference – based upon my knowledge of the reversal motif that undergirds the book.) If the Tweedle brothers do not live in the same house, and if there ARE two houses down the road inhabited respectively by Dum and Dee, the finger-posts would, as indexical signs interpreted according to their intended significance, have different significations and would respectively denote different objects. In making her inference, Alice has provisionally denied this possibility. But I think it may be assumed that Carroll, a professional logician, was aware of the possibility.Why does he not allow Alice to verify her inference by actually reaching the place(s) designated by the finger-posts? Since there is no follow-up to this matter, one must ask what function this brief passage serves in the total context of the book. Since Alice never reaches the

house(s) to which the indicators presumably point, and since the finger-posts have
no subsequent bearing on the story, the incident seems to be present merely to
prepare Alice for her meeting with the Tweedle brothers (enabling her to identify
them when she does meet them) and to provide her with an opportunity to make
her inference about the identical significations of the two signs. Since it has no
other apparent function in the story, the presence of this illustration suggests that
Carroll the logician was playing games with his readers. Whether or not this be the
case, the passage does imply the semiotic principle that two indexical signs which
seem (or are taken) to have identical significations (and to denote the same object)
may actually have been intended to have different significations (and hence to
denote different objects); that two indexical signs which seem (or are taken) to
have different significations (and to denote different objects) may actually have
been intended to have identical significations (and hence to denote the same object);
that signs, regardless of what they purport to denote, may actually denote nothing
(which recalls the Queen's non-existent red rose-tree).

The principle may be illustrated in the analogous realm of written symbols in
the case of a banker's assuming that two signs which he encounters in his accounts
– both of the appearance '$' – are being used to signify the United States dollar,
when actually one of the instances of '$' in this context is intended to signify the
Canadian dollar, which has a different monetary value. The same type of confusion affecting the banker would arise in the case of a history student's assuming
that the symbol 'Pope John XXIII' which he encounters in a textbook is being used
to designate Angelo Roncalli, the immediate predecessor of Pope Paul VI, when
actually his author is using 'Pope John XXIII' to designate Baldassare Cossa, the
first pope of that name and number, who was deposed by the Council of Constance
in 1415. The student, having fallen prey to this confusion, would find references
in his text to 'the Council' highly misleading: for if the term were not more
precisely defined, his predisposition would establish a context of association in
which it would be interpreted to designate Vatican II instead of what the author
intended, the Council of Constance.

Though Carroll's illustrations of the operation of non-linguistic sign-processes
imply certain principles relating to the nature and function of signs in general, it
cannot be determined whether Carroll consciously formulated these principles and
verbalized them to himself. The illustrations exist in their respective narrative
frameworks as brief, self-contained episodes with little or no relationship to subsequent events or to the plot-line as a whole. The painting of the Queen of Hearts'
roses, her inability to identify her prostrate gardeners, Humpty Dumpty's difficulty
in distinguishing individual human faces, the Bellman's blank "map", Alice's immediate classification of the King and the fish as "judge" and "footman", respectively, on the basis of their apparel, and her enigmatic encounter with the two
finger-posts – all of these exist apparently for no other reason than (1) to provide
humorous incident and (2) to make a whimsically-conceived commentary on the

nature and functions of signs. If the former is all that Carroll intended, it is none-theless noteworthy that he chose as a source of humorous incident the operation of sign-processes.

Granted that these illustrations do imply general semiotic principles, what commentary on the nature of signs do they provide? The following, at least: (a) for a sign situation to occur, there must be present something capable of providing a stimulus which can serve as a sign-vehicle for an interpreter; (b) if an interpretable sign-vehicle is not present, no sign can be formed; (c) a sign-vehicle may or may not accurately characterize the true nature of the stimulus-object of which it purports to be an attribute; if it does, the sign to which it gives rise has a signification which corresponds to the inherent nature of the thing providing the sign-vehicle; if it does not, the sign to which it legitimately gives rise upon interpretation will have a signification bearing no correspondence to the inherent nature of the object; (d) the significations of signs may be inaccurate with regard to the true nature of the stimulus-object; (e) if a sign of inaccurate signification is responded to as though the signification WERE accurate, the interpreter's response (and his subsequent actions conditioned by this response) in no way alters the inherent nature of the stimulus-object; (f) classification and naming is a process whereby attributes are taken as signs whose significations correspond to the thing's nature; if an object has no perceptible attributes which could be interpreted as signifying something about the object's nature, the object cannot be classified; if these attributes are such that they give rise to signs of inaccurate signification, the object will be erroneously classified; (g) a sign will necessarily have signification, but it may or may not have denotation, depending on whether or not the association-object actually exists; (h) conventional signs which denote no existing object may be useful for enabling the interpreter to perform certain tasks (meridian lines on navigational charts); (i) two or more discrete signs may have identical significations, and denote the same thing; (j) two or more indexical signs (identifying "pointers" or labels) which are taken to signify and denote different things may actually have been intended to signify and to denote the same thing; conversely, those which seem to the interpreter to have identical significations and to denote the same thing may actually have been intended to signify and denote different things. In a practical situation, the operation of this last principle can be discerned (and the interpreter saved from potential delusion) only by an empirical definition of the signs' respective denotations: Alice could have verified her inference only by proceeding down the path until she came to Tweedledum's house AND the house of Tweedledee.

If these inferred principles are legitimate, they provide a commentary on sign-processes in general. Since language operates through an elaborate system of hier-archically-patterned sign-processes, these principles have a generic relevance to the functional nature of the various kinds of signs which comprise the linguistic code. Linguistic sign-processes may, in part, be described and understood in terms of the principles inferred from Carroll's depiction of non-linguistic sign situations.

4.4 OF LINGUISTIC SIGNS

4.4.1 *The Nature of the Linguistic Sign*

A 'natural' language such as English is a type of code comprised of meaningful elements, finite in number, which are capable of entering into an infinite number of combinations in accordance with a finite set of established rules. These meaningful elements, together with the rules governing their interrelations and usage, constitute and define the language in question. In any act of discourse, one who knows the language will respond to the various constituents of the linguistic code as signs embodying specific kinds of significations. As a subset of signs in general, linguistic signs function in accord with the general process outlined in § 4.2; and the linguistic sign situation may be regarded as a specialized subclass of the general case.

Taken as a group, the linguistic signs comprising English are characterized by their operating as an integrated system on a multiplicity of interacting hierarchical levels of interpretation. In the medium of speech, their sensory vehicle is sound produced by the human vocal tract which acts as a stimulus on the interpreter's auditory system. In the analogous medium of writing, their sensory vehicle is forms perceptible to the interpreter's eye – letters, word-units, word-groups, spaces, and punctuation marks. In the discussion to follow I have confined my remarks to the speech code.

Linguistic signs occurring in the medium of speech may be classified into several types which differ both in the nature of the conceptualized stimuli which evoke them and in the kinds of significations which they have for interpreters. All types, of course, are brought to our perception through the medium of sound; and in this sense, sound may be considered to be the ULTIMATE vehicle for each sign in the speech code. But sounds are only the building blocks from which the higher order constituents are created. In much the same way that a wall is formed through a combination of individual bricks, a building shaped and constituted by several walls in combination, a single architectural complex created by a combination of several buildings, and a city made up of combined groups of these complexes, the higher order constituents of the linguistic code are formed in an incremental fashion into sequential groups, each particular group providing the basis for the existence of the next higher group. It is this progressive formation of successive groups of constituents that requires us to view the linguistic code as a hierarchical structuring of different levels of interpretation. On each level, the IMMEDIATE sign-vehicles (though ultimately reducible to discrete concatenations of articulated sounds) have their own individual character.

Starting at the bottom of the hierarchical scale (at a point technically outside the code itself), we have first the specific sounds, or phones, which the interpreter hears in the stream of speech. Upon identification, these signify respectively the general phone-types which the speaker intends should be apprehended. These phone-types, or phonemes, represented by specific sounds, are the lowest level constituents which are part of the linguistic code proper; entering into various combinations, they form morphs, represented by sound sequences, which in turn comprise the code-elements on the next higher level of interpretation, that of the morpheme (in English, this level is composed of roots, various types of inflection markers, derivational affixes, internal juncture, and intonation contours). Phonemes are sign-vehicles which, when identified, signify through the creation of meaningful contrasts on the morphemic level of interpretation, what code-elements are intended on that level. On the morphemic level, the immediate sign-vehicles are the identifiable units themselves, selectively isolated from whatever morphs may be present that are not recognized as elements of the code. The significations of morphemes go beyond merely indicating what constituents are to be understood on the next higher level of interpretation, that of syntactic structures; in addition to this general type of signification, some morphemes have significations involving things that lie wholly outside the linguistic code, while others have significations that indicate internal relationships between elements of the code. But as the units on the morphemic level enter into various combinations, they do serve to signify what syntactic structures – phrases and sentences – are intended by the speaker. These syntactic structures are themselves sign-vehicles which, upon interpretation, signify what message is intended to be imparted by the speaker.

Since the linguistic code is a complex system of many types of constituents which preserve their individuality while acting in concert to convey messages, the act of interpreting a spoken utterance necessarily involves the interpreter in a large number and variety of sign situations. Moreover, since the integrated operation of linguistic signs to impart a message entails a hierarchical structuring of interpretations (with different types of constituents embodying different kinds of significations), the message finally interpreted from the utterance necessarily incorporates the sum total of the various significations resulting from the sign-processes at each level of interpretation. This is not to say that the interpreter is aware of all of the sign-processes in which he is engaged – for he isn't. Unless a constituent calls attention to itself through presenting some difficulty to his interpretation either of it or of the whole utterance, the interpreter whips through the various intermediate sign-processes with extreme rapidity and is conscious only of the message which the utterance as a whole has imparted to him.

When a speaker begins talking to us, we interpret the fact as a sign signifying that the speaker is engaging in a communication-attempt. This in turn we take to be a sign that the utterance will convey a message, and we respond by listening. Primed to expect a message, we listen selectively to the stream of speech in order to identify those meaningful elements on all levels of interpretation which our knowledge of the language leads us to expect will be present. In an unconscious way, we approach the stream of speech as a phonic code to be 'cracked'.

Any attempt to describe the sign-processes involved in understanding spoken discourse will oversimplify the actual situation by making them appear overly mechanical and schematized. Yet at the same time, because the force of habit renders the process of decoding largely unconscious and effortless, the processes as described will seem more complex to a speaker of the language than he intuitively feels that it is. Thus, it must be remembered that the actual process of interpreting utterances is less mechanical and self-conscious, but more intricate, than my brief discussion will imply. The most fruitful way to discuss linguistic sign-processes is to examine the various types of signification which the constituents of the linguistic code hold for interpreters. For speakers of English, the different types of linguistic signs comprising the code may possess the following kinds of meanings: differential, referential, structural, and contextual.

4.4.2 *Differential Meaning*

The meaningful elements of the linguistic code must be capable of being distinguished from one another on each level of interpretation; for if the interpreter were unable to differentiate them, the code would break down, and the language would cease to function as an instrument of communication. To state it another way, in a given unit of discourse, every meaningful element on each of the hierarchical levels of interpretation must be identifiable, or able to be recognized as being unique and standing in a relationship of functional contrast with all other elements on that particular level. In decoding a message, we identify X as X because it is perceptibly different from Y, Z, or anything else. In order to maintain its functional integrity, English possesses built-in safeguards to make each element uniquely identifiable in any act of discourse. When an element, for any reason, loses its distinct recognition value and becomes indistinguishable from another linguistic sign-vehicle, ambiguity of signification will result – unless it is prevented from occurring by a context of association which informs the interpreter of the intended value – and, as a consequence, the possibility of misunderstanding will arise.

The linguistic code operates through a system of functional contrasts among its elements on each level of interpretation. Each type of linguistic sign – phone, phoneme, morph, morpheme, phrase, sentence, block of unified discourse – is protected from misinterpretation on its level by an internal set of functional contrasts which preserve unitary identity. Thus, every element in the linguistic code has differential meaning: regardless of whatever other types of signification it may possess for an interpreter, when taken as a sign it signifies itself as being an element of the linguistic code and declares its exclusion from other classes of linguistic signs within that system. When the interpreter encounters the element in the stream of speech (whether it be an individual phone; a sequence of sounds comprising a word, phrase, or sentence; a relative change in pitch or stress; an internal juncture;

or a particular intonation contour), he recognizes it as a discrete entity. When X occurs as a stimulus to his hearing in the context of a speech act, the interpreter regards it as a sign-vehicle within the linguistic code and interprets it by 'matching' it with a conceptual counterpart which he knows to be in the code. Thus a sign is created whose signification is the functional identity of X within the language system. It may be seen that differential meaning is strictly equivalent to recognition value. The interpretation of all linguistic sign-vehicles depends on differential meaning, both (a) as it separates the elements of the given code from non-relevant stimuli which may be present in the stream of speech (this selectivity is a function of the interpreter's knowledge of what elements comprise the code), and (b) as it separates and distinguishes one element from another on the same level of interpretation.

In English, the lowest level of the interpretive hierarchy is the phonetic; our conditioning as speakers of the language has trained us to listen for certain specific sounds, or articulated phones, which are intermixed with others in the stream of speech. Primed to listen for only certain phones, we isolate and identify them when they occur, ignoring all of those which do not represent elements in the code of English. We recognize and classify these individual phones by means of a sign-process which, though taking place in a linguistic context of assocation, is properly to be considered pre-linguistic.

On the phonetic level of interpretation, the sign-vehicle is the sum of the acoustic properties of the individual phone uttered by the speaker. In the context of association of an English utterance, the hearer interprets the attributes of the articulated phone by 'matching' them with a conceptualized set of similar attributes possessed by a phone known to be a representative of a specific phone-type which serves as an element in the linguistic code (in this sign situation, the set of conceptualized 'matching' attributes is the association-object). Thus a sign is created whose signification is that the phone in question is a particular representative of a specific class of phones having similar attributes. Through this process, the phone is excluded from all other classes and thus comes to have differential meaning. If the interpreter classifies the perceived phone as the voiceless bilabial stop [p], he has interpreted its acoustic qualities to signify that it is [p] and not the voiced bilabial stop [b], the bilabial nasal [m], or any other phone. As a sign having differential meaning, the phone [p] signifies its own identity, its membership in the class of voiceless bilabial stops, and its exclusion from other classes: it is not [b], [m], [t], etc. But by virtue of its identity, it also signifies – in the context of an English utterance – that it is a particular representative of a specific phoneme /p/. The recognition value of particular phones establishes their identity and, by so doing, reveals them to be members of specific classes of phone-types which act as low-level constituents of the linguistic code.

Whereas the other constituents of the linguistic code have other kinds of signification in addition to their intrinsic differential meaning, phonemes have differential meaning only. In the process of decoding an utterance, the sounds we recognize are those which are particular representatives of phonemes; it is actually phonemes that we are trying to isolate in the utterance, for it is they that will signify the differential meanings possessed by elements on the morphemic level. But we can determine what phonemes are intended only by identifying their concrete phonic representatives. The voiceless bilabial stop [p] which we identify in the stream of speech becomes a sign to us signifying that the phonemic code-element /p/ is intended, and not another phoneme, such as /f/. Since by entering into various combinations phonemes produce morphs, or phonemic shapes, which may in turn constitute the meaningful elements on the morphemic level, and since these morphs may be interpreted as signifying that they are representatives of specific morphemes, it is crucial that the phonemes be accurately identified.

Morphemes are constituents of the code which embody other kinds of meanings – referential, structural, contextual – in addition to differential; it frequently happens that highly divergent significations occur on the morphemic level due to the contrast of different phonemes in the same position in otherwise identical phonemic environments. It is the mutual contrasts of /p/, /b/, /d/, /f/, /r/, and /w/ in otherwise identical environments that respectively produce the different morphemes 'pig', 'big', 'dig', 'fig', 'rig', and 'wig', and both signal and determine their divergent referential significations. Any mistake in identifying the initial phoneme of any item in this series could cause the morpheme in question to be misinterpreted unless the context of association were sufficiently explicit in indicating its intended signification to insure the proper interpretation.

In *Wonderland*, Lewis Carroll illustrates the principle of phonemic signification of morphemic identity. By using a minimal pair (two morphemes containing only one phonemic contrast in otherwise identical environments) the passage illustrates the possession of differential meaning by elements on both the phonemic and morphemic levels; these two types of meaning (phonemic-differential and morphemic-differential) act in concert to signify the differential meanings posssessed on the syntactic level by the two sentences containing, respectively, each morpheme of the minimal pair. Alice is just concluding her conversation with the Cheshire Cat.

"By-the-bye, what became of the baby?" said the Cat. "I'd nearly forgotten to ask."
   "It turned into a pig," Alice answered . . . .
   "I thought it would," said the Cat, and vanished again.

After walking along for a few minutes, Alice is startled when the Cat suddenly reappears; but the Cat has a very good reason for returning:

"Did you say 'pig,' or 'fig'?" said the Cat.
   "I said 'pig'," replied Alice; "and I wish you wouldn't keep appearing and vanishing so suddenly: you make one quite giddy!"
   "All right," said the Cat; and this time it vanished quite slowly. . . .

(*Works*, pp. 73-74)

The passage illustrates what can happen when differential meaning is not explicit. The Cat, expecting the phoneme /p/ to occur in Alice's utterance (in the morpheme 'pig') is not sure that he heard accurately; and since the context of association (physical and verbal) does not make clear which of the two phonemes was intended, he is willing to admit the possibility that /f/ (creating the morpheme 'fig') was the one that Alice actually employed. Because 'pig' and 'fig' themselves exhibit differential meaning on the morphemic level of interpretation – each having its own recognition value in English – and because, as elements of the code, each has its own peculiar referential signification which in turn causes a difference in signification in otherwise identical sentences which might employ them ("It turned into a ——"), the Cat MUST determine which of the two phonemes was employed if he is to understand the message of Alice's utterance.

The Cat is involved in two parallel sign situations in his attempt to identify the crucial morpheme. His assuming that /p/ was intended produces a sign whose signification is the morpheme 'pig'; his assuming /f/, a sign whose signification is 'fig'. Since the intended phoneme is one of two possible alternatives and hence unclear to him, the signs produced at each successive constituent level are consequently twofold in their respective significations also. He has no recourse but to ask Alice to specify what she had said. Alice, on the other hand, has no trouble in differentiating the /p/ and /f/ in the two morphemic alternatives presented to her by the Cat. Her answer ("I said 'pig'") reveals that she has been able to choose one of the alternatives without difficulty, recognizing it immediately and matching it with the morpheme which she had previously uttered. She has understood his question perfectly, her interpretation being the sum total of the significations resulting from the sign-processes on the phonemic, morphemic, syntactic, and contextual levels. In each step of her interpretation, the code is cracked through the agency of differential meaning working in conjunction with the other types of meaning possessed by the various types of code-elements: [p] is not [f], [b], etc.; /p/ is not /f/, /b/, etc.; 'pig' is not 'fig', 'big', 'peg', 'pit', 'fog', 'mix', etc.; 'did' is not 'do', 'must', 'will', etc.; 'did you say' is not 'you did say', 'say you did', 'has he come', etc.; and (in this verbal context) 'or' is not 'ore', 'oar', 'and', 'without', etc. (its recognition value, partly signified by word order, partly by its being unstressed, identifies it as 'or', a morpheme having the structural meaning of indicating disjunction between two syntactic units of similar kinds).

Thus, it is only through the possession of differential meaning by each element on all levels of interpretation that a message can be interpreted unambiguously. In the context of association of the English code, this differential meaning is the sign-vehicle which enables the element to be interpreted as a constituent of the code and which prepares the way for further sign-processes that the element, in that context, entails. But for a unique recognition value to be established, each element must be distinguishable from all other elements on that particular level of interpretation. Otherwise, there would not be a variety of individual sign-vehicles capable of giving rise to signs of diverse significations; the code would break down, and potential interpreters would be confronted with a problem analogous to Humpty Dumpty's in being unable to distinguish between individual human faces: "I shouldn't know you again if we DID meet. . . . you're so exactly like other people. . . . Now if you had the two eyes on the same side of the nose, for instance – or the mouth at the top – that would be SOME help." As Alice says in the epigraph to this chapter, referring to kittens' habit of always purring when spoken to: "If they would only purr for 'yes', and mew for 'no', or any rule of that sort . . . so that one could keep up a conversation! But how CAN you talk with a person if they ALWAYS say the same thing?" No sign-vehicles, no signs; no signs, no significations.

4.4.3 *Referential Meaning*

As a perceived speech phone [p] is interpreted to signify that the phoneme /p/ is being used in the utterance, and as /p/ in combination with other phonemes forms a morph /pig/ which is interpreted to signify that the morpheme 'pig' is intended, so 'pig' itself is interpreted to signify that the particular association-object conventionally associated with 'pig' is the speaker's intended object of discourse. Although when interpreted as a sign within the linguistic code, 'pig' possesses intrinsic differential meaning, it has in addition another kind of meaning: referential – for its signification is a conceptualized association-object which lies wholly outside the confines of the linguistic code. Depending upon the context of association, this association-object will either be a particular animal ("my pig Charley", "that pig in our path") or any member of the general class of porcine quadrupeds ("whenever he wanted fresh meat, he butchered a pig"). Whether the signification be particular or general, the morpheme 'pig' as a conventional sign will refer to something which has real or fictional being outside the language system; and within a context of association that specifies a given animal as object of discourse, it will invariably have, for a knowledgeable interpreter, the power to evoke that particular referent. Hence, morphemes which possess referential meaning, such as the nouns 'pig', 'fig', 'chair', 'Aristotle', 'England', 'love', the verbs 'run', 'walk', 'eat', 'write', the adjectives 'tall', 'heavy', and the adverbs 'quickly', 'hard', have a truly symbolic function. They stand for the things they signify – whether concrete objects, qualities, or notional abstractions – and even in the physical absence of the association-object (if one actually exists; it needn't, of course), are able to evoke it in the mind of the interpreter.

Not only does referential meaning operate on the word level, it also provides a unitary signification for each syntactic structure. On the phrase level, specific referents are symbolized by the phrases "my pig", "your pig", "the man on the bridge", "John the Baptist", "*The City of God*", "a dog", "the dog", "walk quickly", "a tall chair", "tall chairs", "running hard", "Merry England". On the sentence level, specific referents are symbolized by "my pig is running hard",

"Augustine wrote *The City of God*", "the man on the bridge needs a tall chair". A syntactic structure taken as a sign has a referent comprised of the sum total of the significations of the various elements which, singly and in combination, comprise it. But whether phrase or sentence, the syntactic structure will have a unitary signification, embodying referential meaning, in its own right (though what this will be in an actual act of discourse will depend on the total context of association). On the sentence level we may call this referential meaning the sentence's import, or message. It is of course comprised of, and distilled from, the various types of meaning possessed by the code-elements which constitute it: differential, referential, structural, and contextual; but as the signification of the whole sentence, it has its own integrity. [See § 9.1.]

Morphemes which possess referential meaning may or may not have denotation. If the referent actually exists which the sign designates, the sign may be said to denote that referent. If the referent does not physically exist at the time the sign is formed, the sign has designative signification, but no denotation. Examples of non-denotative referential signs are 'John Stuart Mill' (no longer alive), 'unicorns' (never existed), 'all men with four heads' (null class), and 'love', 'truth', etc. (notional abstractions; these signs would have denotation only if they were used to designate something which was taken as representing a particular instance or concrete example of the named condition or quality).

Signs possessing referential meaning will have for any knowledgeable interpreter certain potential informative connotations. The sign 'pig', for example, as a general class-name, will have as its referent the porcine quadruped; its informative connotations will be the peculiar physical and dispositional traits of the animal, that it is widely used for food, and is a source of bacon, ham, pork chops, and sausage. The sign 'pig' may also evoke in the interpreter certain affective connotations; but unlike the informative connotations which are potentially available to anyone, these will necessarily vary from interpreter to interpreter: 'pig' will have divergent affective connotations for a man who is extremely fond of roast pork, and for an orthodox Jew. Lewis Carroll's awareness of the difference between referential and structural meaning, and the contributions of each to the import of utterances, is discussed in § 9.5; his treatment of affective connotations in §§ 10.2 and 10.3.

4.4.4 *Structural Meaning*

Opposed to those elements of the linguistic code which embody referential meaning are those which refer to nothing outside the linguistic code but serve only to signify grammatical relationships between other elements in specific utterances. In addition to their inherent differential meaning, these elements may be said to embody structural meaning. The elements which possess structural meaning in English are (1) morphemes of various kinds and (2) patterns of morphemic distribution. Having little or no referential meaning (or 'content'), these elements are sign-vehicles which are interpreted to signify structural relationships on the levels of word-formation and syntax.

In English, the morphemes which have structural meaning are (a) markers of grammatical inflection such as the '-s ending' which signifies noun plurality, the '-s ending' which signifies third person singular present indicative of verbs, the '-ed suffix' which signifies past tense of weak verbs, and the '-er' and '-est suffixes' which signify degree of comparison in adjectives; (b) the so-called 'function words', such as *and, but, or, of, with, by, for, to, a, the, do* (as in the question "Do you smoke?"), and the modal auxiliaries of the verb system; (c) internal junctures which separate one morpheme from another (that which differentiates between *an aim* and *a name* in speech) and which indicate phrasal grouping (that which in speech differentiates "After he had eaten nothing, more he wanted" from "After he had eaten, nothing more he wanted"); and (d) intonation contours, comprised of linear concatenations of pitch variations and terminal junctures, which conventionally signify whether the speaker's utterance is to be interpreted as statement, question, or "interrupted" discourse. These morphemes which embody structural meaning refer to nothing outside the linguistic code but merely signify, within specific utterances, the particular grammatical functions of, and the relationships between, those elements which do have referential meaning. They of course do contribute to the signification of the utterance as a whole, as well as to the significations of individual phrasal constituents of the whole utterance.

Those elements having structural meaning which are to be conceived as patterns of morphemic distribution function on the levels of syntax and of unified discourse. In this group are (a) function words as joined with content words to form phrases ("*the* man *of* feeling *who* knows *his* mind", "*with* malice *toward* none", "*in a* manner *of* speaking", "*a* man *to be* envied", "John *has* had plenty", "*neither* he *nor* she"); (b) patterns of word order (extremely important for the interpretation of English utterances); (c) co-occurrence relationships, in which the presence of one structural marker necessitates the presence of another ("*a boy* eat*s* the apple", "boy*s* *eat* apples", "he *had* walk*ed*"); and, in the realm of the sentence and of unified discourse, (d) pronoun-antecedent correlations ("*John* decided that *he* [himself] should go", "*Tom* and *Harry* wanted *Sam* to go with *them*. After hesitating a long while, *they* told *him* so", "*To love* is virtuous. The fact should be obvious to anyone who has perception. *It* makes one godlike."). Lewis Carroll's awareness of the importance of structural meaning in the decoding of utterances is discussed in § 9.5.

4.4.5 *Contextual Meaning*

How a linguistic sign-vehicle is to be interpreted depends on the total context of association. Without a context, no sign can be formed (§ 4.2). In this sense, all linguistic signs may be said to possess contextual meaning; for the interpretation we give to a sign-vehicle is a product not only of the physical situation in which the vehicle is perceived and our psychologically-conditioned set of predispositions regarding the interpretation of specific vehicles in specific environments, but also of the various concatenations of differential, referential, and structural meanings provided by the other linguistic signs in the verbal context. How verbal context determines the specific interpretation we give to a particular vehicle can be illustrated by our observing the various interpretations we give to the vehicle *fast* as a consequence of modifying the contextual frame, "She was —— fast". Two interpretations are possible if we put 'considered' in the empty slot.[3] Another, entirely different, is dictated if we put 'running' in the slot; still another by 'stuck'; and yet another by 'ready to'. Moreover, once the vehicle has been interpreted (i.e., the sign created) on the basis of its contextual meaning, it will contribute ITS particular meaning – referential or structural – to the total context, modifying and expanding it, and preparing the way for the interpretation of the next vehicle. Thus, with the completion of each sequential sign-process, the linguistic aspect of the context of association (and perhaps the psychological aspect also) is incrementally enlarged.

But there is another sense in which linguistic signs may be said to have contextual meaning. Certain types of signs are inherently more dependent upon the total context, and upon particular aspects of the total context, for their significations than are others. Included in this group of signs are comparative terms such as *tall* and *heavy*; pronouns; abstract names such as *truth, love, the good*; and some of the morphemes which signal structural meaning, such as *for, on,* and *with*. By nature, these types of signs are potentially more ambiguous in their possible significations than other types; if the total context fails to inform the interpreter of the precise manner in which the sign is to be understood, the interpreter's evoked signification may diverge radically from the speaker's intended signification.

The whole context of association influences the interpreter's understanding of the way in which the sign-vehicle is to be interpreted. This includes the physical environment of the utterance; the interpreter's knowledge of the speaker's frame of reference (the universe of discourse in which he is operating) and of his usual predisposition regarding the significations which specific signs will have in his usage; the interpreter's own predispositions; and the linguistic structure in which the vehicle occurs (the total verbal context). Some of the inherently ambiguous types of signs are particularly sensitive to one or another of these aspects of the total context of association.

The significations of comparative terms such as *tall* and *big*, for example, are

---

[3] The ambiguity of *fast* and of the signification (import) of the whole utterance *She was considered fast* can only be resolved by the total context of association's informing us whether the woman in question is to be regarded as 'swift' or as 'excessively free in her relations with men'. The words *very, awfully,* and *always* would, in the same position, create the same ambiguity as *considered*. But none of these words would cause *fast* to be ambiguous in its signification if the interpreter knew from the total context that *she* referred not to a woman, but to a ship.

predominantly governed by the physical environment: what may be called a tall building in North Branch, Iowa (a six-story hotel) – i.e., tall in comparison with other buildings in the vicinity – would not be called a tall building in New York City. And to a New Yorker who knew nothing about the height of buildings in North Branch, the signification of *tall* as predicated of a building would be something other than the speaker's. Comparative terms such as *heavy* and *ugly* have conventional significations which are predominantly determined by physical and psychological aspects of the context of association. Two sacks of meal, one weighing fifty and the other a hundred pounds, could both be called "heavy" by someone who tries to lift them. But one is demonstrably heavier than the other; and in comparison with the hundred-pound sack, the fifty-pound sack is "light". There is still another dimension to the ambiguity of *heavy*: a single sack of meal weighing fifty pounds may be called "heavy" by a housewife, but not by a stevedore who is accustomed to hefting much greater weights. Thus, because of their respective sets of psychological predispositions, for the housewife and for the stevedore 'heavy' will have divergent significations.

Also predominantly a function of the psychological aspect of the total context are the significations of such abstract terms as *art, love,* and *the good*. Significations of these vehicles taken as signs will be contingent upon the interpreter's awareness of what the speaker intends them to signify (i.e., his knowing the speaker's frame of reference, or psychological predispositions), and upon the interpreter's own set of psychological predispositions.

The signs whose significations are predominantly determined by the linguistic aspect of the total context (i.e., by the other signs which are present in the utterance) are the personal, demonstrative, and relative pronouns and certain 'function words', or morphemic signals of structural meanings. In English, personal pronouns, as substitutes for nouns, can refer to any antecedent which is consistent with them in gender, number, and case. By being substituted for an antecedent sign, a pronoun symbolizes that antecedent. Hence the total referential signification of any pronoun is twofold: its immediate signification is the antecedent sign it stands for; its ultimate signification is the same as that of its antecedent. Since the ultimate signification of a pronoun in a specific utterance is wholly dependent upon the signification of the sign that acts as its referent in the utterance, verbal context is essential to the correct interpretation of any pronoun: ambiguity of ultimate signification will immediately result if the verbal context does not specify what the linguistic referent (or immediate signification) of the pronoun is. Two examples, illustrating the principle as it applies to personal pronouns: "Bill and Tom told Sam and Sue that they would have to go." "Bob gave Sam his book." The same principle applies to demonstrative pronouns when they stand alone, and to relative pronouns when, in certain awkward constructions, they stand at too great a remove from their antecedents: "Charles gave Stuart a copy of *Alice*. This pleased Stuart very much." "Charles gave Stuart a copy of *Alice*, which pleased him greatly." "He didn't like little girls and women who wore short hair." Frequently a modification of the verbal context can easily resolve these ambiguities: "Bob gave his book to Sam." "Bob gave back Sam's book." "Charles gave Stuart a copy of *Alice*, a gift which pleased him much." "He didn't like women who wore short hair or little girls." In speech, intonation, through establishing phrasal groupings, can often resolve potential ambiguities without the speaker's being required to restructure his verbal context.

Finally, certain morphemes which signal structural meanings are capable of being ambiguous in their significations. Usually the total verbal context will automatically prevent these ambiguities from arising. The potential ambiguity of function words may be illustrated by examining an utterance where the verbal context is not sufficiently complete to inform the interpreter which of several possible alternative significations is intended. In the sentence "I walk with ——", the contextual meaning (and hence the structural meaning) of *with* will vary according to which of the following signs fills the slot: *Charles, a limp, a cane, my feet, difficulty, measured tread*. Each of these signs will impart, through the agency of a total context of association, a different structural meaning to *with*. Lewis Carroll's awareness of the potential ambiguity of certain types of structure words is revealed in the following passage from *Sylvie and Bruno*. The Vice-Warden has just discovered his wife, disguised for conspiratorial purposes, trying to hide a tin dagger from him. Demanding to know her reason for having the dagger, His Excellency snarls: "What did you get this dagger for? . . . You ca'n't deceive *me*!"

"I got it for – for – for –" the detected Conspirator stammered, trying her best to put on the assassin-expression that she had been practising at the looking-glass. "For –"
  "For *what*, Madam!"
  "Well, for eighteenpence, if you *must* know, dearest! That's what I got it for, on my –"
  "Now *don't* say your Word and Honour!" groaned the other Conspirator.
  "On my *birthday*," my Lady concluded in a meek whisper.

(*Works*, pp. 349-350)

Structurally, there is a profound difference in whether one gets a dagger "for" eighteenpence or "for" the purpose of assassination. But although My Lady's utterance, interrupted on the ambiguous *for* (note Carroll's repetition of this word to call attention to it) prior to the occurrence of the sign which would provide it with a contextual meaning which in turn would clarify its structural meaning, does reveal the suspended or unresolved signification of *for*, the situation was prepared for by His Excellency's question, "What did you get this dagger for?" The form of the question alone does not technically specify which of the possible significations – purpose or amount paid – he intends for the phrase *for what!* to have. The answer to his question could be either "eighteenpence" or "killing someone". The necessary contextual meaning would have been provided if the question had been differently phrased: "Why did you get this dagger?", "What did the dagger cost?". And had the question had either of these phrasings, My Lady would in all probability not have phrased her answer in such a manner as to perpetuate the potential ambiguity of *for*.

In most utterances, nearly any sign-vehicle (on any level of interpretation: phoneme, morpheme, phrase, sentence, segment of unified discourse) is capable of exhibiting ambiguity of signification if the total context of association does not specify its intended signification. The physical, psychological, and linguistic aspects of the total context should impart contextual meaning to each sign-vehicle in such manner that the intended interpretation of it is assured. This imposed contextual meaning, specifying the signification which the vehicle should be interpreted to embody, in turn signifies the specific referential or structural meaning which the sign is to possess in the utterance. Once the vehicle is interpreted in the light of its contextual meaning, the created sign will add its own signification to the total context of association, thus expanding it: so that when the next vehicle is encountered, a new context of association will be in existence, a new set of conditions which will aid in ITS being properly interpreted.

4.4.6 *Summary*

Although this brief discussion of the nature of linguistic signs is partial and hypothetical – and is not to be taken as representing Lewis Carroll's theoretical notions – it does provide the necessary conceptual framework and terminology to make the subsequent topical discussions meaningful. The major points may be summarized as follows.

Linguistic signs are a subset of signs in general, and linguistic sign-processes conform to those of the generalized sign situation outlined in § 4.2. A 'natural' language such as English is a kind of code, or major sign-system, comprised of a hierarchical structuring of minor sign-systems. The meaningful elements of the linguistic code, though ultimately reducible to auditory stimuli of various types, are of several kinds with regard to both the nature of their conceptualized vehicles and the types of significations which they may possess for knowledgeable interpreters. These elements act singly and in concert to provide a hierarchy of sequential, incremental, and successively more complex levels of interpretation. All linguistic signs possess differential and contextual meaning, and some have in addition referential or structural meaning.

Differential meaning is the recognition value possessed by each linguistic sign, that aspect of a sign's signification which establishes the sign's unique functional identity through the agency of the sign's formal contrasts with all other signs on the same level of interpretation. Contextual meaning is the signification of a sign as dictated by the body of information provided by the total context of association which specifies how individual signs are to be interpreted in specific environments. Referential meaning is that aspect of a sign's signification which, as conceptualized association-object, lies wholly outside the linguistic code. Structural meaning is that aspect of a sign's signification which specifies the logical and grammatical relationships between other code-elements in specific utterances. Those linguistic signs which possess referential meaning may, as part of their signification, designate or identify their association-objects (these which designate or point out are a type of indexical sign, or label; proper names are an example). A sign possessing referential meaning usually will hold for the interpreter, as part of its signification, certain informative connotations which are evoked by the association-object, and it may provide for the evocation of affective connotations as well. A sign may be said to denote only if its association-object actually exists at the time of the sign's creation.

Finally, a potential sign-vehicle which is considered in isolation, without reference to a specific context, cannot be interpreted. It is only within the confines of a specific verbal context that a given stimulus can be interpreted as embodying a particular signification which would approach any of the vehicle's conventionally-established significations. In order to serve the purpose of communication, the elements which comprise the linguistic code must be recognizable as themselves, and must provide for the formation of signs through processes of interpretation which are shared as conventions by both speaker and listener. Specific vehicles, in other words, must be capable of being interpreted in fixed, standardized ways which have been established by convention. Without conventionalized rules governing their interpretation, the elements of the code which provide sign-vehicles are incapable of establishing the context of association which makes interpretation (the creation of signs) possible.

4.5 CARROLL'S EXPLICIT STATEMENTS ON LANGUAGE: FORKS AND HOPE

Carroll's reticence in making formal statements about the nature of language seems to have been a conscious thing with him, for it did not result from a lack of awareness on his part or a lack of encouragement on the part of others. Thomas Banks Strong, the Bishop of Oxford, writing in *The London Times* for January 27, 1932, comments: "At one time, while the 'Symbolic Logic' was in process of being written Dodgson used to correspond with me at great length. . . . I tried to raise the general question of the relation of words and things, but he always declined to write upon this problem: if the words were clear and certain in their meaning, the results of combining them must be clear and certain too" (p. 11). It was, then, Carroll's choice not to write formally on the relation of words and things. With the exception of several conventional statements in the expository sections of his *The Game of Logic* (1886; 1887) and *Symbolic Logic* (1896), his straightforward comments on the nature of meaning are very few, and scattered about in unexpected contexts.

(1) In a letter of December 8, 1891 to Alice Liddell Hargreaves, the original "Alice", now an adult woman, he writes:

My dear Mrs. Hargreaves: I should be so glad if you could, quite conveniently to yourself, look in for tea any day. You would probably prefer to bring a companion; but I must leave the choice to you, only remarking that if your husband is here he would be

[most] very welcome (I crossed out most because it's ambiguous; most words are, I fear).

(Quoted by Caryl Hargreaves in "The Lewis Carroll
that Alice Recalls", *The New York Times Magazine*
[May 1, 1932], p. 15)

(2) In an undated (but presumably late) letter to "the Lowrie Children", he says:

As to the meaning of the Snark? I'm very much afraid I didn't mean anything but non-sense! Still, you know, words mean more than we mean to express when we use them: so a whole book ought to mean a great deal more than the writer meant.

(Quoted in Hatch, *Letters to Child-friends*,
pp. 242-243)

(3) In "The Stage and the Spirit of Reverence", an article he wrote for the magazine *The Theatre* in 1888, he says:

... no word has a meaning *inseparably* attached to it; a word means what the speaker intends by it, and what the hearer understands by it, and that is all.

I meet a friend and say "Good morning!" Harmless words enough, one would think. Yet possibly, in some language he and I have never heard, these words may convey utterly horrid and loathsome ideas. But are *we* responsible for this? This thought may serve to lessen the horror of some of the language used by the lower classes, which, it is a comfort to remember, is often a mere collection of unmeaning *sounds*, so far as speaker and hearer are concerned.

(Quoted in Collingwood, *The Lewis Carroll
Picture Book* [1899], p. 183)

(4) In the "Appendix, Addressed to Teachers" with which he concludes *Symbolic Logic*, he states unequivocally the arbitrary nature of word-meanings:

... I maintain that any writer of a book is fully authorised in attaching any meaning he likes to any word or phrase he intends to use. If I find an author saying, at the beginning of his book, "Let it be understood that by the word '*black*' I shall always mean '*white*', and that by the word '*white*' I shall always mean '*black*'," I meekly accept his ruling, however injudicious I may think it.

(*Symbolic Logic*, 4th ed. [1897], p. 166).

This statement is foreshadowed in a letter to Edith Rix written in 1885, where, speaking of the forthcoming *Game of Logic* (or possibly of the projected three-part *Symbolic Logic*, if he had conceived it at that time), he says, "I shall take the line 'any writer may mean exactly what he pleases by a phrase so long as he explains it beforehand' " (Quoted in Collingwood, *Life*, p. 242). It is also foreshadowed in Humpty Dumpty's statement in *Through the Looking-Glass* (1871): "When *I* use a word ... it means just what I choose it to mean – neither more nor less." [4]

---

[4] This philosophical position parallels that of George Boole, whose *An Investigation of the Laws of Thought* (1854) Carroll was reading in 1884 (*Diaries*, II, 430). We don't know whether Carroll had read the book prior to 1884 or not. Early in Boole's book the following statements occur (the quotations are from the edition issued by Dover Publications): "There exist, indeed, certain general principles founded in the very nature of language, by which the use of symbols,

These are the only generalized statements about the nature of words that I have
been able to discover in Carroll's writings. There are a few statements of a specialized nature in *Symbolic Logic* which will be mentioned later in conjunction with
the topics to which they are relevant. With the exception of Humpty Dumpty's
dictum, the above statements were uttered in serious contexts and may, I think,
be taken at face value. In summary form: (1) most words are ambiguous; (2) words
mean more than we mean to express when we use them; (3) no word has a meaning
inseparably attached to it: it merely means what the speaker intends by it and what
the interpreter understands by it; (4) word-meanings are totally arbitrary.

In view of his statement in (3), I think that (2) should be interpreted as referring
to the personal connotations which a word may have for a given interpreter in
addition to its established conventional signification and irrespective of the user's
intended meaning. The statement implies an awareness on Carroll's part of the
swarm of associations which surrounds most words as a function of the interpreter's
previous experience with them and with their association-objects. Since these personal associations (informative and affective connotations) vary with individual
interpreters (and speakers), they create a potential ambiguity of reference which
can result in misunderstanding. Statement (3) implies an awareness on Carroll's
part of the 'one word-one meaning' fallacy which the General Semanticists of the
twentieth century have been vigorous in pointing out, and which is instrumental in
creating delusion in everyday life. It also seems to imply a realization that the
meaning of a word depends upon the total context – physical, psychological, and
verbal – in which it is uttered and perceived. From (4) it follows that if communication is to occur, there must be some convention governing word-usage, whether in
the form of a general rule adopted by the speech community at large, or in the
form of an arbitrary stipulation of meaning applicable in a particular act of discourse. Illustrations of these principles will be encountered frequently in the course
of this study.

If there is little that is unique or startling in these assumptions – (3) and (4)

---

which are but the elements of scientific language, is determined. To a certain extent these elements are arbitrary. Their interpretation is purely conventional: we are permitted to employ
them in whatever sense we please. But this permission is limited by two indispensable conditions, – first, that from the sense once conventionally established we never, in the same process
of reasoning, depart; secondly, that the laws by which the process is conducted be founded
exclusively upon the above fixed sense or meaning of the symbols employed" (p. 6). "That
Language is an instrument of human reason, and not merely a medium for the expression of
thought, is a truth generally admitted" (p. 24). "The elements of which all language consists
are signs or symbols. Words are signs" (p. 25). "A sign is an arbitrary mark, having a fixed
interpretation, and susceptible of combination with other signs in subjection to fixed laws
dependent upon their mutual interpretation" (p. 25). "... a sign is an *arbitrary* mark. It is
clearly indifferent what particular word or token we associate with a given idea, provided that
the association once made is permanent. The Romans expressed by the word 'civitas' what we
designate by the word 'state'. But both they and we might equally well have employed any other
word to represent the same conception" (p. 26).

probably caused some raised eyebrows among his Victorian readers – they do reveal that Carroll had thought much about the nature of words and had reached conclusions quite sophisticated for his time and very much in accord with the tenets of semantic theory subscribed to by many twentieth-century students of language. It is fortunate that the four statements above are of a general propositional nature, for they may thus serve as concrete bases for the inferential method that must be employed throughout this study.

5

THE PROCESS OF CLASSIFICATION

"But if I'm not the same, the next question is 'Who in the world am I?' ... I'm sure I'm not Ada ... for her hair goes in such long ringlets, and mine doesn't go in ringlets at all ...".

Alice's Adventures in Wonderland, Chapter II

However, this bottle was *not* marked "poison," so Alice ventured to taste it, and, finding it very nice (it had, in fact, a sort of mixed flavour of cherry-tart, custard, pineapple, roast turkey, toffy, and hot buttered toast), she very soon finished it off.

Alice's Adventures in Wonderland, Chapter I

5.1 CARROLL'S DEFINITION OF 'CLASSIFICATION'

As logician, Lewis Carroll was required to study the properties and functions of names, and to investigate and test the validity of modes of definition and classification. His interest in these matters was not confined to his professional life, but also found expression in his literary work. Illustrations of the process of classification abound in Carroll's writing; but before turning to them, we should prepare the ground with tools that Carroll himself has left us. At the end of his life, having thought about the matter for fifty years, Carroll defined 'classification' in his *Symbolic Logic* (1896). This and his definition of 'name' I wish to quote in full, for they provide the only formal statements on these important matters to be found in his writing. Moreover, they reveal the scrupulosity with which he habitually defined his terms in his technical works. I have deferred his definition of 'name' until Chapter 6.

If these definitions seem narrow in scope it is because Carroll's purpose in writing *Symbolic Logic* was simply to provide a healthful mental recreation for young people. He was not concerned with presenting an elaborate treatise on names and naming after the manner of John Stuart Mill; he was merely giving his readers the minimal information necessary to work the logic problems presented in later sections of the book.

Carroll begins his exposition by stating that the universe contains 'Things' such as "I", "London", "roses", "redness", and "the letter which I received yesterday". These things have 'Attributes' such as "large", "red", and "which I received yesterday". Any attribute or set of attributes may be called, for convenience, an 'Adjunct'. Having established his terminology, he continues with his definition of 'classification'. The square brackets are Carroll's.

'CLASSIFICATION', or the formation of Classes, is a Mental Process, in which we imagine that we have put together, in a group, certain Things. Such a group is called a 'Class.'

This Process may be performed in three different ways, as follows: –

(1) We may imagine that we have put together all Things. The Class so formed (i.e. the Class "Things") contains the whole Universe.

(2) We may think of the class "Things," and may imagine that we have picked out from it all the Things which possess a certain Adjunct *not* possessed by the whole Class. This Adjunct is said to be 'peculiar' to the Class so formed. In this case, the Class "Things" is called a 'Genus' with regard to the Class so formed: the Class, so formed, is called a 'Species' of the Class "Things": and its peculiar Adjunct is called its 'Differentia'.

As this Process is entirely *Mental*, we can perform it whether there *is*, or *is not*, an existing Thing which possesses that Adjunct. If there *is*, the Class is said to be 'Real'; if *not*, it is said to be 'Unreal,' or 'Imaginary.'

[For example, we may imagine that we have picked out, from the Class "Things," all the Things which possess the Adjunct "material, artificial, consisting of houses and streets"; and we may thus form the Real Class "towns." Here we may regard "Things" as a *Genus*, "Towns" as a *Species* of Things, and "material, artificial, consisting of houses and streets" as its *Differentia*.

Again, we may imagine that we have picked out all the Things which possess the Adjunct "weighing a ton, easily lifted by a baby"; and we may thus form the *Imaginary* Class "Things that weigh a ton and are easily lifted by a baby."]

(3) We may think of a certain Class, *not* the Class "Things," and may imagine that we have picked out from it all the Members of it which possess a certain Adjunct *not* possessed by the whole Class. This Adjunct is said to be 'peculiar' to the smaller Class so formed. In this case, the Class thought of is called a 'Genus' with regard to the smaller Class picked out from it: the smaller Class is called a 'Species' of the larger: and its peculiar Adjunct is called its 'Differentia'.

[For example, the Class "towns having four million inhabitants," which Class contains only *one* Member, viz. "London."]

Hence, any single Thing, which we can name so as to distinguish it from all other Things, may be regarded as a one-Member Class.

[Thus "London" may be regarded as the one-Member Class, picked out from the Class "towns," which has, as its Differentia, "having four million inhabitants."]

A Class, containing two or more Members, is sometimes regarded as *one single Thing*. When so regarded, it may possess an Adjunct which is *not* possessed by any Member of it taken separately.

[Thus, the Class "The soldiers of the Tenth Regiment," when regarded as *one single Thing*, may possess the Attribute "formed in square," which is *not* possessed by any Member if it taken separately.]

(*Symbolic Logic, Part I: Elementary*,
4th ed. [London, 1897], pp. 1½-2½)

Classification is a mental process by which an object, after it has been examined and its attributes determined, is grouped with other objects possessing similar attributes. As a process it leads to the act of naming: when the object has, on the basis of its attributes, been assigned to its appropriate class, it is given the name which is applicable to all members of that class.

5.2 CAUSES OF ERROR IN CLASSIFICATION

5.2.1 *A Thing's Possessing Misleading Attributes*

We have seen that Alice was able to classify the fish she met in the wood as "footman" on the basis of his attributive livery (interpreting it as signifying his occupation) and, at the Knave's trial, to classify the King of Hearts as "judge" because of his great wig (§ 4.3). But as was pointed out, her act of classification and naming could have been erroneous if – in spite of the apparently unambiguous characterizing attributes – the fish had not been a footman, and the King not a judge. Similarly, had the Queen classified the flowers on the rose-tree as "red-roses" on the basis of their apparent attribute of redness, she would have been in error. Since things are classified according to their attributes, responded to as signs signifying the true nature of the things, accurate classification can occur only if the attributes possessed by a thing accurately represent its nature. That which we see lying on a friend's coffee-table and take to be a book because of its tooled leather cover and gilt-edged pages may, upon our opening it, turn out to be a cigar box. Classification may be rendered extremely difficult or even impossible by a thing's possessing attributes which are not indigenous to members of its class but are rather the inherent defining characteristics of things which are members of another class.

5.2.2 *Errors Which Lie with the Classifier*

But erroneous classification can result from other causes than a thing's possessing misleading or equivocal attributes. It can also arise from the classifier's failure to grasp the total significance of an attribute or his failure to see additional attributes which would place the object in another generic class altogether. Ignorance of a thing's attributes may stem from such external causes as darkness, fog, or distance, which obscure characteristics, or from perceptual limitation on the part of the classifier, as in the case of his being color-blind. It may also be caused by the classifier's lack of requisite knowledge or experience, or by his carelessness in determining a thing's attributes. With the exception of failures caused by external hindrances or perceptual limitations which sometimes cannot be helped, most errors in classification arising from the classifier's ignorance (and not from misleading or equivocal attributes in the thing itself) are the result of over-hasty generalization, the making of an inductive inference before sufficient data have been collected and assessed. Such would seem to be the problem of the Professor in *Sylvie and Bruno:*

"But you must explain to me, please," the Professor said with an anxious look, *"which* is the Lion, and *which* is the Gardener. It's *most* important not to get two such animals confused together. And one's very liable to do it in their case – both having mouths, you know –"

"Doos oo *always* confuses two animals together?" Bruno asked.

"Pretty often, I'm afraid," the Professor candidly confessed. "Now, for instance, there's the rabbit-hutch and the hall-clock. ... One gets a little confused with *them* – both having doors, you know. Now, only yesterday – would you believe it? – I put some lettuces into the clock, and tried to wind up the rabbit!"

(Works, pp. 354-355)

Errors can also occur when the classifier does not attempt to assess attributes objectively but is content to make his classification according to a pre-conceived notion of what a thing should be. In Chapter II of *Through the Looking-Glass,* the Live Flowers, upon seeing Alice, immediately classify her as a member of their generic class (though with the peculiar attribute of being able to walk about). The Rose feels that Alice is the "right colour", but the Tiger-lily wishes that her "petals curled up a little more". Alice, without contradicting their classification of her, stresses her generic difference from the Flowers by asking, "Are there any more people in the garden besides me?". Her verbal distinction is lost upon them.

"There's one other flower in the garden that can move about like you," said the Rose. "I wonder how you do it ... but she's more bushy than you are."

In her rigid frame of reference, the Rose is unable to see the possibility that the peculiar attribute of mobility might suggest that Alice and the Red Queen are not to be classed as flowers at all. She persists in her erroneous classification, unable to make the hypothetical leap to conceive of a class of things, not Flowers, whose members are as sentient and rational as those of her own class. The conversation continues in a predictable fashion:

"Is she like me?" Alice asked eagerly, for the thought crossed her mind, "There's another little girl in the garden, somewhere!"

"Well, she has the same awkward shape as you," the Rose said: "but she's redder – and her petals are shorter, I think."

"They're done up close, like a dahlia," said the Tiger-lily: "not tumbled about, like yours."

"But that's not *your* fault," the Rose said kindly. "You're beginning to fade, you know – and then one ca'n't help one's petals getting a little untidy."

Alice didn't like this idea at all ...

(Works, p. 160)

In "The Angler's Adventure", written when he was thirteen and included in the earliest family magazine, *Useful and Instructive Poetry* (1845; published, 1954), Carroll presents the case of a fisherman who, in spite of his ingenious attempts at classification, is unable to identify the creature dangling from his hook:

> No tail it had, it could not be a beast,
> No wings, it could by no means be a bird.
> Its flesh, when tasted, proved a luscious feast,
> And yet, methought, its name I'd never heard.
>
> Speckles it had of most enchanting hue,
> An unknown foreign creature it appeared;
> It might be anything, perhaps a Jew,
> I almost wondered it had not a beard.
>
> . . . . . .
>
> By thinking over Buffon's history,
> And Bewick's Birds, and Isaak Walton's book,
> I seemed to penetrate the mystery,
> The name of that which hung upon my hook.
>
> Remembering Isaak Walton's own instructions
> And other anglers' who have gone before us,
> By algebra, and eke the help of fluxions,
> I made it out, it was a Plesiosauras!
>
> > (*Useful and Instructive Poetry*, ed. Derek Hudson
> > [New York, 1954], pp. 35-36)

When the angler shows the object to his maid, she immediately identifies it as a toad. Evidently the angler had not seen a toad before; if he had, he would not have been forced to resort to such a rigorous process of classification. Although his attempt ends in failure, his method is sound up to a point: he determines the creature's physical attributes, studies them separately and in the aggregate, and goes to the established authorities to find catalogues of creatures classed according to their attributes. This is both legitimate and wise. But a toad is not a Plesiosaurus: in his method of classification algebra and calculus were perhaps not as helpful as he thought. This poem is a whimsical trifle, but it does show Carroll's early interest in the process of classification and naming. It also foreshadows the method of classification outlined thirty years later in "Fit the Second" of *The Hunting of the Snark* (1876). The Bellman tells his crew "the five unmistakable marks/ By which you may know, wheresoever you go,/ The warranted genuine Snarks":

> "Let us take them in order. The first is the taste,
>   Which is meagre and hollow, but crisp:
> Like a coat that is rather too tight in the waist,
>   With a flavour of Will-o'-the-Wisp.

The second attribute is "its habit of getting up late", the third is its "slowness in taking a jest", the fourth is its "fondness for bathing machines", and

> "The fifth is ambition. It next will be right
>   To describe each particular batch:
> Distinguishing those that have feathers, and bite,
>   From those that have whiskers, and scratch.
>
> > (*Works*, p. 763)

In view of the difficulty of ascertaining these five general attributes, a person might be hard put to identify a Snark as such if he did encounter one. In Carroll's poem the Snark remains a shadowy creature never pictured or physically described. But there is one type of Snark, called a "Boojum", which is not at all difficult to identify. The peculiar attribute possessed by members of this sub-class is the power to make the beholder "softly and suddenly vanish away, and never be met with again". A Boojum, in allowing no possibility of erroneous classification, greatly simplifies the classifier's task.

With most objects, however, errors in classification can occur when the classifier has not sufficiently studied the implications of the observed attributes and is too hasty in assigning the object to a given class. Two illustrations of this type of error are found in *Wonderland*.

In Chapter V, Alice, having grown very tall after eating part of the Caterpillar's mushroom, finds her head bobbing about among the tree-tops at the end of a long prehensile neck. She frightens a Pigeon who immediately classifies her as a serpent on the basis of the attributes possessed by her lithe and sinuous neck. When Alice denies that she is a serpent and declares that she is a little girl, the Pigeon does not believe her. The Pigeon has seen a good many little girls, "but never *one* with such a neck as that!" Convinced that Alice is lying, the Pigeon says contemptuously, "I suppose you'll be telling me next that you never tasted an egg!"

"I *have* tasted eggs, certainly," said Alice, who was a very truthful child; "but little girls eat eggs quite as much as serpents do, you know."

"I don't believe it," said the Pigeon; "but if they do, then they're a kind of serpent: that's all I can say."

(*Works*, pp. 61-62)

At the trial in Chapter XI, there is a similar illustration of erroneous classification when the King of Hearts calls the Hatter as a witness:

"Take off your hat," the King said to the Hatter.

"It isn't mine," said the Hatter.

"*Stolen!*" the King exclaimed, turning to the jury, who instantly made a memorandum of the fact.

(*Works*, p. 117)

Both the Pigeon and the King have fallen prey to fallacious reasoning. As Daniel F. Kirk has pointed out, the Pigeon fails to realize that "it might be convenient to have besides the terms 'little girl' and 'serpent' a third called 'little girls with necks like serpents'" [*Charles Dodgson, Semeiotician* (University of Florida Press, 1963), p. 67]. Since "egg-eating" is an attribute of the members of the class "serpent", the Pigeon fallaciously assumes that anything possessing this attribute is necessarily a member of the class "serpent".[1] The King of Hearts, in classifying the hat as

---

[1] In his article "Logic and the Humour of Lewis Carroll", *Proc. of the Leeds Philosophical and Literary Society*, VI (May, 1951), Peter Alexander says of this passage: "This may be looked at in two ways – either as a reference to the way in which definitions come to be

"stolen" upon learning that it doesn't belong to the Hatter, makes an unwarranted inference: he classifies the object too quickly, without studying the implications of the attribute "not mine". The King falls prey to gross oversimplification in postulating his dichotomous choice: the hat either belongs to the Hatter, or is a stolen hat. He has made no provision for other classifications that are suggested by the attribute "not owned by the Hatter": "stolen" is a possibility, to be sure; but so are "borrowed", "being bought on the installment plan", and – as is the case here – "kept to sell as merchandise".

5.3 CAUSES OF DIFFICULTY IN CLASSIFYING

5.3.1 *Difficulties Caused by the Lack of Available Class-Names*

A different problem of classification is faced by Alice when she uses the fish's livery to assign him to the class "footman". It will be recalled that Alice had some difficulty in making her classification: "She considered him to be a footman because he was in livery: otherwise, judging by his face only, she would have called him a fish." Which of the two sets of attributes should she employ in assigning a name to the creature – those of its facial features, or those of its uniform? Alice is experiencing the dilemma faced by the Pigeon. It is inconceivable to her that a thing might be both a fish and a footman; to her, the two classes are mutually exclusive. She settles the matter by choosing the livery as her basis for classification, and names the creature "footman". As Daniel Kirk has indicated, a third class is required for greater precision, analogous to that which the Pigeon should have conceived ('little girls with necks like serpents') – and Carroll himself as narrator (not Alice) coins the name 'Fish-Footman' immediately after Alice's act of naming.

The obstacle presented to precise classification by a lack of available class-names is explicitly stated in Chapter IX of *Through the Looking-Glass*. Alice, having

---

modified or as a particular logical fallacy. First, the fallacy. It is that called by traditional logicians 'the fallacy of affirming the consequent' and can be brought out by restating the argument in this way – If this is a serpent it will eat eggs. It does eat eggs. Therefore it is a serpent [1] which is invalid because the premisses do not warrant the conclusion that *only* serpents eat eggs.

"Considered now as a reference to definitions the passage points to the fact that definitions outlive their usefulness and if not abandoned must be modified or 'brought up to date'. The pigeon regards serpents as egg-stealers and is not interested in little girls until she discovers that they, too, eat eggs. For her purpose the classification of little girls with serpents then becomes a useful one because the cry of 'Serpent!' will indicate that egg-stealers, of whatever kind, are about.

"This practice of making a definition wider because it becomes useful to include more things under it is common in science, but we commit the fallacy of affirming the consequent if we do not recognise when we do it that we *are* changing the meaning of our word. We do this in argument much more often than we realise" (pp. 559-560).

reached the Eighth Square and been made a Queen, arrives at the banquet which
is being given in her honor.

> She was standing before an arched doorway, over which were the words "QUEEN ALICE"
> in large letters, and on each side of the arch there was a bell-handle; one was marked
> "Visitors' Bell," and the other "Servants' Bell."
>   "I'll wait till the song's over," thought Alice, "and then I'll ring the – the – *which* bell
> must I ring?" she went on, very much puzzled by the names. "I'm not a visitor, and I'm
> not a servant. There *ought* to be one marked 'Queen,' you know –"
>
> (*Works*, p. 258)

Alice is here faced with an insoluble problem. To gain admittance, she must ring
one of the two bells; in order to ring, she must classify herself as either "visitor" or
"servant". But with her attribute of "queenhood", she does not qualify for either
class. She is certainly not a servant, and since the arch over the doorway is inscribed
"QUEEN ALICE" (a label designating that the precincts within "belong" to her), she
is not strictly a visitor either. She, as Queen, has merely arrived to take possession
of what is rightfully hers by virtue of her reaching the Eighth Square. The exhaustive
division of the available bell-pulls into two classes, from both of which Alice is
excluded as Queen and bell-ringer, makes it impossible for her to gain admittance
by ringing a bell. "There OUGHT to be one marked 'Queen,' you know" – and so
there ought, if she is to gain admittance by ringing. Fortunately the door opens of
its own accord.

5.3.2 *Difficulties Caused by Equivocal Attributes*

In addition to errors in classification that are caused by some limitation on the
part of the classifier, such as his ignorance of the existence of some attributes or
his being unaware of their significance, unwarranted inferences arrived at through
invalid reasoning, and preconceptions or 'tunnel vision' which prevent him from
seeing more than one possibility for a thing's classification, there are errors capable
of being produced by the difficulties presented to accurate classification by the
nature of the observed attributes themselves. Attempts at classification can be
defeated by an apparent lack of significant attributes, as in the case of the Queen
of Hearts' being unable to identify her prostrate gardeners, or by the observed
attributes' being equivocal in their significations. This last difficulty is illustrated
in *Through the Looking-Glass* when Alice tries to classify the ornamental band
which circles Humpty Dumpty's middle.

> "What a beautiful belt you've got on!" Alice suddenly remarked. ... "At least," she
> corrected herself on second thoughts, "a beautiful cravat, I should have said – no, a belt,
> I mean – I beg your pardon!" she added in dismay, for Humpty Dumpty looked
> thoroughly offended, and she began to wish she hadn't chosen that subject. "If only I
> knew," she thought to herself, "which was neck and which was waist!"
>   Evidently Humpty Dumpty was very angry, though he said nothing for a minute or
> two. When he *did* speak again, it was in a deep growl.

"It is a – *most* – *provoking* – thing," he said at last, "when a person doesn't know a cravat from a belt!"

"I know it's very ignorant of me," Alice said, in so humble a tone that Humpty Dumpty relented.

"It's a cravat, child, and a beautiful one, as you say. . . ."

(Works, p. 212)

The problem faced by Alice is analogous to that encountered by biologists when they attempt to classify as "plant" or "animal" one of those borderline creatures such as Euglena, which possesses attributes characteristic of both classes. Humpty Dumpty settles the question by fiat; but even that does not help Alice to know "which is neck and which is waist" (the reader should refer to Tenniel's illustration to see how this ambiguity is pictured). Indeed, neck and waist seem to be one and the same.

One of the most amusing (though somewhat disturbing) illustrations of classification hindered by ambiguity in the characterizing attributes is that of the Pig-Baby's metamorphosis in Chapter VI of *Wonderland*. During the chaotic scene in the Duchess' kitchen before Alice is given the baby to nurse, there is an intimation of what is to come when the Duchess suddenly addresses the infant as "Pig!". As soon as Alice is given the baby, she is aware that it is a peculiar child – "a queer-shaped little creature" which "held out its arms and legs in all directions, 'just like a starfish'". When Alice takes it from the Duchess, it is "snorting like a steam-engine", apparently because of the peppery atmosphere of the kitchen. But the baby's wheezing soon changes to an unmistakable "grunt".

"Don't grunt," said Alice; "that's not at all a proper way of expressing yourself."

Not proper for a human baby, of course.

The baby grunted again, and Alice looked very anxiously into its face to see what was the matter with it. There could be no doubt that it had a *very* turn-up nose, much more like a snout than a real nose: also its eyes were getting extremely small for a baby: altogether Alice did not like the look of the thing at all. "But perhaps it was only sobbing," she thought, and looked into its eyes again, to see if there were any tears.

No, there were no tears. "If you're going to turn into a pig, my dear," said Alice, seriously, "I'll have nothing more to do with you. Mind now!" The poor little thing sobbed again (or grunted, it was impossible to say which), and they went on for some while in silence.

Alice was just beginning to think to herself, "Now what am I to do with this creature [note Alice's choice of name for it], when I get it home?" when it grunted again, so violently, that she looked down into its face in some alarm. This time there could be *no* mistake about it: it was neither more nor less than a pig, and she felt that it would be quite absurd for her to carry it any further.

So she set the little creature down, and felt quite relieved to see it trot away quietly into the wood. "If it had grown up," she said to herself, "it would have made a dreadfully ugly child: but it makes rather a handsome pig, I think." And she began thinking over other children she knew, who might do very well as pigs. . . .

(Works, pp. 70-71)

Initially there is no difficulty whatsoever in classifying the object as a human baby. But as the change progresses, and the physical attributes which place it in the class "human baby" begin to disappear in favor of those which are characteristic of members of the class "pig", an ambiguous borderline state is reached, where the Pig-Baby's noises can be classified with certainty as neither "sobs" nor "grunts". Alice's awareness of this ambiguous state is revealed in her selection of the name 'creature' to refer to it: the physical attributes have become so equivocal that she cannot assign it to any class other than the general one, "member of the animal kingdom". Finally the change is complete; the characterizing attributes have become sufficiently unequivocal for Alice to feel safe in classifying the object as "pig". The attributes which would have been grotesque and ugly in a human child now suit it, in its new classification, admirably. And Alice is led to think of her own acquaintances who, on the basis of their physical (and perhaps behavioral) attributes, might do very well as pigs if the metamorphosis could be effected.

Another problem in classification is presented to Alice in *Wonderland* when the Caterpillar, leaving the mushroom on which he has been sitting, tells her that one side of the plant will make her grow taller, the other side shorter.

Alice remained looking thoughtfully at the mushroom for a minute, trying to make out which were the two sides of it; and, as it [the cap, presumably] was perfectly round, she found this a very difficult question. However, at last she stretched her arms round it as far as they would go, and broke off a bit of the edge with each hand.

"And now which is which?" she said to herself, and nibbled a little of the right-hand bit to try the effect.

(*Works*, p. 59)

The Caterpillar states that this circular mushroom-cap has TWO sides: "one" and "the other". Since the object presents no characterizing attributes which might distinguish the two "sides", the rim of the mushroom-cap cannot be classified into separate parts by Alice, but must stand as a whole. After making the best effort of which she is capable to ascertain two widely separated areas, Alice tests the respective fragments empirically to determine their attributes. The right-hand bit, which she nibbles first, causes her to shrink. This instance of Alice's having to classify two things possessing no discernible attributes was not in the original manuscript version, "Alice's Adventures under Ground" (1862): in the earlier version, the Caterpillar merely says of the mushroom, "The top will make you grow taller, and the stalk will make you grow shorter." When Carroll revised the manuscript for general publication in 1865, he changed the mushroom sequence in order to provide Alice with a problem in classification.

Alice is faced with an insoluble problem in classification in Chapter V of *Through the Looking-Glass*. In her examination of the merchandise in the Sheep's little shop, she is frustrated in her attempts to identify the objects upon the shelves: "whenever she looked hard at any shelf, to make out exactly what it had on it, that particular shelf was always quite empty, though the others round it were crowded as full as they could hold".

"Things flow about so here!" she said at last in a plaintive tone, after she had spent a minute or so in vainly pursuing a large bright thing that looked sometimes like a doll and sometimes like a work-box, and was always in the shelf next above the one she was looking at. "And this one is the most provoking of all – but I'll tell you what –" she added, as a sudden thought struck her. "I'll follow it up to the very top shelf of all. It'll puzzle it to go through the ceiling, I expect!"

But even this plan failed: the 'thing' went through the ceiling as quietly as possible, as if it were quite used to it.

"Are you a child or a teetotum?" the Sheep said, as she took up another pair of needles. "You'll make me giddy soon, if you go on turning round like that."

(*Works*, pp. 202-203)

The difficulty in classification apparent in this episode may stem from Carroll's depiction of the consequences of Alice's dream state. If so, the problem arises from the classifier's inability to grasp significant attributes – a situation analogous to one's being unable to identify an object looming before him in a thick fog. But if the difficulty is not a result of Alice's dream state, Carroll may be suggesting that the nature of the "thing" itself is what prevents its classification. Alice cannot give the thing a name because she cannot determine the attributes which would inform her of its genus. As she pursues it with her eyes, she is never able to get it into focus, to pin it down. She has only a vague general impression that it is "a large bright thing" which looks "sometimes like a doll and sometimes like a work-box". Unable to classify it with any greater precision, she puts it in the class "things" (note Carroll's use of single quotation marks indicating that the word 'thing' is Alice's) and assumes that it will behave like a member of the class "material things" in being forced to stop its upward rise when it reaches the ceiling. Contrary to her expectation, and to the behavior of material things in her own world, the object vanishes through the ceiling; this implies that Alice's vague classification of it was erroneous, or that material things in Looking-Glass Land have modes of behavior quite different from those in her own world (which Carroll's reversal motif would lead one to expect).

If Carroll is suggesting that this "thing" cannot be classified and named because of something in its nature that prevents its physical attributes from being determined, the attributes themselves are not ambiguous in the manner of those which are possessed by Humpty Dumpty's "neck-waist" and "cravat-belt", and by the Pig-Baby's "sob-grunt". Instead, like those of the mushroom's "two sides", they are simply enigmatic. They cannot be ascertained AS attributes because the object which possesses them cannot be clearly perceived. Alice does not classify the object AS "doll" or "work-box", but only as being "like", or similar to, members of those classes. A provisional comparative classification is the best that she can make: at times the object's attributes approach those possessed by members of the class "doll", at others, those of the class "work-box".

The only attributes which Alice is able to determine with any degree of certainty are: that the object is "large" and "bright", that it looks sometimes like a doll and sometimes like a work-box, that it is always on the shelf next above the one that she is looking at, that it has the ability to rise through the ceiling, and that it will not allow its attributes to be clearly perceived. These attributes, although distinctive, do not provide the basis for the "thing's" being included in any specific class with which Alice is acquainted. Yet she persists in thinking of it as a member of a familiar class, an object which could immediately be identified if only it could be clearly seen: she seems unwilling to admit the possibility that the "thing" belongs to a class (unnamed in her experience) whose members possess as defining characteristics those specific attributes which she HAS been able to determine. If her hypothesis is correct, and the "thing" is a member of a familiar class merely unable to be identified as such, then functionally, as regards the process of classification, Alice's difficulty is analogous to the Queen of Hearts' inability to identify her gardeners because of a lack of distinguishing attributes.

Carroll seems in this passage to be illustrating the general principle that classifi-cation can often be extremely difficult to accomplish. He is suggesting that some-times it can at best be only approximate. Not always, however; for as was seen in the epigraph to this chapter, objects possessing complex attributes sometimes can be classified precisely; the contents of the bottle which Alice sampled in Wonder-land had "a sort of mixed flavour of cherry-tart, custard, pineapple, roast turkey, toffy, and hot buttered toast". In this instance, Alice is able to differentiate and name each of the individual flavors which make up the composite taste; and although she has no specific name for the "mixed flavour" itself, she nonetheless has a clear idea of its specific attributes and could describe the taste to someone else by enumerating these attributes. Such is not the case with the "thing" she encounters in the shop. Those of its attributes which she is able to determine do not give her a clear idea of what the object is; nor would they, if she listed them for someone else, give HIM any concrete notion of the "thing" either. Classification is a process which often can be very difficult and treacherous: there are not many things which are so easily classified, and so certain in their classification, as that type of Snark called a "Boojum".

5.4 SUMMARY

Yet, as a process which ends in the bestowing of names upon objects, classification is necessary for the effecting of both thought and communication. If men were not able to assign objects to specific generic classes on the basis of their common attributes, generalizations could not be made. Abstract thought would be impossible;

and men would be forced to rely upon indexical signs for communication, confining themselves to discussion of concrete particular objects present before them, or of objects which they as individuals had experienced in common.[2]

Carroll saw that obstacles to naming can often arise through some deficiency on the part of the classifier, and through inherent ambiguities in the attributes of the thing being classified. Usually, erroneous classifications occur because of failures in the classifier's perception or in his method: he does not take sufficient note of the thing's attributes (or for some reason is unable to determine what they are), he over-simplifies, over-generalizes, or draws invalid inferences from observed data because of some preconceived notion about the nature of the object he is classifying. Often, however, the attributes of the object are themselves misleading or ambiguous. In such cases, the object may be assigned to a specific class by fiat (as in Humpty Dumpty's identifying his ornamental band as "cravat"), left unclassified (Alice never does learn whether the line of demarcation formed by the band is "neck" or "waist" – and Tenniel's illustration does not help the reader to decide), or subjected to empirical test (as when Alice finds by nibbling that it is the right-hand side of the mushroom which makes her shrink). In some cases an object may defy its classification into any existing genus – either because no appropriate class has been postulated by the classifier, and no name provided for members of such a class (in which case classification can occur only if such a class IS postulated, and a word – such as 'Fish-Footman' – is coined to name the members), or because the classifier cannot ascertain the object's attributes with sufficient precision to hazard even a guess as to its generic nature.

The act of classification (and naming), though performed unconsciously and with great speed in a majority of situations, is rendered slow and difficult by objects and attributes which are unfamiliar, ambiguous, or unclear. Carroll realized that the process of classification, though often quite simple, was potentially intricate, and liable to error. He saw that erroneous classifications can, if acted upon as though they were accurate, produce confusion in human thought and communication, and create situations potentially dangerous to mental health and social order. Of the Hatter's hat, the King cried, "Stolen!" – and the jury instantly made a memorandum of the fact.

---

[2] Such a state of affairs is treated by Jonathan Swift in Book III of *Gulliver's Travels* when he pursues to a logical and absurd conclusion the scheme of certain projectors at the Academy of Lagado to abolish all words and carry on discourse with objects which could be taken from place to place.

6

NAMES

"What's in a name? that which we call a rose
By any other name would smell as sweet ..."

Shakespeare, *Romeo and Juliet*, II, i

6.1 CARROLL'S DEFINITION OF 'NAME'

The final step in a given process of classification is the act of naming. Lewis Carroll was aware that classification is often difficult to perform and always open to the possibility of error. He was aware that strict accuracy in assigning names to things is often impossible, and that the names bestowed often must be approximate, or provisional. But he was also aware that classification and naming can occur with sufficient accuracy and precision to make it possible for men to refer to things, to make generalizations about them, to think abstractly, to draw valid inferences from verbal data, and to communicate effectively. Since in all of these operations objects are conceptualized through the agency of the names assigned to them, it is of crucial importance that the nature and function of names be understood by the men using them. Lewis Carroll gave much thought to the theoretical nature and practical use of names, and evidence of his interest is found throughout his fictional works. Before beginning a discussion of the topic, it will be profitable to look at his formal definition of 'name' as it is found in *Symbolic Logic*. The square brackets are Carroll's.

The word "Thing", which conveys the idea of a Thing, *without* any idea of an Adjunct, represents *any* single Thing. Any other word (or phrase), which conveys the idea of a Thing, *with* the idea of an Adjunct represents *any* Thing which possesses that Adjunct; i.e., it represents any Member of the Class to which that Adjunct is *peculiar*.

Such a word (or phrase) is called a 'Name'; and, if there be an existing Thing which is represents, it is said to be a Name of that Thing.

[For example, the words "Thing," "Treasure," "Town," and the phrases "valuable Thing," "material artificial Thing consisting of houses and streets," "Town lit with gas," "Town paved with gold," "old English Book."]

Just as a Class is said to be *Real*, or *Unreal*, according as there *is*, or *is not*, an existing

Thing in it, so also a Name is said to be *Real*, or *Unreal*, according as there *is*, or *is not*, an existing Thing represented by it.

> [Thus, "Town lit with gas" is a *Real* Name: "Town paved with gold" is an *Unreal* Name.]

Every Name is either a Substantive only, or else a phrase consisting of a Substantive and one or more Adjectives (or phrases used as Adjectives).

Every Name, except "Thing", may usually be expressed in three different forms: –

> (*a*) The Substantive "Thing", and one or more Adjectives (or phrases used as Adjectives) conveying the ideas of the Attributes;
>
> (*b*) A Substantive, conveying the idea of a Thing with the ideas of *some* of the Attributes, and one or more Adjectives (or phrases used as Adjectives) conveying the ideas of the *other* Attributes;
>
> (*c*) A Substantive conveying the idea of a Thing with the ideas of *all* the Attributes.

> [Thus, the phrase "material living Thing, belonging to the Animal Kingdom, having two hands and two feet" is a Name expressed in Form (*a*).
>
> If we choose to roll up together the Substantive "Thing" and the Adjectives "material, living, belonging to the Animal Kingdom," so as to make the new Substantive "Animal," we get the phrase "Animal having two hands and two feet," which is a Name (representing the same Thing as before) expressed in Form (*b*).
>
> And, if we choose to roll up the whole phrase into one word, so as to make the new Substantive "Man," we get a Name (still representing the very same Thing) expressed in Form (*c*).]

A Name, whose Substantive is in the *plural* number, may be used to represent either (1) Members of a Class, *regarded as separate Things*; or (2) a whole Class, *regarded as one single Thing*.

> [Thus, when I say "Some soldiers of the Tenth Regiment are tall," or "The soldiers of the Tenth Regiment are brave," I am using the Name "soldiers of the Tenth Regiment" in the *first* sense; and it is just the same as if I were to point to each of them *separately*, and to say "*This* soldier of the Tenth Regiment is tall," "*That* soldier of the Tenth Regiment is tall," and so on.
>
> But, when I say "The soldiers of the Tenth Regiment are formed in square," I am using the phrase in the *second* sense; and it is just the same as if I were to say "The *Tenth Regiment* is formed in square."]

> (*Symbolic Logic, Part I: Elementary,*
> 4th ed. [London, 1897], pp. 4½-5)

Note that Carroll's exposition of the three forms in which names can be expressed involves in (a), (b), and (c) a progressive condensation or "rolling up" of attributes into substantives of a structurally simpler form. This condensation is a process of verbal abstraction whereby each successive term is less precise in its listing of specific attributes than the one before. The attributes are still present in the new and simpler term, but implied rather than stated.

Carroll states in his definition that a name is a word or phrase which "represents" a given thing. It "conveys the idea of a Thing, WITH the idea of an Adjunct ["Attribute or set of Attributes"]". When a thing is given a name, a verbal symbol is selected to stand for the thing and to indicate its membership in a certain class. All things which possess the attributes that qualify them for membership in this class are entitled to representation by this name. Names have two distinct functions: they "convey the idea of a Thing" *i.e.*, they identify the thing which is being referred to and, as sign-vehicles, evoke in the interpreter a notion of the thing as association-object) and they "convey the idea of the Thing's attributes" *i.e.*, to a knowledgeable interpreter, they provide information about the thing in the sense that they evoke a body of associations, or informative connotations, regarding the association-object). The word *man*, for example, refers to a "material, living thing, belonging to the animal kingdom, having two hands and two feet, the capacity for rational thought, the ability to use language", and so forth. The word *man* is thus a general name, referring to any member of the class whose members possess these peculiar attributes. As Carroll tells us, a class may contain only one member: "Any single Thing, which we can name so as to distinguish it from all other Things, may be regarded as a one-Member Class" (*Symbolic Logic*, p. $2\frac{1}{2}$). He uses *London* as his example, since at the time of his writing, London was the only member of the genus "Towns" which possessed the attribute "having four million inhabitants". *London*, being the name of the sole member of a one-member class, "towns having four million inhabitants", is an 'individual' or 'proper' name. Yet, like other names, *London* does more than merely identify the thing it stands for; it also conveys, to a knowledgeable interpreter, information ABOUT the thing: in this instance, by virtue of Carroll's definition, it implies the city's population.

John Stuart Mill, whose *System of Logic* Carroll was reading in 1855, defines general and individual names as follows: a general name is

a name which is capable of being truly affirmed, in the same sense, of each of an indefinite number of things. An individual or singular name is a name which is only capable of being truly affirmed, in the same sense, of one thing. . . . Thus *man* is capable of being truly affirmed of John, Peter, George, and other persons without assignable limits: and it is affirmed of all of them in the same sense; for the word man expresses certain qualities, and when we predicate it of those persons, we assert that they all possess those qualities. But *John* is only capable of being truly affirmed of one single person, at least in the same sense. For although there are many persons who bear that name, it is not conferred upon them to indicate any qualities, or anything which belongs to them in common; and cannot be said to be affirmed of them in any *sense* at all, consequently not in the same sense. "The present king of England" is also an individual name. For, that there never can be more than one person at a time of whom it can be truly affirmed, is implied in the meaning of the words.

(John Stuart Mill, *A System of Logic* [New York, 1852], p. 18)

6.2 THE FUNCTION OF NAMES: J. S. MILL AND LEWIS CARROLL

Since incidents involving 'proper' names play a prominent role in Carroll's fiction, further comment should be made upon them at this time. One of the striking aspects of John Stuart Mill's highly influential treatise on names is his assertion that only general names can convey information about the things they represent (his term for this is 'connotation'); that individual, or proper, names do not indicate or imply attributes, but merely 'denote' (or identify; my term for this is 'designate') the individuals who are called by them.[1] Since, for Mill, whatever information is conveyed by names *i.e.*, whatever 'meaning' they possess) is a product of their connotation and not of their 'denotation', it is obvious that proper names, which merely identify the thing they symbolize, have "strictly speaking, no signification. ... A proper name is but an unmeaning mark which we connect in our minds with the idea of the object, in order that whenever the mark meets our eyes or occurs to our thoughts, we may think of that individual object" (Mill, *Logic*, p. 23).

Carroll does not make this distinction between general and proper names. In his definition in *Symbolic Logic*, all of the names treated are "connotative" in Mill's sense (*e.g.*, "A connotative term is one which denotes a subject and implies an attribute" [Mill, *Logic*, p. 20]). In Carroll's brief discussion of names, the only proper name cited is 'London', the symbol selected to stand for the single member of a particular "Individual" class. He defines London as he would any other thing, by genus and differentia: "London is the TOWN which has four million inhabitants" (*Symbolic Logic*, p. 7). Carroll's treats 'London' as a special type of general name, equivalent to Mill's "connotative individual name":

[1]   In Mill's system, the third major division of names is into CONNOTATIVE and NON-CONNOTA-TIVE [his term 'denote' is to be taken to signify the same thing as my term 'designate']: "A non-connotative term is one which signifies a subject only, or an attribute only. A connotative term is one which denotes a subject and implies an attribute. By a subject is here meant anything which possesses attributes. Thus John, or London, or England, are names which signify a subject only. Whiteness, length, virtue, signify an attribute only. None of these names, therefore, are connotative. The word white, denotes all white things, as snow, paper ... and implies, or as it was termed by the schoolmen, CONNOTES, the attribute *whiteness*. The word white is not predicated of the attribute, but of the subjects, snow, &c.; but when we predicate it of them we imply, or connote, that the attribute of whiteness belongs to them. [...] All concrete general names are connotative. The word *man* ... denotes Peter, Paul, John, and an indefinite number of other individuals, of whom, taken as a class, it is the name. But it is applied to them, because they possess, and to signify that they possess, certain attributes. [...] Proper names are not connotative: they denote the individuals who are called by them; but they do not indicate or imply any attributes as belonging to those individuals. When we name a child by the name Mary, or a dog by the name Caesar, these names are simply marks used to enable those individuals to be made subjects of discourse. It may be said, indeed, that we must have had some reason for giving them those names rather than any others: and this is true; but the name, once given, becomes independent of the reason. A man may have been named John because that was the name of his father; a town may have been named Dartmouth, because it is situated at the mouth of the Dart. But it is no part of the signification of the word John, that the father of the person so called bore the same name; nor even of the word Dartmouth, to be situated at the mouth of the Dart. If sand should choke up the mouth of the river, or an earthquake change its course, and remove it to a distance from the town, there is no reason to think that the name of the town would be changed. That fact, therefore, can form no part of the signification of the word; for otherwise, when the fact ceased to be true, the name would cease to be applied. Proper names are attached to the objects themselves, and are not dependent upon the continuance of any attribute of the object" (John Stuart Mill, *A System of Logic* [New York, 1852], pp. 20-21).

... although we may give to an individual a name utterly unmeaning, which we call a proper name, – a word which answers the purpose of showing what thing it is we are talking about, but not of telling anything about it; yet a name peculiar to an individual is not necessarily of this description. It may be significant of some attribute, or some union of attributes, which being possessed by no object but one, determines the name exclusively to that individual. [His examples are 'the sun', 'God' (when used by a Christian), 'the first emperor of Rome', and 'the father of Socrates'.]

(Mill, *A System of Logic*, p. 22)

Since Carroll did not discuss proper names in a formal fashion, it is difficult to say whether he would have agreed with Mill that they do nothing more than identify, or designate, the object which they stand for. All of the names discussed by Carroll in *Symbolic Logic* serve both to identify and to convey information about the things they represent. Yet in his fictional works he seems to have been intrigued by the question, Do proper names tell anything about the object they designate? Moreover, he was fascinated by the possibility of a person's losing or forgetting his name, and by the effects this would have upon the person.

Before discussing Carroll's literary treatment of proper names, I wish to examine his conception of names in general. There is no certainty that the definition of 'name' which he recorded toward the end of his life is that which he subscribed to in his earlier years. Yet there is a strong possibility that he had formulated his notions on the nature and functions of names in the 1850's and 1860's while he was engaged in his intensive and systematic study of mathematics and logic.

6.3 CARROLL'S CONCEPTION OF NAMES IN GENERAL

6.3.1 *Terminology: 'Denotation', 'Designation', 'Connotation'*

Before proceeding, it is necessary to establish our terminology. As a type of linguistic sign, names function in accord with the general sign-process outlined in § 4.2. Since names have as their significations conceptualized association-objects which lie wholly outside the linguistic code, they embody referential meaning; and inasmuch as they are able to stand for their referents in acts of discourse, they are symbols. (See also §§ 4.4.3 and 4.4.6 for discussion of this and the following points.) In a given act of discourse, the signification of a 'general' name such as *city* may be either ANY member of the class of things so named (without unique specification) or a PARTICULAR member of the class; the signification of a 'proper' name such as *London* is always a particular thing (perhaps best conceived as the sole member of a one-member or 'Individual' class).

Signs embodying referential meaning have designative as well as (potential) connotative signification: designative, in that they identify, point out, or 'label' their referents as objects of discourse; connotative, in that they evoke in a knowledgeable interpreter a body of personal associations, informational and (perhaps) attitudinal, which stem from his previous experience with the symbol and with the referent. While fulfilling both a designative and a connotative function, names may or may not denote their referents, denotation being contingent on whether the referents do or do not actually exist at the time when the sign-process occurs. In giving 'denotation' this signification, I diverge from the practice of John Stuart Mill (and others), which is to use 'denotation' to refer to the identifying or labeling function of names – which process of identification I prefer to call 'designation'. As I have previously intimated (§ 4.3), names – and especially those that symbolize PARTICULAR referents – are a kind of indexical sign, or identifying label, which, like finger-posts, "point to" their conceptualized association-objects as objects of discourse. Whereas in this study 'designation' refers to that part of a name's signification which indicates and identifies the referent, 'connotation' refers to that part of a name's signification which embodies the attributes (real or fancied) of the referent which are evoked in the mind of the interpreter.

A name 'connotes' when it suggests or implies (i.e., evokes in the mind of the interpreter) the attributes of the thing designated by it. It will be useful to differentiate two types of connotation. Availing myself of two terms which have been brought into prominence by the General Semanticists, I have used 'informative connotation' to refer to the process by which a name "suggests or implies" those attributes of a thing which have caused it, through the general agreement of classifiers, to be placed in the specific class whose members possess that name. 'Affective connotation' I have used to refer to the process by which a name evokes in an interpreter those real or imagined attributes of a thing which produce emotional responses. When used in the plural, each of these terms should be taken to refer to the attributes themselves – whether these are commonly shared by all interpreters, or purely personal – which are conveyed by the name. Affective connotations necessarily will vary from interpreter to interpreter. Moreover, it is obvious that affective connotations may bear little or no correspondence to the informative connotations of a name, and quite as little to the inherent nature of the thing which possesses the name. For example, a person who, upon hearing the name *man,* thinks "Nature's greatest mistake!" reveals the affective connotations which the name holds for him. These connotations have little relation either to the informative connotations ("member of the animal kingdom, having two hands and two feet, the capacity for rational thought, and the ability to use language") or to the referent designated (a specific person, any single member of the class "men", or – conceivably – any given member of the class "human beings"). I have deferred discussion of affective connotation to Chapter Ten; in the remainder of this chapter, I have concentrated on the designative and informative functions of names.

6.3.2 *Designation: the 'Labeling' Function of Names*

Carroll's definition of 'name' establishes any name's symbolic status: a name is a linguistic token which stands for a given thing to which it has been assigned on the basis of that thing's inclusion in a given class. Insofar as they identify the thing they stand for, names are analogous to labels affixed to specific objects. A passage in *Through the Looking-Glass* illustrates Carroll's awareness of this 'labeling' function of names and, incidentally, his awareness of the way in which language can be used to talk about language. The White Knight wishes to sing for Alice a song whose tune is his own invention:

". . . The name of the song is called '*Haddocks' Eyes*.' "

"Oh, that's the name of the song, is it?" Alice said, trying to feel interested.

"No, you don't understand," the Knight said, looking a little vexed. "That's what the name is *called*. The name really *is* '*The Aged Aged Man*.' "

"Then I ought to have said 'That's what the *song* is called'?" Alice corrected herself.

"No, you oughtn't: that's quite another thing! The *song* is called '*Ways and Means*': but that's only what it's *called*, you know!"

"Well, what is the *song*, then?" said Alice, who was by this time completely bewildered.

"I was coming to that," the Knight said. "The song really *is* '*A-sitting On A Gate*': and the tune's my own invention."

(Works, p. 244)

Carroll is here demonstrating that verbal symbols may be used to refer to other verbal symbols. Alice is confused because she does not realize what the Knight is doing when he states one linguistic expression to be the call-name of another. In the words of Martin Gardner in *The Annotated Alice* (New York, 1960), p. 306: "To a student of logic and semantics all this is perfectly sensible. The song *is* 'A-sitting on a Gate'; it is *called* 'Ways and Means'; the *name* of the song is 'The Aged Aged Man'; and the name is *called* 'Haddocks' Eyes.' Carroll is distinguishing here among things, the names of things, and the names of names of things." Ernest Nagel has discussed this passage in his treatment of call-names in the article "Symbolic Notation, Haddocks' Eyes and the Dog-Walking Ordinance", printed in *The World of Mathematics*, Vol. III, ed. James R. Newman (New York, 1956), pp. 1878-1900. He considers Alice's difficulty to be "the type of misunderstanding that may arise from the failure to distinguish between fragments of discourse (such as names) and what linguistic expressions are about or designate" (pp. 1886-1887); Alice does not realize from the White Knight's speech that he is talking about linguistic expressions as such. According to Nagel, when we assert something about a linguistic expression, "the statement should contain as a constituent not *that expression* but a *name* for the expression. Now there is a widely used current device for manufacturing names for written and printed expressions: it consists in placing an expression within single quotation marks, and using the complex made up out of the expression and its enclosing quotation marks as the name for the expression itself" (p. 1884). Note that Carroll has conformed to this convention in the quoted passage. He was aware of the necessity for distinguishing levels of symbolization by some arbitrary and conventional means; but Alice, merely LIS-

TENING to the Knight's speech, had no way of knowing that the problematical expressions were intended to be taken as set apart from the rest of the utterance in single quotation marks. This passage reveals Carroll's sophistication in realizing that if language is used to discuss language, if names are to be given names, if labels are themselves to be labeled, there must be some conventional way of distinguishing the symbol from the thing symbolized. In written and printed discourse the conventional notation of single quotation marks provides the practical means by which a metalanguage can be established. There is theoretically no limit to the hierarchy of successive metalanguages capable of being thus formed.[2]

A moment ago I said that, as symbol standing for a given thing, a name is analogous to a label identifying the object to which it is affixed. Labels and names are markers which indicate to an interpreter: "here is x object". Thus, Alice is able to determine the respective identities of the look-alike Tweedle brothers when she comes upon them:

... Alice knew which was which in a moment, because one of them had 'DUM' embroidered on his collar, and the other 'DEE.' "I suppose they've each got 'TWEEDLE' round at the back of the collar," she said to herself.

They stood so still that she quite forgot they were alive, and she was just going round to see if the word 'TWEEDLE' was written at the back of each collar, when she was startled by a voice coming from the one marked 'DUM.'

"If you think we're wax-works," he said, "you ought to pay, you know. Wax-works weren't made to be looked at for nothing. Nohow!"

"Contrariwise," added the one marked 'DEE,' "if you think we're alive, you ought to speak."

(*Works*, pp. 180-181)

[2] Ernest Nagel feels that when the White Knight finally resolves Alice's difficulty by declaring, "The Song really *is* 'A-sitting On A Gate'," either Carroll himself or the printer blundered in leaving quotation marks around the right-hand expression in the identity. "For the 'object' designated by the left-hand expression in this identity could not possibly be the 'object' designated by the right-hand expression, since the former is the song whose tune is claimed by the Knight to be his own invention, while the latter is a certain linguistic expression whose name is exhibited on the right-hand side of the identity. What the Knight obviously meant to say is that:
    The Song = A-sitting On A Gate."
Nagel's paradigm of the four identities given by the Knight is this:
    The call-name of the name of The Song = 'Haddocks' Eyes'
    The name of The Song   = 'The Aged Aged Man'
    The call-name of The Song   = 'Ways and Means'
    The Song   = A-sitting On A Gate
He concludes by casting the text of the dialogue between Alice and the Knight into the notation of symbolic logic. (Ernest Nagel, "Symbolic Notation, Haddocks' Eyes and the Dog-Walking Ordinance", in *The World of Mathematics*, Vol. III, ed. James R. Newman [New York, 1956], pp. 1889-90.)
Roger W. Holmes, in his article "The Philosopher's *Alice in Wonderland*", *Antioch Review*, XIX (1959), 133-149, likewise sees an inconsistency in this last identity given by the White Knight. Holmes feels that Carroll, in giving "A-sitting On A Gate" as the song itself, "was definitely pulling our leg. ... To be consistent, the White Knight, when he had said that the song *is* ... could only have burst into the song itself" (p. 139).

In this passage, labels uniquely identify, and purport to denote differences in, two apparently identical objects. Note Carroll's use of single quotation marks to indicate 'DUM', 'DEE', and 'TWEEDLE' as objects of discourse and to distinguish them, as expressions, from his and Alice's levels of discourse. Note too that Carroll does not refer to the brothers by name. Adopting Alice's point of view, he chooses instead to refer to them as "the one marked 'DUM' " and "the one marked 'DEE' ", which expressions become, in the context of this passage, the functional names of the two individuals. When, a few lines later, Carroll begins referring to the individuals as "Tweedledum" and "Tweedledee", he dispenses with the periphrastic expressions as being no longer of use in referring to the objects. Their function had been to serve as provisional names – a way of talking about the objects until their identities had been ascertained, a feat rather mysteriously accomplished by Alice's reciting the familiar nursery rhyme recounting their quarrel. As soon as the rhyme containing their names has been uttered, Carroll begins calling them by their proper names. Since Tweedledum IS the one marked 'DUM', and Tweedledee the one marked 'DEE', Alice finds in this case that labels CAN accurately identify their objects.

6.3.3 *Informative Connotation: The ability of Names to Convey Information About the Thing Designated*

In addition to identifying the object to which it refers, a label may also convey information about the object. The word 'MEN' painted on a door in a public building is a conventional abbreviation for 'MEN'S TOILET'; it designates the presence of a men's toilet and its location (behind the door), and it conveys to passers-by (i.e., evokes in their minds) the attributes possessed by men's toilets: that men might be found in the room, and that women are neither expected nor welcome inside. In like manner, the word 'POISON' on the label of a bottle designates that something poisonous is present in the bottle, and connotes the substance's attribute, "harmful if taken internally". Carroll illustrates this connotative function of labels explicitly. In *Wonderland*, Alice, having reached the bottom of the rabbit hole, finds a bottle labeled with the words 'DRINK ME':

... but the wise little Alice was not going to do *that* in a hurry. "No, I'll look first," she said, "and see whether it's marked '*poison*' or not"; ... she had never forgotten that, if you drink much from a bottle marked "poison," it is almost certain to disagree with you, sooner or later.

However, this bottle was *not* marked "poison," so Alice ventured to taste it, and, finding it very nice ... she very soon finished it off.

(Works, p. 22)

Alice assumes that the absence of a label marked "poison" guarantees that the substance in the bottle is not poisonous. She was running a great risk in drinking this unnamed and uncharacterized fluid, for the absence of such a label does not assure the drinker that it is not poisonous. (Contrariwise, a bottle labeled "poison" might not, in fact, contain a poisonous substance, though a potential drinker would be quite justified in refusing to sample its contents.) Alice was a trusting soul to assume that if the liquid were poisonous, it would be labeled as such; she responds to the ABSENCE of a label designating the presence of poison as a sign equivalent in its signification to that of a label reading "NOT POISON" – an interpretation reinforced by the actual label, "DRINK ME", which, though logically noncommittal with regard to the poisonous or non-poisonous nature of the liquid, implies to her that the substance is harmless.

Since Tweedledum and Tweedledee WERE correctly identified by the names embroidered on their shirt collars, and since the contents of the bottle were NOT poisonous (the liquid only made Alice shrink), Carroll is illustrating in these passages the obvious fact that labels often can be relied upon to characterize objects accurately. We usually do rely upon them, in fact. A man opens a door marked "MEN" confident that he will find himself in a washroom, and not a women's washroom; no one in his right mind who knows the significance of the label drinks out of a bottle marked "POISON". It is necessary, for the purposes of effective thought and communication, for people to feel that labels (and names generally) can be trusted to identify and characterize their objects accurately. But since, as Carroll amply demonstrates, signs can be inaccurate and thus misleading in their designation, it is also necessary that people exercise considerable caution in trusting them. If the Tweedle brothers had traded shirts before meeting Alice, if the persons wearing the shirts had not been the Tweedle brothers at all, or if the embroidery had been mere ornament for the collars and not symbols designating the wearers' identities, Alice would have been deceived by her credulity.

6.3.4 *Labels Inaccurate in Designation and False in Connotations*

Labels may not be accurate in their designations. If they are not – if, in other words, there actually is no referent which they purport to symbolize – they are useless as identifying markers and, insofar as they evoke informative connotations regarding a non-existent referent, deceptive. Lewis Carroll was highly conscious of the powers which false labels have to mislead and deceive their interpreters. In *Sylvie and Bruno*, he has the Vice-Warden of Outland use a map intentionally to confuse the Baron Doppelgeist, a visiting dignitary unfamiliar with the country:

... the Baron was ... much bewildered by the Vice-Warden's habit of pointing to one place while he shouted out the name of another.

(*Works*, p. 337)

The Baron is confused because the true name in each case is printed on the map in conjunction with the place to which the Vice-Warden is pointing. If these printed names had not been before his eyes, he would have taken the Vice-Warden's shouted names at face value and not been confused. But he is able to see that the printed names (the referents) are not accurately symbolized by the shouted names (the labels).

Alice, during her fall down the rabbit hole into Wonderland, is greatly disappointed when she takes a jar labeled "ORANGE MARMALADE" from a shelf and finds it to be empty (*Works*, p. 18). The label is false not only because it does not accurately designate the contents of the jar, but also because it does purport to designate (and denote) something not present. Carroll's illustration, recalling that of the red paint on the Queen of Hearts' white-roses, suggests the analogous situations to be found in a totalitarian dictatorship's calling itself a "democracy", or in the widespread tendency of American politicians of every stamp and hue to invoke as support for their respective platforms "the principles of the Founding Fathers". When labels are used indiscriminately and carelessly with regard to their accuracy of designation (subverting their conventional acceptations), it is only a short step to their conscious abuse, as in Orwell's nightmare world of *1984*, where the populace is conditioned to believe that "WAR IS PEACE", "FREEDOM IS SLAVERY", "IGNORANCE IS STRENGTH".

The principle illustrated by Alice's falsely labeled jar has far-reaching consequences in the realm of human behavior. The General Semanticists of the twentieth century, following the lead of Alfred Korzybski and S. I. Hayakawa, often use the metaphor "maps without territories" to refer to those situations in which men hold beliefs (based upon misinformation or erroneous reasoning) that have no correspondence to the world of reality. Superstitions, factual errors held to be true, and stereotypes of various sorts (the product of over-generalization) constitute "maps" which represent no existing "territories". Hayakawa says that no harm will come from the possession of such a "map" unless someone uses it to plan a trip.[3] This is true; but men being what they are, the course of human history is littered with the wrecks of those who did plan their journeys by means of such "maps".

6.3.5 *Names Without Designative Signification; Their Defeat of Communication Attempts Through Non-Understanding*

While falling down the rabbit hole, Alice employs two words which have no designative signification in the context of their utterance.

Down, down, down. Would the fall *never* come to an end? "I wonder how many miles I've fallen by this time?" she said aloud. "I must be getting somewhere near the centre of the earth. Let me see: that would be four thousand miles down, I think ... but then I wonder what Latitude or Longitude I've got to?" (Alice had not the slightest idea what Latitude was, or Longitude either, but she thought they were nice grand words to say.)

(Works, p. 19)

'Latitude' and 'Longitude' as used here are empty labels in two distinct senses. As Daniel Kirk has pointed out, "Since these words denote arbitrary, man-made divi-

---

[3] S. I. Hayakawa, *Language in Thought and Action* (New York, 1949), p. 33.

sions of the Earth's surface, they have no application at its center." [4] Symbolizing nothing which can have relevance for the physical context in which they are uttered, these labels (in the sense of their common acceptations) have no designative signification whatsoever; in this context, in spite of their having the appearance of actual names, they are merely meaningless noise. But, as used by Alice, they are devoid of meaning in yet another way. Carroll tells the reader that Alice has not the slightest idea what things the names 'Latitude' and 'Longitude' refer to. Thus, even if she were on the earth's surface where the names do have designative signification, she would not, in her ignorance, be able to interpret them as signs; for her they would evoke no association-objects which would provide significations. Since she has never ascertained their conventional symbolic reference, as far as she is concerned (except for her vague awareness that they are names referring to geographical location), they are mere noise.

A further example of "maps without territories" occurs in *Sylvie and Bruno* when Arthur Forester, the intellectual hero of the adult portion of the novel, is forced to endure the pseudo-intellectual chatter of a "bluestocking". The narrator comments:

[Arthur] had placed himself next to the young lady in spectacles, whose high rasping voice had already cast loose upon Society such ominous phrases as "Man is a bundle of Qualities!", "the Objective is only attainable through the Subjective!". Arthur was bearing it bravely: but several faces wore a look of alarm, and I thought it high time to start some less metaphysical topic.

(Works, p. 418)

The terms used by the young lady are so vague and abstract that they have no meaning for her audience (and most probably none for her either). Since she has not bothered to explain what she intends for the words to signify, the names 'bundle of Qualities', 'Qualities', 'the Objective', and 'the Subjective' have no specific designations and therefore no informative connotations. Such "words", utterly without signification of any type, are rendered unfit for purposes either of thought or communication.[5] Unfortunately this does not prevent their widespread

---

[4]   Daniel F. Kirk, *Charles Dodgson, Semeiotician* (University of Florida Press, 1963), p. 52.
[5]   J. S. Mill says of this ever-present danger in the use of words: "One of the chief sources ... of lax habits of thought, is the custom of using connotative terms without a distinctly ascertained connotation, and with no more precise notion of their meaning than can be loosely collected from observing what objects they are used to denote. ... [General similarities in objects often cause them to be classed under a single common name without an analytic apprehension of the particular attributes – without seeing what it is that they possess in common, giving them resemblance.] ... When this is the case, men use the name without any recognized connotation, that is, without any precise meaning; they talk, and consequently think, vaguely. ... Even philosophers have aided in this perversion of general language from its purpose; sometimes because, like the vulgar, they knew no better; and sometimes in deference to that aversion to admit new words, which induces mankind, on all subjects not considered technical, to attempt to make the original small stock of names serve with but little augmentation to express a constantly increasing number of objects and distinctions, and, consequently to express them in a manner progressively more and more imperfect.

use among both the general public and the learned (who should know better). Of this latter group, those who habitually engage in abstract thinking – theologians, sociologists, and art critics, for example – are particularly prone to be victimized by such language; though of course not all of them are.

When words 'empty' of concrete signification are used in attempts at communication, the attempts usually fail because of non-understanding on the part of the interpreter. In "The Three Voices" (1856), a poem parodying Tennyson's "The Two Voices", Carroll demonstrates in a whimsical fashion the demoralizing effects of a consistent use of highly abstract language. The parody deals with a man cast into despondency by the unfathomable (and therefore unanswerable) arguments of a contentious and predatory woman whom he meets on the seashore. The dialogue is for the most part nonsensical – Carroll's carrying to the logical extreme Tennyson's abstract language in "The Two Voices". Note how the woman, by speaking in vague generalities, provides neither her victim nor the reader with anything like a coherent argument, and at one point causes her companion to become hopelessly muddled while trying to meet her on her own ground.

> She urged "No cheese is made of chalk":
> And ceaseless flowed her dreary talk,
> Tuned to the footfall of a walk.
>
> Her voice was very full and rich,
> And, when at length she asked him "Which?"
> It mounted to the highest pitch.
>
> . . . .
>
> She waited not for his reply,
> But with a downward leaden eye
> Went on as if he were not by –
>
> Sound argument and grave defence,
> Strange questions raised on "Why?" and "Whence?"
> And wildly tangled evidence.
>
> When he, with racked and whirling brain,
> Feebly implored her to explain,
> She simply said it all again.
>
> Wrenched with an agony intense,
> He spake, neglecting Sound and Sense,
> And careless of all consequence:
>
> "Mind – I believe – is Essence – Ent –
> Abstract – that is – an Accident –
> Which we – that is to say – I meant –"

"To what degree this loose mode of classifying and denominating objects has rendered the vocabulary of mental and moral philosophy unfit for the purposes of accurate thinking, is best known to whoever has most reflected on the present condition of those branches of knowledge" (*A System of Logic* [1852], pp. 25-26; square brackets mine).

When, with quick breath and cheeks all flushed,
At length his speech was somewhat hushed,
She looked at him, and he was crushed.

.   .   .   .

Then, having wholly overthrown
His views, and stripped them to the bone,
Proceeded to unfold her own.

"Shall Man be Man? And shall he miss
Of other thoughts no thought but this,
Harmonious dews of sober bliss?"

(Works, pp. 870-871)

6.3.6   The Ability of Names to be Inaccurate in their Designations

While names may be devoid of designative signification altogether and thus produce
failures in communication-attempts through non-understanding on the part of the
interpreter, they sometimes may be simply inaccurate in their designations. An
example of this principle occurs in Chapter IV of *Wonderland* when the White
Rabbit, seeing Alice, calls out angrily:

"Why, Mary Ann, what *are* you doing out here? Run home this moment, and fetch me
a pair of gloves and a fan!"

Alice is so frightened that she runs off in the direction he indicates without
attempting to explain his mistake:

"He took me for his housemaid," she said to herself as she ran. "How surprised he'll be
when he finds out who I am! But I'd better take him his fan and gloves – that is, if I can
find them."

(Works, p. 43)

The name 'Mary Ann' does not accurately label Alice; but she must have some
similarity in appearance to the housemaid (perhaps her human form?) which caused
the White Rabbit to make his error in classification. The conferring of a false name
upon Alice does not, of course, change her in any way: she does not become Mary
Ann, and she retains the knowledge of her own identity. To the Rabbit, the name
'Mary Ann' designates his housemaid and connotes that the object so named will
run errands for him. Since Alice does not inform the Rabbit of his mistake and acts
upon his orders as though his name for her WERE accurate as a label, he has no
reason to doubt that his act of naming was correct. From this illustration may be
inferred the principle that, although a name (as label) may not in fact accurately
designate the object to which it is affixed, it may – unless proved false by empirical
evidence – serve functionally for men's use. Once again we are reminded of the
Queen of Hearts' roses. Although she might be deluded by appearances into thinking
that the gardeners had planted a red rose-tree, beneath the paint both the flowers
and the tree remain unaltered. In like manner, the names given to things in no way

affect their essential nature; and things which are erroneously named can sometimes still be conjured with.

In *Sylvie and Bruno*, for example, Arthur Forester deludes the bespectacled bluestocking into thinking that the reason we see things right-side-up when their images are upside-down on our retinas, is that the brain is inverted:

"What we call the *vertex* of the Brain is really its *base*: and what we call its *base* is really its *vertex*: it is simply a question of *nomenclature*."

This last polysyllable settled the matter. "How truly delightful!" the fair Scientist exclaimed with enthusiasm.

(Works, p. 417)

And in *Through the Looking-Glass*, while Alice is helping the Tweedle brothers arm for battle, Carroll gives another illustration of this principle:

"Do I look very pale?" said Tweedledum, coming up to have his helmet tied on. (He *called* it a helmet, though it certainly looked much more like a saucepan.)

(Works, p. 193)

Finally, the principle is alluded to in *Wonderland* when the Cheshire Cat is explaining to Alice how he knows that he is mad:

"To begin with," said the Cat, "a dog's not mad. You grant that?"

"I suppose so," said Alice.

"Well, then," the Cat went on, "you see a dog growls when it's angry, and wags its tail when it's pleased. Now *I* growl when I'm pleased, and wag my tail when I'm angry. Therefore I'm mad."

"*I* call it purring, not growling," said Alice.

"Call it what you like," said the Cat.

(Works, p. 72)

If *growling* and *purring* WERE two names conventionally used to designate one and the same thing (as the Cat seems to think), one could indeed call the thing by either name as he "liked". Of course, in conventional usage *growling* and *purring* do not designate one and the same thing as referent. But the Cat's concluding statement does imply the valid principle that regardless of what name is given to a thing, the thing itself is not affected by the signification of the label: the Cat's using one name for both phenomena does not make a purr into a growl. A further principle may be inferred from the Cat's final statement: that more than one name CAN be given to a single thing with equal validity. This last holds true, however, only if the various names given to the thing are not contradictory in their conventional significations. An illustration of what can happen when this rule is violated occurs at the trial in *Wonderland*, when the King asks Alice what she knows about the theft of the tarts:

"Nothing whatever," said Alice.

"That's very important," the King said, turning to the jury. They were just beginning to write this down on their slates, when the White Rabbit interrupted: "*Un*important, your Majesty means, of course," he said, in a very respectful tone, but frowning and making faces at him as he spoke.

"*Un*important, of course, I meant," the King hastily said, and went on to himself in an undertone, "important – unimportant – unimportant – important –" as if he were trying which word sounded best.

Some of the jury wrote it down "important," and some "unimportant." Alice could see this, as she was near enough to look over their slates; "but it doesn't matter a bit," she thought to herself.

(Works, p. 124)

Perhaps it doesn't matter in the nonsensical context of this particular trial; but outside of this context, such contradictory significations of the names used would matter a great deal. A given thing (such as a witness's testimony) cannot be both important and unimportant with reference to something which it materially affects (the jury's consideration of a verdict). In *Through the Looking-Glass* Alice sees this clearly when the Red Queen says of a nearby hill:

"*I* could show you hills, in comparison with which you'd call that [one] a valley."

"No, I shouldn't," said Alice . . . "a hill *ca'n't* be a valley, you know. That would be nonsense –"

(Works, pp. 162-163)

It would indeed. A hill may be called many things: "hillock", "rise", "topographical elevation", "*kopje*", "*Hügel*" – but never, in the conventional acceptation of the word, "valley". The attributes of the thing named which are connoted by the word *hill* in conventional usage do not correspond with those connoted by the word *valley*.

However, Tweedledum's calling a saucepan his "helmet" does not in any way contradict the attributes of the thing as connoted by the name 'saucepan'. The thing was made to be a saucepan (not a helmet) and therefore possesses those physical attributes characteristic of saucepans (which enable Alice to identify it as such) and suited to its intended function. Still, it CAN be used as a protective head-covering, and thus can function as a helmet. Tweedledum classifies the object as "helmet" on the basis of its temporary function; but this change of name does not alter the fact that the thing was constructed to be, and still has the physical attributes of, a saucepan. He may call it what he likes; and as long as he does not thereby contradict the specific attributes which provide the basis for its primary classification, he may validly affix a new label to the object on the basis of its expanded function. But it remains a saucepan still.

6.4 THE IDENTIFYING FUNCTION OF NAMES

6.4.1 *General Names as Indexical Signs; the Usefulness of Names*

If a given thing can have many different names legitimately applied to it, and if names can, while accurately designating and characterizing the things to which they refer, be thus fluid, interchangeable, and capable of expansion to encompass additional functions of the thing named, what is their precise value as instruments of thought and communication? What's IN a name, after all? Alice seems to have an answer in the following passage, but the Gnat is not much help:

"What sort of insects do you rejoice in, where *you* come from?" the Gnat inquired.
  "I don't *rejoice* in insects at all," Alice explained, "because I'm rather afraid of them – at least the large kinds. But I can tell you the names of some of them."
  "Of course they answer to their names?" the Gnat remarked carelessly.
  "I never knew them do it."
  "What's the use of their having names," the Gnat said, "if they wo'n't answer to them?"
  "No use to *them*," said Alice, "but it's useful to the people that name them, I suppose. If not, why do things have names at all?"
  "I ca'n't say," the Gnat replied.

(Works, p. 173)

Note that in her concluding question Alice shifts from "insects" to a consideration of "things" in general. It is people who assign names to things, and they do so because names are useful in providing convenient labels for referring to and thinking about things. Alice's concluding question, if framed in general terms, may, I think, be taken to imply the usefulness of both general and individual, or proper, names.

Initially, while discussing insects, she is thinking of their general or classification names, such as "dragon-fly", "horse-fly", and "butterfly"; and in her world, things do not answer to their classification-names. The Gnat, in assuming that insects in Alice's world WILL answer to their names, seems to be interpreting 'name' in the sense of individual, or 'personal', names, taking it for granted that an insect would answer to its name as Alice would to hers, or a dog to 'Fido'. But in Alice's world, insects – and most other objects animate and inanimate – are rarely given personal names. Should the necessity arise for differentiating a particular object from the other members of its class, the object might merely be pointed to, or its general name converted into an indexical sign by the addition of a demonstrative qualifier: "*this* lamp", "*that* dog". It is unnecessary to assign individual or personal names to most objects in Alice's world, for in the first place, the names would be of no use to the objects; and in the second, the general names (with their ability to be converted into indexical signs) are sufficient for men to identify the objects and to think about them. Moreover, it would be impractical to give each member of a numerous class its own individual name: similarities which determine class membership would be obscured, men's memories would be intolerably burdened, and generalized thought and communication would be rendered virtually impossible. Proper, or individual, names are reserved for those creatures which CAN respond to them, such as people and certain of the more intelligent domestic animals, and for places and relatively non-numerous things (perhaps unique) which, though unable to derive benefit from their names themselves, must be able to be designated specifically.

6.4.2 *Personal Names as Indexical Signs*

Proper names are of great value when persons are referred to as individuals. General names applicable to people, such as 'man', 'history professor', 'truck driver', and so on, even when converted into indexical signs by the addition of a demonstrative qualifier, are usually not sufficiently specific to serve as a means of designating individual people. In the words of Sir Alan Gardiner, human beings "look alike, or at all events the distinguishing marks are not conspicuous enough for the individuality of each to be upheld by words more meaningful than proper names. It is of importance for the theory of proper names that these accompany their owners, as a rule, from the cradle to the grave, and consequently identify these owners at every conceivable stage and in every situation. Indeed, we may pertinently note that a personality sometimes undergoes temporary eclipse by change of name, as in the case of girls who marry or prominent men when elevated to the peerage" (*The Theory of Proper Names,* 2nd ed. [Oxford, 1954], p. 47). If a person's given name should be made unavailable to anyone wishing to refer to that person (as Gardiner suggests that it might), the task of designating that person becomes much more difficult. Yet it can be done. The problem and its solution are illustrated by Lewis Carroll when he has the Gnat ask Alice: "I suppose you don't want to lose your name?"

"No, indeed," Alice said, a little anxiously.
    "And yet I don't know," the Gnat went on in a careless tone: "only think how con-
venient it would be if you could manage to go home without it! For instance, if the
governess wanted to call you to your lessons, she would call out 'Come here –,' and there
she would have to leave off, because there wouldn't be any name for her to call, and
of course you wouldn't have to go, you know."

The Gnat does not seem to realize that the governess would have recourse to a substitute if Alice's given name were not available. Alice knows better:

"That would never do, I'm sure," said Alice: "the governess would never think of
excusing me lessons for that. If she couldn't remember my name, she'd call me 'Miss,'
as the servants do."

                                                                    (*Works*, p. 175)

If Alice's personal name did not come to mind, the governess would employ a general name indexically, in direct address: 'Miss', 'little girl', or 'young lady' would serve equally well.

    Another example of a loss of personal name circumvented by substitutions occurs in *The Hunting of the Snark*. In this case, however, the substituted names are not of the type used by the governess in Alice's hypothetical illustration. They are, rather, utterances of various sorts – expletives, nonsense phrases, and common nouns – used as personal names. The Baker is the crew-member in question:

He had forty-two boxes, all carefully packed,
　　With his name painted clearly on each:
But, since he omitted to mention the fact,
　　They were all left behind on the beach.

The loss of his clothes hardly mattered, because
　　He had seven coats on when he came,
With three pair of boots – but the worst of it was,
　　He had wholly forgotten his name.

He would answer to "Hi!" or to any loud cry,
　　Such as "Fry me!" or "Fritter my wig!"
To "What-you-may-call-um!" or "What-was-his-name!"
　　But especially "Thing-um-a-jig!"

While, for those who preferred a more forcible word,
　　He had different names from these:
His intimate friends called him "Candle-ends,"
　　And his enemies "Toasted-cheese."
                                        (*Works*, p. 758)

With regard to his personal name, the Baker is a man without a label (having left all forty-two behind). Unable to recall his given name, he is willing to settle for a variety of substitutes, each of which then functionally becomes a personal name. The crew-members, who in the absence of his label (presumably all forty-two were the same) cannot designate him by the name his parents gave him, decide to name him arbitrarily. They are fortunate that he is willing to submit to such a variety of names; but it would have been almost as easy, and much more efficient, for them to have cooperated in the selection of a single name such as 'the Baker' for referring to him, and 'Baker' for addressing him. If each crew-member kept his private name for the Baker to himself, it must have been difficult for them to talk about him with one another; for one man would not, in the absence of some stipulation to the effect, know that the Baker was the other's object of discourse. If, on the other hand, the crew-members made no secret of their individual labels for the Baker, they would all know that "any loud cry" or expletive ("Fry me!") could refer to him – and this supposition would be confirmed when they saw the Baker come running in answer to the call.

　Although this passage is basically nonsense like the rest of *The Hunting of the Snark*, there are some serious implications to be drawn from it. (1) If men are to be able to refer to a thing, they must have a name for it. (2) The conferring of personal names is purely arbitrary: a name may be chosen and bestowed on a thing by a single individual, or by a group of individuals who have agreed among themselves upon a specific name that will designate that thing. (3) If an individual confers a name privately, he must – if communication is to occur with others about the object – inform other men of what he intends that name to designate. (4) A single name bestowed upon a thing by the mutual agreement of members of a group will serve to enable that group to communicate about the thing. (5) If each of many individuals applies his own private name to a thing and does inform others of his action, there is a danger that specificity of designation will be lost: i.e., if too many labels for the same thing are employed in current usage, confusion may result simply because no one would be able to keep them all in mind. This is particularly true when the labels used are not highly distinctive; for there is the possibility of confusing the thing so labeled with other things of similar labels ("His intimate friends called him 'Candle-ends,'/And his enemies 'Toasted-cheese'": confusion might result if the Bellman told the ship's cook, an enemy of the Baker, "Let's have toasted-cheese for supper," or if he left a memorandum for the cabin-boy, a friend of the Baker, "Throw old candle-ends overboard."). (6) If, in the case of a variety of personal names being applied to a single individual, the object named is willing to "answer" to all of these names, all are valid for referring to him (in view of the number and variety of his names, their lack of specificity, and their potentially ambiguous designations and uses, the Baker must have been continually kept hopping). (7) Many names may legitimately designate (and denote) a single object. (8) If their designative signification is identical, one name may validly be substituted for another.

6.5 THE INFORMATIVE FUNCTION OF NAMES

6.5.1 *The Relationship of the Name to the Thing Named*

Although there are other ways of referring to a person than by means of the personal name with which he was labeled at birth (and some of these alternatives might be much more descriptive than the original name), it is usually by means of the original personal name that individuals ARE designated in situations which require particular specificity of reference. General names are not specific enough (i.e., they are too connotative of the attributes possessed by all members of the class which they name) for precise designation of individuals unless they are used as indexical signs in direct address, or demonstratively, as in "*that* little girl".

In discussing the names of insects in Alice's world, the Gnat seems to be taking the word 'names' to refer to proper names (which insects do not possess), or perhaps to their general names used indexically in direct address. Alice is interpreting the word to refer to general names, which men assign to insects to indicate their class-membership; and she realizes that the insects themselves have no knowledge of either their general names or their membership in a specific class. Whether the Gnat has a personal name or not (if he does, Alice never learns it), he would undoubtedly answer to his general name used indexically: "Come here, Gnat." And presumably the other insects in Looking-Glass Land would also. What the Gnat does not realize (probably because he cannot conceive of such a thing), and what Alice DOES know, is that in Alice's world, insects are incapable of comprehending human speech. The names given to them are of no "use" whatever to them. Names are of use only to men, who employ them as a means of referring to the things which bear them: without names to identify them, no objects could become the subject of discourse.

An illustration of this principle occurs shortly after Alice has left the Gnat (or it has left her, as the case may be). She enters the wood where nothing has a name and immediately loses her personal and her general name.[6] Note that the objects in the wood cannot be referred to individually except by means of indexical signs.

"Well, at any rate it's a great comfort," she said as she stepped under the trees, "after being so hot, to get into the – into the – into *what*?" she went on, rather surprised at not being able to think of the word. "I mean to get under the – under the – under *this*, you know!" putting her hand on the trunk of the tree. "What *does* it call itself, I wonder? I do believe it's got no name – why, to be sure it hasn't!"

She stood silent for a minute, thinking: then she suddenly began again. "Then it really *has* happened, after all! And now, who am I? I *will* remember, if I can! I'm determined to do it!" But being determined didn't help her much, and all she could say, after a great deal of puzzling, was "L, I *know* it begins with L!"

Just then a Fawn came wandering by: it looked at Alice with its large gentle eyes, but didn't seem at all frightened. "Here then! Here then!" Alice said, as she held out her hand and tried to stroke it; but it only started back a little, and then stood looking at her again.

"What do you call yourself?" the Fawn said at last . . .

[6]   Throughout his career Lewis Carroll was fascinated by the possibility of a person's losing or forgetting his personal name. In *Alice's Adventures under Ground* (1862; published 1886) and in its revised version, *Wonderland* (1865), Alice thinks at one point that she must have been changed in the night for one of her acquaintances, since the events she is experiencing are so odd in comparison with yesterday's. She is unable to answer the Caterpillar's question, "Who are you?". In *Through the Looking-Glass* (1871) there are many references to loss of name: in Chapter II, the Red Queen tells Alice, "Remember who you are!"; in Chapter III, though Alice has not yet forgotten her name, the passengers in the railway carriage seem to think she has – one of them says, "So young a child ought to know which way she's going, even if she doesn't know her own name!"; later the Gnat discusses with her the hypothetical results accruing to loss of name and mentions the wood where things have no names; later still, Alice enters the wood and becomes nameless (being deprived of both personal and general name); in Chapter IX, after the White Queen has said that in a recent thunderstorm she was so frightened that she couldn't remember her own name, Alice thinks to herself: "I never should *try* to remember my name in the middle of an accident! Where would be the use of it?". In *The Hunting of the Snark* (1876) the Baker forgets his name and, having no label, must submit to whatever labels people choose to give him. In *Sylvie and Bruno* (1889) there are two incidents concerning loss of name. In one the possibility is threatened (but only because of Bruno's misunderstanding of a common speech idiom), in the other, realized. (1) [Sylvie and Bruno, having arrived in Dogland, are about to be granted an audience with the King:] . . . the Sentinel turned to the children, and said "Give me your names."

"We'd rather not!" Bruno exclaimed, pulling Sylvie away from the door. "We want them ourselves. Come back, Sylvie. Come quick!" [*Works*, p. 379.]
(2) [The Professor, having just been awakened from a deep sleep:] "Would you have the kindness to mention," he said . . . "whereabouts we are just now – and *who* we are, beginning with me?"

I thought it best to begin with the children. "This is Sylvie, Sir; and *this* is Bruno."

"Ah, yes! I know *them* well enough!" the old man murmured. "It's *myself* I'm most anxious about." [*Works*, p. 428.]

"I wish I knew!" thought poor Alice. She answered, rather sadly, "Nothing, just now."
"Think again," it said: "that wo'n't do."

Alice thought, but nothing came of it. "Please, would you tell me what *you* call your-self?" she said timidly. "I think that might help a little."

"I'll tell you, if you'll come a little further on," the Fawn said. "I ca'n't remember *here*."

So they walked on together through the wood, Alice with her arms clasped lovingly round the soft neck of the Fawn, till they came out into another open field, and here the Fawn gave a sudden bound into the air, and shook itself free from Alice's arm. "I'm a Fawn!" it cried out in a voice of delight. "And, dear me! you're a human child!" A sudden look of alarm came into its beautiful brown eyes, and in another moment it had darted away at full speed.

Alice stood looking after it, almost ready to cry with vexation at having lost her dear little fellow-traveler so suddenly. "However, I know my name now," she said: "that's *some* comfort. Alice – Alice – I won't forget it again. . . ."

(*Works*, pp. 177-179)

Martin Gardner has said of this passage, "The wood . . . is in fact the universe itself, as it is apart from symbol-manipulating creatures who label portions of it because . . . 'it's useful to the people that name them.' The realization that the world by itself contains no signs – that there is no connection whatever between things and their names except by way of a mind that finds the tags useful – is by no means a trivial philosophic insight" (*The Annotated Alice* [New York, 1960], p. 227). Several principles may be inferred from this passage which reflect Carroll's speculations upon the nature of names.

Alice, approaching the wood, calls it by its name, 'the wood where things have no names'. But when she has entered the wood, she is unable to recall this name; not only does she find that she has been deprived of both her personal and her general name, but also that the other objects which she encounters while in the wood – individual trees and the Fawn – are nameless too. When she cannot think of the name of the tree which she puts her hand against, she says that "it's got no name". She is quite correct, both from her own immediate viewpoint in being unable to come up with one, and in a literal sense (she is actually stating one of the attributes of the tree as object). Things IN the wood have no names: this particular tree is one of the many which are permanent fixtures of the wood, one of those which, taken as a group, constitute the wood AS wood. It does not, and cannot by definition, have a name. And as long as the wood preserves its peculiar attribute of denying names to things within it, this tree, being within the wood and an integral part of it, never will have a name. The Fawn and Alice have no names while within the wood; but once they have left it, each immediately remembers his own name and what the other is called.

Since neither the physical attributes nor the basic traits of disposition (friend-liness, gentleness) of Alice and the Fawn are affected by their loss of name, I think we may accept Martin Gardner's reading of the passage – that it reveals Carroll's insight that "there is no connection whatever between things and their names except by way of a mind that finds the tags useful." When Alice and the Fawn leave the wood, the Fawn's taking fright is a reaction not to Alice, who behaves no differently than when she had no name, but to her name only, 'human child'. Note that it is her GENERAL name which the Fawn responds to, the classification-name which connotes to the Fawn all of those attributes possessed by human beings which produce terror in deer. The Fawn's violent reaction to Alice's general name will be discussed further in § 10.2 in connection with the affective connotation of words.

Alice is more concerned about her loss of personal name than about her loss of general name; and understandably, for with it goes her identity, her sense of individuality. She does not seem disturbed by the thought that with the loss of her classification-name, she becomes, at the very most, a mere Thing. The Fawn, however, presumably having no personal name, is merely at a loss to recall its general name. It knows, though, that once they have left the wood, they will know each other truly. When they emerge from the wood, the Fawn recalls its own general name and Alice's. Though informed by the Fawn of her general name, Alice does not share its "delight" in the recovered knowledge of class-membership. She is preoccupied only with the restoration of her personal name, that which is most immediate to her; it is normally of little concern to her that she is "a human child". Certainly her class-membership is of less importance to her than it is to the Fawn, who does not remain to learn her personal name. 'Alice' would probably be meaningless to him; certainly it would not inspire fear. It is her general name, conveying information about her human nature, that terrifies him.

What semantic principles may be inferred from this passage? (1) The things existing in the phenomenal world do not possess names inherently as part of their nature. (2) Things which have not been named cannot serve as objects of thought or discourse for rational creatures, in any abstract sense. (3) Things are given names by men so that they CAN become objects of abstract thought and discourse; names are thus of use to men. (4) The names which men assign to things may be of two types: general (arbitrarily chosen and bestowed on the basis of a process of classification), such as 'wood', 'tree', 'fawn', and 'human child'; and personal (arbitrarily chosen and bestowed to confer individuality for purposes of singular identification), such as 'Alice' and 'the Fawn'. (5) General names both designate the objects to which they refer, and convey information about them. (6) [provisionally] Personal names, to one unfamiliar with the attributes of the individual so named, convey little or no information about the individual. (7) A name may possess affective connotations for a given interpreter (i.e., evoke emotional responses on the basis of the interpreter's personal associations regarding the name and the thing it designates). (8) These affective connotations may arise from the informative connotations conveyed by the name (the Fawn was frightened by Alice's being a HUMAN child). (9) These affective connotations may persist in spite of empirical evidence to the contrary that the object so named does not possess attributes warranting the emotional response evoked by the name (Alice's consistent lovingkindness denies the basis for the Fawn's fear). (10) A thing may have more than one name assigned to it with equal validity of designation and denotation ('Alice', 'human child', ['little girl', 'person of gentle disposition', . . .]). (11) The nature of a thing (i.e., the aggregate of its physical and other peculiar attributes) is not materially affected by the thing's being nameless. (12) Since the names originally given to things are labels arbitrarily chosen by men and applied by them to things, there is no inherent connection between the things and the names which stand for them (the thing called "Alice" could have been christened "Mabel" without its being materially affected; the things which men have agreed to call "trees" could have been called something else without there being any effect on the things themselves). (13) Insofar as names are labels, or convenient tags, applied to things by men, names are capable of being removed or changed without this affecting the things themselves.

6.5.2 *The Kind of Meaning Conveyed by Personal Names*

I said above that if the Fawn HAD heard his companion refer to herself as "Alice" without his being otherwise made aware of her human nature, he would not have been frightened as he was by the name 'human child'. Except for the Fawn's being aware that a thing called "Alice" was being singled out as an object of discourse, and his knowledge, based on previous experience with the conventions of bestowing proper names, that 'Alice' is a name usually applied to female human children (and it cannot be assumed that the Fawn had this knowledge), the name would, by itself, provide him with no information whatever about the thing. There is nothing in the name 'Alice' which would suggest to an interpreter unacquainted with the thing so named and unfamiliar with any other objects so named the peculiar attributes possessed by human beings. What sort of thing is identified by 'Alice'? "A female human being", one might say, if he had had previous experience with things possessing that name. But 'Dinah', after all, was the name of Alice's cat. The Fawn would have had no reason to be frightened by the informative connotations of Alice's name; because for him, the name would have held none. Its only meaning would be to indicate to him that "Alice" was what his companion called herself.

The notion that proper names have merely a designative function, and possess no informative connotations for an interpreter who has no previous acquaintance with the object so named or with other objects so named, is apparently denied in *Through the Looking-Glass* when Alice is confronted with Humpty Dumpty's statement that proper names must convey specific information about the things they label. The passage requires close scrutiny, for an assessment of Humpty Dumpty's position is crucial to determining Carroll's assumptions regarding the connotation of proper names.

"Don't stand chattering to yourself like that," Humpty Dumpty said, looking at her for the first time, "but tell me your name and your business."

"My *name* is Alice, but –"

"It's a stupid name enough!" Humpty Dumpty interrupted impatiently. "What does it mean?"

"*Must* a name mean something?" Alice asked doubtfully.

"Of course it must," Humpty Dumpty said with a short laugh: "*my* name means the shape I am – and a good handsome shape it is, too. With a name like yours, you might be any shape, almost."

"Why do you sit out here all alone?" said Alice, not wishing to begin an argument.

(Works, p. 209)

He is right, of course: there is nothing in the name 'Alice' which would, for anyone not previously acquainted with the thing so named, suggest the shape (or any other attributes) of the thing. But, according to Humpty Dumpty, a proper name SHOULD convey information about the object possessing it. Peter Alexander has said of this passage: "We are led to see that there is a great deal in a name – certainly more in Looking-Glass Land and Wonderland than in ours. Humpty Dumpty is shocked to learn that Alice's name MEANS nothing. . . . Proper names, apparently, have to mean something – and what they mean is dictated by what they name." [7] So it would seem on the surface; but I think that Alexander's view is an over-simplification.

Let us look for a moment at the names of the creatures which Alice meets in Looking-Glass Land. Most of the creatures are labeled with indexical general names: 'the Gnat', 'the Red Queen', 'the White Knight', 'the Unicorn', 'the Pudding', 'the Tiger-lily', 'the Fawn'. The only specifically personal names are those possessed by: Tweedledum and Tweedledee; Haigha and Hatta, the White King's Anglo-Saxon Messengers; Pudding and Mutton, to whom Alice is formally introduced at the banquet (and it is only during the introductions that these proper names are used); Lily, "one of the White Pawns"; and Humpty Dumpty.

Carroll is able to deny personal names to most of his characters because there is no opportunity presented for them to be confused with other members of their respective classes. Within the context of the narrative nearly all of the creatures are unique representatives of their respective classes. This is the case whether, like the Red Queen and the White King, they themselves constitute and exhaust their respective classes (there is only one Red Queen on the chess-board), or whether,

---

[7] Peter Alexander, "Logic and the Humour of Lewis Carroll", *Proc. of the Leeds Philosophical and Literary Society*, VI (May, 1951), 558. After commenting that in Looking-Glass Land proper names seem to have general significance, he continues by saying: "On the other hand, our ways with common [general] names are not cavalier *enough* for Humpty Dumpty", who reserves the right to apply whatever meaning he chooses to such general names as 'glory' and 'impenetrability.' Alexander sees this reversal of conventions governing the function of names as one of the mirror-image reversals which Carroll employs to contrast Alice's world with the land behind the Looking-Glass. As paraphrased by Martin Gardner (*The Annotated Alice* [New York, 1960], p. 263), Alexander's position is made clearer than in his own exposition: "In real life proper names seldom have a meaning other than the fact that they denote an individual object, whereas other words have general, universal meanings. In Humpty Dumpty's realm, the reverse is true. Ordinary words mean whatever Humpty Dumpty wants them to mean, whereas proper names like 'Alice' and 'Humpty Dumpty' are supposed to have general significance."

like the Gnat, the Tiger-lily, and the Fawn, they are single representatives of classes which potentially have many members in Looking-Glass Land. Being particular representatives of their respective classes and the only ones that Alice encounters, they may be adequately identified by *the* being prefixed to their general names. Even though there are two White Knights on the chess-board, Alice meets only one of them; and he therefore may safely be labeled "the White Knight". Had both White Knights confronted her at the same time, there would have had to be some arbitrary means for differentiating them. With the exception of 'Pudding' and 'Mutton' (general names used as proper names only for the purpose of allowing Alice to be formally introduced to the objects bearing them), all of the proper names in *Through the Looking-Glass* serve to prevent the things they label from being confused with other members of the things' respective classes. 'Tweedledum' and 'Tweedledee' distinguish the physically identical brothers; 'Haigha' and 'Hatta' differentiate the White King's Anglo-Saxon Messengers; 'Lily' indicates which of the eight White Pawns that Alice replaces in the game. In a book where proper names are used primarily to distinguish individual members of a class from one another, how is 'Humpty Dumpty' being used? There is no other character in the book with whom Humpty Dumpty could be confused. Yet, since Carroll does not follow his consistent pattern of prefixing the name with an article ('the Humpty Dumpty') which would suggest that it is to be taken as an indexical general name, 'Humpty Dumpty' is obviously intended to be construed as a proper name.

When Humpty Dumpty tells Alice that a proper name must convey information about the object it designates, she is understandably startled, for in her world the convention is that proper names do not, in themselves, convey information about their referents' attributes. Alice doubts the validity of his assertion but, "not wishing to begin an argument", changes the subject. Why does Lewis Carroll not allow Alice to defend her views? He raises the question, establishes doubt in his heroine's (and the reader's) mind, and leaves the matter unresolved. He is, I think, once again playing with his readers, posing a puzzle to test their ingenuity. If Humpty Dumpty's name does indeed suggest his shape, is the reader supposed to accept without question that Humpty Dumpty is correct in saying that all proper names must convey information, or – as Peter Alexander does – that in Looking-Glass Land, if NOT in Alice's world, such is the case?

I wish to advance the following as a possible solution to the questions raised by this passage. Carroll himself is quite explicit in providing a clue to the answer. It will be helpful to keep in mind what I have said about the function of proper names in *Through the Looking-Glass,* and about the name 'Humpty Dumpty' as being atypical in not serving to differentiate Humpty Dumpty from other individuals with whom he might be confused.

The clue which Carroll provides comes at the beginning of Chapter VI, and immediately precedes the passage under discussion. At the end of Chapter V, Alice had been walking toward an egg which was placed on a shelf in the Sheep's little store. The shop undergoes a gradual transformation as she approaches the egg: the furnishings become trees, a brook appears in her path; and before reaching the egg she finds that the shop has vanished altogether and that she is standing in a wood. She expects the egg to turn into a tree also.

However, the egg only got larger and larger, and more and more human: when she had come within a few yards of it, she saw that it had eyes and a nose and a mouth; and, when she had come close to it, she saw clearly that it was HUMPTY DUMPTY himself. "It ca'n't be anybody else!" she said to herself. "I'm as certain of it, as if his name were written all over his face!"

Alice had expected to meet Humpty Dumpty at some time in her progress to the Eighth Square (in Chapter II, the Red Queen had told her that she would); but when she does encounter the nursery-rhyme character, whose rhyme she later recites, she is able to recognize him immediately on the basis of his physical attributes: "she saw clearly that it was HUMPTY DUMPTY himself. 'It ca'n't be anybody else!' " When he takes no notice of her, Alice studies his appearance:

"And how exactly like an egg he is!" she said aloud, standing with her hands ready to catch him, for she was every moment expecting him to fall.
"It's *very* provoking," Humpty Dumpty said after a long silence, looking away from Alice as he spoke, "to be called an egg – *very*!"
"I said you *looked* like an egg, Sir," Alice gently explained. "And some eggs are very pretty, you know," she added, hoping to turn her remark into a sort of compliment.
(*Works*, p. 208)

Indeed, Alice has not classified him as an egg, but merely noted some similarities between his physical attributes and those possessed by eggs. When Humpty Dumpty thinks mistakenly that she HAS called him an egg, he rejects this classification angrily. Carroll, moreover, does not say that Humpty Dumpty is to be classified as "human": the text merely says that the thing "got more and more human" as Alice approached; further on, Carroll refers to him in the narration, though still from Alice's point of view, as "the queer creature". These facts indicate (and the conclusion is borne out by Tenniel's illustrations) that Humpty Dumpty can be classified neither as an egg nor as a human being. Alice's ability to identify him by name as the nursery-rhyme character immediately upon determining his physical attributes indicates that the thing to which she gives the label 'Humpty Dumpty' is the sole member of that class whose members possess the physical attributes (or peculiar shape) which entitle them to be classified as "humpty dumpties". But there is only one Humpty Dumpty, and that is the character in the nursery rhyme (in the context of *Through the Looking-Glass,* Alice meets him just before his fall). Since he is unique, he constitutes a class in himself. His name, therefore, is similar to 'London', cited in Carroll's *Symbolic Logic* as the symbol which stands for the single member of the individual class "TOWNS having four million inhabitants", or to John Stuart Mill's "connotative individual names" such as 'the sun', 'God' (when used by a Christian), and 'the father of Socrates'. As I mentioned earlier, Carroll seems – on the basis of his treatment of 'London' – to regard "connotative individual names" as a special type of general name. 'London', being the name of the sole member of the class "TOWNS having four million inhabitants", will connote that attribute of population to knowledgeable interpreters. 'Humpty Dumpty', being the name of the unique member of the class of things having a shape both egglike and manlike, will connote that attribute of shape to knowledgeable interpreters. Thus his name "means" the shape he is.

It is obvious from his arrogant behavior and inflated sense of self-importance that Humpty Dumpty is aware of his uniqueness. But from his point of view, Alice is also unique: as a resident of Looking-Glass Land, he has probably never met an Alice before. Therefore, when he assumes out of hand that her name must mean something, he is taking her name not as an arbitrarily-bestowed and inherently meaningless proper name (as it would be according to the conventions of her world), but as a "connotative individual name" like his own. 'Humpty Dumpty' is the name of both an individual and a class; in its latter function it conveys information about Humpty Dumpty's shape. But 'Humpty Dumpty' functions as a personal name also; and in this role, its signification is primarily designative in that it serves to identify the object so named. Alice interprets it as a personal name only. She does not regard it as a classification-name, because in her world she has not been accustomed to recognizing the possibility of personal names having this double function. Humpty Dumpty cannot understand why such an obviously unique creature (in Looking-Glass Land) as an Alice should not have a name that would connote its physical attributes. Alice, on the other hand, cannot understand why a familiar nursery-rhyme figure (whom she had known about for a very long time) should have a name that indicates his physical shape. Given his frame of reference, it is reasonable that Humpty Dumpty would assume Alice's name to have the same dual function as his own: granted his premise, his only error is assuming that 'Alice' should connote information about the SHAPE of the object so labeled. It reveals his personal limitations, and perhaps his colossal ego, not to be aware that other attributes than shape might be connoted by (what he takes to be) a "connotative individual name".

Such is my reading of this problematical passage. Alice's initial impulse to argue with Humpty Dumpty suggests that Carroll is not subscribing to the notion that proper names must directly convey information about the things which they designate. Carroll does not allow her to take issue with Humpty Dumpty because he wants his readers to exercise their ingenuity in resolving the question. And to enable them to do so, Carroll has provided them with a clue in Alice's ability to classify Humpty Dumpty – on the basis of his physical attributes alone – as neither an egg nor a human being, but as "Humpty Dumpty HIMSELF". The illustration implies that although there ARE "connotative individual names" which may be interpreted functionally as a sort of general name, Alice is justified in asking, "MUST a name mean something?" For in her experience, most proper names are merely arbitrarily-selected labels which in themselves convey no intrinsic information about their referents. Whatever information they DO connote comes not from their specifying their objects' attributes by virtue of class-membership, but simply through the interpreter's prior personal knowledge of the attributes of the object so designated. To a person who knows nothing about London, the name 'London' will not connote the attribute "having four million inhabitants".

Although Carroll nowhere makes a formal statement with regard to the inability of proper names to convey informative connotations, I think that we are tentatively able to infer from this passage that he probably subscribed to Mill's doctrine, that they serve merely to identify objects and, as labels, to connote nothing whatever about the attributes of their referents. This passage is as close as Carroll ever comes to discussing the connotation of proper names; and Alice's disagreement with Humpty Dumpty, though not allowed by the author to develop into an argument, is, I think, indicative of Carroll's own views.

As a label, 'Alice' identifies the heroine but does not tell anything about her: the name, like 'Dinah', might belong to many little girls, to many grown women, to many pet cats. As it identifies her in the specific context of Looking-Glass Land, where she is presumably unique as an Alice, the name would come to have a great deal of connotative potential for anyone who has become acquainted with her. A proper name, in Sir Alan Gardiner's phrase, "provides a key to information" for anyone who has learned the specific attributes of the object so named.[8] Thus, for anyone who has learned the specific attributes possessed by this particular Alice, the name 'Alice' alone will, on occasions subsequent to the first meeting, bring those attributes to mind. In parting from her, Humpty Dumpty says that since Alice's facial features are so similar to other people's, he will not be able to identify her if he sees her again. But, assuming that he has never met a creature named "Alice" before and that he will not meet another one at some later time, it is probable that even in Alice's absence, his hearing her name on a subsequent occasion would bring to mind those attributes which she displayed at this meeting: "the human child who spoke to me the other day, who insulted me by calling me an egg, who couldn't tell that I was wearing a cravat, and who said that her name meant nothing – a rather dull child altogether". Thus would Alice's proper name come to connote her attributes in Looking-Glass Land; and thus would it in her own world. For although she is not unique as an Alice in her own world, she is, to

---

[8] Sir Alan Gardiner, *The Theory of Proper Names*, 2nd ed. (Oxford, 1954), p. 32: "Ordinary words, among which general names play a prominent part, directly convey information; proper names merely provide the key to information. To hark back to Mill's own example, *York* certainly does not mean *cathedral-town*, but it provides any knowledgeable listener with a datum which, after only the slightest interval for reflection, will bring to his consciousness the fact that the town he is beholding possesses a cathedral; the same name will doubtless recall to his memory other information as well. Ultimately *York* will prove much more informative than *cathedral-town*, but in itself it does no more than establish the identity of the town spoken about."

the people with whom she comes into contact and who have occasion to refer to her by name, one of a rather limited number of Alices of their acquaintance, and relatively easy to distinguish from the rest. To these people, 'Alice' will bring to mind her peculiar attributes as informative connotations since the name will effectively, in their experience, have come to designate the sole member of an individual class. A proper name will thus function as an "individual connotative name" if the interpreter has prior knowledge of the attributes of the object which the name designates.

6.5.3 *The Kind of Meaning Conveyed by General Names*

Proper names such as 'Alice', 'Dinah', 'Scipio', 'York' (a major cathedral-town, the given name of York Powell, and – currently – a brand of cigarette), 'Pierre', 'Charlotte', and 'Barnes & Phillips' will connote little or no information about their referents to anyone not previously familiar, either through experience or hearsay, with the things' attributes. General names, on the other hand, do convey information about the attributes of the things they designate. By identifying its referent as a member of a particular class of things, a general name will connote to a knowledgeable interpreter those attributes of its referent which are possessed by all members of that class. It is necessary only that the interpreter be aware of the attributes characteristic of members of that class, of the conventions which govern the name's usage, and of the implications regarding its interpretation in the immediate context of association. We know when we hear the word 'tree' in a context which specifies the association-object to be an item of vegetation that the particular referent in question, even if it is not present to our sight, possesses certain attributes in common with all other things which are named "trees", though we may not know particular facts about it, such as its species (oak, maple, spruce) or its peculiar attributes as object (its being dead, or living, or scarred with lightning, or hollow).

Though all general names convey information about the things they name to interpreters familiar with the conventions of their usage, some general names are analytically more descriptive than others. That is, they have by virtue of their form and literal import a logical meaning which describes the object named. The word 'stone', for example, does not have this inherently descriptive quality. But such words as 'automobile' (which suggests the quality of self-propulsion), *'aardvark'* (which, to one who knows Afrikaans, signifies 'earth-pig'), 'astronaut' (which indicates the referent's occupational activities), 'typewriter' (which reveals the machine's function), '[baseball] diamond' (which indicates the object's shape), 'hydrogen' (which suggests the object's chemical properties), and 'fingernail' (which specifies the physical location of the object) are within themselves analytically descriptive. AS WORDS they say something about the objects which they name. When such names are initially selected, men decide on them in order to indicate the attributes which are possessed by the object to be named (and as may be seen from these few examples, the attributes which form the basis for name-selection may be of various kinds). This is not to say, of course, that the attributes necessarily DETERMINE what name is to be chosen for the object; men merely USE the attributes as the basis for applying descriptive names.

In Looking-Glass Land, however, it would appear that, in some cases at least, attributes do determine the names given to objects. An instance of this occurs when Alice asks the Live Flowers if they are not frightened with no one in the garden to protect them.

"There's the tree in the middle," said the Rose. "What else is it good for?"
"But what could it do, if any danger came?" Alice asked.
"It could bark," said the Rose.
"It says 'Bough-wough!'" cried a Daisy. "That's why its branches are called boughs!"
(*The Annotated Alice*, ed. Martin Gardner
[New York, 1960], p. 202)

Later in the book, Alice discusses Looking-Glass Insects with the Gnat. The insects of Alice's world often have names which are not at all descriptive of their physical attributes; she thinks of the names 'Horse-fly', 'Dragon-fly', and 'Butterfly'. With the possible exception of 'Horse-fly', which may signify that type of fly characteristically found in the vicinity of horses, the literal import of the names is not generally recognized by people who use them in Alice's world. If the names are taken literally, as being descriptive of the insects' physical attributes, the things so described become, to a rational mind, fabulous monsters indeed.

While in Alice's world general names of insects are often arbitrarily framed and not descriptive of the things to which they are applied, in Looking-Glass Land many of the insects have names which were evidently given to them precisely because of their physical attributes. The Gnat shows Alice a Rocking-horse-fly, which, consistent with Tenniel's illustration depicting it as a rocking-horse, is "made entirely of wood, and gets about by swinging itself from branch to branch", and a Bread-and-butter-fly, whose wings are "thin slices of bread-and-butter" and whose body is a crust. The names of these creatures seem to have been chosen on the basis of, and to describe, the insects' attributes. The names suggest how these creatures came to be classified; and, in so doing, they imply the definitions of the things themselves. Thus: "A Rocking-horse-fly is an insect which [like a rocking-horse] is made entirely of wood and gets about by swinging itself from branch to branch"; "a Bread-and-butter-fly is an insect whose wings are thin slices of bread-and-butter and whose body is a crust." In that they embody the definitions of the things they stand for, these names are similar to '*aardvark*' and 'automobile'. By virtue of their concrete descriptiveness, names of this type also tend to imply in a self-reflexive fashion their own definitions AS WORDS. A person in Alice's world who analyzed the word 'automobile' as used in a normal context might be strongly disposed to define it as "a name used to stand for a thing which is self-propelled". However, he could not be certain, from anything conveyed by the word itself, that his analytical definition of it is accurate with regard to its acceptation in general usage: 'ringworm' is used to refer to a fungus disease; 'rockhound' to a person who delights in collecting geological specimens.

In Alice's world, most words do not imply the definitions of the things they name. And even those that do, such as '*aardvark*' and 'automobile', can be used arbitrarily to refer to things whose attributes in no way coincide with those suggested by the names. Since names have no inherent meanings, but are merely arbitrary labels whose functional significations have been established by convention, even those whose overt descriptiveness seems to provide a clue to their referential use (i.e., a clue to their definitions as words) cannot be taken at face value. Since the knowledge of how a word is being used in a given context is necessary for the achievement of effective thought and communication, and since words do not provide this information with absolute certainty, it is necessary for the men using them to make clear what meaning they wish their words to have in specific contexts. The process by which conventions are established for the use of words is called "nominal definition"; as process, it stipulates or explains what significations words are to be understood to have in specific instances of their use. Lewis Carroll's interest in nominal definition will be the next topic to be taken up.

7

NOMINAL DEFINITION

"Let us consider the false appearances that are imposed upon us by words, which are framed and applied according to the conceit and capacities of the vulgar sort: and although we think we govern our words, and prescribe it well ... yet certain it is, that words, as a Tartar's bow, do shoot back upon the understanding of the wisest, and mightily entangle and pervert the judgment. So as it is almost necessary in all controversies and disputations to imitate the wisdom of the mathematician, in setting down *in the very beginning* the definitions of our words and terms, that others may know how we accept and understand them, and whether they concur with us or no. For it cometh to pass, for want of this, that we are sure to end where we ought to have begun, which is in questions and differences about words."

> Sir Francis Bacon, *Of the Advancement of Learning*, as quoted in John Horne Tooke's *The Diversions of Purley*, 3rd ed. [1840], p. 16

The executioner's argument was, that you couldn't cut off a head unless there was a body to cut it off from: that he had never had to do such a thing before, and he wasn't going to begin at *his* time of life.

The King's argument was that anything that had a head could be beheaded, and that you weren't to talk nonsense.

> *Alice's Adventures in Wonderland*, Chapter VIII

7.1 LEXICAL AND STIPULATIVE DEFINITION

As Alice intimates in her discussion with the Gnat, names are useful to men because they provide convenient labels by which things may be identified, thought about, and discussed. But FOR them to be useful, their intended designations must be clear to the men using them. If men do not know precisely what thing a given label is to be understood to designate, the label can produce obscurity of thought and, by its vagueness or ambiguity, cause attempts at communication to fail through non-understanding or misunderstanding on the part of interpreters.

To avoid being victimized by words, men have recourse to nominal definition, a process whereby words are defined according to their use. Nominal definition makes explicit what meaning a word is to have in a given situational context: it establishes what a word is to be taken to signify; or, to state it another way, it identifies the thing which the word is to be understood to designate. The signification may be one which is accepted by the entire linguistic community in which the word is habitually used, or it may be one which is peculiar to an individual act of discourse. If, in a given context, the intended signification of a word is one which is conventionally established and generally accepted by all or a portion of the members of the speech community, that signification may be called the word's "lexical definition". The definitions of words which are recorded in standard dictionaries are of this type.

On the other hand, if the intended signification of a word deviates radically from the word's generally-accepted lexical definitions and is peculiar to a specific act of discourse such as a given individual's private train of thought, a conversation between two men, or a written communication, that signification may be called the word's "idiosyncratic definition". If, in a specific act of discourse, a word is used idiosyncratically (*i.e.*, its intended signification diverges from that of general conventionalized usage) or in such manner that its intended signification is not clear to the interpreter, the user must explicitly state what he intends for the word to signify if he is to prevent confusion in his audience. This specified signification may be called the word's "stipulated definition", and the process by which the intended signification is asserted, "stipulative definition". Stipulative definition is called for when the user intentionally gives his words idiosyncratic significations, when he wishes merely to clarify his discourse, or when the interpreter is unable to comprehend the utterance because the terms used are vague, ambiguous, or unfamiliar. It is called for when the speaker is charged by his audience: "What do you mean by that?" or by its equivalent, "Define your terms!"

7.2 CARROLL AND LEXICAL DEFINITION

Although stipulative definition will be the main emphasis of this chapter, some mention should be made of Lewis Carroll's interest in the lexical definitions of words. As early as 1845, when he was thirteen years of age, Carroll's interest in the problem of meaning may be seen in his "Quotation from Shakespeare with slight improvements" in the family magazine, *Useful and Instructive Poetry* (1845; published 1954). He is parodying Prince Hal's soliloquy at the bedside of his apparently deceased father (*2 King Henry IV*, IV, v). Though presumably asleep, King Henry is able to interject comments into his son's speech:

> P. ". . . Yet not so sound, and half so deeply sweet,
>   As he whose brow with homely biggin bound
>   Snores out the watch of night."
> K.   Harry I know not
>   The meaning of the word you just have used.

P. What word, my liege?

K.   The word I mean is "biggin."

P. It means a kind of woolen nightcap, sir,
   With which the peasantry are wont to bind
   Their wearied heads, ere that they take their rest.

K. Thanks for your explanation, pray proceed.

.   .   .   .

P.   "... My gracious lord! my father!
   This sleep is sound indeed, this is a sleep
   That from this golden rigol hath divorced
   So many English –"

K.   What meaneth rigol, Harry?

P. My liege, I know not, save that it doth enter
   Most apt into the metre.

K.   True, it doth.
   But wherefore use a word which hath no meaning?

P. My lord, the word is said, for it hath passed
   My lips, and all the powers upon this earth
   Can not unsay it.

K.   You are right, proceed.

(*Useful and Instructive Poetry*, ed. Derek Hudson
[New York, 1954], pp. 25-26)

In both of these instances, King Henry is asking his son for the lexical definitions of the words in question. Hal is able to define *biggin* according to its general acceptation, 'a kind of woolen nightcap'; but he cannot do the same for *rigol* ('circle', here referring to the crown). Since neither man knows what *rigol* is understood to signify in general usage, and since no idiosyncratic definition is stipulated for it by Hal, in this context it is utterly without signification – simply a space filler that enters "most apt into the meter". The King is justified in demanding to know why a word that has no meaning should be used at all. Implied is the question, Can a word have no meaning? The answer is, Certainly – in particular contexts of association; but if such is the case, it should not be regarded as a word, for it is not functioning as a sign but existing merely as noise. This answer is not given in Carroll's text; Prince Hal will not admit that he has no justification for uttering a meaningless sequence of sounds in a supposedly meaningful speech – he skirts the issue by asserting bluntly that the meaning doesn't matter, the word has been said, and that's that. In taking this way out, he is investing the "word" with an autonomous power of its own, independent of man's control. The word *rigol* presumably did have meaning for Shakespeare's audience; and simply because in Carroll's parody neither the King nor the Prince know this generally accepted meaning does not imply that the word has no lexical definition. It merely indicates that in the context of their dialogue *rigol* has no signification.

7.2.1 *Humpty Dumpty's Definitions of the "Jabberwocky" Neologisms*

Prince Hal is an equivocator; but one may be sure that Humpty Dumpty, in the same situation, would not have appealed to the sovereignty of the word as absolute and autonomous power in order to evade his responsibility in providing a meaning. He would have faced the matter squarely and GIVEN the word an arbitrary signification. He is not the least bit hesitant about defining the "hard words" which troubled Alice in her reading of "Jabberwocky". Although in view of his strong opinions on stipulative definition ("When *I* use a word it means just what I choose it to mean – neither more nor less.") there is some basis for doubting that his explanations represent the words' general acceptations, the glosses are presented as lexical definitions.

"You seem very clever at explaining words, Sir," said Alice. "Would you kindly tell me the meaning of the poem called 'Jabberwocky'?"

"Let's hear it," said Humpty Dumpty. "I can explain all the poems that ever were invented – and a good many that haven't been invented just yet." . . . .

[He hears the first stanza.]

"That's enough to begin with," Humpty Dumpty interrupted: "there are plenty of hard words there. '*Brillig*' means four o'clock in the afternoon – the time when you begin *broiling* things for dinner."

"That'll do very well," said Alice: "and '*slithy*'?"

"Well, '*slithy*' means 'lithe and slimy.' 'Lithe' is the same as 'active.' You see it's like a portmanteau – there are two meanings packed up into one word."

"I see it now," Alice remarked thoughtfully: "and what are '*toves*'?"

"Well, '*toves*' are something like badgers – they're something like lizards – and they're something like corkscrews."

"They must be very curious-looking creatures."

"They are that," said Humpty Dumpty; "also they make their nests under sun-dials – also they live on cheese."

"And what's to '*gyre*' and to '*gimble*'?"

"To '*gyre*' is to go round and round like a gyroscope. To '*gimble*' is to make holes like a gimlet."

"And '*the wabe*' is the grass-plot round a sun-dial, I suppose?" said Alice, surprised at her own ingenuity.

"Of course it is. It's called '*wabe*' you know, because it goes a long way before it, and a long way behind it –"

"And a long way beyond it on each side," Alice added.

"Exactly so. Well then, '*mimsy*' is 'flimsy and miserable' (there's another portmanteau for you). And a '*borogove*' is a thin shabby-looking bird with its feathers sticking out all round – something like a live mop."

"And then '*mome raths*'?" said Alice. 'I'm afraid I'm giving you a great deal of trouble."

"Well, a '*rath*' is a sort of green pig: but '*mome*' I'm not certain about. I think it's short for 'from home' – meaning that they'd lost their way, you know."

"And what does '*outgrabe*' mean?"

"Well, '*outgribing*' is something between bellowing and whistling, with a kind of sneeze in the middle: however, you'll hear it done, maybe – down in the wood yonder – and, when you've once heard it, you'll be *quite* content. Who's been repeating all that hard stuff to you?"

"I read it in a book," said Alice. . . .

(*Works*, pp. 215-217)

If, on the basis of his philological knowledge, Humpty Dumpty is reporting the generally accepted meanings of these words, the information he imparts is "as sensible as a dictionary". If he is merely guessing at their possible meanings (he admits some difficulty with *mome*), he might easily be giving Alice false information without realizing it. It is quite possible that Carroll is using Humpty Dumpty to satirize the amateur philological speculators of his time who committed ludicrous etymological errors through ignorance of historical relationships of languages, through false analogies and hasty generalizations. If Humpty Dumpty is merely inventing the definitions as he goes along (his incremental treatment of *toves* looks suspicious), he is imparting no information at all, but is simply enlarging his ego at Alice's expense.

It is interesting to compare Carroll's definitions of the "Jabberwocky" words in *Through the Looking-Glass* (c. 1870-71) with those that he concocted for his "Stanza of Anglo-Saxon Poetry" in *Mischmasch* (1855). There is more 'etymology' in the original gloss; and in Humpty Dumpty's version the earlier definitions, almost without exception, have been improved and refined. The changes in the definitions (some of them quite radical) indicate that Carroll did not conceive of the words as having fixed specific meanings. Although the term "portmanteau" was applied to these words for the first time by Humpty Dumpty, Carroll's awareness of the process of blending was present in the original – for there too *slithy* was said to be compounded of 'slimy' and 'lithe'. The 1855 version of the gloss is given complete in § 3.3.4.

7.2.2 Carroll's Neologisms; "Portmanteau" Words, or Blends

Humpty Dumpty does not define for Alice the unfamiliar words in "Jabberwocky" after the first stanza, and it is probable that Carroll had no specific meanings for them in mind. In the preface to *The Hunting of the Snark* (1876), a poem employing some of the "Jabberwocky" words, he says in addition to explaining how the vowels in *slithy, toves,* and *borogoves* should be pronounced:

This also seems a fitting occasion to notice the other hard words in that poem. Humpty-Dumpty's theory of two meanings packed into one word like a portmanteau, seems to me the right explanation for all.

For instance, take the two words "fuming" and "furious." Make up your mind that you will say both words, but leave it unsettled which you will say first. Now open your mouth and speak. If your thoughts incline ever so little towards "fuming," you will say "fuming-furious"; if they turn, by even a hair's breadth, towards "furious," you will say "furious-fuming"; but if you have that rarest of gifts, a perfectly balanced mind, you will say "frumious."

Supposing that, when Pistol uttered the well-known words –

"Under which king, Bezonian? Speak or die!"

Justice Shallow had felt certain that it was either William or Richard, but had not been able to settle which, so that he could not possibly say either name before the other, can it be doubted that, rather than die, he would have gasped out "Rilchiam!"

(Works, pp. 754-755)

Carroll's explanation of the "Jabberwocky" words as blends is to be taken with considerable reservation. He implies that the words were consciously formed by the author's deciding in each case to incorporate the meanings of two separate words into one significant form by uttering the words simultaneously. The resulting neologism would supposedly then contain in its signification the individual significations of the words which comprise it. Is the reader seriously expected to believe that *frumious* contains the significations of both 'fuming' and 'furious'? And are all of the other "hard words" in the poem, as Carroll intimates, similarly compounded?

Taking Carroll at his word, Eric Partridge attempts to determine in each case what the compounding elements probably were. In an interesting essay, "The Nonsense Words of Edward Lear and Lewis Carroll", in *Here, There and Everywhere* (London, 1950), pp. 162-188, Partridge maintains that all of Carroll's neologisms in "Jabberwocky" are portmanteau words, except for *gyre, whiffle, burble,* and *beamish,* which he holds to be revivals of archaic and dialectal words. He is highly ingenious in attempting to determine the probable components of the respective blends (Examples: *vorpal,* a blend of *voracious* + *narwhal*; *uffish,* a possible combination of *uberous,* 'fruitful' + *officious,* in its now rare sense 'efficacious' + the adjectival *ish.*). My own feeling is, that although some of the "Jabberwocky" words may indeed be blends after the manner of 'slithy' (*galumphing,* for example, which seems to have something of *gallop* and *triumph* in it, and *chortle,* a combination of *chuckle* and *snort*), it is more likely that most occurred to Carroll spontaneously in their final form. The definitions given for the words in the "Stanza of Anglo-Saxon Poetry" (1855) indicate that Carroll was not consciously creating blends in any word except *slythy.* Even there, the statement that it is composed of 'lithe' and 'slimy' may have occurred to him after the word was conceived. In short, I think that in spite of Carroll's published statement that Humpty Dumpty's theory will account for all of the words, such is not actually the case. There is no other evidence that the words are all portmanteaus than this tentative assertion in the preface to *Snark,* and there is some evidence to the contrary. *Mimsy,* called a portmanteau by Humpty Dumpty, is not so designated in the etymological gloss of 1855. And in a letter to Maud Standen of December 18, 1877, Carroll says:

I am afraid I can't explain "vorpal blade" for you – nor yet "tulgey wood"; but I did make an explanation once for "uffish thought" – It seems to suggest a state of mind when the voice is gruffish, the manner roughish, and the temper huffish. Then again, as to "burble": if you take the three verbs "*b*leat," "m*ur*mur," and "war*ble*," and select the bits I have underlined, it certainly *makes* "burble": though I am afraid I can't distinctly remember having made it in that way.[1]

(*Letters to Child-friends*, ed. Hatch, p. 73)

The principle of blending, as described by Carroll in the *Snark* preface, seems to entail a conscious fusion of two words: that is, one starts with the separate words and creates a blend by trying to say them simultaneously.[2] In the letter just quoted, Carroll seems in his explanation to be starting with the portmanteau itself and isolating its individual components, not the reverse. This letter, too, seems to indicate that Carroll had no specific meanings in mind when he coined his "Jabber-wocky" words, but in nearly every case (with the exception of *slithy* and possibly *chortled* and *galumphing*) merely recorded forms which spontaneously occurred to him. When called upon to give an 'etymology', he merely fabricated his derivations from plausible choices. The explanation of *frumious* is, like his discussion of *burble*, an afterthought.[3] This is not to say that Carroll was unaware of conscious and unconscious blending as a source of word-formation, but merely that he did not create all of the "Jabberwocky" words on that principle.

Carroll's neologisms in *Through the Looking-Glass, The Hunting of the Snark*, Knot VIII of *A Tangled Tale* (*grurmstipth*, a Kgovjnian word for an omnibus), and *Sylvie and Bruno* (where, with the exception of Arthur Forester's *sillygism*, most are the transcriptions of erroneous pronunciation) were not invented to illustrate the process of word-formation, but merely to serve the cause of humor.[4] In his

---

[1] In his biography of Carroll (*The White Knight* [Philadelphia, 1963], second impression), Alexander L. Taylor asserts that *vorpal* "seems to be concocted out of Verbal and Gospel by taking alternate letters from each" (p. 81). This, I think, is going too far in order to support a personal thesis about Dodgson's religious views.

[2] Linguists recognize the existence of 'portmanteau' words in the general word-stock of English, and regard blending as an historically-attested source of word-formation. In the words of Eric Partridge, "The earliest blends were, as the latest will doubtless be, the result of confusion: a speaker begins to express an idea before he has formulated it in his mind; he commences a word and immediately continues with another, or the corresponding part of another, word of different yet associated meaning. ... One can easily picture to oneself the perplexity experienced by those etymologists who, in the days before their frequency became recognized, dealt with blends" ("The Nonsense Words of Edward Lear and Lewis Carroll", in *Here, There and Everywhere* [London, 1950], pp. 178-179).

[3] In *The Field of Nonsense* (London, 1952), Elizabeth Sewell says of *frumious*: ". . . it seems curious that Humpty Dumpty should have got by so easily on his portmanteau theory, for when one looks at it, it becomes very unsatisfactory. It would fit a pun well enough, in which there are precisely that – two meanings (or more than two) packed up in one word. But *frumious* . . . is not a word, and does not have two meanings packed up in it; it is a group of letters without any meaning at all. What Humpty Dumpty may have meant, but fails to say, is that it looks like two words, 'furious' and 'fuming', reminding us of both simultaneously. It is not a word, but it looks like other words, and almost certainly more than two" (pp. 119-120).

[4] Eric Partridge (above, note 2) classifies the nonsense words of both Edward Lear and Lewis Carroll into several individual types, and argues convincingly that Carroll's coining of neologisms was influenced by the practice of the older man. Although there is no proof for this hypothesis since neither Lear nor Carroll ever mentioned the other, it is probable that Lear's practice did influence Carroll. The men were contemporaries, were engaged in the same

stating of Humpty Dumpty's theory of portmanteau words and in his creation of such terms as *slithy, chortle, snark* ('snake + shark'?), and Bruno's *muddlecome table* (for 'multiplication table'), Carroll anticipated the practice of James Joyce in *Finnegan's Wake*.[5] Although, as is attested by their presence in both the *Oxford English Dictionary* and *Webster's Third New International Dictionary,* the words *chortle* and *galumph* have been accepted into the English language (albeit their lexical definitions are left rather vague in these dictionaries), Carroll was not attempting to graft his neologisms onto the stock of the linguistic community. If he had been, he would have stipulated meanings for them. I think that the definitions given by Humpty Dumpty should be regarded merely as Carroll's (perhaps satirical) illustration of the scholarly ascertainment of lexical definitions of archaic words. And as mentioned earlier, there is every possibility that, given his peculiar cast of mind, Humpty Dumpty was making up the "meanings" as he went along.

7.3 CARROLL AND STIPULATIVE DEFINITION

Lexical definition is the reporting of those meanings of a word which are conventionally held by the speech community at large. Stipulative definition is the specifying of what meaning a word is to be understood to have in a particular act of discourse. Stipulative definition is required whenever new words are introduced into an established general vocabulary, when – in a particular context – established words are used in an unusual or specialized manner, and when an interpreter fails to understand an utterance because of the words' vagueness, ambiguity, or unfamiliarity.

Carroll attempted to introduce several new symbols into the language of mathematics; and – as was not the case with his purely literary neologisms discussed

---

kind of writing, and shared to a certain extent the same circle of acquaintances. Carroll probably read Lear's work. If he did, he would certainly have been impressed by Lear's wordplay. Carroll's work is entirely his own, however; at most he was indebted to Lear only for the method of framing portmanteaus.

[5] J. S. Atherton, in "Lewis Carroll and *Finnegan's Wake*", *English Studies*, XXXIII (1952), 1-15, demonstrates that James Joyce employs many of the linguistic devices used by Carroll and that *Finnegan's Wake* contains many references to Carroll and to the *Alice* books. Atherton's thesis is that Joyce did not consciously borrow Carroll's idea of making portmanteau words, but that after he had developed the technique himself, he suddenly became aware that he had been anticipated by Carroll. Atherton maintains that Joyce came to Carroll's works for the first time after he had begun writing *Finnegan's Wake*; and after the revelation, worked references to Carroll into the book. This hypothesis is borne out by Joyce's own admission in a letter to Harriet Shaw Weaver of May 31, 1927, published in *Letters of James Joyce*, ed. Stuart Gilbert (New York, 1957), pp. 254-256. He comments that many reviews say that he is imitating Lewis Carroll in the fragments of *Finnegan's Wake* already published, and says: "I never read him till Mrs Nutting gave me a book, not *Alice*, a few weeks ago – though, of course, I heard bits and scraps. But then I never read Rabelais either though nobody will believe this. I will read them both when I get back [to Paris]" (p. 255).

above – he took great pains to establish what they should be taken to signify. In *The Formulae of Plane Trigonometry* (1861) he invented a group of figures to represent the trigonometric ratios, and the term *Goniometry,* 'the measurement of angles by angular units'. In *An Elementary Treatise on Determinants* (1867) he introduced a notational symbol and the word *determinantal.* In the preface to this latter book, he apologizes for his innovations: "New words and symbols are always a most unwelcome addition to a Science, especially to one already burdened with an enormous vocabulary, yet I think the Definitions given of them will be found to justify their introduction, as the only way of avoiding tedious periphrasis." [6]

In technical fields where a specialized vocabulary is employed, the usefulness and convenience of neologisms as abbreviations MAY justify their introduction. But there are dangers in introducing them which, from his apologetic note, Carroll seems to have been aware of: the possibility of over-burdening the vocabulary (and men's memories) with unnecessary or redundant terms, and the possibility of creating a language too esoteric for usefulness even among the specialists who habitually employ it. The current proliferation of jargon in many technical fields – notably psychology, sociology, many branches of philosophy, linguistics, and literary criticism – illustrates these dangers. If carried to excess, the introduction of new terms can produce vagueness of thought and failure of communication.

On the other hand, if there are not a sufficient number of specialized terms which can serve as convenient abbreviations for more complex expressions, men will be forced to rely on 'tedious periphrasis' – and this too can cloud thought and render communication difficult. Carroll's reluctance to coin neologisms in his technical writings while feeling free to do so in his literary work where it did not really matter indicates that in his professional writing he preferred periphrasis to the creation of an arbitrary jargon which would require a great deal of initial stipulative definition. That this periphrastic form of expression CAN be tedious (and confusing), the reader has seen in Carroll's definitions of 'Classification' and 'Name' in *Symbolic Logic* (quoted in this study respectively in § 5.1 and § 6.1).

As mathematician and logician, Carroll was acutely conscious of the necessity for words in particular contexts to be precisely defined. In his technical writings he was often excessively scrupulous in stipulating what his terms were to be taken to mean. D. B. Eperson has said of Carroll's geometrical work, *Notes on Euclid* (1860):

... in this he even out-Euclids Euclid by defining the terms "problem" and "theorem": "a problem is something to be done", whilst "a theorem is something to be believed, for which proof is given". I think it is doubtful if there is really much to be gained by definition of this sort, but it is interesting to note Dodgson's love of logic, the study of which developed into one of his chief mental pursuits. The process of defining one's

---

[6]   *An Elementary Treatise on Determinants* (London, 1867), p. iii.

terms can be continued *ad infinitum et ad nauseam.* Why draw the line at defining 'problem' and 'theorem'? Why not also define 'definition'?

("Lewis Carroll – Mathematician", *Mathematical Gazette*, XVII [May, 1933], 93-94)

In all of his technical writings Dodgson established the conventions of terminology at the outset. And the same precision that he practiced himself, he demanded of others. In *Euclid and His Modern Rivals* (1879) it was the rivals' slipshod definitions and inconsistencies of language that provoked his most withering scorn. Toward the end of his life he became quite disturbed over the lack of agreement among logicians as to whether the proposition "Some x is z" establishes the actual existence of x. In discussing this problem in a letter to Edith Rix in 1885, he concludes with a statement of considerable importance for this study:

Dear Edith, – I have been a severe sufferer from *Logical* puzzles of late. I got into a regular tangle about the "import of propositions," as the ordinary logical books declare that "all x is z" doesn't even *hint* that any x's exist, but merely that the qualities are so inseparable that, if ever x occurs, z must occur also. As to "some x is z," they are discreetly silent; and the living authorities I have appealed to, including our Professor of Logic, take opposite sides! Some say it means that the qualities are so connected that, if any x's *did* exist, some *must* be z – others that it only means compatibility, *i.e.*, that some *might* be z, and they would go on asserting, with perfect belief in their truthfulness, "some boots are made of brass," even if they had all the boots in the world before them, and knew that *none* were so made, merely because there is no inherent impossibility in making boots of brass! Isn't it bewildering? I shall have to mention all this in my great work on Logic – but *I* shall take the line "any writer may mean exactly what he pleases by a phrase so long as he explains it beforehand." But I shall not venture to assert "some boots are made of brass" till I have found a pair! ...

(Quoted in Collingwood's *Life and Letters of Lewis Carroll* [New York, 1898], p. 242)

The possibility of defining words to suit ourselves, asserted openly in this letter, is dealt with in *Through the Looking-Glass,* published nearly fifteen years earlier. Humpty Dumpty is Carroll's spokesman; the passage is the one of Carroll's which is most frequently quoted by students of language. Humpty Dumpty has just explained to Alice why un-birthday presents are better than birthday presents. A person can receive three hundred and sixty-four un-birthday presents a year, but there is "only ONE [day] for birthday presents, you know. There's glory for you!"

"I don't know what you mean by 'glory,'" Alice said.

Humpty Dumpty smiled contemptuously. "Of course you don't – till I tell you. I meant 'there's a nice knock-down argument for you!'"

"But 'glory' doesn't mean 'a nice knock-down argument,'" Alice objected.

"When *I* use a word," Humpty Dumpty said, in rather a scornful tone, "it means just what I choose it to mean – neither more nor less."

"The question is," said Alice, "whether you *can* make words mean so many different things."

"The question is," said Humpty Dumpty, "which is to be master – that's all."

Alice was too much puzzled to say anything; so after a minute Humpty Dumpty began again. "They've a temper, some of them – particularly verbs: they're the proudest – adjectives you can do anything with, but not verbs – however, *I* can manage the whole lot of them! Impenetrability! That's what *I* say!"

"Would you tell me please," said Alice, "what that means?"

"Now you talk like a reasonable child," said Humpty Dumpty, looking very much pleased. "I meant by 'impenetrability' that we've had enough of that subject, and it would be just as well if you'd mention what you mean to do next, as I suppose you don't mean to stop here all the rest of your life."

"That's a great deal to make one word mean," Alice said in a thoughtful tone.

"When I make a word do a lot of work like that," said Humpty Dumpty, "I always pay it extra."

(Works, pp. 213-214)

Humpty Dumpty's assumption that he can dictate meanings to the words he uses has provoked much comment. One critic has said, "With Humpty Dumpty's method of dealing with words, chaos is come again." [7] Another has asked, "*May* we, like Humpty-Dumpty, make our words mean whatever we choose them to mean? One thinks of a Soviet delegate using 'democracy' in a U.N. debate. May we pay our words extra, or is this the stuff that propaganda is made of? Do we have an obligation to past usage? In one sense words are our masters, or communication would be impossible. In another, we are the masters; otherwise there could be no poetry." [8]

7.4 THE ARBITRARY NATURE OF WORD-MEANINGS; THE NEED FOR OBSERVING CONVENTIONS OF USAGE

That Carroll himself subscribed to Humpty Dumpty's view of the arbitrary nature of word-meanings is attested in a serious article which he published in *The Theatre* magazine in 1888 (see § 4.5): "... no word has a meaning INSEPARABLY attached to it; a word means what the speaker intends by it, and what the hearer understands by it, and that is all". Carroll's position, stated here unequivocally, implies that since words have, of themselves, no intrinsic meanings to be conveyed, men are free to decide what significations they wish their words to have in particular contexts. But, as illustrated in Alice's conversation with Humpty Dumpty, Carroll also saw that if men expect to communicate by means of such arbitrarily-defined words, they must inform their hearers what meaning they intend the words to have. Since Humpty Dumpty does not feel obligated to do so and keeps his idiosyncratic definitions to himself, Alice is baffled by his use of the word *glory*. When she learns that it is being used to signify 'a nice knock-down argument', she objects that it cannot be made to do so since that is not its generally accepted meaning – an invalid objection, as Humpty Dumpty points out. Alice's further objection, that a word cannot be

---

[7] Patricia Meyer Spacks, "Logic and Language in 'Through the Looking Glass'", *ETC.*, XVIII (April, 1961), 95.

[8] Roger W. Holmes, "The Philosopher's *Alice in Wonderland*", *Antioch Review*, XIX (1959), 137.

made to signify whatever the user wishes, is answered by Humpty Dumpty's decla-
ration of mastery over the words he uses. Alice is puzzled into silence by this remark
(as Carroll probably intended his young readers to be); but, having learned Humpty
Dumpty's method of handling words, she is not disturbed by his cryptic and unfamiliar use of *impenetrability*. In a pragmatic fashion she immediately asks him
what he intends that word to mean and accepts his explanation, only wondering
"in a thoughtful tone" (Carroll's hint, perhaps, that his readers should think about
it too) that a word can be made to signify so much.

Since words may be defined arbitrarily by their users, there is nothing in the
nature of the word itself to prevent its being used to signify Humpty Dumpty's
complex of ideas. *Impenetrability* is merely an abbreviation for the ideas expressed
in the phrase, "we've had enough of that subject, and it would be just as well if
you'd mention what you mean to do next, as I suppose you don't mean to stop here
all the rest of your life". Richard Robinson has said of this type of abbreviation:

By the stipulative substitution of a word for a phrase, language is abbreviated. What can
now be said could also have been said previously, . . . but it can now be said in fewer
words, because the thing can now be indicated by a single name, whereas formerly a
descriptive phrase was required. . . . Abbreviation not merely shortens discourse; it also
increases understanding. We grasp better what we can hold in one span of attention, and
how much we can thus hold depends on the length of the symbols we have to use in
order to state it.

                                                        (*Definition* [Oxford, 1950], p. 68)

However, there are dangers incurred by using a single word to refer to a highly
complex phrase which embodies many ideas:

Abbreviation, the replacement of a phrase by a name, involves the disappearance of
words reminding us of the complexity of a thing. Most names, whether names of simple
or of complex objects, fail to mirror by their structure any complexity in the object. . . .
To abbreviate a phrase into a word, therefore, is always to set up a cause that may lead
men to overlook an important complexity or relation, or to find mystery where there is
none. He who forgets that 'five' is an abbreviation for 'one and one and one and one
and one', and similarly with other names for numbers, may find it mysterious and
wonderful that seven plus five must equal twelve.

                                                        (Richard Robinson, *Definition*, p. 79)

Whether or not Humpty Dumpty "pays it extra" for its work, the stipulated definition of *impenetrability* in this instance IS, as Alice shrewdly sees, a "great deal"
for one word to mean. The complexity of Humpty Dumpty's thought is not mirrored
in the word he selects to represent it; consequently there is a danger that even after
he has explained what he intends for the word to signify, Alice will not grasp or be
able to retain the full signification of the term. To be useful, an abbreviation must
provide for a knowledgeable interpreter a key to an understanding of the thing it
represents (the longer phrase and the welter of ideas embodied in the phrase). If
the phrase for which it is substituted contains so numerous or heterogeneous a
body of ideas that the interpreter has difficulty in remembering them all, or in
grasping the totality in a single act of interpretation, perhaps a single word CAN

embody too great a condensation of signification. Thus, Carroll seems to be aware that a word required to do "a lot of work" may not convey to an interpreter the entirety of the speaker's intended meaning, and that, as a result of this, an attempt at communication may not wholly succeed.

Though Lewis Carroll felt that words could be made to mean whatever men wished them to, he also saw that if a word is used to signify something other than its acceptation in general usage, this peculiar signification must be explained by its user if communication is to be possible. In the "Appendix, Addressed to Teachers" which concludes his *Symbolic Logic,* he makes a further statement of his position. He is following up his intention to do so stated in the letter to Edith Rix of 1885 quoted above.

The writers, and editors, of the Logical text-books which run in the ordinary grooves . . . take, on this subject [the "existential Import" of Propositions], what seems to me to be a more humble position than is at all necessary. They speak of the Copula of a Proposition "with bated breath", almost as if it were a living, conscious Entity, capable of declaring for itself what it chose to mean, and that we, poor human creatures, had nothing to do but to ascertain *what* was its sovereign will and pleasure, and submit to it.

In opposition to this view, I maintain that any writer of a book is fully authorised in attaching any meaning he likes to any word or phrase he intends to use. If I find an author saying, at the beginning of his book, "Let it be understood that by the word '*black*' I shall always mean '*white*', and that by the word '*white*' I shall always mean '*black*'," I meekly accept his ruling, however injudicious I may think it.

And so, with regard to the question whether a Proposition is or is not to be understood as asserting the existence of its Subject, I maintain that every writer may adopt his own rule, provided of course that it is consistent with itself and with the accepted facts of Logic.

(Symbolic Logic, 4th ed. [1897], pp. 165-166)

This is precisely Humpty Dumpty's theoretical position. It implies many things about the nature and function of words, which Richard Robinson has eloquently summarized as follows:

Humpty Dumpty claimed the most entire freedom to give any meaning to any word.

There is much justice in this claim. It is a slogan suggesting many of those truths about words which the linguistic layman ignores or denies. It includes the assertion that stipulation has no truthvalue . . .; stipulation is free in that no stipulative definition can justly be rejected on the ground that it is false. It is also a proper protest against the pedantic grammarian's demand that we should always use our words in the same senses as Samuel Johnson or some other 'authority', and never in any sense not found in the *Oxford English Dictionary*. It is a proper protest against all tyrannous demands, from whatever source, that insist upon everybody's using a word in a particular sense . . . It suggests a proper protest against the layman's assumption that common meanings are known and clear, and that there is some one 'correct' meaning for each word, in contrast to which all other meanings that may be given to it are 'incorrect'. It upholds the ancient truth, which it goes so much against our grain to believe, that words are conventional not natural signs, that there is no necessary or natural connexion between a word and a thing, no 'predestined' meaning for a given word . . . no sacredness or divine authority about any rule of meaning. It is a just protest against the inability to contemplate the possibility that what one has always meant by some word does not exist, the possibility, for example, that there cannot be such a thing as one has always meant by 'murder', or 'virtue', or 'responsibility', because one has included in one's meaning an uncausedness that does not exist, or that what one has always thought one meant by 'simultaneous' is something that can never be demonstrated to occur, whereas by stipulating a new definition we can make simultaneity into an empirical property. It is a just protest against the common habit of insisting on the question 'But what really *is x*?' even after it has been shown that '*x*' is an ambiguous or vague or inapplicable word.

(Robinson, *Definition*, pp. 72-73)

I think that it may safely be assumed that Carroll, in adhering to a belief in the arbitrary nature of word-meanings, was aware of many or all of these implications. But he was also aware that, although men have the power to give words idiosyncratic meanings, their privilege carries with it – if communication is their aim – the obligation to define their arbitrary usage. Humpty Dumpty, for all his insight into the theoretical nature of words, was deficient in his understanding of their practical employment for purposes of communication. His tendency to 'overwork' words, causing them to embody more significations than could easily be grasped and retained by an interpreter, has already been mentioned. But of even graver import for the achievement of successful communication is his practice of using familiar words in other than their general acceptations without due explanation.

If words drawn from the general stock of the linguistic community are used without peculiar stipulations, it must be in accordance with their past usage. For in the absence of some indication of idiosyncratic usage, interpreters will automatically assume that the words' general acceptations are intended. If there are no stipulations and the word IS being used to signify something other than its familiar and expected signification, and if the verbal context in which it is uttered does not sufficiently inform the interpreter that such is the case, misunderstanding may occur. The verbal context of Humpty Dumpty's utterance indicates to Alice that 'glory' is being used in an unusual fashion – to her mind, incorrectly. She is right in telling Humpty Dumpty that *glory* does not mean 'a nice knock-down argument': it doesn't, in conventional usage; and Humpty Dumpty has not bothered to inform her that he is using it idiosyncratically. There is nothing in the word itself, or in the verbal context of its utterance, which would have enabled her even to guess at the meaning which Humpty Dumpty intended for the word to convey. In a sense, with Humpty Dumpty's use of words, "chaos *is* come again" – not because of his using words idiosyncratically, but because of his failure to inform his listener of his practice.

One of the most important functions of stipulative definition is that of clarifying language which is vague, ambiguous, or (because of unfamiliarity) nonsensical to the interpreter. The role of stipulative definition in preventing and dispelling misunderstanding is deferred until the next chapter, which treats the general topic of "Ambiguity". At this point I shall illustrate the function of stipulative definition in preventing and clearing up non-understanding on the part of the interpreter.

7.5 STIPULATIVE DEFINITION A SAFEGUARD
AGAINST NON-UNDERSTANDING

When communication fails because of the interpreter's non-understanding of the words of an utterance, it is usually because the words are either unfamiliar to him and therefore meaningless, or vague in their significations to the extent that they impart no ascertainable meaning. For example, the interpreter's unfamiliarity with the words in question is responsible for the instances of non-understanding illustrated in the following two passages. The first occurs in Chapter III of *Wonderland* where, after the assorted creatures have heard the Mouse's history lecture, Alice admits that she has not been dried by it at all.

"In that case," said the Dodo solemnly, rising to its feet, "I move that the meeting adjourn, for the immediate adoption of more energetic remedies –"
   "Speak English!" said the Eaglet. "I don't know the meaning of half those long words, and, what's more, I don't believe you do either!" . . .
   "What I was going to say," said the Dodo in an offended tone, "was, that the best thing to get us dry would be a Caucus-race."
   "What *is* a Caucus-race?" said Alice . . .
   "Why," said the Dodo, "the best way to explain it is to do it."

(Works, p. 37)

The limitations of the Eaglet's vocabulary make it impossible for him to comprehend the Dodo's pompous diction. When the Eaglet makes his pointed protest, the Dodo paraphrases the sense of his initial utterance (with additional information) in simpler language. This restatement is, in essence, a stipulation of intended meaning – not, in this case, of individual words, but of the utterance as a whole. Since the word *Caucus-race* is unfamiliar to Alice, it therefore signifies nothing to her. She asks the Dodo in effect, "What do you mean by 'Caucus-race'?" It is unclear whether in Wonderland the word *Caucus-race* is an established word with a standard lexical definition, or simply a coinage peculiar to the Dodo. Whichever the case, he is willing to stipulate his meaning for the word by demonstrating the process to which the word refers.

   In Chapter V of *Through the Looking-Glass,* Alice finds herself rowing a boat in the company of the old Sheep. Alice is not accustomed to rowing; and the Sheep, by assuming on her part more knowledge of the activity than she actually possesses, merely confuses her by giving advice.

"Feather!" cried the Sheep . . .
   This didn't sound like a remark that needed any answer: so Alice said nothing, but pulled away. There was something very queer about the water, she thought, as every now and then the oars got fast in it, and would hardly come out again.
   "Feather! Feather!" the Sheep cried again . . . "You'll be catching a crab directly."
   "A dear little crab!" thought Alice. "I should like that."
   "Didn't you hear me say 'Feather'?" the Sheep cried angrily . . .
   "Indeed I did," said Alice: "you've said it very often – and very loud. Please where *are* the crabs?"
   "In the water, of course!" said the Sheep . . . "Feather, I say!"

"*Why* do you say 'Feather' so often?" Alice asked at last, rather vexed. "I'm not a bird!"

"You are," said the Sheep: "you're a little goose."

(*Works*, pp. 203-204)

Alice, who has little experience in rowing boats, is not aware that *Feather!* as used by the Sheep is not a noun, but the imperative form of the verb, 'to feather' – a technical term referring to the rotation of the oar blades to an almost horizontal position while moving them back for the next stroke. Her failure to feather her oars causes the blades (left vertical) to drag in the water, which gives her the impression that they are stuck fast. For Alice, the Sheep's word is nonsensical; in exasperation she casts about for a possible signification and comes up with "birds", the only things she can think of to which the word *feather* might be applied. The Sheep does not see fit to stipulate what she means by "Feather!" even when Alice asks her to, evidently assuming that Alice should know what she means and that if she doesn't, she is "a little goose". The failure in communication which results from Alice's ignorance and the Sheep's refusal to explain what she intends *feather* to signify creates total lack of understanding and a flare-up of tempers on both sides. Alice fails to interpret *feather* altogether, in any significant way; but she *mis*interprets the phrase *catching a crab*. This too is a technical term in rowing with which she is unfamiliar; it refers to the rower's being tipped or unseated either when his oar misses the water entirely, or when the blade drags in the water on the recovery. Alice does "catch a crab" a moment later and is thrown to the floor of the boat by the handle of the oar. Yet, ignorant of the meaning of *catching a crab* in a rowing context, she persists in taking the phrase in its literal and conventional rather than its metaphorical and technical sense, and looks overboard to find the crab that she has "caught". Had the Sheep explained to her what the phrase meant when she saw that Alice did not understand it, the accident would probably have been prevented.

While non-understanding may result from the interpreter's being unfamiliar with either the conventional or idiosyncratic meaning of a given word or phrase, it may also result from vagueness, or lack of specific signification, in the term itself. Vagueness occurs when a word standing in a specific context fails to evoke a concrete signification in the interpreter's mind – i.e., there is no specific association-object for the interpreter to fasten upon and link up with the word's occurrence. We have already seen how vague words are like "maps without territories" (§§ 6.3.4 and 6.3.5): in *Sylvie and Bruno*, the bespectacled young woman who uttered such "ominous phrases" as *Man is a bundle of Qualities* and *the Objective is only attainable through the Subjective* was using terms whose significations her audience could not possibly apprehend – for they had no significations. If the young woman herself had some referents in mind which she intended her words to signify, it would only have been through stipulative definition that she could have communicated these meanings. However, since she herself probably had nothing specific in mind for the words to refer to, she would have been sadly embarrassed if her audience had demanded that she define her terms. Finally, it should be noted that the vagueness of her individual words renders the utterances in which they occur wholly meaningless also.

At the same picnic where we learn that man is a bundle of qualities, there are two other conversations which illustrate how non-understanding can result from vagueness of language and the interpreter's unfamiliarity with certain words; moreover, they illustrate how a speaker may consciously exploit the ignorance of the interpreter to confuse him. In the first instance, a pompous "authority" on art uses language so vague that his esthetic pronouncements are meaningless to a would-be interpreter:

"... for any one who has a soul for *Art*, such a view is preposterous. *Nature* is one thing. *Art* is another. *Nature* shows us the world as it *is*. But *Art* – as a Latin author tells us – *Art*, you know – the words have escaped my memory –"

"*Ars est celare Naturam*," Arthur interposed with delightful promptitude.

"Quite so!" the orator replied with an air of relief. "I thank you! *Ars est celare Naturam* – but that isn't it." And, for a few peaceful moments, the orator brooded, frowningly, over the quotation.

(Works, p. 416)

If he does not stipulate his definitions more precisely than he has, there is little possibility of his audience's understanding what the orator intends for *Art* and *Nature* to signify. Arthur Forester, taking him for a charlatan, capitalizes upon his unfamiliarity with the Latin language by giving him a twisted version of *ars est celare artem*. In his ignorance, the art expert initially accepts the erroneous quotation as being accurate and a valid support for his "thesis" (whatever it is). Arthur's willful creation of confusion by using words with which his victim is unfamiliar is further demonstrated by his unraveling the bluestocking who has already oppressed the party by her pretensions to intellectuality:

"Talking of Herbert Spencer," he began, "do you really find no *logical* difficulty in regarding Nature as a process of involution, passing from definite coherent homogeneity to indefinite incoherent heterogeneity?"

Amused as I was at the ingenious jumble he had made of Spencer's words, I kept as grave a face as I could.

"No *physical* difficulty," she confidently replied: "but I haven't studied *Logic* much. Would you *state* the difficulty?"

"Well," said Arthur, "do you accept it as self-evident? Is it as obvious, for instance, as that 'things that are greater than the same are greater than one another'?"

"To *my* mind," she modestly replied, "it seems *quite* as obvious. I grasp *both* truths by intuition. But *other* minds may need some logical – I forget the technical terms."

"For a *complete* logical argument," Arthur began with admirable solemnity, "we need two prim Misses –"

"Of course!" she interrupted. "I remember that word now. And they produce –?"

"A Delusion," said Arthur.

"Ye – es?" she said dubiously. "I don't seem to remember that so well. But what is the *whole* argument called?"

"A Sillygism."

"Ah, yes! I remember now. But I don't need a Sillygism, you know, to prove that mathematical axiom you mentioned."

"Nor to prove that 'all angles are equal', I suppose?"

"Why, of course not! One takes such a simple truth as that for granted!"

(*Works*, pp. 425-426)

The words uttered by Arthur, purporting to be those of Herbert Spencer, are inherently so vague in this context that the young woman (who, as Carroll pictures her, probably has not read Spencer with any understanding) cannot possibly tell whether he is making sense or not. If she had asked Arthur to explain what each word in the utterance was to be taken to mean, he, to preserve his joke, would have had to become even more vague and abstract, substituting for these words other terms equally meaningless. But realizing that her pride will not allow her to admit that the sentence is unintelligible to her, Arthur is able to exploit her ignorance of logical terminology to confuse her even more, feeling certain that she will not challenge his use of *prim Misses, Delusion,* and *Sillygism.*[9]

Carroll's poem "The Three Voices", mentioned in the last chapter (§ 6.3.5), has as its main point the demoralizing effect upon an individual of non-understanding. It will be recalled that, during a conversation on the sea-shore, a man is reduced to gibbering bewilderment by the statements of a woman he has met – statements which, though dogmatically uttered, are essentially meaningless. The following is typical:

> "Thought in the mind doth still abide
> That is by Intellect supplied,
> And within that Idea doth hide:
>
> "And he, that yearns the truth to know
> Still further inwardly may go,
> And find Idea from Notion flow:
>
> "And thus the chain, that sages sought,
> Is to a glorious circle wrought,
> For Notion hath its source in Thought."

Unable to comprehend her language, the man feels his mind going; but nothing he or she can say can clarify the meaning of the words. As the conversation progresses, and the man sinks deeper and deeper, he finally begs her to be more specific; but she does not, will not, cannot (?) stipulate what her words are to be taken to mean:

> When he, with racked and whirling brain,
> Feebly implored her to explain,
> She simply said it all again.

---

[9] A passage quite similar to this – employing mock logic, vague language, and the use of 'angles' as illustrations – occurs in Chapter Seven of Oliver Goldsmith's *The Vicar of Wakefield* (1766), in which the Vicar's son Moses is befuddled and put to rout in an argument with the Squire.

After they have parted, the man remains on the shore crushed and baffled. He wonders at the waters clear,

> And why he had so long preferred
> To hang upon her every word:
> "In truth," he said, "it was absurd."
>
> .   .   .   .
>
> "Her speech," he said, "hath caused this pain.
> Easier I count it to explain
> The jargon of the howling main,
>
> Or, stretched beside some babbling brook,
> To con, with inexpressive look,
> An unintelligible book."

(For the complete poem see *Works*, pp. 865-877)

This is a fine summary statement of the effects produced on an interpreter by vague language. In many such cases – not this one, apparently – the interpreter's non-understanding can be dispelled by the speaker's stipulating what he intends for the words' signification to be.

7.6 SUMMARY

Lewis Carroll, aware that no word has a signification inseparably attached to it, saw that men are able to stipulate what meanings they wish their words to have. But he also saw that communication can occur only if conventions of usage are observed. These conventions may be those adopted by the speech community in general, or an arbitrary set established in private between individuals in the context of a single act of discourse. He saw that whenever the meaning given to a word deviates from the word's general acceptation, its deviant signification must be made clear to potential interpreters. The means for accomplishing this clarification is the process of stipulative definition.

As a type of covenant between men as to the manner in which words are to be used, stipulative definition has several functions. It is a necessary means for limiting the signification of a word in a given act of discourse (that is, for excluding un-intended significations from the interpreter's consideration), for explaining the conventions to be observed in such an act of discourse (as in the case of an author's setting forth in a preface what he intends for specific symbols to represent in the context of his book), for allowing the introduction of new words into an established vocabulary, and for clarifying language which is vague or unfamiliar to a given interpreter. The last-named function serves to remedy lapses of communication that occur through non-understanding on the part of the interpreter. Another function of stipulative definition is the prevention of misunderstanding through the clearing up of ambiguities. This is dealt with in the next chapter.

8

AMBIGUITY

"I never make bets," Clara said very gravely. "Our excellent preceptress has often warned us –"
"You'd be none the worse if you did!" Mad Mathesis interrupted. "In fact, you'd be the better, I'm certain!"
"Neither does our excellent preceptress approve of puns," said Clara.

Lewis Carroll, *A Tangled Tale*, Knot III

8.1 PREFATORY STATEMENT

In addition to clarifying vague language and explaining the idiosyncratic use of words with conventionally established meanings, stipulative definition is useful in resolving ambiguities. Verbal ambiguity occurs whenever an utterance – be it a word, phrase, sentence, or group of sentences – is capable of having for the interpreter more than one signification in a given context. It has already been shown that Lewis Carroll considered most words to be ambiguous (§ 4.5). The present chapter illustrates his exploitation of this realization in his literary works. As will be seen, he was aware of other types of ambiguity than that possessed by individual words. He saw that sentence structure itself could create ambiguities, and on several occasions he used this syntactic ambiguity (sometimes called "amphiboly") as a source of humor. This chapter deals first with lexical ambiguity and then proceeds to a consideration of syntactic ambiguity and contextual ambiguity.

8.2 LEXICAL AMBIGUITY

8.2.1 *The Nature and Functional Cause of Lexical Ambiguity*

Lexical ambiguity occurs when a word having two or more distinct significations in conventional usage occurs in a verbal context which does not make clear to the interpreter which one of these significations is intended. Words which, viewed in isolation outside of any context, are potentially capable of being interpreted in more than one way depending upon the particular context they are placed in, may be called "equivocal". A word such as *oxygen* which has only one meaning allotted to it by convention is NOT equivocal: but a word such as *iron* which has several distinct potential meanings in conventional usage IS equivocal. When equivocal words occur in contexts that do not specify which one of their possible significations is to be understood by the interpreter as having been intended – that enable him to choose between two or more significations with equal validity – these words cease to be equivocal and become "ambiguous". Most words in the general lexicon of English are equivocal in that they each have potentially a variety of possible significations. Excluded from this generalization are the numerous specialized terms peculiar to the working vocabularies of various technical fields such as mathematics, biology, chemistry, physics, musicology, medicine, law, psychology, etc. Thus, most words – being equivocal – may be viewed as being potentially ambiguous: teetering on the brink, so to speak, of full-fledged ambiguity, needing only the agency of a careless or willful context of association to push them over the edge.

According to John Stuart Mill, in a statement which Lewis Carroll undoubtedly read, an equivocal word is in reality not a single word with several possible meanings, but two or more words which accidentally coincide in sound.[1] That which is called an equivocal 'word' is actually as many different words as there are meanings which it is potentially capable of having. *Track*, for example, is the name of many different things. It may designate the rails along which trains move, the spoor of an animal, the turf course where horses race, the cinder course where men run races in the springtime sporting event (comprised of running, pole vaulting, high jumping, and discus throwing) which also bears the name, or the path of a sub-atomic particle through a cloud chamber. As it refers to these various things individually, *track* is not one symbol, but six. For convenience, however, men generally speak of such equivocal symbols not as homophones, but as a single word signifying various things. Thus, the word *mouse* is said to mean 'a type of rodent', 'a young woman', or 'a black eye'. As long as one realizes that the symbol *mouse* as it refers to these three things, is actually three separate symbols, each with its own signification, he may safely regard *mouse* for the sake of convenience as a word which is capable of having three distinct meanings. Usually the context in which the word is perceived will inform the interpreter which of the possible meanings is intended; but occasionally the context allows for no clear decision, and the word proves capable of being taken in more than one of its possible senses. In a context such as the following, the equivocal *mouse* becomes ambiguous: "He picked up a mouse last night down at the waterfront." The three-fold ambiguity of *mouse* is reinforced by the ambiguity of *picked up,* and by the physical location where the picking up occurred.

If the interpreter does not see that a word is ambiguous in its context, he may

[1]   John Stuart Mill, *A System of Logic* (New York, 1852), p. 30.

unwittingly choose a meaning not intended and thus misinterpret the utterance. On the other hand, if he does see the ambiguity, he is puzzled to know which of the possible meanings he should select; for he sees that, depending upon his choice, the utterance as a whole may have two or more alternative senses. It is at this point that he should ask the speaker to stipulate which one of the possible meanings he intends the word to have.

The type of verbal joke called a "pun" is created by the conscious use of an equivocal word to produce an ambiguity. This word will have at least two distinct meanings, each of which will profoundly affect the meaning of the total utterance. For the joke to be successful, the ambiguity of the key word must be recognized, the alternative meanings of both the word and the utterance must be isolated and then juxtaposed in the interpreter's mind. The works of Lewis Carroll are filled with puns, as well as with disparaging comments about puns. Punning was a Victorian vice – or so Carroll seemed to regard it; but he could not resist the temptation when it presented itself. More attention will be given to Carroll's puns in § 8.2.2.

8.2.2 *Multiple Definition*

Since Carroll believed that most words are equivocal and capable of becoming ambiguous in certain contexts, it is reasonable to assume that he was undoubtedly aware that for purposes of clear thinking and successful communication, people must realize that words are capable of multiple definition. This assumption is borne out by turning to Carroll's writings. In a letter of February 1, 1881, he writes to an unspecified Edith:

I have waited since Jan. 27 to thank you for your letter and present, that I might be able to say the "scales" had come – But as they still don't come, I will wait no longer. Thank you for all your birdthday wishes, and for the "scales" whatever they are. Oh! how puzzled I am to guess what they will be like. First I think "Dear little thoughtful Edith! She knew I was always an invalid, taking heaps of medicine – and she was afraid I should take too much – so she is sending me a nice pair of medicine-scales to weigh it out grain by grain." Then I think "Oh no, she knows I am fond of music: so she is sending me a set of scales to practise on the pianoforte or the orguinette." Then again I say "Oh, how stupid I am! why of course it's a *fish* she's sending me. A nice scaly salmon, just to remind me of Eastbourne, wrapped up in seaweed, and sprinkled with sand." When it comes, I wonder which of these guesses will turn out to be right!

(*Letters to Child-friends*, ed. Hatch, pp. 158-159)

In *Through the Looking-Glass,* Alice reveals her awareness that words can have a multiplicity of meanings when the White Knight explains how he once fell into a huge helmet he had invented and had an extremely difficult time in getting out again. He became stuck inside when the other White Knight, thinking it was his own helmet, put it on. Alice comments that he must have hurt the other Knight, "being on top of his head".

"I had to kick him, of course," the Knight said, very seriously. "And then he took the helmet off again – but it took hours and hours to get me out. I was as fast as – as lightning, you know."

"But that's a different kind of fastness," Alice objected.

The Knight shook his head. "It was all kinds of fastness with me, I can assure you!" he said.

(Works, pp. 241-242)

The use of *fast* in this passage is not strictly ambiguous, because Alice has no difficulty in seeing that the Knight is defining it erroneously for the context. *Fast* and *fastness* are certainly equivocal symbols to Alice; but there is some indication that the Knight does not recognize that they may be used to refer to different concepts such as 'speed' and 'fixity'. Or if he does recognize this possible multiplicity of reference, perhaps he is succumbing to the fallacious thinking ascribed to him by Peter Alexander: "the view that if things have the same name there must be some good reason for this – a familiar enough view in philosophy which has led many astray but which has peculiar attractions".[2] A moment before, the Knight had fallen prey to the same type of confusion: "You see the wind is so *very* strong here. It's as strong as soup" (*Works*, p. 238). Strength may indeed be predicated of both wind and soup, but not in the same sense: in this context, *strong* is TWO words and not one as the Knight implies in his comparison. Or, in more conventional terms, *strong* is a word having two distinct meanings, unable respectively to be applied to both wind and soup.

While Alice demonstrates a realization that words may be subject to multiple definition, Sylvie – the fairy heroine of Carroll's last fantasy – does not seem to have this realization, at least in the following passage (though her error may be due simply to her ignorance of the second meaning of *singular*):

"What a singular boy!" the Lord Chancellor whispered to himself: but Bruno had caught the words.

"What do it mean to say 'a *singular* boy'?" he whispered to Sylvie.

"It means *one* boy," Sylvie whispered in return. "And *plural* means two or three."

"Then I's welly glad I *is* a singular boy!" Bruno said with great emphasis. "It would be *horrid* to be two or three boys! P'raps they wouldn't play with me!"

A few moments later, the Other Professor says to Bruno, who has kept Sylvie's definition of 'singular' in mind:

"you said 'this Cat's very kind to the Mouses.' It must be a singular animal!"

"So it *are*," said Bruno, after carefully examining the Cat, to make sure how many there were of it.

(Works, pp. 722-723)

Failure on Sylvie's part to interpret the equivocal word according to its intended meaning (in her case, through ignorance of the symbol's alternative meaning,

---

[2] Peter Alexander, "Logic and the Humour of Lewis Carroll", *Proc. of the Leeds Philosophical and Literary Society*, VI (May, 1951), 556-557.

"exceptional" or "strikingly individual") misleads Bruno into making the same error, and the misunderstanding is compounded.

In Wonderland, misinterpretation of an equivocal word causes a misunderstanding between Alice and the Hatter.

"Take some more tea," the March Hare said to Alice . . .
"I've had nothing yet," Alice replied in an offended tone: "so I can't take more."
"You mean you ca'n't take *less*," said the Hatter: "it's very easy to take *more* than nothing."
"Nobody asked *your* opinion," said Alice.

(*Works*, p. 81)

The difficulty arises from the ambiguity of the word *more,* reinforced by the ambiguity of the word *nothing.* Alice takes the Hare's use of *more* to be "[Take some tea] *in addition to that which you have already had*" – an interpretation based on the idiom in Alice's world *some more,* meaning 'an additional quantity'. Since she has had no tea, she feels that the March Hare is mocking her and becomes offended. When she says, "I've had nothing yet, so I can't take more", the meaning of her statement is: "Since I have not yet had any tea, I cannot take any tea in addition to that which I have already had." The word *nothing* is ambiguous in the context of her utterance. By *nothing* Alice means "no tea"; but the Hatter, exercising a rigorous logic, takes the word in its literal sense. Not realizing her intended meaning for the word *more,* he assumes that she has made a logical error and hastens to correct her: it is, after all, quite easy to take "more than nothing", which is "some". If Alice had been more careful in her choice of words, or instead of snapping at the Hatter had stipulated what meaning she intended for her words to have, the difficulty would not have arisen.

In *Sylvie and Bruno* there are a few examples of Carroll's humorous use of ambiguity which approach the standard of those in *Alice.* One of these occurs when Bruno is telling of a goat which sang a song:

"It singed right froo. I *sawed* it singing with its long beard –"
"It couldn't sing with its *beard*," I said, hoping to puzzle the little fellow: "a beard isn't a *voice*."
"Well then, *oo* couldn't walk with Sylvie!" Bruno cried triumphantly. "Sylvie isn't a *foot*!"
I thought I had better follow Sylvie's example, and be silent for a while. Bruno was too sharp for us.

(*Works*, p. 493)

Realizing that *with* is an ambiguous word in this context, the narrator attempts to confuse Bruno by taking it to mean 'by means of' while knowing full well that Bruno intends it to signify 'possessing' or 'with the attribute of'. Bruno's syntax enables the narrator to interpret *with* ambiguously: if the child had placed his modifying phrase closer to *it* and not in proximity to *singing,* the opportunity for willful misinterpretation would not have been presented. Bruno, while adhering to his initial statement, beats the narrator at his own game by showing him that *with* in the sense of 'by means of' is absurd when applied to relationships of association. There is, however, a further distinction in Bruno's two uses of *with* which is not brought out in the text and which the child seems not to be aware of (unless, of course, he is playing an even more subtle trick on the narrator than is apparent on the surface): idiomatic usage does not hold the relationship of accompaniment with reference to an attribute or possession ["with a beard"] to be identical to the relationship of accompaniment with reference to human companionship ["with Sylvie"]. A narrator *with a girl* entails in this context a relationship of association not at all parallel to that of a goat *with a beard*.

The point is, of course, that *with*, a function word embodying structural meaning, is fully as equivocal as many content words which embody referential meanings. And *with* is not alone among the function words in possessing this quality. We have already seen (§ 4.4.5) in the conversation from *Sylvie and Bruno* between My Lady and the Vice-Warden of Outland that *for* and *on* are equivocal and capable of becoming ambiguous in certain contexts. The divergent significations potentially held by equivocal function words are, of course, structural meanings. As is the case with content words, it is the context of association that determines which one of the possible structural meanings of the function word is to be understood. If the context does not specify a particular signification, and two or more remain available to the interpreter, the function word will become ambiguous in that context.

A further illustration of Carroll's awareness that function words can be fully as equivocal as content words is encountered in *Through the Looking-Glass* when Alice asks Humpty Dumpty,

"Why do you sit out here all alone?" . . .
  "Why, because there's nobody with me!" cried Humpty Dumpty. "Did you think I didn't know the answer to *that*? Ask another."

(*Works*, p. 209)

Humpty Dumpty interprets the *why* of her question causally, in such manner that the meaning of her total utterance becomes, "As you sit out here, what is the reason for your being alone?" Her intended meaning for *why* was merely 'for what purpose'. Humpty Dumpty's taking Alice's *why* in a causal sense may not be mere perversity on his part; Carroll is perhaps suggesting that ambiguity can be created by a speaker's failure to make clear through intonation pattern and stress which of two possible alternative interpretations for an utterance is to be understood. In my dialect of American speech, for example, a different type of answer would be expected according to whether I uttered the question thus:

```
                           ___
                          |    |
_____|    |_____
2                         3  1
```

why do you sit out here all alone # [with primary stress on 'alone']
(*Answer:* "Because there's nobody with me.")

or thus:

3   2   21 $\sqrt{}$ 2
why do you sit out here all alone ‖ [with primary stress on 'why']
(*Answer:* "Because I want to be by myself.")

There may have been some distinction similar to this operating in Carroll's mind
when he framed his dialogue (though in view of the embryonic state of phonological studies in mid-nineteenth-century England, it is extremely unlikely that he
had other than a vague and intuitive notion of the role that stress patterns and
intonation contours play in signalling differential meanings in utterances). And of
course my tentative phonological hypothesis as an attempt to suggest a reason for
Humpty Dumpty's misunderstanding of Alice's question may be wholly false in
terms of Carroll's conscious intention. Humpty Dumpty's taking of Alice's query
as a riddle to be solved may indeed have been perversity: he was certainly capable
of it. Nonetheless, the passage does illustrate Carroll's awareness of the equivocal
nature of the function word *why*. But he quickly passes over the failure of Alice's
attempt at communication without authorial comment, leaving the reversal of
expectation produced by Humpty Dumpty's reply to stand as a puzzling surprise
for the reader.

He was not always so reticent in his manipulation of ambiguities that provide
humorous incident. Frequently he took delight in calling the reader's attention to
the functional ambiguity of equivocal terms in specific contexts. For example,
ambiguity is explicitly pointed out by Carroll when in *Sylvie and Bruno* the wife
of the Sub-Warden of Outland expresses her joy at the prospect of her husband's
becoming "Vice-Warden":

"He would distinguish himself as a Vice!" my Lady proceeded, being far too stupid to
see the double meaning of her words. "There has been no such Vice in Outland for many
a long year, as he would be!"

(*Works*, p. 304)

Carroll here feels compelled to make an overt comment about double meanings
because of the possibility that his young readers, not habitual users of the term
Vice, might miss the joke. He calls attention to his puns frequently in this book,
though not always so obviously. In the following examples the square brackets
are mine.

[The Vice-Warden wishes the Professor to preside at his election as Emperor of Outland:]
    "I fear I ca'n't, your Excellency!" the old man faltered. "What will the Warden –"
    "True, true!" the Vice-Warden interrupted. "Your position, as Court-Professor,
makes it awkward, I admit. Well, well! Then the Election shall be held without
you."
    "Better so, than if it were held *within* me!" the Professor murmured with a be-
wildered air, as if he hardly knew what he was saying.

(*Works*, pp. 353-354)

[After the Chancellor has pulled the monstrous child Uggug out of the room by his ear, my Lady asks where the child is:]

"He left the room a few minutes ago – with the Lord Chancellor," the Sub-Warden briefly explained.

"Ah!" said my Lady ... "Your Lordship has a very *taking* way with children! I doubt if any one could *gain the ear* of my darling Uggug so quickly as *you* can!" For an entirely stupid woman, my Lady's remarks were curiously full of meaning, of which she herself was wholly unconscious. ... "He is a clever boy," she continued with enthusiasm, "but he needs a man like your Lordship to *draw him out!*"

The Chancellor bit his lip, and was silent. He evidently feared that, stupid as she looked, she understood what she said *this* time, and was having a joke at his expense. He might have spared himself all anxiety: whatever accidental meaning her *words* might have, she *herself* never meant anything at all.

(Works, pp. 309-310)

The degenerate puns in these passages require little comment. The Professor's confusion of the alternative senses of *without* reveals how far Carroll had declined in imaginative vigor since *Through the Looking-Glass* of twenty years before (and there are many puns in *Sylvie and Bruno* that are much more feeble than these [3]). In the second passage, the unintended double meanings are merely a function of

---

[3] Here is a random sampling of further quibbles from *Sylvie and Bruno* (1889); there are many, many more. Page references are to *The Complete Works of Lewis Carroll* (New York, 1937); the square brackets are mine.

(a) [The Sub-Warden praising the Chancellor for his speech:] "You did that speech very well indeed. Why, you're a born orator, man!"

"Oh, that's nothing!" the Chancellor replied, modestly. ... "Most orators are *born*, you know." [p. 290]

(b) [Of the Professor, who has just rushed out of the room, nearly trampling Bruno in his haste:] "*Isn't* he learned?" the Warden said, looking after him with admiring eyes. "Positively he runs over with learning!"

"But he needn't run over *me!*" said Bruno. [p. 294]

(c) [The Sub-Warden's wife speaking to the Professor:] "You were teaching my son before breakfast, I believe?" my Lady loftily remarked. "I hope he strikes you as having talent?"

"Oh, very much so indeed, my Lady!" the Professor hastily replied, unconsciously rubbing his ear, while some painful recollection seemed to cross his mind. "I was very forcibly struck by His Magnificence, I assure you!" [pp. 304-305]

(d) [The Mad Gardener speaking to Bruno:] "I wonder you've got the face to tell me such fibs!" ... To which Bruno wisely replied, "Oo don't want a *face* to tell fibs wiz – only a *mouf*." [p. 322]

(e) [After Uggug shoots an arrow at a target, a hole is found in the bull's-eye:] "See!" said the Professor, pointing out a hole in the middle of the bull's-eye. "His Imperial Fatness had only *one* shot at it; and he went in just *here!*"

Bruno carefully examined the hole. "Couldn't go in *there*," he whispered to me. "He are too *fat!*" [p. 373]

(f) [In Dogland, Sylvie and Bruno are about to be granted an audience with the Dog-King:] "When His Majesty speaks to you," the Sentinel hastily whispered to Bruno, "you should prick up your ears!"

Bruno looked doubtfully at Sylvie. "I'd rather not, please," he said. "It would hurt."

"It doesn't hurt a bit!" the Sentinel said with some indignation. "Look! It's like this!" And he pricked up his ears like two railway signals. [p. 379]

the interpreter's psychological context – for they are double meanings only to the Lord Chancellor. What the Chancellor takes to be consciously ambiguous expressions are, the narrator hastens to inform the reader, really nothing of the kind. Carroll calls attention to his puns by italicizing the ambiguous words, as though he were afraid his readers would miss them. There is also an excessive use of exclamation points to emphasize the presence of puns. The only matter of interest in this latter passage is the narrator's comment that words can have accidental meanings which are unintended by the speaker and which are available to the interpreter because of the peculiar set of associations that the words hold for him.

A further illustration of ambiguity produced by the interpreter's set of personal associations linked to a given word is found in *Through the Looking-Glass* where, because she has seen the White Knight fall from his horse many times, Alice interprets his word *off* in a way that the Knight does not intend. Alice is about to cross the brook into the Eighth Square, and the Knight says in taking leave of her:

"But you'll stay and see me off first?" . . .
  "Of course I'll wait," said Alice . . .
  So they shook hands, and then the Knight rode slowly away into the forest. "It wo'n't take long to see him *off*, I expect," Alice said to herself, as she stood watching him. "There he goes! Right on his head as usual!"

                                                            (*Works*, p. 248)

Carroll's use of italics to set off the equivocal word in its punning sense is not as objectionable here as it becomes in his later books. It even suggests the possibility that Alice herself is consciously making the pun, being fully aware of the Knight's intended meaning but seeing another equally applicable to the situation.

In *Wonderland*, while the Mouse is reciting history (the "driest" thing he knows) to dry out the group of animals after their swim in the pool of tears, a misunderstanding arises from ambiguity in both word and syntax. The passage in question underwent considerable revision between its appearance in the manuscript "Alice's Adventures under Ground" (1862) and its publication in final form in *Wonderland* (1865). I have given both versions, for the revision reveals an aspect of Carroll's practice in selecting materials which is of considerable importance to this study. In the original version the passage is as follows:

"I proceed. Edwin and Morcar, the earls of Mercia and Northumbria, declared for him; and even Stigand, the patriotic archbishop of Canterbury, found it advisable to go with Edgar Atheling to meet William and offer him the crown. William's conduct was at first moderate – how are you getting on now, dear?" said the Mouse, turning to Alice as it spoke.
  "As wet as ever," said poor Alice, "it doesn't seem to dry me at all."
                    (*Alice's Adventures Under Ground* [London, 1886], p. 26)

In the revision:

"I proceed. 'Edwin and Morcar, the earls of Mercia and Northumbria, declared for him; and even Stigand, the patriotic archbishop of Canterbury, found it advisable –'"
  "Found *what*?" said the Duck.

"Found *it*," the Mouse replied rather crossly: "of course you know what 'it' means."

"I know what 'it' means well enough, when *I* find a thing," said the Duck: "it's generally a frog, or a worm. The question is, what did the archbishop find?"

The Mouse did not notice this question, but hurriedly went on, " '– found it advisable to go with Edgar Atheling to meet William and offer him the crown. William's conduct at first was moderate. But the insolence of his Normans –' How are you getting on now, my dear?" it continued, turning to Alice as it spoke.

"As wet as ever," said Alice in a melancholy tone: "it doesn't seem to dry me at all."

(*Works*, pp. 36-37)

The Duck, interrupting before the Mouse has finished his sentence, interprets the word *it* as a pronoun of unclear reference, the direct object of the verb *found*. The Duck wishes to know what *it* refers to; he does not seem to realize that *found it advisable* is merely an abbreviated way of saying *found [that] it [was] advisable*. Even if the Duck does realize that ellipsis has occurred, he still interprets *it* as referring to some object unspecified: and he is right. The Mouse, who has formulated the entire sentence in his mind, knows that *it* is a pronoun referring to the phrase *to go with Edgar Atheling,* and he seems to expect the Duck to know this also, although the phrase has not yet been uttered. He testily remarks, "of course you know what 'it' means": it means simply "going with Edgar Atheling". The sentence in its entirety could be rephrased: "The archbishop found [that] it [was] advisable [for him] to go with Edgar Atheling", or "The archbishop found [his] going with Edgar Atheling [to be] advisable." The incomplete syntax of the Mouse's sentence prevents the Duck from seeing that, far from being a pronoun of uncertain reference and the simple object of *found, it* is actually a use of the pronoun as an anticipatory subject of the entire clause which is the object of *found*. The problem is resolved when the Mouse finishes the sentence; but before its resolution, the difficulty provides Carroll with one of the most delightful bits of "nonsense" in *Wonderland*. The problem arises from a twofold cause: a syntactic ambiguity existing at the moment of the Duck's interruption, and the possibility of a pronoun's being able to refer to a multiplicity of things. Pronouns are among the most equivocal of words, since they may have as many different referents as are consistent with their grammatical gender, number, and case. Unless the verbal or physical context of their utterance makes specific their immediate signification (the antecedent sign in the utterance which they stand for) – and hence their ultimate signification (the thing outside the utterance which the antecedent sign refers to) – pronouns such as *it, they, them, he, she, this,* and *that* can create unresolvable ambiguities (see § 4.4.5).

That Carroll was aware of this property of pronouns is apparent from the passage just quoted. A comparison of this with the original version reveals that while he was revising "Under Ground" for publication as *Wonderland*, Carroll saw an opportunity for additional play with language which would both point a moral and adorn his tale. He inserted the digression provided by the Duck as a humorous illustration of misunderstanding produced by lexical and syntactic ambiguity. That he was fully conscious of what he was about is confirmed by his precise use of single quotation marks to indicate that *it* was to be regarded as a linguistic expression under discussion. Note that the Duck's question, "What did the archbishop find?" (a request for stipulative definition) is ignored by the Mouse; but that in finishing his sentence the Mouse does provide the answer. Carroll is, once again, playing with his readers, setting them a problem ("Of course you know what 'it' means") and providing them with the answer indirectly stated. A thoughtful child might indeed, with the Duck, wonder what *it* means in the Mouse's utterance; but he would have to puzzle out the answer for himself.

8.2.3 *The Effects of Lexical Ambiguity on Communication Attempts: Non-Understanding or Misunderstanding*

Lexical ambiguity, resulting from a word's having more than one possible interpretation in a given context, may or may not be recognized as such. If it is, but the intended meaning of the word is not made clear through stipulation or additional contextual information, the interpreter will be unable to decide which of the word's possible senses should be understood. He may be fully aware of the alternative meanings of the utterance resulting from the lexical ambiguity; but if he chooses not to commit himself to one of the alternative interpretations, if he prefers to remain neutral and refuses even to make a guess as to which meaning was intended, he cannot be said to have understood the utterance in any real sense according to its intent. The communication attempt has failed through the interpreter's non-understanding. If, on the other hand, he does choose one of the alternatives and guesses correctly, well and good; if he guesses wrongly, the communication attempt has failed through misunderstanding.

This latter case is the same in its effect as the situation which arises when a given lexical ambiguity is NOT recognized as such. Not realizing that a lexical ambiguity has occurred which affects the meaning of the whole utterance, the interpreter may inadvertantly choose a meaning not intended by the speaker and thus misunderstand the utterance.

When a communication attempt fails through non-understanding, the interpreter is usually aware of the failure (though the awareness may be only a fleeting impression in an on-going stream of discourse, and he may be unable to isolate the cause of the failure). If he is able to pinpoint the cause of difficulty, he can ask the speaker to stipulate what he intends for the ambiguous word to mean.

When a communication attempt fails through misunderstanding, the interpreter will never be aware that the failure has occurred unless some subsequent action, situation, or utterance reveals to him that he has interpreted the ambiguous utterance wrongly. This applies equally whether the ambiguity is initially recognized or not. In those cases mentioned above in which the interpreter is aware of the ambiguity but decides to follow one of the possible interpretations rather than remain neutral, he will never know (if nothing occurs subsequently to inform him) that he has guessed wrongly. And in those cases – probably much more frequent – in which the interpreter is not aware that an ambiguity is present, he will have no reason to doubt (unless there is some future test of his interpretation) that he has understood the utterance perfectly. It is sobering to think that there may be more instances of unsuspected misunderstanding in this world than are dreamt of in our complacency.

8.2.4 *Homophonic Ambiguity*

In § 8.2.2 we saw evidence of Carroll's consciousness of the capacity of words to have multiple significations and his awareness that, if confusion is to be prevented, men in general must realize that words are capable of multiple definition. The word *scales*, for example, potentially has many possible interpretations in conventional usage, as do *fast, strong, singular, more, with, why,* and *it*. These words can be ambiguous in either spoken or written discourse; but there is a type of lexical ambiguity which is possible only in a speech context: that produced by homophones, different words which sound the same. Homophones deceive the ear but not the eye, for they usually have different forms when represented in writing. In *Wonderland*, we see Carroll's use of homophonic ambiguity particularly well in three instances. The first occurs when the Mouse is about to recite his personal history.

"Mine is a long and a sad tale!" said the Mouse, turning to Alice, and sighing.
    "It *is* a long tail, certainly," said Alice, looking down with wonder at the Mouse's tail; "but why do you call it sad?" And she kept on puzzling about it while the Mouse was speaking . . .

After talking for a moment, the Mouse breaks off impatiently:

"You are not attending!" said the Mouse to Alice severely. "What are you thinking of?"
    "I beg your pardon," said Alice very humbly: "you had got to the fifth bend, I think?"
    "I had *not*!" cried the Mouse, sharply and very angrily.
    "A knot!" said Alice, always ready to make herself useful, and looking anxiously about her. "Oh, do let me help to undo it!"
    "I shall do nothing of the sort," said the Mouse, getting up and walking away. "You insult me by talking such nonsense!"

(*Works*, pp. 39-41)

At the Knave of Hearts' trial, the King falls prey to homophonic ambiguity:

"I'm a poor man, your Majesty," the Hatter began, in a trembling voice, "and I hadn't begun my tea – not above a week or so – and what with the bread-and-butter getting so thin – and the twinkling of the tea –"
    "The twinkling of *what*?" said the King.
    "It *began* with the tea," the Hatter replied.
    "Of course twinkling *begins* with a T!" said the King sharply. "Do you take me for a dunce? Go on!"

(*Works*, p. 119)

In each of these three illustrations some adverse consequence follows from the hearer's mistaking the uttered word for another of identical sound and thus interpreting the whole utterance in a manner not intended by the speaker. In the first, Alice is puzzled by the Mouse's calling his tail "sad", and her misunderstanding of the word *tale* affects her view of his history: as he proceeds, and she continues to puzzle about his "tail", she visualizes his tale as a winding narrative tail-like in configuration (emblematically represented in Carroll's text as a zig-zag column with type decreasing in size toward the bottom of the page). Her misunderstanding of *tale* does not become apparent to the Mouse; as far as he can tell, she understands him perfectly. This type of communication failure, which occurs and runs its logical course without either party ever being made aware of the misunderstanding, may have consequences ranging from comic to grave. Although Carroll has treated the matter in a humorous fashion, and there are no profound consequences in this instance, the illustration – by showing that such a type of unsuspected misunderstanding CAN result from homophonic ambiguity – is quite serious in its implications. In the second illustration and, to a lesser extent, in the third, the consequences of the interpreters' misunderstanding of the ambiguous words are more immediately serious: communication breaks down completely, and tempers flare. Alice mistakes the Mouse's word *not* for *knot*; and he, not following her thought but retaining his own intended meaning for the sound-sequence, takes her *knot* for *not*. From his point of view, when she says "Let me help to undo it!", she IS talking nonsense; and he becomes angry at what he takes to be an insult to his intelligence. The King reacts similarly to the Hatter's *T* – a misunderstanding potentially quite dangerous for the Hatter.

8.2.5 *The Inherent Ambiguity of Comparative Terms*

A further cause of misunderstanding brought about through lexical ambiguity is the equivocal nature of certain words whose primary meanings are to be interpreted comparatively. Such words as *tall, dark, heavy, old,* and *fast* (conveying the idea of speed) are relative terms (see § 4.4.5). Their specific meanings will vary with the user's conception of tallness, darkness, and so on, and with the interpreter's conception also. Thus, what might be considered heavy by one man might be considered light by another. The physical context, too, affects the word's meaning in a given instance of use. A fifty-pound sack of flour might be called "heavy", but not as "heavy" as a hundred-pound sack would be called. A speed of forty miles per hour was considered "fast" in the early days of the automobile, but today it is "slow" in comparison with a rate of ninety miles per hour. Moreover, what would be considered a "fast" speed for an automobile today is negligible in comparison with the speed of a jet airliner. It may be seen how easily misunderstanding could arise from two people's using one of these comparative terms in different senses. If the specific meaning which the word was intended to have were not stipulated by the user, misunderstanding might occur through the interpreter's taking the word according to his own frame of reference; if he then used the word to represent HIS meaning without stipulation, the original user might in turn misunderstand him.

Lewis Carroll was conscious of the equivocal nature of comparative terms. In his *Eight or Nine Wise Words about Letter Writing* (1890), he says,

Remember the old proverb "*Cross-writing makes cross reading.*" "The *old* proverb?" you say, inquiringly. "*How* old?" Well, not so *very* ancient, I must confess. In fact, I'm afraid I invented it while writing this paragraph! Still, you know, "old" is a *comparative* term. I think you would be *quite* justified in addressing a chicken, just out of the shell, as "Old boy!", *when compared* with another chicken, that was only half-out!

(*Works*, p. 1217)

In *Through the Looking-Glass* when the Red Queen objects to Alice's use of the word *garden* to refer to the plot of ground outside of Looking-Glass House, she suggests that general names too may be comparative terms capable of multiple definition.

"when you say 'garden' – *I've* seen gardens, compared with which this would be a wilderness."
Alice didn't dare to argue the point, but went on: "–and I thought I'd try and find my way to the top of that hill –"
"When you say 'hill,'" the Queen interrupted, "*I* could show you hills, in comparison with which you'd call that a valley."
"No, I shouldn't," said Alice, surprised into contradicting her at last: "a hill *ca'n't* be a valley, you know. That would be nonsense –"
The Red Queen shook her head. "You may call it 'nonsense' if you like," she said, "but *I've* heard nonsense, compared with which that would be as sensible as a dictionary!"

(*Works*, pp. 162-163)

The word *garden* designates a plot of ground which has undergone a certain degree of cultivation; but, as word, it does not specify how much cultivation. The name may be legitimately applied to many plots of ground, varying in their degrees of cultivation from those whose paths are laid out with geometric precision and whose hedges are trimmed into ornamental shapes, to those which have been allowed to "run wild" and retain an uncultivated appearance. Alice, it will be noticed, does not disagree with the Queen's assertion that the word *garden* is a comparative term. She does, however, take issue with the statement that a hill can be called a "valley" for reasons which were discussed in § 6.3.6. If the Queen had said, "I could show you hills in comparison with which you'd call that a mountain", she might have gotten a less violent response from Alice, since *hill* and *mountain* both refer to the same KIND of object and merely differentiate (in their informative connotations) degrees of size and elevation above the surrounding territory. In practice, it might be difficult to say whether a given outcropping should be called a "hill" or a "mountain". When do hills, on the basis of size, cease to be "hills" and become "mountains"? Although there is a difference between the informative connotations of *hill* and *mountain*, this difference is one of degree rather than kind. However, the difference between the connotations of *hill* and *valley* is one of kind rather than degree: the attributes respectively possessed by hills and valleys stand in a relationship of opposition. Whereas a mountain might conceivably be called a "large hill", a valley could not logically be called any sort of hill. *Nonsense* in its literal signification admits of no degrees: a statement either makes logical sense or it does not. If the Queen has heard nonsense in comparison with which the self-contradictory *hills can be valleys* is "as sensible as a dictionary", one would very much like to know exactly what sort of statement she has in mind.

In *Sylvie and Bruno Concluded* (1893) Arthur Forester is made to comment upon the comparative force of the word *good*. Present by implication in this passage is an awareness on Carroll's part of the rather serious misunderstandings which could arise from men's confusing the word's many possible significations. Arthur points out two fallacies in the trite sentiment that a rich man often does "good" by employing people who would otherwise be out of work, and that this is "better" than pauperizing them by merely giving them money. The first is the "fallacy of *ambiguity* – the assumption that '*doing good*' (that is, benefiting somebody) is necessarily *a good thing to do* (that is, a *right* thing)". The second is "the assumption that, if one of two specified acts is *better* than another, it is necessarily a *good* act in itself". He calls this second assumption an example of "the fallacy of *comparison* – meaning that it assumes that what is *comparatively* good is therefore *positively* good", and goes on to say,

Nothing illustrates a fallacy so well as an extreme case, which fairly comes under it. Suppose I find two children drowning in a pond. I rush in, and save one of the children, and then walk away, leaving the other to drown. Clearly I have '*done good*,' in saving a child's life? But –. Again, supposing I meet an inoffensive stranger, and knock him down, and walk on. Clearly that is '*better*' than if I had proceeded to jump upon him and break his ribs? But –"

(*Works*, p. 547)

Words which refer to some abstract quality, such as *good, bad, evil, ugly, handsome, beautiful, nice, wise, happy,* and *stupid* have, in their comparative force, a multiplicity of possible meanings that can be overlooked by users and interpreters. As Arthur demonstrates, they can be quite misleading if carelessly used, since they characterize their specific subjects only in comparison with something else which could be characterized by the same word. When confronted with such words, interpreters must attempt to determine both the immediate signification which the user has in mind, and the implied comparison. Such words tend not to characterize the thing of which the quality is predicated in any absolute sense, but merely to indicate their users' attitudes toward the thing designated as "good", "bad", "beautiful", or "stupid". Delusion arises when an interpreter takes the word to characterize the thing in an absolute sense, and loses sight of its comparative force and its reflection of the user's attitude toward the thing.

8.3 SYNTACTIC AMBIGUITY

Words are equivocal for a variety of reasons: some because they have acquired a multiplicity of significations through conventional usage over long periods of time; some because of phonetic similarity with other words; some, such as pronouns, because of inherent vagueness unless they are given a specific referent by verbal or physical contexts; some because they have only a relative signification; and some because of their intensely personal connotations. Words which are equivocal in their potential significations when viewed in isolation from any context can become ambiguous when put into contexts that do not make their intended signification clear. But it is not only words that can produce ambiguities in discourse: sentence structure, too, can make entire utterances equivocal. Syntactic ambiguity serving humorous ends is not found to any great extent in the writings of Lewis Carroll. He seems to have avoided it for some reason, though of course, being a logician, he was quite aware of its being a potential cause of misunderstanding. There is one example of syntactic ambiguity in a letter to Ethel Hatch of August 19, 1884. He ends the letter with:

LOVE TO BE

(This doesn't mean "future love" – nor does it mean "lavish all your affection on the verb "to be" [sic] – and BE isn't short for "Beatrice.")

(*Letters to Child-friends*, p. 189)

As the editor, Evelyn Hatch, interprets it, 'BE' stands for 'Beatrice and Evelyn', the names being those of Ethel's two sisters (*Letters to Child-friends*, p. 186). Other examples of syntactic ambiguity already noted occur in Bruno's account of his seeing the Goat "singing with its long beard" and in the Duck's misinterpreting the Mouse's word *it* to signify an object, such as a frog or worm, which the archbishop found. It may be seen from these examples that ambiguous syntax may force a word in the sentence to become ambiguous also. Syntactic and lexical meaning are closely related. 'With' becomes ambiguous when placed in conjunction with 'singing', whereas it would not have been so if placed in the vicinity of 'Goat'. In the example above, the equivocal nature of 'BE' causes the entire phrase to become ambiguous. Had Carroll written "LOVE TO BEA" or "LOVE TO BEATRICE/EVELYN", the phrase could not possibly have meant "future love" or "lavish all your affection on the verb 'to be' ". The logical import of a whole utterance is often determined by a close interaction of the words and the syntax; lexical or syntactic ambiguity can easily produce ambiguity of import for the entire sentence.

8.4 CONTEXTUAL AMBIGUITY; CONSCIOUS EQUIVOCATION WITH THE INTENTION OF DECEIVING

Of more concern to Lewis Carroll than purely syntactic ambiguity were problems of interpretation which arise from the logical import of whole utterances, particularly ambiguities of sense which stem from the speaker's conscious manipulation of language to deceive the interpreter. On May 4, 1849, when he was seventeen, he wrote to his sister Elizabeth about an example of dissembling he had come upon in Macaulay's *History of England*.

I have not yet been able to get the 2nd vol: Macaulay's *England* to read: I have seen it however & one passage struck me when 7 bishops signed the invitation to the pretender, & King James sent for Bishop Compton (who was one of the 7) and asked him 'whether he or any of his ecclesiastical brethren had had anything to do with it?' He replied after a moment's thought, 'I am fully persuaded, your majesty, that there is not one of my brethren who is not as innocent as myself.' This was certainly no actual lie, but certainly as Macaulay says, it was very little different from one. On the next day the King called a meeting of all the bishops, when Compton was present, but the other 6 absented themselves. He then for form's sake put the question to each of them 'whether they had had anything to do with it?' Here was a new difficulty which Compton got over by saying, when it came to his turn, 'I gave your lordship *my* answer yesterday.' It certainly showed talent, though exerted in the wrong direction . . .

(Diaries, I, p. 17)

The type of equivocation indulged in by Bishop Compton evidently fascinated Carroll, for thirteen years later the guards in *Alice's Adventures under Ground* resort to the same method of self-defense when they have been unable to find the Queen of Hearts' gardeners. Ordered to behead the gardeners, they search fruitlessly for them, not realizing that Alice has put them in her pocket (in *Wonderland* she hides them under a flowerpot). When the Queen shouts, "Are their heads off?", the soldiers, fearing for their own, evade the question by answering, "Their heads are gone, if it please your Majesty!"

Carroll himself indulged in equivocation in a series of letters to Ella Monier-Williams, daughter of the Sanskrit scholar, written in 1873. He had borrowed her journal of her Continental tour, and she his; he then played an elaborate joke on her by convincing her that he had arranged to have excerpts from her diary published in *The Monthly Packet*. Extracts from three letters reveal Carroll's skill at equivocation:

MY DEAR ELLA,

I return your book with many thanks: you will be wondering why I kept it so long. I . . . hope you will not be annoyed at my sending three short chapters of extracts from it, to be published in *The Monthly Packet*. I have not given any names in full, nor put any more definite title to it than simply "Ella's Diary, or The Experiences of an Oxford Professor's Daughter, during a Month of Foreign Travel."

I will faithfully hand over to you any money I may receive on account of it, from Miss Yonge . . .

. . . .

[Extract from next letter:]

I grieve to tell you that *every word of my letter was strictly true*. I will now tell you more – that Miss Yonge *has not declined* the MS., but she will not give more than a guinea a chapter. Will that be enough?

. . . .

[Extract from next letter:]

I'm afraid I have hoaxed you too much. But it really was true. I "hoped you wouldn't by annoyed at my etc.," for the very good reason that I hadn't done it. And I gave no *other* title than "Ella's Diary," nor did I give *that* title. Miss Yonge hasn't declined it – because she hasn't seen it. And I need hardly explain that she hasn't given more than three guineas!

(Letters to Child-Friends, pp. 88-89)

The ambiguity of this type of equivocation resides in the whole utterance: when, though the literal sense of the statement is true, the interpreter is misled by the context and apparent import of the sentence, and by his own expectation (the psychological context, engendered by the equivocator), to understand something other than what the sentence literally states. Desiring to deceive his audience, the equivocator takes advantage of and capitalizes on the interpreter's set of expectations which are a function of the context of discourse; he achieves this expectation in the interpreter by choosing words which convey connotations above and beyond the literal imports they would normally have. Thus the Queen of Hearts' soldiers, knowing that she is expecting the gardeners to have been beheaded, use the word *gone*, assuming that she will take it in its equivocal sense of 'removed' instead of in its equally legitimate (and literally true) sense, 'not present'. Bishop Compton relies upon the affective connotations of the word *innocent* to give the king the impression that he is saying that he is not guilty; analysis of the statement reveals that he has not asserted his innocence at all, nor has he admitted his and the other bishops' guilt. The sentence as spoken conveys no information at all as to the guilt or innocence of the men as a group. The bishop's statement could have been expressed, "I am fully persuaded that all of my brethren are as innocent as myself", and still have been equivocal in its context. But it would not have had the equivocal force of the negative statement which he gives: "I am fully persuaded that there is not one of my brethren who is not as innocent as myself." In the first place, it approaches much closer to being an outright lie, since *innocence* is stressed; and in the second, the double use of *not* both clouds the import of what he is saying and reinforces the connotation he is hoping to establish in the king's mind of "not guilty".

In Carroll's equivocation with Ella Monier-Williams, the verbal context he establishes in the first letter prepares the girl psychologically to take his sending of her diary to *The Monthly Packet* as an accomplished fact. Once that assumption has been fixed in her mind, the rest of his statements will not be taken literally, but in such manner as to fit that context. In conventional usage, when someone says, "I hope you will not be annoyed at my sending x", we commonly understand the statement to mean "I have sent or am going to send x, and I hope that you will not be annoyed at my doing so". When he says, "I have not given any names in full," we assume that he has given some in part – not that he has given none at all. And when he says, "I have not put any more definite title to it than 'z'", we assume that 'z' has been given it as a title. If not, why should the statement be made at all? Carroll's promise to send Ella whatever money Charlotte Yonge pays for the manuscript merely reinforces the notion of a *fait accompli*.

In the second letter Carroll is backing off a bit, for Ella had evidently expressed surprise or dismay in her intervening letter. He underlines his equivocal expression to call attention to it; and as a result, the literal sense of 'has not declined' obtrudes more than the literal sense of the deceptive expressions in the first letter. 'Miss Yonge HAS NOT DECLINED the MS.' would suggest to a thoughtful person that it is not certain that she has accepted it, either. The matter-of-fact statement about her giving not more than a guinea a chapter tips the scales away from the growing doubt that she has accepted it to a more neutral position – that, if she hasn't declined it and perhaps not accepted it, she may be withholding her decision until payment can be settled. Ella seems to have become excited about the prospect of becoming a published author, for Carroll is moved in his last letter to explain the hoax in a somewhat apologetic fashion [the editor, Evelyn Hatch, says, "At first she was not taken in, but was convinced by his next letter that his statement must be true. Naturally she felt some disappointment at the final explanation, but in the end she could not help laughing with him over the joke" (*Letters to Child-friends*, p. 87). Ella's own account, accurately summarized by Hatch, is found in Collingwood's *The Lewis Carroll Picture Book*, pp. 224-228.]

Negative expression is important to the equivocations of both Bishop Compton and Lewis Carroll. It is true that if Charlotte Yonge has accepted the manuscript, she has not declined it; but her not declining it does not necessarily indicate that she has accepted it. 'I have not given any names in full' does not indicate that some have been given in part. 'She will not give more than a guinea a chapter' does not indicate that she WILL give a guinea a chapter – or anything at all, for that matter. A person who sets out to equivocate may often insure his success by using the negative form of expression in a literal fashion; in conventional usage, people commonly take the sense of a qualified negative to signify the truth of a tacit affirmative not covered by the qualification.

8.5 SAFEGUARDS AGAINST AMBIGUITY
IN COMMUNICATION ATTEMPTS

While Carroll saw that the equivocal nature of most words and some syntactic structures provides the possibility for the creation of ambiguity by people who intend to deceive, he realized that most ambiguity occurs not through willful deception, but through accident. He saw that inadvertent ambiguity could largely be avoided by greater care and precision in the use of words and the framing of sentences. In *Eight or Nine Wise Words about Letter Writing*, he cautions his readers:

... if it should ever occur to you to write, jestingly, in *dispraise* of your friend, be sure you exaggerate enough to make the jesting *obvious*: a word spoken in *jest*, but taken as earnest, may lead to very serious consequences. I have known it to lead to the breaking-off of a friendship. Suppose, for instance, you wish to remind your friend of a sovereign you have lent him, which he has forgotten to repay – you might quite *mean* the words "I mention it, as you seem to have a conveniently bad memory for debts," in jest; yet there would be nothing to wonder at if he took offence at that way of putting it. But, suppose you wrote "Long observation of your career, as a pickpocket and a burglar, has convinced me that my one lingering hope, for recovering that sovereign I lent you, is to say 'Pay up, or I'll summons yer!'" he would indeed be a matter-of-fact friend if he took *that* as seriously meant!

(*Works*, pp. 1216-17)

To be responsible users of language, men must be aware of the ability of language to create ambiguity of import. If they wish to communicate, they must see to it that their intended meaning is clear to potential interpreters. The intended significations of inherently equivocal words and sentences must be made explicit, whether by means of stipulative definition, careful establishment of verbal contexts, or – as in the above quotation – psychological preparation of the interpreter through some device such as unmistakable exaggeration. If these precautions are not observed, ambiguity may arise in discourse; if it does, and is recognized as such, the interpreter will be puzzled as to which of the possible meanings is the one intended (though he may ask the user to stipulate his meaning if he is present); if it is not recognized, the interpreter may unwittingly choose a meaning not intended by the speaker and thus misunderstand the utterance.

Implicit in Carroll's illustrations of misunderstanding caused by ambiguity is an awareness of the necessity for users of language to scrutinize their language closely. In the words of Peter Alexander,

... language is the vehicle of logic, the matter in which the form is embodied, and, as certain philosophers never tire of pointing out, perhaps with some truth, can mislead us because it was not invented simply to exhibit logical forms. A language invented for such a purpose would have no ambiguous words, every word would have a quite fixed and definite meaning; all play on words and much poetry would be impossible. It is no wonder, then, that much of Carroll's humour should arise from an exploitation of such ambiguities, of the ways in which we may be misled by our language, perhaps as a warning against being so misled.[4]

I think that Carroll may have been issuing a warning to his readers about the pitfalls which language provides for its users. Certainly I would agree with Derek Hudson's opinion that "no child can read *Alice* without gaining an increased understanding of the importance of words" – the concrete effect of "a message that came naturally from a student of language and logic: 'Pay attention to what you are saying!'"[5] But Carroll's paramount aim was to delight and entertain, not (in his earlier works, at least) to admonish and instruct. He saw that language, by virtue

---

[4] Alexander, p. 556.
[5] Derek Hudson, *Lewis Carroll* (= *Writers and Their Work Series*, No. 96) (London, Longmans, Green, 1958), p. 23.

of its inherent potential for creating ambiguities and of its illogical conventions of usage, was an admirable vehicle, ready to hand, for creating humorous situations in his works and for providing tests for his young readers' ingenuity.

As Alexander suggests, language was not invented to exhibit logical forms; it developed in a somewhat haphazard fashion over thousands of years, changing continually to fit the current needs of its users. Because of the nature of its historical development, ordinary language is not well suited for strictly logical discourse (Cf. § 4.1.1). Words are equivocal in their potential meanings, syntax can produce ambiguity, intended meaning is not always reflected in the literal sense of the linguistic forms chosen to express it. Hence the need, seen in the nineteenth century by such men as Boole and met constructively in the twentieth by a host of logicians, to create a new language capable of removing from statements the possibility of ambiguity. The elaborate and self-contained system represented by modern symbolic logic was invented to express the MEANING of propositions and arguments in such manner as to avoid the pitfalls of vagueness and ambiguity inherent in the linguistic forms of ordinary language. As Irving Copi has phrased it,

Arguments formulated in English or in any other natural language are often difficult to appraise because of the vague and equivocal nature of the words in which they are expressed, the ambiguity of their construction, the misleading idioms they may contain, and their pleasing but deceptive metaphorical style. . . . The special symbols of modern logic permit us to exhibit with greater clarity the logical structures of propositions and arguments which may be obscured by their formulation in ordinary language. It is an easier task to divide arguments into the valid and the invalid when they are expressed in a special symbolic language, for in it the peripheral problems of vagueness, ambiguity, idiom, metaphor, and amphiboly do not arise.[6]

Lewis Carroll's experiments with symbolic logic were different in kind from the investigations of twentieth-century logicians and are not the main subject of this study. Nonetheless he was quite aware of the various problems which language presents to thought and communication that have continued to occupy the attention of modern logicians. The problems resulting from ambiguity were among those that intrigued him most.

[6]   Irving M. Copi, *Symbolic Logic* (New York, 1954), pp. 7-8.

9

SOUND AND SENSE

"The game's going on rather better now," [Alice] said ...

"'Tis so," said the Duchess: "and the moral of that is – 'Oh, 'tis love, 'tis love, that makes the world go round!' "

"Somebody said," Alice whispered, "that it's done by everybody minding their own business!"

"Ah, well! It means much the same thing," said the Duchess, ... "and the moral of *that* is – 'Take care of the sense, and the sounds will take care of themselves.' "

. . . .

"I quite agree with you," said the Duchess; "and the moral of that is – 'Be what you would seem to be' – or, if you'd like it put more simply – 'Never imagine yourself not to be otherwise than what it might appear to others that what you were or might have been was not otherwise than what you had been would have appeared to them to be otherwise.' "

"I think I should understand that better," Alice said very politely, "if I had it written down: but I ca'n't quite follow it as you say it."

Alice's Adventures in Wonderland, Chapter IX

9.1 THE IMPORT OF STATEMENTS

9.1.1 *Introductory: Ways of Viewing Import*

As was pointed out in § 4.4.1, an utterance, such as a statement of predication, has a unitary signification in its own right which, though ultimately comprised of the sum total of the individual significations of the various types of linguistic signs that constitute it (on all of the sequential and incremental levels of interpretation), is to be conceived as having its own unique integrity. The whole utterance, then, functions as a sign-vehicle which, upon interpretation, gives rise to a sign of such and such a specific signification. If the utterance is a statement of predication, this unitary signification may be called the statement's IMPORT. The present chapter deals in part with Lewis Carroll's interest in the ability of statements to have, by virtue of their linguistic form, imports for interpreters which are divergent from those which the speaker intended them to convey.

There are several ways of viewing the concept of 'import'. From the point of view of their semantic 'content' (the message which they impart), statements may have both LITERAL IMPORT and IDIOMATIC IMPORT. The first is what a statement signifies by virtue of the peculiar linguistic forms which comprise it, each form being interpreted according to its usual primary sense, or general acceptation, in conventional usage. The words are understood in terms of their lexical definitions (those which are commonly and typically accepted by the speech community at large), and the syntactic patterns likewise according to their conventionalized significations. Idiomatic import, on the other hand, is what a statement signifies by virtue of certain peculiar conventions of usage pertaining to it AS PARTICULAR STATE-MENT. There are certain expressions which are recognized by members of the speech community as individual items in the language, subject, by convention, to a specific and particular mode of interpretation. The standardized signification which convention prescribes for such an expression is the expression's idiomatic import.

All statements have literal import; not all have idiomatic import. And frequently literal and idiomatic import for a given statement do not coincide. Two examples are *He is a rolling stone* and the current hipster expression *I'm nowhere*. In the first, the literal import is that "he" is being equated to a rock proceeding forward along a surface by axial rotation; the idiomatic import, that "he" is a restless wanderer unable to settle down and make something of himself. In the second, the literal import is an assertion that the speaker exists in no location – in interpreta-tion which would be regarded as nonsensical; the idiomatic import, that the speaker is 'out of it', 'squaresville', unable to 'swing', fit in with, or relate to a given situation. A statement such as 'Lewis Carroll died in 1898' has literal import, but not idiomatic import, as I've defined the latter term. Expressions which have idiomatic import frequently deviate in form from the habitually encountered structures of the language. Idiomatic import tends to diverge radically from the literal import of those expressions which possess it; and it may be a function of syntax (*I'm going too*, AREN'T I ?; *the bigger the better*), of lexicon (*the last remark but one*; *Tuesday week*; *every other day*, meaning 'alternate days'), of irony and metaphor (*he could care less!*, meaning 'he doesn't care at all'; *she's a dog*, meaning 'ugly'; *he's dead*, meaning 'extremely tired').

Another way of viewing import is from the standpoint of statements' functioning as vehicles for communication attempts. In the framework of a communication attempt, a statement has two types of import: the signification which the speaker structures his utterance to convey is the statement's INTENDED IMPORT; the significa-tion which that utterance has for the interpreter is the statement's RECEIVED IMPORT. If, in a given communication attempt, intended and received import coincide, communication has occurred. We have already seen in Chapter Eight that intended import and received import do not always coincide (i.e., that attempts at communi-cation sometimes fail) because of vagueness in the utterance itself, because of lexical and syntactic ambiguity, or because of the interpreter's response to the affective connotations incidentally embodied in the utterance rather than to its literal import. The present chapter will deal in part with the breakdowns of communication attempts that come about because of the speaker's failure to frame his utterance in such manner as to convey his intended import.

A third way of looking at a statement's import is in terms of the sign-process. Although it is functionally meaningless to talk of the signification of a statement without assuming an interpreter who has performed an act of interpretation (since a sign cannot exist until the sign-vehicle has been interpreted), it IS the case that an utterance is framed to BE interpreted; and, since statements have this quality of potential interpretability, it is meaningful, I think, to talk of a statement's POTENTIAL IMPORT as it exists prior to any specific act of interpretation that is performed. This is to postulate the existence of the utterance as linguistic form (having been uttered by the speaker with an intended import for it in mind), as an articulated body of code-elements subject to conventional explication. As linguistic form, framed according to the conventions of the speech community with regard to lexicon and syntax, it has, in its own right, a potential import (literal and perhaps idiomatic) in terms of conventional usage. Until it is interpreted by a second party, its import(s) must be regarded as potential only, and not realized. When an act of interpretation occurs, this potential import becomes actual: and the resulting signification is the statement's received import. If a speaker frames his statement in such manner that its potential literal import does not, according to conventional standards of usage, coincide with the import he intended it to convey, the interpreter's received import, derived in accordance with those standards, will not coincide with the intended import. Thus it may be said that statements, once uttered, have potentially a literal import, based on linguistic convention, which is independent of the speaker's intended import. Potential import, prescribed by the conventions of usage that govern interpretation, thus may or may not coincide with what the speaker had in mind for his utterance to convey.

9.1.2 *The Responsibility of Speakers to Make Their Intended Import Clear*

Words can be made to mean whatever the user chooses. Thus, to Humpty Dumpty, *glory* means 'a nice knock-down argument'; to the White Knight, *fast* signifies 'all kinds of fastness'. As with words, so with statements. To the Duchess in the passage quoted above, the statement *'tis love that makes the world go round* is equivalent in meaning to *it's everybody minding their own business that makes the world go round*. The Duchess is free to stipulate that *love* is equivalent in meaning to *everybody minding their own business*, but her definition of *love* is highly subjective. Not everyone would agree that the two statements mean "much the same thing". Still, if she does define *love* to mean 'everybody minding their own business', for her the word does mean that, regardless of how others might disagree. On the basis of general usage, the standard against which the potential import of all statements in ordinary language must be measured, the two propositions have quite divergent significations since their respective literal imports are different. If communication is to occur, conventions must be observed; for in the absence of a peculiar stipulation of intended meaning, interpreters will take statements according to their conventionalized literal import unless they recognize the utterance as one of those exceptional cases having idiomatic import.

In view of the Duchess' own logical difficulties and loose use of language throughout her conversation with Alice, one should take her assertions about the nature of language with considerable reservations. There is, however, a grain of truth in her comment about sounds and sense (modeled upon the adage, "Take care of the pence, and the pounds will take care of themselves"). To the extent that, for purposes of communication, men must embody their ideas in sound-sequences which have been given specific significations agreed upon by users of the language, sound (the linguistic forms) does follow from sense (the ideas to be imparted), and sense is embodied in sound. The Duchess' comment has some value as a rule for making communication possible: a person must know what he intends to say before he can find the proper sounds to convey his thought. However, since language itself can obscure a speaker's intended meaning even when there is no conscious effort on his part to deceive, it is not sufficient for a person merely to know what he means to say and to assume that the linguistic forms that comprise his utterance will function automatically to convey his meaning to others. He must also say what he means: he must select the proper sound-sequences and express them in a form that will not mislead his listeners. In other words, it is not sufficient for a speaker to 'take care of his own sense' (i.e., to determine what he wishes to convey) and frame his utterance so as to be clear to himself, paying no special heed to the signs which are to represent his thought to others. For sounds will not necessarily 'take care of themselves' in making his sense clear to a given listener. If, on the other hand, the speaker gives due attention to the sense of his utterance, making sure that the words and syntax do represent his intended import accurately according to the conventions of usage, the sounds (linguistic forms) of the utterance WILL "take care of themselves" and, through their literal import, convey his meaning to an interpreter who is knowledgeable in the conventions of the language's use.

The Duchess' intended import for the expression *Be what you would seem to be* may or may not be accurately embodied in the alternative statement *Never imagine yourself not to be otherwise* ... (I leave the final judgment to the symbolic logicians); but whether it is or is not potentially, the latter utterance does not convey that meaning to Alice. The statement's syntax, its confusing repetition of words, and its excessive use of negative constructions merely bewilder her; she is not able to interpret it at all, and thus is denied access to a received import. The Duchess may know what she intends the sentence to signify, but she has not "taken care" of the sense of the utterance, its potential literal import. Since her word choice and syntax are an obstacle to communication, since she has not made the sense of the utterance clear, the sounds are not able to "take care of themselves" and convey even their own literal import (let alone the Duchess' intended import) to Alice. Functionally, the sentence is nonsensical to Alice; it is doubtful that she could understand it any better if she COULD see it written down.

9.1.3 *Equivalence of Import in Verbally Dissimilar Statements*

Usually, however, utterances used in attempts at communication do have literal import that can be ascertained. And as is the case with words, two or more of which can designate the same referent, statements may, in spite of verbal dissimilarity, embody the same signification. In *Wonderland*, for example, Alice finds herself in a hallway lined with locked doors and attempts to open them with a golden key which she discovers on a table. "But alas!" says Carroll, "either the locks were too large, or the key was too small, but at any rate it would not open any of them" (*Works*, p. 21). This is another of Carroll's jokes on his readers; for by means of the disjunctive formula, *either . . . or*, he sets up an expectation in the reader's mind to have alternative reasons presented for Alice's being unable to unlock the doors: "She could not open the doors because either *x* or *y*." Actually, however, the two 'reasons' given are functionally equivalent in their explanation of the difficulty. Although the literal imports of the two statements offered as alternatives are indeed different – *the key was too small* [for the locks]; *the locks were too large* [for the key] – the statements each signify precisely the same relationship of incongruity existing between the key and the locks. Since the relationship designated is the same in each case, the LOGICAL IMPORT of the two expressions is equivalent. Since both statements have the same logical import, there is no disjunction as Carroll implies by means of his conventional formula: the alternatives offered are merely '*z*' and '*z*'. This is not to say that the literal imports of the two statements is the same. One stresses the key's inability to open the locks, the other stresses the locks' inability to be tumbled by the key. Dissimilarity of literal import in two statements does not necessarily affect their equivalence in logical import.

Another example of this type occurs in *Sylvie and Bruno*. The Professor asks the children what they had for dinner.

"A little piece of a dead crow," was Bruno's mournful reply.
"He means rook-pie," Sylvie explained.
"It *were* a dead crow," Bruno persisted.

(Works, p. 372)

A little piece of a dead crow and *rook-pie* are two names which in this context designate a single referent: the meat-dish which Sylvie and Bruno had for dinner. They therefore have identical significations. Although the literal imports of the two statements, *We had a piece of a dead crow for dinner* and *We had rook-pie for dinner,* are different since the lexical definitions (and the informative connotations) of the two names are different, the statements have logical imports which are equivalent IN THIS CONTEXT. Sylvie's definition of *a little piece of a dead crow* as 'rook-pie' is not as subjective as the Duchess' definition of *love* as 'everybody minding their own business'. The Duchess' definition of *love* is a personal and arbitrary stipulation. Sylvie's definition of Bruno's term is merely a statement of the conventional name used in polite society for "a piece of a dead crow" cooked and served in such and such a manner; and it is given to "explain" for the Professor Bruno's idiosyncratic name for the dish, which is so unconventional as to be misleading (she may also be attempting, through the substitution of a name less explicit in its informative connotations, to shield herself from the realization that she has been eating dead crow). The logical import of Sylvie's and Bruno's respective statements is simply: "There is an x, such that x is crow-meat that we had for dinner." It is true that the lexical signification of *a piece of a dead crow* is not the same as that of *rook-pie*. Sylvie's term includes the meaning of Bruno's, for rooks baked into pies are presumably dead. The informative connotations of *rook-pie* include the deadness of the crow, the quality of the pie's being cooked, and perhaps (for a given eater of rook-pies) something about the form, appearance, and taste of the dish. The informative connotations of *a little piece of a dead crow* do not include the crow's being an ingredient in a pie or being cooked. Nor is there any indication as to what part of the crow is designated by *a little piece*. The affective connotations of the two names, the emotional associations which the names hold for interpreters, are markedly different. Bruno's name for the article of food is potentially highly charged with unpleasant associations for persons accustomed to referring to the dish by its conventional and rather neutral name. The name *rook-pie*, though somewhat descriptive of the object to anyone who has tasted that article of food, would probably possess for most people no other affective connotations than "I like it" or "I don't like it" – for the name superficially obscures the fact, which would be decidedly repugnant to many people, that the dish so designated is actually dead crow.

Although the statements implied in the answers of Sylvie and Bruno, while literally different, are identical in logical import, such is not the case with the two statements which Alice encounters on the finger-posts pointing respectively "TO TWEEDLEDUM'S HOUSE" and "TO THE HOUSE OF TWEEDLEDEE". Let us assume for the sake of this discussion that the two pointers do indeed designate the same location. Regardless of their designating the same building, the posts bear statements which are divergent in literal import. One says '[This sign points] TO TWEEDLEDUM'S HOUSE', and the other '[This sign points] TO THE HOUSE OF TWEEDLEDEE'. We may disregard the grammatical dissimilarity in the names of the two houses, since it represents merely alternative forms of the genitive and does not affect the logical imports of the statements. Neither statement, taken alone, asserts or implies that the Tweedle brothers live in the same house; but if the observer knew for certain that the brothers DID inhabit the same building, for him the logical imports of the two statements would be identical, and he might interpret 'TO TWEEDLEDUM'S HOUSE' as though it included the information, 'TO THE HOUSE OF TWEEDLEDEE'. Functionally, either statement would then have the added informative connotations (based on the interpreter's prior knowledge) which would enable him to regard either signpost as a sign of expanded signification: for him, the statements on the two finger-posts would simply be two ways of saying the same thing – '[This sign points] TO THE HOUSE OF TWEEDLEDUM AND TWEEDLEDEE'. But in the absence of this prior knowledge, the statements have different logical imports; for, as we have seen earlier (§ 4.3), on the basis of their literal imports alone, they may refer to different buildings.

9.2 DIVERGENCE OF INTENDED AND LITERAL IMPORT

9.2.1 *The Literal Import of Statements*

Carroll enjoyed puzzling his readers with questions concerning the meaning of statements. While Alice is falling down the rabbit hole, she drowsily asks herself "Do cats eat bats?" over and over, sometimes phrasing it "Do bats eat cats?". Carroll comments drily, "for, you see, as she couldn't answer either question, it didn't much matter which way she put it" (*Works*, p. 20). It is difficult to know whether he was being serious in this comment, or merely setting a problem for his readers. Peter Alexander, in dealing with this passage, wonders if Carroll would have subscribed to the views of Logical Positivism. Alice has no way of verifying the truth of the proposition implied by either question since she cannot refer them to the test of experience.

Perhaps he *is* supporting the view that if a question cannot be answered by the methods of science it is nonsensical and therefore illegitimate – for indeed, if a question is nonsensical it doesn't matter how it is phrased. Or, on the other hand, he may simply be pointing to the obvious truth that some questions cannot be given clear and certain answers – and issuing a warning against confusing the two sorts of question. The most we can say on this point, from internal evidence, at least, is that he is approving of those conclusions of Logical Positivism which would probably be accepted nowadays by most philosophers as valuable and necessary criticisms of traditional philosophy, but not necessarily of its fundamental, and more extreme, doctrine.[1]

Since, while falling down the rabbit hole, Alice has no way of testing the truth of the proposition contained in either question, it does not matter for her, in this physical context, how the initial question she asks ("Do cats eat bats?") is phrased. It contains no meaningful proposition for her, and is mere noise. Regarded outside of this peculiar context, in a situation where either question could be empirically

[1] Peter Alexander, "Logic and the Humour of Lewis Carroll", *Proc. of the Leeds Phil. and Lit. Soc.*, VI (May, 1951), 562.

answered, the two implied statements do have different imports, and it would matter a great deal which way the initial question was expressed.

Later in *Wonderland*, Alice falls into a logical trap while talking to the Hatter and March Hare at the Mad Tea Party. The Hatter sets her a riddle, "Why is a raven like a writing-desk?", which, though Alice does not realize it, has no answer. Pleased by the riddle, she says "I believe I can guess that."

"Do you mean that you think you can find out the answer to it?" said the March Hare.
"Exactly so," said Alice.
"Then you should say what you mean," the March Hare went on.
"I do," Alice hastily replied; "at least – at least I mean what I say – that's the same thing, you know."
"Not the same thing a bit!" said the Hatter. "Why, you might just as well say that 'I see what I eat' is the same thing as 'I eat what I see'!"
"You might just as well say," added the March Hare, "that 'I like what I get' is the same thing as 'I get what I like'!"
"You might just as well say," added the Dormouse, which seemed to be talking in its sleep, "that 'I breathe when I sleep' is the same thing as 'I sleep when I breathe'!"
"It *is* the same thing with you," said the Hatter . . .

(*Works*, pp. 75-76)

From Alice's point of view, the intended imports of the two statements, 'I believe I can guess that' and 'I think that I can find out the answer to it', are the same; for according to the conventional usage in her world, 'I can guess that' is equivalent in meaning to 'I can find out the answer to it', as the meaning of *believe* is to that of *think*. The March Hare, however, exhibiting that literal turn of mind characteristic of the creatures which Alice meets in Wonderland and behind the Looking-Glass, does not see the two statements as identical in import. And literally, of course, they aren't. The words *guess* and *find out* have different informative connotations in general usage: *guess* implies establishing an hypothesis, making an inferential leap; *find out* implies discovery through a process of reasoned inquiry which results in greater certainty than mere hypothesis. The words *think* and *believe*, though able to be used in common speech to signify basically the same mental operation, have respectively, as used in these statements, their own shades of connotation: *believe* connotes a greater degree of certainty than *think*, which connotes a degree of reservation or doubt.

The March Hare is correct in seeing that the two statements do not have the same literal import; but in making this distinction he is being much more precise than Alice. The Hare feels that if Alice intends *x*, she should say *x*; but Alice feels ("Exactly so.") that she has said the equivalent of *x*. The Hare, not realizing that in her frame of reference – the conventional usage of her world – she HAS stated the equivalent of *x*, adheres to his literal interpretation and will be satisfied only if she uses the words that he prescribes. If Alice had stopped with "I do say what I mean", she would have made clear to the Hare that in her mind the two statements are equivalent in import. And he would have had to be content with her stipulated definition of his longer statement. But she makes the error of assuming that the converse, 'I mean what I say', has the same import as her original statement, 'I say what I mean'. The Hatter and Hare are quick to point out that technical converses do not necessarily have the same meaning: 'I see what I eat' is not equivalent in import to 'I eat what I see'. A further complexity is introduced by Carroll when the Hatter declares that the Dormouse's pair of converses, 'I breathe when I sleep' and 'I sleep when I breathe', are, when predicated of the Dormouse, "the same thing". Both statements may indeed be true when predicated of the Dormouse; but their being able to be applied to him with equal validity does not signify that the meanings of the two expressions are the same. Each has its own logical import.

In *Sylvie and Bruno*, an idiomatic comparison, logically unsound but used frequenty in everyday discourse, provides Carroll with an opportunity to baffle his readers with verbal sleight-of-hand. The final tautology is worthy of the Professor, who has invented a means of carrying one's-self – an operation not at all tiring because "whatever fatigue one incurs by *carrying,* one saves by *being carried*" (*Works*, p. 376):

[The Narrator admonishes Bruno to copy Sylvie's behavior:]
 "*She's* always as busy as the day is long!"
 "Well, so am *I*!" said Bruno.
 "No, no!" Sylvie corrected him. "*You're* as busy as the day is *short*!"
 "Well, what's the difference?" Bruno asked. "Mister Sir, isn't the day as short as it's long? I mean, isn't it the *same* length?"
 Never having considered the question in this light, I suggested that they had better ask the Professor . . .
 "My dears," he said after a minute, "the day is the same length as anything that is the same length as *it*."

(*Works*, pp. 370-371)

In conventional usage, the phrase *as busy as the day is long* signifies that the person of whom it is predicated is busy 'all day long', or 'always busy'. It is not to be interpreted literally as a comparison, for the things signified by the terms cannot logically be compared. The absurdity is apparent in the following invalid comparison: "A giraffe is as tall as a pig is fat." Sylvie interprets the narrator's idiomatic phrase in a literal fashion, and plays a variation on it which reveals the absurdity that can result from taking according to its literal import a statement whose intended import is idiomatic: "[Bruno] is as busy as the day is short." Bruno does not see the joke; he diverts the conversation from the disturbing subject of his laziness to a consideration of the signification of the words *long* and *short* when applied to a day. Bruno's questions about the day's length relative to its duration are not clearly phrased. What he means is, "Isn't the duration of the day the same whether we view the day as long or short?" *Long* and *short* are comparative terms whose meaning depends upon the subjective predispositions of the user and interpreter. Bruno's phrasing quibbles on 'length' as it signifies duration and a measure-

ment of duration; it is sufficiently unclear for the Professor to be confused by it.
The old man's tautology does have a meaning: that x is equal in length to anything
that is equal in length to x – but the statement conveys no information about the
day's relative length or shortness.

In *Sylvie and Bruno* there is another illustration of confusion arising from the
meanings of statements; but in this instance the confusion occurs in the speaker,
and not in the audience. The Chancellor, in league with the Sub-Warden to usurp
power from the Warden, addresses a mob of citizens who have marched upon the
palace. The Chancellor's speech is monitored by a henchman outside the window
who is greatly disturbed by the official's bad oratory. The Chancellor says:

"But your *true* friend is the *Sub-Warden*! Day and night he is brooding on your wrongs
– I should say your *rights* – that is to say your *wrongs* – no, I mean your *rights* –"
("Don't talk no more!" growled the man under the window. "You're making a mess of
it!")

(*Works*, pp. 289-290)

Depending upon which word is used, the statement has two separate literal imports;
Carroll, depicting the Chancellor's confusion and his desire not to misrepresent his
intended meaning, provides his readers with an opportunity to study the implications of the respective utterances. *He is brooding upon your wrongs* and *He is
brooding upon your rights* (disregarding the puns which Carroll is exploiting) could
be construed to have the same logical import: that the Sub-Warden is deeply concerned about the condition of the people of Outland – when their rights have been
denied them, the people have been wronged. But the literal imports of the two
statements are different. The informative connotations of the first are that the
Sub-Warden is worrying about the wrongs which the people have sustained, presumably with the intention of rectifying the injustice. The second statement implies
that the Sub-Warden is pondering the people's rights with the intention of securing
them. The Chancellor's difficulty in deciding which word to use may stem from his
indecision as to which of the two sets of informative connotations he wishes to
impart and also, perhaps, from his awareness that the words *wrongs* and *rights*
have separate sets of affective connotations and his not being sure which of the
two sets he wishes to exploit. Or, being a poor orator, he may simply be confused
by the punning senses of the words, which designate a relationship of opposition:
"right" versus "wrong".

9.2.2 *Literal Interpretation as an Obstacle to Communication: Divergence Between Literal and Idiomatic Import*

In its everyday use, language is not employed in a strictly logical manner. Language
is a conventionalized system of signs by means of which people refer to things,
make statements about things, reveal their feelings and attitudes towards things,
express emotional states, issue commands, attempt to influence the thoughts of

others persuasively, communicate information of various types, and maintain social cohesion. Logical discourse, which involves the use of linguistic forms (according to arbitrarily-established and relatively inflexible rules) for postulating relationships and conducting sound argument, is a specialized application of language which does not make up the greatest part of its use in everyday affairs. The common uses of language – particularly those that act in a directive capacity, express emotional states or produce them in others, and serve to cement social unity – often give rise to conventional formulaic expressions which, having distinct recognition value as particular formulas, are interpreted in conventionally prescribed ways. Frequently illogical in their literal import when analyzed according to the rules of logical discourse, these formulas convey a standardized meaning (idiomatic import) as their intended import which cannot be gained from a literal interpretation alone. English is rich in idiomatic formulas, many of which are comprised of metaphorical statement, such as the phrase, "He is a rolling stone."

Lewis Carroll was intrigued by the possibilities for humor which could result from the literal interpretation of metaphorical idioms. The creatures in Wonderland and behind the Looking-Glass tend to be governed by a relentless logicality, neither understanding the loose statement characteristic of Alice's world nor allowing her to get by with it in theirs. Alice is constantly being brought up short and made to see the illogicality of the conventions of English usage. In Chapter IX of *Through the Looking-Glass,* when Alice is about to undergo her examination for queenhood, the Red Queen, alluding to a previous remark by Alice, demands:

"What do you mean by 'If you really are a Queen'? What right have you to call yourself so? You ca'n't be a Queen, you know, till you've passed the proper examination. . . ."

"I only said 'if'!" poor Alice pleaded in a piteous tone.

The two Queens looked at each other, and the Red Queen remarked, with a little shudder, "She *says* she only said 'if' –"

"But she said a great deal more than that!" the White Queen moaned, wringing her hands. "Oh, ever so much more than that!"

"So you did, you know," the Red Queen said to Alice. . . .

"I'm sure I didn't mean –" Alice was beginning, but the Red Queen interrupted her impatiently.

"That's just what I complain of! You *should* have meant! What do you suppose is the use of a child without any meaning? Even a joke should have some meaning – and a child's more important than a joke, I hope. You couldn't deny that, even if you tried with both hands."

"I don't deny things with my *hands,*" Alice objected.

"Nobody said you did," said the Red Queen. "I said you couldn't if you tried."

(*Works*, p. 251)

Matter-of-fact the Queens are, quick to see illogicality in the utterances of Alice (she DID say more than 'if'), but not without flaws in their own reasoning. Although the Queen is correct in asserting that she did not imply that Alice denies things with her hands, and seems to expect Alice to be as literal in her interpretation of other people's utterances as she herself is, she is guilty of fallacious thinking in comparing a child to a joke. She is punning upon the word *meaning* without realizing it. One wonders what the Queen's reply would have been if instead of saying, "I don't deny things with my hands", Alice had said: "A child ca'n't be compared to a joke, you know. A child ca'n't have meaning in the same way that a joke can." A moment later the Red Queen asks:

> "Do you know languages? What's the French for fiddle-de-dee?"
> "Fiddle-de-dee's not English," Alice replied gravely.
> "Who ever said it was?" said the Red Queen.
>
> (*Works*, p. 254)

Earlier in the book, the White King, eating hay to overcome faintness, exhibits the same literal turn of mind:

> "There's nothing like eating hay when you're faint," he remarked to her, as he munched away.
> "I should think throwing cold water over you would be better," Alice suggested: "– or some sal-volatile."
> "I didn't say there was nothing *better*," the King replied. "I said there was nothing *like* it." Which Alice did not venture to deny.
>
> (*Works*, p. 225)

As Peter Alexander says of this passage, "Here we are being shown the literal meaning, usually slurred over, of one of our most common idioms. Alice, again, is being corrected, not this time for assuming that the same verbal expression refers to different things [as she did in the case of the White Knight's use of *fast*] but for assuming that two different verbal expressions refer to the same state of affairs." [2] In conventional usage, the phrase *there's nothing like x* [*for some purpose*] is commonly taken to mean "there's nothing better than *x*" for that purpose, or "for this purpose, *x* is without peer". This is the statement's idiomatic import. But Alice is not in her own world where people can get by with such approximate statements.

Another encounter of this type occurs when Humpty Dumpty asks Alice "How old did you say you were?" in a context where she has not previously mentioned her age.

> Alice made a short calculation, and said "Seven years and six months."
> "Wrong!" Humpty Dumpty exclaimed triumphantly. "You never said a word like it!"
> "I thought you meant 'How old *are* you?' " Alice explained.
> "If I'd meant that, I'd have said it," said Humpty Dumpty.
>
> (*Works*, p. 211)

Humpty Dumpty would have been satisfied with her answer only if she had said, "I've not yet said how old I am." Carroll in this instance explicitly shows what, in Alice's world, convention takes to be the idiomatic import of Humpty Dumpty's question, and how this differs from the literal import. Another idiomatic expression is exploited by Carroll a moment later. Humpty Dumpty, speaking of his cravat,

---

[2]   Alexander, p. 557.

says that it was given him for "an un-birthday present". Alice does not know what he means, and makes the polite noises which in her world indicate this lack of understanding. Humpty Dumpty takes her request for more information (or stipulative definition) as a statement of apology.

> "I beg your pardon?" Alice said with a puzzled air.
> "I'm not offended," said Humpty Dumpty.
> "I mean, what *is* an un-birthday present?"
> "A present given when it isn't your birthday, of course."
>
> (*Works*, pp. 212-213)

The same idiomatic expression runs afoul of the White King's literal turn of mind. Speaking of his Anglo-Saxon Messengers, he says "I must have *two,* you know — to come and go. One to come, and one to go."

> "I beg your pardon?" said Alice.
> "It isn't respectable to beg," said the King.
> "I only meant that I didn't understand," said Alice. "Why one to come and one to go?"
>
> (*Works*, p. 224)

In both of these instances, Alice is forced to resort to stipulative definition to explain her intended import for the expression. *Sylvie and Bruno* has its share of instances where idioms are interpreted literally in such manner that lack of communication and logical absurdity result. For example, a young lady asks Bruno, "You're not more than seven, are you, dear?"

> "I'm not so many as *that*," said Bruno. "I'm *one.* Sylvie's *one.* Sylvie and me is *two.* . . ."
> .   .   .   .
>   "When I asked if you were *seven,* you know, I didn't mean 'how many *children*?' I meant 'how many *years* –'"
> "Only got *two* ears," said Bruno. "Nobody's got *seven* ears."
>
> (*Works*, p. 608)

The ambiguity created by conventional elision of *years* makes possible Bruno's misinterpretation of the lady's *You're not more than seven.* Seven what? People, of course. Bruno takes the utterance according to its literal import. The further misunderstanding comes about as a result of the young lady's failure to make a noticeable hiatus between *many* and *years*; Bruno does not recognize the juncture, and the sound-sequence – being phonetically identical to that of *many/ears* – becomes homophonically ambiguous.

When Bruno meets the mysterious old man in the adult portion of the novel, he asks, "What does he call his-self?"

> "He calls himself 'Mein Herr,'" Sylvie whispered in reply.
> Bruno shook his head impatiently. "That's what he calls his *hair*, not his *self*, oo silly!" He appealed to me. "What doos he call his *self*, Mister Sir?"
> "That's the only name *I* know of," I said. "But he looks very lonely. Don't you pity his grey hairs?"

"I pities his *self*," said Bruno, still harping on the misnomer; "but I doesn't pity his *hair*, one bit. His *hair* ca'n't feel!"

(Works, p. 612)

After falling prey to the homophonic ambiguity of the old man's name (a reasonable mistake, since Bruno does not know the German expression as a form of address), the boy interprets the narrator's metaphorical idiom *pity his grey hairs* literally and thereby shows its essential absurdity.

The young lady who inquired into Bruno's age with such unsatisfactory results makes the error of telling Bruno that she has a sister at home "exactly like your sister".

"They'd be very extremely useful to each other," Bruno said, thoughtfully. "And they wouldn't want no looking-glasses to brush their hair wiz."
"Why not, my child?"
"Why, each one would do for the other one's looking-glass a-course!" cried Bruno.

(Works, pp. 608-609)

The young lady's intended import for 'exactly like your sister' is simply an assertion of similarity between her sister and Sylvie. No speaker of English would normally take the statement according to its literal import to mean that two people were in every respect identical, for common sense rejects such an interpretation as absurd. Bruno, of course, does take it literally, providing Carroll with a humorous illustration which reveals both the illogicality often found in conventional usage and also the possibility that such expressions can, when they are taken at face value and not as loose metaphors, result in absurdities which might NOT be recognized as such by common sense. In formal philosophy, the use of the expression 'the same' for things actually only similar (implying identity when only similarity is warranted) can cause great confusion.

It is apparent from these quoted illustrations that Carroll himself was amused at the illogicality of idiomatic usage and that he enjoyed pointing this illogicality out to his readers by treating metaphorical expressions in a strictly logical fashion, interpreting them according to the letter and not according to the "spirit" in which they are used. He was fascinated by yet another characteristic habit of conventional usage that offered the possibility for humorous exploitation: the substantive use of such words as *nobody, nothing,* and *no one.*

9.2.3 *The Existential Treatment of the Null Class*

A null class is a class containing no existing members. Such, for example, are the class of men who are sixty feet tall, and those consisting of (respectively) the man who assassinated President Cleveland, unicorns, gryphons, and three-headed Sunday school teachers. The word *nobody*, like *unicorn*, designates an object that does not exist; yet it is a useful expression which may stand as the subject of a proposition. Carroll peoples his books with concrete representatives of specific null classes, using as characters a Gryphon, a Unicorn, a Mock Turtle, a Bread-and-butter-fly, and – on several occasions – Nobody. By exploiting the ability of the term 'nobody' to be used substantively, Carroll provides for himself another means for presenting illustrations of communication failure.

In *Wonderland*, the King of Hearts says of the letter brought up as evidence at the Knave's trial that it must have been written to somebody, "unless it was written to nobody, which isn't usual, you know" (*Works*, p. 125). In *Through the Looking-Glass*, the White King asks Alice to look down the road to see if the Anglo-Saxon Messengers are in sight.

"I see nobody on the road," said Alice.
   "I only wish *I* had such eyes," the King remarked in a fretful tone. "To be able to see Nobody! And at that distance too! Why, it's as much as *I* can do to see real people, by this light!"

(*Works*, p. 223)

Carroll pushes this device to its logical extreme a moment later when the King asks the Anglo-Saxon Messenger, who has arrived in the interim, "Who did you pass on the road?"

"Nobody," said the Messenger.
   "Quite right," said the King: "this young lady saw him too. So of course Nobody walks slower than you."
   "I do my best," the Messenger said in a sullen tone. "I'm sure nobody walks much faster than I do!"
   "He ca'n't do that," said the King, "or else he'd have been here first. . . ."

(*Works*, p. 225)

Peter Alexander has said of this passage, "There are, of course, two confusions – an illicit assumption that the noun 'nobody' stands for a person, in which sense the King uses it to compliment the Messenger, and the confusion with this of one of our familiar idioms ('Nobody walks slower than you'), in which sense the Messenger takes the King's intended compliment as an insult." [3] The King and the Messenger, each with a different signification for the word *nobody* in mind, talk at cross purposes. The Messenger is using the word in the same sense that Alice did earlier, as a symbol that names a class which has no members. The King, taking the word to designate a PERSON so named, remains logically consistent throughout the conversation, enabling Carroll to comment indirectly upon the potential hazards for communication inherent in the use of such words.

In a letter to Sydney Bowles of May 22, 1891, Carroll plays another variation on the theme: he had evidently slighted the girl inadvertantly, and he uses a personified Nobody to make a graceful apology.

I *am* so sorry, and so ashamed! Do you know, I didn't even know of your *existence*? And it was *such* a surprise to hear that you had sent me your love! I felt just as if Nobody

---

[3]   Alexander, p. 563.

had suddenly run into the room, and given me a kiss! (That's the thing which happens to me, *most* days, just now.)

(*Letters to Child-friends*, ed. Hatch, p. 221)

The most elaborate use of this existential treatment of Nobody occurs in *Euclid and His Modern Rivals*. Here we meet Nobody face to face in the person of Herr Niemand, the phantasm who has undertaken the formidable task of defending the modern rivals against the arguments of Minos, Euclid's defender. Herr Niemand claims to be a member of the Syllabus Committee of the Association for the Improvement of Geometrical Teaching:

Min. (*astonished*) You! A German professor! No such member is included in the final list of the Committee, which a friend showed me the other day.

Nie. The final list, was it? Well, ask your friend whether, since the drawing up of that list, any addition has been made: he will say 'Nobody has been added.'

Min. Quite so.

Nie. You do not understand. *Nobody – Niemand* – see you not?

Min. What? You mean –

Nie. (*solemnly*) I do, my friend. *I* have been added to it!

Min. (*bowing*) The Committee are highly honoured, I am sure.

Nie. So they ought to be, considering that I am a more distinguished mathematician than Newton himself, and that *my* Manual is better than Euclid's! Excuse my self-glorification, but any moralist will tell you that I – I alone among men – *ought* to praise myself.

Min. (*thoughtfully*) True, true. But all this is word-juggling – a most misleading analogy. However, as you now appear in a new character, you must at least have a new name!

Nie. (*proudly*) Call me *Nostradamus*!

. . . .

Min. Nostra, the plural of nostrum, 'a quack remedy'; and *damus*, 'we give.' It is a suggestive name.

(*Euclid and His Modern Rivals*,
2nd ed. [1885], pp. 181-183)

Thus does Charles Dodgson dispose of the Syllabus Committee. Note how his play with the literal import of *Nobody's geometry manual is better than Euclid's* reinforces his entire argument against the modern rivals which called the treatise into being. Mere word-juggling it may be; but juggling of any sort requires practiced skill – both in dexterity and in precise timing – to keep the juggled objects from falling to the ground. Carroll's playthings here are sound and sense: the equivocal nature of the term 'nobody' allows it to signify either a class without members or to act as the name for a hypostatic entity. Depending upon which interpretation is given the word, statements containing it as a subject may be construed either as universal negative propositions or as particular affirmative propositions. Respectively, *Nobody is a more distinguished mathematician than Newton* may mean either 'No mathematician is more distinguished than Newton' or 'Nobody [Herr Niemand] is a more distinguished mathematician than Newton'. These alternatives could be paraphrased respectively, 'Newton is in the first rank of distinguished mathematicians' and 'Newton is not as distinguished a mathematician as Nobody [Herr Niemand]'. Carroll's juggling of sound and sense in this passage is quite dexterous, because he is able to keep both sets of interpretations in the air simultaneously. The reader is made aware of the double meanings; and, though forced by the context to accept *nobody* as the name of a hypostatic entity, is nonetheless compelled by the skillful wording of the passage to apprehend the other set of meanings as well. Indeed, Carroll's satirical point against the modern rivals depends upon the reader's taking 'nobody' to designate a class without members. His cleverness in this passage has its antecedent in Homer's *Odyssey*, where the wily Odysseus convinces the Cyclops that "no man" put out his eye.

9.2.4 *Summary*

Lewis Carroll saw that intended import could be obscured or misrepresented by the linguistic forms used to express it: vagueness and ambiguity could be caused by equivocal words and syntactic constructions, and by the disparity that frequently exists between a statement's literal import and its idiomatic import. Linguistic forms have potentially a conventionalized sense of their own which, in a given context, may not be the signification which the speaker intends them to convey. Thus the interpreter's received import MAY not coincide with the speaker's intended import. Many idioms in English convey particular standardized meanings in general usage which – because of their metaphorical phrasing and content – would be nonsensical or ludicrous for their context if they were interpreted literally. When recognized as idioms, these expressions do function to convey the speaker's intended meaning. They fail to do so when, because of the interpreter's ignorance of the convention or his misunderstanding of the speaker's intention, their literal import becomes dominant, and the intended import is obscured. We have seen Carroll's humorous exploitation of these principles in his forcing a literal interpretation upon such common expressions as 'I beg your pardon', 'How old did you say you were?', 'I only said 'if'', 'You can't be more than seven', 'You're as busy as the day is long', 'There's nothing like eating hay when you're faint', 'Don't you pity his grey hairs?', 'A sister exactly like yours', and in his causing 'Nobody' to be taken as the name of a hypostatic entity. In revealing the essential illogicality of some of the language's most common expressions, he was, I have no doubt, trying to awaken his readers to the resources and limitations of English, encouraging them to pay attention to what they were saying, and warning them against carelessness in their linguistic habits.

9.3 CARROLL'S CONCERN WITH PRECISION
AND CLARITY OF EXPRESSION

9.3.1 *Carroll's Interest in Standards of Usage*

Carroll's own attempts to make his technical writing clear and precise often led
him into excessive stipulation of intended meaning, tedious periphrasis, and dry-as-
dust exposition. But the "jealousy of error" which had been noted by his headmaster at Richmond Grammar School caused him throughout his life to demand
precision, clarity, and concreteness of expression in other people as well, whether
they were his academic colleagues, the correspondents who answered the serialized
puzzles in *A Tangled Tale*,[4] his child-friends, or Euclid's modern rivals.

His passion for precision naturally caused him to be interested in questions of
English usage – in grammatical "correctness", in the ways in which utterances are
framed, in punctuation, pronunciation, and spelling (Cf. § 3.3.2 and § 3.3.5). For
example, a rigorous logic compelled him to adopt unconventional spellings of
can't, won't, and *traveller*; and, as always with his symbolic innovations, he gave
an elaborate justification for his practice. This particular defense occurs in the
preface to *Sylvie and Bruno Concluded* (1893):

... critics have objected to certain innovations in spelling, such as "ca'n't," "wo'n't,"
"traveler." In reply, I can only plead my firm conviction that the popular usage is *wrong*.
As to "ca'n't," it will not be disputed that, in all *other* words ending in "n't," these letters
are an abbreviation of "not"; and it is surely absurd to suppose that, in this solitary instance, "not" is represented by "'t"! In fact "can't" is the *proper* abbreviation for "can it,"
just as "is't" is for "is it." Again, in "wo'n't," the first apostrophe is needed, because the
word "would" is here *abridged* into "wo": but I hold it proper to spell "don't" with only
one apostrophe, because the word "do" is here *complete*. As to such words as "traveler,"
I hold the correct principle to be, to *double* the consonant when the accent falls on that
syllable; otherwise to leave it *single*. This rule is observed in most cases (e.g. we double
the "r" in "preferred," but leave it single in "offered"), so that I am only extending, to
other cases, an existing rule. I admit, however, that I do not spell "parallel," as the rule
would have it; but here we are constrained, by the etymology, to insert the double "l".

(*Works*, pp. 509-510)

Although Carroll was a precisionist in matters of grammar, spelling, and pronunciation, he saw that humor could be gained from calculated deviations from standard
usage. Such a deviation is Alice's surprised "Curiouser and curiouser!" when in
Wonderland she suddenly grows tall after eating a cake that she finds at the bottom
of the rabbit hole. Carroll feels constrained to comment parenthetically: "she was
so much surprised, that for the moment she quite forgot how to speak good English"
(*Works*, p. 26). In like manner, the narrator of *Sylvie and Bruno* is made to
comment on Sylvie's ecstatic response to Bruno's beautifying her garden: "she ...

---

[4] Lewis Carroll, *Works*, pp. 1025-78; or the Dover Publications edition of *A Tangled Tale*
(New York, 1958), pp. 77-152.

gave her verdict – in a hurried whisper and without the slightest regard to grammar
– 'It's the loveliest thing as I never saw in all my life before!' " (*Works*, p. 403).
Carroll does not feel called upon to comment on the grammatical infelicities of
most of his characters who normally speak substandard English; for they are made
to do so in accord with the literary convention that peasants, laborers, servants,
and the uneducated in general would naturally use incorrect grammar. In the case
of Alice and Sylvie, his two refined heroines, he feels that he must make some
apologetic mention that their infelicities are but momentary lapses. That he would
consciously put 'bad' grammar into the mouths of his lower-class characters and
self-consciously give his two idealized heroines conspicuously 'bad' grammar on
certain occasions indicates that Carroll was keenly sensitive to the form in which
utterances were expressed; that to him, a person's speaking 'correctly' was merely
a matter of training and habit; that he knew that even normally 'correct' speakers
can sometimes be caught off guard and startled into substandard usage.

9.3.2 *Bruno's Deviations from Standard Usage: Errors by Analogy*

Bruno's brand of substandard usage is another matter. Following the literary convention of the time of putting baby talk into the mouths of young children, Carroll
strives both to be 'cute' and to capitalize upon the substandard qualities of baby
talk to create humor through erroneous pronunciation and grammatical constructions. Bruno's idiolect is a particular representation of the kind of usage that might
be characteristic of very young children who are attempting to adapt their speech
habits to the conventions required by adult usage. Most of his grammatical blunders
are errors by analogy. For example, the comparative forms of adjectives and
adverbs give him some trouble: " 'It's a miserable story!' said Bruno. 'It begins
miserably, and it ends miserablier' " (*Works*, p. 729); "more wonderfuller" and "a
betterer reason" (p. 721). Past tenses of verbs are another source of difficulty. He
often frames past tenses of weak verbs on the analogy of strong verbs [*jamp* for
'jumped'; *wug* for 'wagged' (p. 492)], the past tenses of weak verbs with a super-
fluous *-ed* [*slipted, tripted* (p. 453); *peepted* (p. 721); *tumbleded* (p. 742)], and
the past tenses of strong verbs on the analogy of weak verbs [*stinged, knewed*
(both forms used here) (p. 453); *singed* for 'sang,' *sawed* for 'saw' (p. 493); *tooked,
camed in* (p. 721)]. Here is an example in context:

> "Once," Bruno began again, "Sylvie and me writed –"
> "Wrote!" Sylvie whispered.
> "Well, we *wroted* a Nursery-Song . . ."

> (*Works*, pp. 410-411)

In addition to these errors by analogy, Bruno also has difficulty in making the
grammatical number of nouns and verbs consistent, in interpreting and using
idiomatic expressions, and in understanding and reproducing standard pronuncia-
tions. Many of these errors in pronunciation are merely approximations to the

correct sound and do not particularly affect the sense of the utterance: *pruffickly* for 'perfectly', *wiss* for 'wish', *nuffin* for 'nothing', *welly* for 'very', *conkery* for 'contrary', and *imporkant* for 'important'. Some are merely whimsical, such as *lizard bandages* for 'disadvantages' (p. 360), *umbrella-sting* for 'embarrassing' (p. 608), and *dindledums* for 'dandelions' (pp. 454-455). Others, however, do affect the sense of the utterance as a whole by virtue of the additional associations which the erroneous sound-sequence brings to the context. In these instances, where an added dimension of meaning is imposed upon the original utterance, Carroll is anticipating the method of James Joyce in *Finnegan's Wake*. Examples are: *seedling discontent* for 'seething discontent' (p. 303); *shave me* for 'save me' [where the indicated operation is almost carried out, and would have been if My Lady had possessed a razor] (p. 346); *a compliment* for 'accompaniment' (p. 421); *Muddle-come table* for 'multiplication table' (p. 529); *illconvenient* for 'inconvenient' (p. 360); and *flightened* for 'frightened' (p. 555). Deviations from standard canons of usage (regardless of their cause) may give rise to utterances which themselves can provide obstacles to communication.

9.4 OBSTACLES TO COMMUNICATION PRESENTED
BY THE UTTERANCE ITSELF

9.4.1 *Obstacles Presented by Pronunciation*

Communication attempts may fail through misunderstanding the intended sense of an utterance if the interpreter misapprehends the speaker's pronunciation, or if he in repeating the speaker's utterances to a third party fails to reproduce the speaker's pronunciation accurately. Bruno fails to grasp the Professor's articulation of two words in the following utterance (probably because he does not know the words the Professor is using), and then fails to reproduce their pronunciation in his "repetition" of the statement to Sylvie; the Professor says: "All of me, that isn't *Bonhommie,* is Rumination!"

> "*What* did he say, Bruno?" Sylvie enquired, as soon as we were safely out of hearing.
> "I *think* he said 'All of me that isn't Bone-disease is Rheumatism.' ..."
>
> (*Works*, p. 743)

Bruno's mistake in apprehending the Professor's pronunciation changes the literal import of the utterance and hence its received import in the mind of the inter-preter; in passing on the erroneous pronunciation, Bruno forces Sylvie, too, to misapprehend the intended sense of the Professor's original utterance. A further example of communication difficulty produced by misapprehension of pronuncia-tion is Bruno's misunderstanding of Sylvie's word *revenge*:

> "revenge is a wicked, cruel, dangerous thing!"
> "River-edge?" said Bruno. "What a funny word! I suppose oo call it cruel and danger-ous' cause, if oo wented too far and tumbleded in, oo'd get drownded."

"No, not river-edge," I explained: "revenge" (saying the word very slowly). But I couldn't help thinking that Bruno's explanation did very well for either word.

(Works, p. 393)

In *Sylvie and Bruno* much is made of "The Unpronounceable Monosyllable" – *y'reince* – which, Carroll tells the reader, "was nothing but 'your Royal Highness' condensed into one syllable" (*Works*, p. 289). The method of condensation which forms *y'reince* is similar to that which Carroll claimed was the means for obtaining *frumious* from 'fuming' and 'furious' (§ 7.2.2); but *y'reince* is not a 'portmanteau' in the same sense that (according to Carroll) *slithy* and *frumious* are. Whereas the Jabberwocky words supposedly have two meanings packed into them (a fusion of the separate meanings of the component parts), *y'reince* has only the meaning possessed by 'your Royal Highness', of which term it is merely a shortened form. But to one not familiar with the conventions of its use, *y'reince* would probably not be recognizable as an abbreviation for 'your Royal Highness', and for him, the signification of the longer term would be inaccessible. Thus, *y'reince* presents a potential obstacle to the success of a communication attempt employing it.

In Knot X of *A Tangled Tale* there is an instance of misunderstanding brought about by the speaker's deviation from standard pronunciation. Mad Mathesis and Clara have just addressed a query to the butler: –

"Yes, m'm, Master *is* at home, m'm" ... (N.B. – It is only a butler of experience who can manage a series of three M's together, without any interjacent vowels.) "And the *ole* party is a-waiting for you in the libery."

"I don't like his calling your father an *old* party," Mad Mathesis whispered to her niece, as they crossed the hall. And Clara had only just time to whisper in reply, "He meant the *whole* party ..."

(Works, p. 1022)

The misunderstanding in this passage caused by the butler's "dropping" of an initial [h] is a pale shadow in comparison with one which occurs in the short story "Wilhelm Von Schmitz" (1854), written thirty years earlier. There the misunderstanding is caused by the same dialectal trait, but it is of a rather more serious nature. The hero of the story, thinking that the Cockney waiter wishes to "acquire the heart" of his own beloved Sukie, attacks the man with the intention of strangling him. He is set straight when the waiter says,

"My 'ope were, Sir, to hacquire her Hart of waiting at table, which she do perdigious well, sure-ly: seeing that I were thinking of happlying for to be 'eadwaiter at the 'otel."

(Works, p. 1105)

The butler's ability to solve the problem of juncture presented by a series of "M's" without interjacent vowels is greatly to his credit. He at least managed to be understood, which is more than can be said of the young lady who asked Bruno how "many/ears" he possessed.

The subject of juncture evidently interested Carroll; for in addition to giving these two examples of problematical pronunciation, he also reveals elsewhere that he had thought about the possible effects that variations in juncture could have upon the form of words. In "Answers to Knot V" of *A Tangled Tale,* he defends himself against a correspondent who criticized him for calling a zero "ought" instead of "nought". He justifies his practice by citing the parallel case of *adder.*

That creature was originally "a nadder": then the two words took to bandying the poor "n" backwards and forwards like a shuttlecock, the final state of the game being "an adder." May not "a nought" have similarly become "an ought"? Anyhow, "oughts and crosses" is a very old game. I don't think I ever heard it called "noughts and crosses."

(Works, p. 1045)

An illustration of syntax obscured by pronunciation (in this case, the lack of variation in intonation contours necessary to signal phrasal units) is found in Carroll's early story "The Walking-Stick of Destiny", composed in 1849 or 1850, and included in *The Rectory Umbrella,* one of the family magazines. The speaker in question is the Baron Muggzwig, of whom Carroll says:

In his ordinary conversation he was, to say the least of it, misty and obscure, but after dinner or when at all excited his language certainly verged on the incomprehensible. This was perhaps owing to his liberal use of the parenthesis without any definite pause to mark the different clauses of the sentence. He used to consider his arguments unanswerable, and they certainly were so perplexing, and generally reduced his hearers to such a state of bewilderment and stupefaction, that few ever ventured to attempt an answer to them.[5]

Being asked what he "would like to be done with regard to Signor Blowski", the Baron answers:

"And though I have no wish to provoke the enmity which considering the provocations I have received and really if you reckon them up they are more than any mortal man let alone a Baron for the family temper has been known for years to be beyond nay the royal family themselves will hardly boast of considering too that he has so long a time kept which I shouldn't have found out only that rascal Blowski said and how he could bring himself to tell all those lies I can't think for I always considered him quite honest and of course wishing if possible to prove him innocent and the walking-stick since it is absolutely necessary in such matters and begging your pardon I consider the toad and all that humbug but that's between you and me and even when I had sent for it by two of my bandits . . ."[6]

Like the Duchess in framing her moral "Never imagine yourself not to be otherwise than what it might appear to others that what you were or might have been was not otherwise than what you had been would have appeared to them to be otherwise", the Baron Muggzwig (assuming, of course, that he himself knows what he intends his utterance to mean) does not give due attention to the sense of his sounds. He has failed in his responsibility to his hearers to make his syntax clear.

---

[5] Lewis Carroll, *The Rectory Umbrella and Mischmasch,* ed. Florence Milner (London, 1932), pp. 69-70.
[6] Lewis Carroll, *The Rectory Umbrella and Mischmasch,* pp. 72-73.

In the first place, he has used too many parenthetical expressions, parentheses within parentheses, making the sense difficult to follow; secondly, he has not indicated to his audience by vocal inflections where the parentheses occur. His utterance cannot be otherwise than what Carroll calls it – "incomprehensible". Since the words employed by the Baron are of a common sort with established lexical definitions, the utterance's being gibberish is due to a syntactic rather than a lexical cause. As with the Duchess' moral, the hearer feels that he could understand the utterance if he had some means for sorting out the various clauses and determining which are to be subordinated to which.

9.4.2 *Obstacles Presented by Unfamiliar Idiom or by the Speaker's Operating in a Frame of Reference Not Recognized by the Interpreter*

In Carroll's works there are two striking examples of utterances which make no sense to the interpreter although the words and the syntax are apparently clear and intelligible. In *Wonderland*, Alice fails to comprehend the Hatter's statement about his watch because she does not yet realize that for him, the time is always fixed at tea-time. She cannot understand because she does not know the frame of reference in which he is operating.

"What a funny watch!" she remarked. "It tells the day of the month, and doesn't tell what o'clock it is!"

"Why should it?" muttered the Hatter. "Does *your* watch tell you what year it is?"

"Of course not," Alice replied very readily: "but that's because it stays the same year for such a long time together."

"Which is just the case with *mine*," said the Hatter.

Alice felt dreadfully puzzled. The Hatter's remark seemed to her to have no sort of meaning in it, and yet it was certainly English. "I don't quite understand you," she said, as politely as she could.

(Works, p. 77)

In *Sylvie and Bruno Concluded*, non-understanding occurs because the speaker uses words in a fashion unidiomatic to English.

"... there's the dinner to finish," the Professor said with a bewildered smile: "and the heat to bear. I hope you'll enjoy the dinner – such as it is; and that you won't mind the heat – such as it isn't."

The sentence *sounded* well, but somehow I couldn't quite understand it; and the Other Professor seemed to be no better off. "Such as it isn't *what?*" he peevishly enquired.

"It isn't as hot as it might be," the Professor replied, catching at the first idea that came to hand.

"Ah, I see what you mean *now!*" the Other Professor graciously remarked. "It's very badly expressed, but I quite see it *now!*"

(Works, pp. 722-723)

9.5 CARROLL'S AWARENESS OF THE RESPECTIVE ROLES
OF REFERENTIAL AND STRUCTURAL MEANING

Carroll saw that the intended import of an utterance could be obscured – even when the words were drawn from the common vocabulary of English – by unidiomatic usage, by the operation of the speaker in a frame of reference unrecognized by the interpreter, and by confused or misleading syntax. But he also saw that syntax could serve to impart to lexical gibberish an illusion of sense. The first stanza of "Jabberwocky" has provoked much comment among students of language because, although many of the words it contains convey no meaning of any sort, the poem as a whole does possess the power to SUGGEST meanings. The first stanza reads:

> 'Twas brillig, and the slithy toves
>   Did gyre and gimble in the wabe:
> All mimsy were the borogoves,
>   And the mome raths outgrabe.

Alice says of the poem as a whole:

"It seems very pretty . . . but it's *rather* hard to understand!" (You see she didn't like to confess, even to herself, that she couldn't make it out at all.) "Somehow it seems to fill my head with ideas – only I don't exactly know what they are! . . ."

(Works, p. 155)

Since the first stanza is almost devoid of referential meanings, the vague "ideas" which fill Alice's head must stem from the associations which the sounds evoke for her, and from the structure of the utterance. Charles C. Fries holds the view that her "ideas" are "without doubt the structural meanings for which the framework contains the signals"; and he isolates the structural signals as follows:

> Twas ——————, and the ————y ———s
>   Did ——— and ———— in the ———;
> All ———y were the ————s,
>   And the ——— ————s ——————.[7]

To a speaker of English this framework will be familiar, and will immediately suggest certain functions for the nonsense words which fit in the blank spaces. According to Fries, "these 'ideas' seem vague to the ordinary speaker because in the practical use of language he is accustomed to dealing only with total meanings to which lexical content contributes the elements of which he is conscious".[8] Following Fries, Charles F. Hockett sees the "grammatical 'skeleton'" of the stanza to be the operative agent in suggesting "ideas" to Alice. These "ideas" are the relationships and functions of the nonsense words themselves as hinted at by the structure: "The framework itself asserts nothing about anything, but it is familiar to Alice, and to us, because as we speak English, we constantly use bits of it in

[7] Charles C. Fries, *The Structure of English* (New York, 1952), p. 70.
[8] Fries, p. 71.

utterances which *do* purport to deal with the world around us." [9] The grammatical structure of English consists of certain formulaic patterns which, through custom, convey a meaning of their own quite independent of the given 'content' words that may be present in the available formulaic slots (see § 4.4.1). Hockett illustrates his point by framing two sentences on Carroll's model which reveal the essential identity of the respective structural meanings:

"'Twas morning, and the merry sunbeams did glitter and dance in the snow; all tinselly were the treetops, and the happy fairies frolicked.
'Twas stormy, and the tall pines did quiver and tremble in the gale; all dark were the streets, and the weary villagers slept." [10]

The structural signals which suggest to Alice the functions of the nonsense words are (1) word order, which is that of conventional English; (2) function words, such as *it, and, the, did, in, all, were*; (3) inflectional markers, such as *-s* (noun plural) and indications of verb tense and number; and (4) co-occurrence phenomena, such as '*were* the ———*s*'. A certain type of meaning often resides in content words alone, deprived of an articulating structure. Hockett concludes his discussion of Carroll's stanza by showing that the content words of his two analogous examples will produce by themselves – without the aid of the structural framework – a telegraphic meaning of their own. But the total meaning will have to be guessed at: "The effect is easier to feel than to describe – like an extreme variety of headline English, or like certain types of Chinese poetry (particularly in word-by-word English translation), where many of the structural relationships are left to the reader's imagination." Respectively, the two examples read:

"morning merry sunbeam glitter dance snow tinselly treetop happy fairy frolic;
stormy tall pine quiver tremble gale dark street weary villager sleep." [11]

If we follow his lead and list the content words of the "Jabberwocky" stanza in like form, we can easily see that no telegraphic message whatever is present – that Alice's apprehension of vague meaning must have come from the structure alone:

brillig slithy tove gyre gimble wabe mimsy borogove mome rath outgrabe.

At the time of her initial reading of the poem, Alice FEELS that it means something. In her discussion with Humpty Dumpty about the nonsense words, we see that the grammatical skeleton has enabled her to know how certain of the nonsense words function. She asks him, "What are '*toves*'?", which question implies that she recognizes *toves* as a 'thing' word; moreover, her use of the verb *are* indicates that she has taken the final *-s* of *toves* to signify 'noun plural'. Further, she asks Humpty Dumpty, "What's to '*gyre*' and to '*gimble*'?" Her use of the infinitive shows that

[9]   Charles F. Hockett, *A Course in Modern Linguistics* (New York, 1958), p. 263.
[10] Hockett, p. 262.
[11] Hockett, p. 264.

she has construed them as 'action' words, presumably on the basis of the function word *did*. *Wabe* Alice takes to be a 'thing' word which names a physical location – presumably on the basis of the formula 'in the ——'. (For her entire conversation with Humpty Dumpty, see § 7.2.1.)

It may be seen that Carroll possessed a realization of the difference between structural and referential meaning, of the respective roles they play in making a whole utterance meaningful, and of the fact that conventional syntactic patterns exert a subtle but extremely important influence upon our understanding of English utterances. By inserting meaningless forms into the positions normally occupied by content words and retaining the formulaic patterns of conventional morphology and syntax, by having Alice comment that the incomprehensible poem somehow "filled her head with ideas", and by having her, in her conversation with Humpty Dumpty, reveal through the phrasing of her questions that she understood the functions of some of the nonsense words by virtue of the structural markers, Carroll makes it clear that he had an awareness (perhaps intuitive only and not consciously verbalized to himself) that the purely functional structure of English utterances conveys its own meaning which is independent of the referential meaning, and that the two types of meaning, structural and referential, are closely related in a functional sense and are both essential to our understanding of the whole import of English utterances.

9.6 SUMMARY: THE SUCCESS OF COMMUNICATION ATTEMPTS DEPENDENT UPON SPEAKER, INTERPRETER, UTTERANCE: FAILURES VIEWED AS NON-UNDERSTANDING OR MISUNDERSTANDING

I have grouped together in this chapter a variety of matters which seem to me essentially related. I have called the general topic "Sound and Sense" because Carroll's interest in these matters can be reduced to a consideration of the form of utterances, and the implications which form has for the import of utterances as regards speaker, interpreter, and context of association. As noted earlier, Carroll felt that a word "means what the speaker intends by it, and what the hearer understands by it, and that is all". Whole utterances (either one word used in a specifically meaningful way or several words linked together into a syntactic structure) have in addition to these two possible meanings, a third: that which resides potentially in the literal import of the utterance itself, analytically viewed in terms of the speech community's general conventions of usage.

In the Duchess' statement, "Take care of the sense, and the sounds will take care of themselves", we have an expression of a valid linguistic principle subject to certain qualifications. A speaker must take care of his own sense; that is, he must know what he means to say and select the proper words and syntax to express that sense to a knowledgeable interpreter. But he must also say what he means; the utterance must accurately represent his intended meaning and, through its literal import, say nothing in itself that he does not intend. The speaker thus must take care of the sense of his utterance as well, to insure that it is clear and precise and neither vague nor ambiguous in its context. Once this has been done, once the speaker has chosen linguistic forms which accurately embody his intended import and scrutinized the literal import of the framed utterance to exclude unintended meanings, he may be reasonably sure that the sounds will convey to an interpreter who is familiar with his conventions of usage the meaning that he intends to impart. In this fashion, the sounds may be said to "take care of themselves". Conventions of usage will insure proper understanding in a knowledgeable interpreter except on those occasions when the words used have accidental affective connotations for the interpreter which may distort his apprehension of the speaker's intended meaning. Such occasions are always difficult and usually impossible for the speaker to foresee; he can guard against them to a certain extent by using words that do not have inherently a strong emotional charge, but at best his attempts at preventing such occurrences can only be minimal.

When attempts at communication fail because the utterance is so framed that it conveys no meaning at all to an interpreter, the failure may be ascribed to NON-UNDERSTANDING on the part of the interpreter. An utterance may be functionally meaningless because of (1) an overly complex syntax (as in the Duchess' moral, "Never imagine yourself not to be otherwise . . ."), (2) an overly complex syntax coupled with a lack of vocalized inflections indicating structural units (as in the Baron Muggzwig's speech), (3) unidiomatic word-use (as in the case of the Professor's hoping that the party will enjoy the heat "such as it isn't"), (4) the speaker's operating in a universe of discourse of which the interpreter is unaware (as in the case of the Hatter's saying of his watch, "Which is just the case with *mine*"), or (5) meaninglessness in the sounds themselves (as in the case of the 'content' words in the first stanza of "Jabberwocky").

When an utterance is so framed that its structure does not make clear in what way inherently equivocal words are to be taken, ambiguity can be created and attempts at communication can fail through MISUNDERSTANDING on the part of the interpreter. Misunderstanding can occur (1) when pronunciation is 'erroneous' according to the standards of normal usage (the butler's use of "ole party"), (2) when juncture is not made explicit ("many/ears"), or (3) when an interpreter misapprehends the speaker's pronunciation (Bruno's taking of *Bonhommie* and *Rumination* to be respectively *Bone-disease* and *Rheumatism*).

Carroll's insight into the fact that utterances have, by virtue of their words and syntax, a potential import in terms of conventional usage independent of the speaker's intended import and the interpreter's received import led him to exploit for humorous purposes the literal interpretation of metaphorical idioms. In the *Alice* books the interpreters are generally the characters whom Alice meets; their literal interpretation of her idiomatic expressions (and failure to grasp her intended import) stems either from their ignorance of the conventions of usage in Alice's world, or from a rigidly literal turn of mind. In a sense, the use of language in Wonderland and Looking-Glass Land is much more precise than it is in Alice's world. In *Sylvie and Bruno*, misunderstanding arising from the literal interpretation of idiomatic expressions tends to be due less to strict literalism than to ignorance of convention on the part of the interpreters. The effect of bringing a literal interpretation to metaphorical idioms is to reveal the essential absurdity of many of the types of utterance which pass as currency in English usage; it reveals the illogicality which is entrenched in the language through long habit and acceptance.

Carroll was also fascinated by the fact that although 'sounds' (the linguistic forms) of utterances might be different, their 'sense' (logical import) in a given context could very well be the same. That is, regardless of what words were chosen to convey a given thought, the designative import of two utterances differently phrased could be the same in a given context (*a piece of a dead crow* is equivalent in import to *rook-pie* when both names are used to designate the same meat-dish; *the lock was too large* is equivalent in import to *the key was too small* when each expression designates a single relationship of incongruity between the two objects).

It is interesting that most of Carroll's illustrations of communication difficulties occur in speech contexts. It would seem that he was well aware that language is, in its communicative role, essentially oral, and that writing is largely an attempt to reproduce in concrete form the sounds of speech. Thus, most of his illustrations dealing with non-understanding and misunderstanding occur because sound-sequences are nonsensical or ambiguous – the linguistic forms of the utterance itself, lexical and syntactic, AND the specific phones comprising them as articulated by the speaker. The Duchess' maxim will stand as valid if slightly rephrased: "Take care of the sense (both your own and that of the utterance), and, if you are speaking to an interpreter who is familiar with the conventions of the language you are using and you have made sure that your articulation is conventionally correct and clear, the sounds in which you frame your utterance (i.e., the words and syntactic structures you select) will, in large measure, take care of themselves in making your intended meaning understood."

10

WORD MAGIC

"... I suppose every child has a world of his own – and
every man, too, for the matter of that. I wonder if *that's*
the cause for all the misunderstanding there is in Life?"
The Narrator, *Sylvie and Bruno Concluded*, Chapter IV

10.1 INTRODUCTORY COMMENTS

In addition to their having the ability to serve men as instruments of thought and
communication, words also have the power to influence men's minds by evoking
emotional responses which often have no relation either to the thing which the
word symbolizes, or to the informative connotations about the thing which the
word conveys. Lewis Carroll's awareness of the affective power of words is the
subject of the present chapter. I call the topic "Word Magic" because the influence
which words exert on men's minds is the result of a process for the most part non-
rational, is in many ways mysterious since it involves complex psychological needs
and drives not fully understood, and is instrumental in producing a state of super-
stitious awe similar to that which is accorded to supernatural forces.

In Carroll's writing, word magic occurs frequently and seems to stem from two
closely related yet distinctive causes. The first of these is the affective connotations
which words may possess, the swarm of personal associations surrounding most
words which may determine a given interpreter's response both to the word and to
the thing signified by it. Thus, word magic may arise because of the meanings which
individual words hold for given interpreters. The second cause is men's tendency
to invest words with an autonomous existence and power of their own, to regard
the word itself as some sort of magical token having supernatural powers over
natural phenomena. Sometimes the affective force of such words lies in the meanings
they embody, but not always. Words can have affective force by virtue of their
sound alone. Carroll's characters often delight in uttering words which are unusual
or exceptionally long; and much of the fascination which such words hold for them
lies in their SOUND, and not in their sense. When this is the case, it is almost as
though the speaker's physical act of uttering the word (regardless whether the

sound has any meaning for him) in some way entails his mastery over it; yet, in granting the word this influential status, in taking some kind of comfort in the act of articulating it, the speaker is in a sense admitting the word's mastery over him. We shall examine these matters in greater detail in the ensuing sections.

10.2 AFFECTIVE CONNOTATIONS

"Words", said Lewis Carroll, "mean more than we mean to express when we use them" (see § 4.5). This statement seems to imply an awareness on Carroll's part of the capability of most words to evoke personal associations in the minds of interpreters. These personal associations may be informative connotations in addition to those which the speaker is trying to impart (though still representing aspects of the word's primary signification in general usage), or they may be purely subjective and represent the wholly personal "meanings" which the word holds for particular interpreters. These purely personal meanings are not part of the word's primary signification in general usage but are peculiar to a given interpreter on the basis of his past experience with the word and with the thing it symbolizes. They often carry an emotional charge which renders the word capable of producing emotional responses when it is encountered. These emotional responses may be directed toward the thing which the word symbolizes, or, as often happens, toward the word itself. The personal associations which a word has for a given interpreter that are capable of producing emotional responses in him are the word's "affective connotations".

The word *Communist*, for example, designates either a specific individual or any single member of the class of individuals who subscribe to the economic ideology set forth in the writings of Karl Marx. The informative connotations of the word include the fact that the person so designated adheres to this economic philosophy, and – for an interpreter familiar with the tenets of Marxist theory – something about the economic beliefs which the person holds. For anyone with formulated attitudes regarding Communists and Communism, the word *Communist* will possess a body of affective connotations as well which may evoke emotional responses to the person so designated ranging potentially from a sense of comradeship and good feeling, through neutrality, to irrational hate. Verbalized, these affective connotations might variously be expressed, depending upon the respective interpreters' attitudes, as: "a man to be trusted", "one of us", "dirty Red", "one who has seen the true light", "the Enemy", "misguided soul", "the cause of all our woes", and (particularly in America) "one of those engaged in the international conspiracy to destroy Our Way of Life". Sometimes, when an interpreter has fallen prey to stereotyped thinking, his emotional response to the word may be in the nature of a conditioned reflex, involving nothing so defined or verbalized as the affective connotations just listed, but rather being merely an immediate feeling of approbation or revulsion. The affective connotations which the name possesses for an interpreter may have little or no relation either to the object designated by the term (the specific Communist in question may NOT be dedicated to destroying the interpreter's Way of Life) or to the informative connotations of the term ("adherent to the economic teachings of Karl Marx").

It will be recalled that in *Through the Looking-Glass* the Fawn remained on friendly terms with Alice as long as neither of them possessed a classification-name (§ 6.5.1). When, upon leaving the wood where things have no names, the Fawn remembers its own name and classifies Alice as "a human child", it bolts away in terror. It is not Alice, but her NAME, that the Fawn reacts to so violently; and specifically, it is to the affective connotations which the word *human* holds for him as Fawn: "[human beings are] the enemies of deer". I say "affective connotations" instead of "informative" because the attribute of being an enemy of deer is not necessarily a characteristic of those things classified as "human beings". It is neither part of the acceptation of the term in general usage, nor is it, as attribute, possessed by all men. Some human beings are enemies of deer, some are not. The Fawn has fallen prey to stereotyped thinking in assuming that anything which may be classified as a human being will harm deer if given the chance. Alice has demonstrated no behavior that could be called hostile, and in fact she has been just the opposite – friendly, gentle, and loving. In allowing her name alone to determine his reaction to her as object, the Fawn is permitting the associations which the word *human* holds for him to override and deny the evidence he has gained through personal experience that her attributes are otherwise than what his stereotype demands. Therefore, when he has observed nothing in her actions to warrant such a response, his reaction of fear upon learning her name is irrational.[1]

Since almost any word which has 'content' (which is not merely a 'function' word, or structural marker) may come to have personal associations for individual interpreters, and since these associations will of necessity vary from mind to mind, failure in communication attempts may be caused by divergence in the affective or informative connotations which a given word may have respectively for a speaker and an interpreter. Such a divergence is usually not foreseeable by the speaker when he is selecting his words, for he has no way of knowing what personal associations a given word may have for his hearer. When such a divergence occurs, the discrepancy in meanings may not be recognized by either the speaker or the hearer. If it remains unrecognized, the disparity in meanings can result in men talking at

---

[1] I grant that it is possible that the Fawn, suddenly apprehending his own nature with the recovery of his name, may assume that Alice's gentle behavior in the wood was atypical and that she, upon recovering HER name, will revert to her "normal" behavior (i.e., become hostile to deer). If this were so, the Fawn might indeed be justified in regarding Alice, as "human child", with suspicion and fear. However, I think that this interpretation is over-subtle, and that we will be closer to the mark if we take the Fawn's reaction simply as an illustration of the power of affective connotations of words to induce emotional responses which pervert judgment.

cross purposes (or using the same sounds in different senses) without realizing it.
Thus, in spite of a speaker's precision of thought, in spite of his care in framing
his utterance to convey his intended meaning, and in spite of the interpreter's
good-will in attempting to apprehend accurately the intended sense of the utterance,
the sounds selected, by virtue of the personal associations which they hold for the
interpreter, may convey to him a sense NOT intended by the speaker and one quite
independent of the literal import of the utterance.

It will be recalled that in *Sylvie and Bruno* the Lord Chancellor, having pulled
the child Uggug out of the room by his ear, is greatly disturbed when the boy's
mother uses the terms 'a taking way with children', 'gain the ear', and 'draw him
out' while speaking to him about her son (§ 8.2.2). Because of the personal associations which the words hold for him, the Lord Chancellor assumes that My Lady
knows of his action and is slyly referring to it through *double entendre*. Carroll, in
the voice of the narrator, hastens to assure his readers that My Lady, not knowing
of the Chancellor's action, does NOT intend the additional meanings which the
Chancellor is able to see: "my Lady's remarks were curiously full of meaning, of
which she herself was wholly unconscious". Here we have a graphic illustration of
the principle that "words mean more than we mean to express when we use them".

10.3 EUPHEMISM

Although almost any word which embodies referential meaning is potentially
capable of possessing affective connotations for a particular interpreter, some words
may be so highly charged with emotional overtones that their utterance becomes
intolerable for particular individuals or groups (which groups may range in size
almost to the whole of the speech community). When the emotional associations
surrounding a given thing are extended to the word which symbolizes it, men often
will avoid using the word because of the emotional shock it has come to provide
for them as individuals and for other men. Words symbolizing "taboo" referents
may themselves thus come to be "taboo". When this has occurred and the thing
symbolized by the word must for some reason be made an object of discourse, men
often resort to euphemism – the substitution of a less emotionally-charged word
for the one of strong and undesirable affective connotations.

Lewis Carroll was conscious of the operation of euphemistic substitution, and
gave illustrations of it on several occasions. In his *Russian Journal*, he records an
instance of euphemism that occurred in his own experience. While in Paris on the
return trip from Russia, he went to the Convent of S. Thomas, Rue de Sevres, to
procure some of the salve made there for the treatment of the "tic-doloreux".

I had interviews with two of the Sisters, & the elder, who appeared to have most
authority, assured me in very fluent French, much of which was lost on me, that they
never sold it, & only gave it to their own poor. As this appeared to be an exhaustive

division of the category "modes of distribution of ointment" I was very nearly giving up the quest in despair – but there was an indication of some other process for obtaining it being practicable, & after much beating about the bush I said "then you cannot *sell* it me, but you will *give* me some, and permit me to give something, for your poor?" "Oui', Certainment!" was the eager reply, & so the delicately-veiled bargain was at last concluded.

(Russian Journal, pp. 120-121)

In "Novelty and Romancement" (1856), the poetic hero who has yearned all his life for "romancement" misinterprets a sign-board reading "ROMAN CEMENT" as advertising the object of his desire as a purchasable commodity. He contacts a mechanic who works at the place, and makes an appointment for the following morning

when I would personally inspect "the article" (I could not bring myself to utter the beloved word itself).

(Works, p. 1087)

If he had been able to utter the word, and had not resorted to the vague euphemism, the mechanic, noting his pronunciation, would have set him straight on the nature of the commodity sold at the establishment.

In *Wonderland,* the words *cat* and *dog* have powerful affective connotations for the Mouse which Alice meets while swimming in the pool of tears. Thinking that the Mouse does not understand English, Alice asks it a question in French, which – it is interesting to note – the Mouse has no difficulty in understanding.

... she began again: "Où est ma chatte?" which was the first sentence in her French lesson-book. The Mouse gave a sudden leap out of the water, and seemed to quiver all over with fright. "Oh, I beg your pardon!" cried Alice hastily, afraid that she had hurt the poor animal's feelings. "I quite forgot you didn't like cats."

"Not like cats!" cried the Mouse in a shrill passionate voice. "Would *you* like cats, if you were me?"

"Well, perhaps not," said Alice in a soothing tone: "don't be angry about it. ..."

After speaking for a moment about her cat Dinah, Alice sees that the Mouse has become extremely agitated and says, "We wo'n't talk about her any more if you'd rather not."

"We, indeed!" cried the Mouse, who was trembling down to the end of his tail. "As if *I* would talk on such a subject! Our family always *hated* cats: nasty, low, vulgar things! Don't let me hear the name again!"

(Works, pp. 32-33)

In the original version of this passage, as found in "Alice's Adventures under Ground", the Mouse's final sentence was "Don't talk to me about them any more." Carroll's making the change indicates that he was consciously illustrating the principle of word magic; for in the revised version, it is obvious that the Mouse is adversely affected by the name alone (and the Mouse's reaction is equally violent whether the name is given in English or in French). Knowing that the names 'cat' and 'dog' hold painful associations for the Mouse, Alice later resorts to euphemism in referring to the things designated by them.

"You promised to tell me your history, you know," said Alice, "and why it is you hate – C and D," she added in a whisper, half afraid that it would be offended again.

(Works, p. 39)

In *Sylvie and Bruno Concluded* there is an example of euphemism used not only to neutralize an emotionally-charged word, but also to put a false coloration on an unpleasant matter. Once again the illustration involves cats and mice; but in this case, the viewpoint expressed is the cat's. Bruno has said of a fat tabby that has entered the room, "This Cat's very kind to the Mouses." The Other Professor is skeptical: "But how do you know it's kind to the Mouses – or, more correctly speaking, the *Mice*?"

"'cause it *plays* with the Mouses," said Bruno; "for to amuse them, oo know."

"But that is just what I *don't* know," the Other Professor rejoined. "My belief is, it plays with them to *kill* them!"

"Oh, that's quite a *accident*!" Bruno began, so eagerly, that it was evident he had already propounded this very difficulty to the Cat. "It 'splained all that to me, while it were drinking the milk. It said 'I teaches the Mouses new games: the Mouses likes it ever so much.' It said 'Sometimes little accidents happens: sometimes the Mouses kills theirselves.' It said 'I's always *welly* sorry, when the Mouses kills theirselves.' . . ."

(Works, p. 723)

Here is euphemism that amounts to equivocation, employed by a speaker who intends to deceive. "Accident" indeed! The mice "kill themselves", no doubt, by happening to get in the way of the cat's paw, or somehow managing to get their heads into its mouth. This kind of deceitful euphemism, or "whitewashing", is frequently employed by politicians, advertisers, and apologists of many types who wish to make the worse appear the better cause.

10.4 THE SOVEREIGNTY OF THE WORD

10.4.1 *The Power of Language to Influence Events; Ritual and Charm*

Although words often come to exert emotional influence upon men's minds by virtue of their affective connotations, they often are capable of doing so not primarily through any specific meaning they may possess for the interpreter, but merely because of men's tendency to regard them as having an autonomous authority and potency independent of men's understanding and use of them. It is not only in primitive societies that words come to be regarded as having super-natural powers over natural forces, as having some sort of divine origin and in-evitable concrete relationship to the things they name, as having through their sound alone, or their ritual repetition, the ability to function as charms. Lewis Carroll saw that it was a general human tendency to endow words with sovereign powers and to allow them to be a dominant force in the conditioning of men's behavior and in the conduct of men's affairs. His insight into the prevalence of word magic of this sort among even such sophisticated students of language as formal logicians is attested by his statement in *Symbolic Logic* that many professional logicians "speak of the Copula of a Proposition 'with bated breath', almost as if it were a living, conscious Entity, capable of declaring for itself what it chose to mean, and that we, poor human creatures, had nothing to do but to ascertain WHAT was its sovereign will and pleasure, and submit to it" (*Symbolic Logic,* 4th ed., p. 165). Moreover, many logicians "have somehow acquired a perfectly MORBID dread of negative Attributes, which makes them shut their eyes, like frightened children, when they come across such terrible Propositions as 'All not-x are y'" – a state of mind which Carroll calls "unreasoning terror" (*Symbolic Logic*, p. 172).

The operation of word magic is manifested in a variety of ways. Words and phrases may sometimes be considered to have the force of charms influencing in some unexplainable way natural forces or states of being in the world of reality. As M. M. Lewis has said, "If a derivation is simple enough and repeated often enough it will frequently gain a strong motive power of itself, whatever its validity." [2] The use of formulaic phrases to exert some supernatural influence upon the things of the real world is illustrated in *The Hunting of the Snark*.

> "Just the place for a Snark!" the Bellman cried,
>   As he landed his crew with care;
> Supporting each man on the top of the tide
>   By a finger entwined in his hair.
>
> "Just the place for a Snark! I have said it twice:
>   That alone should encourage the crew.
> Just the place for a Snark! I have said it thrice:
>   What I tell you three times is true."
>
> (*Works*, p. 757)

The Baker, in expressing his fear of meeting with a Boojum and therefore having to softly and suddenly vanish away, requires a three-fold statement of a particular phrase and becomes insistent upon the third repetition when the Bellman wishes to cut him off:

> "It is this, it is this that oppresses my soul,
>   When I think of my uncle's last words:
> And my heart is like nothing so much as a bowl
>   Brimming over with quivering curds!
>
> "It is this, it is this –" "We have had that before!"
>   The Bellman indignantly said.
> And the Baker replied "Let me say it once more.
>   It is this, it is this that I dread!
>
> (*Works*, p. 765)

[2] M. M. Lewis, *Language in Society* (London, 1947), p. 177.

The Butcher and the Beaver, having ventured alone into a desolate valley in their hunt for the Snark, are frightened by a shrill scream. The Butcher identifies the animal that made the scream, feeling compelled for some reason to utter its name three times – as though this would insure the accuracy of his identification, or perhaps cause the beast itself to become that which the Butcher says it is.

> "'Tis the voice of the Jubjub!" he suddenly cried.
> (This man, that they used to call "Dunce.")
> "As the Bellman would tell you," he added with pride,
>   "I have uttered that sentiment once.
>
> "'Tis the note of the Jubjub! Keep count, I entreat.
>   You will find I have told it you twice.
> 'Tis the song of the Jubjub! The proof is complete.
>   If only I've stated it thrice."
>
> (*Works*, p. 770)

Of these three passages, the first and third seem to indicate a belief on the part of the Bellman and Butcher that their three-fold repetition of their respective phrases will insure the truth of the assertion contained in the formula. Their repetitions are of the nature of magical incantations, verbal charms which supposedly will influence natural phenomena. If the Bellman's statement is not uttered three times, there will be no assurance that its assertion is true; if it IS uttered three times, there can be no doubt of the assertion's truth, for it will be true of necessity. The second passage seems to illustrate word magic of another sort. The Baker's three-fold repetition of *It is this, it is this* does not seem to have the same type of function as the formulas of the Bellman and Butcher. Rather than acting as a charm to influence external reality, it seems to be the reflection of some psychological need that the Baker is experiencing. He insists upon the third repetition. To what end? It seems to have only subjective significance; he is for some reason compelled to utter the formula three times, as though there is some personal benefit – perhaps security or peace of mind – in his doing so.

10.4.2 *Therapeutic Powers of Words*

Words can, in themselves, be therapeutic or comforting to individuals, even when they lack designative signification for the user. In *Wonderland*, Alice, having not the faintest idea what the words *Latitude* and *Longitude* refer to, nonetheless utters them because, as Carroll tells the reader, "she thought they were nice grand words to say" (*Works*, p. 19). At the Knave of Hearts' trial, she takes pleasure in identifying the legalistic fixtures of the courtroom; and the legal terminology she has acquired gives her an almost sensual delight:

"I suppose they are the jurors." She said this last word two or three times over to herself, being rather proud of it: for she thought, and rightly too, that very few little girls of her age knew the meaning of it at all. However, "jurymen" would have done just as well.

(*Works*, p. 115)

In *Through the Looking-Glass,* Alice, having said good-bye to Humpty Dumpty
and received no answer, lets her accumulated irritation boil over in words. This is
obviously a therapeutic relief, or working out of aggressive feelings: note that she
is comforted –

. . . "of all the unsatisfactory –" (she repeated this aloud as it was a great comfort to have
such a long word to say) "of all the unsatisfactory people I *ever* met –"

(Works, p. 221)

And in *Phantasmagoria* (1869) the narrator is stopped in the middle of a song he
is singing by the occurrence of a word to which he responds emotionally:

> *And art thou gone, beloved Ghost?*
> > *Best of Familiars!*
> *Nay then, farewell, my duckling roast,*
> *Farewell, farewell, my tea and toast,*
> > *My meerschaum and cigars!*
>
> *The hues of life are dull and gray,*
> > *The sweets of life insipid,*
> *When* thou, *my charmer, art away –*
> *Old Brick, or rather, let me say,*
> > *Old Parallelepiped!"*
>
> Instead of singing Verse the Third,
> > I ceased – abruptly, rather:
> But, after such a splendid word
> I felt that it would be absurd
> > To try it any farther.

(Works, p. 852)

In these four examples, only in the case of *jurors* is the sense of the word stressed
as being of cardinal importance to the person speaking. In the other examples, the
SOUND of the word is that which evokes the speaker's emotional response; and
even *jurors* is repeated "two or three times over". The other words are described
simply as "nice", "grand", "long", and "splendid". As regards their effect on the
speaker (who is also the listener), meaning doesn't matter: their emotional force
stems primarily from their length or unfamiliarity, from the physical act of articulating them, and from their sound. *Jurors* is important to Alice because her ability
to use the word indicates her command over its meaning and use. However, the
fact that she repeats it two or three times indicates that it holds an emotional sway
over her. *Unsatisfactory* is important to Alice because its meaning enables her to
verbalize her feeling of irritation at Humpty Dumpty's rudeness; but of even greater
importance to her than its meaning is its providing her, by virtue of its length, with
a satisfying and somehow definitive expression of her frustration. In a moment of
stress, "it was a great comfort to have such a long word to say".

10.4.3 *The Affectiveness of Long, Unfamiliar, or Foreign Words*

Unfamiliar words and words of exceptional length often inspire a sort of super-
stitious awe in listeners not accustomed to hearing them. Even if they are nonsensical
in that they convey no meaning to the interpreter, there is something about foreign
words and long words in general which induces an emotional response to sound
alone. In "The Vision of the Three T's" (1873), Carroll comments wryly upon this
tendency of people to regard utterances in foreign languages with deferential respect
and reverential awe. The passage, though humorous in its context, reflects an actual
state of affairs: the growing importance of German scholarship and England's (and
perhaps Carroll's) essential insularity. An Oxford professor is speaking to the main
characters, Piscator and Venator:

. . . now-a-days, all that is good comes from the German. Ask our men of science: they
will tell you that any German book must needs surpass an English one. Aye, and even
an English book, worth naught in this its native dress, shall become, when rendered into
German, a valuable contribution to Science!

    VEN. Sir, you much amaze me.

    PROF. Nay, Sir, I'll amaze you yet more. No learned man doth now talk, or even so
much as cough, save only in German. The time has been, I doubt not, when an honest
English "Hem!" was held enough, both to clear the voice and rouse the attention of the
company, but nowadays no man of Science, that setteth any store by his good name, will
cough otherwise than this, Ach! Euch! Auch!

(Works, p. 1154)

The emotional effect of Latin is illustrated in Knot VII of *A Tangled Tale*. Two fat
women leaving a cab become stuck in the door.

"I tell you the cab-door isn't half wide enough!" she repeated, as her sister finally
emerged, somewhat after the fashion of a pellet from a pop-gun . . .

    "Some folks is too wide for 'em," growled the cab-driver.

    "Don't provoke me, man!" cried the little old lady . . . "Say another word and I'll put
you into the County Court, and sue you for a *Habeas Corpus*!" The cabman touched his
hat, and marched off, grinning.

    "Nothing like a little law to cow the ruffians, my dear!" she remarked confidentially
to Clara. "You saw how he quailed when I mentioned the *Habeas Corpus*? Not that I've
any idea what it means, but it sounds very grand, doesn't it?"

(A Tangled Tale, in the Dover Publications
edition of *Pillow Problems and A Tangled Tale*
(New York, 1958), pp. 46-47; also in *Works*,
p. 1008)

Judging by the cabman's grinning response, it would seem that the little old lady
was more awed by the Latin term than he. Nonetheless, she uses it for the specific
purpose of "cowing" the man, since she feels certain that it will probably have that
effect. So sure is she that it will overawe the man, she assumes that it has done so
in spite of the fact that the man had NOT visibly "quailed". The sound of the word,
and not its meaning, is the effective agent invoked by the little old lady to subdue

the cab-driver; and it is this aspect of sound which, by thinking it "grand", she succumbs to herself.

In English, the long words which produce emotional responses are often Latinate in origin. Their effect perhaps lies in their carrying with them as a result of their derivation an air of scholarly authority – scientific, juridical, ecclesiastical – which, because of the words' restricted use and magisterial sound, conveys to hearers ignorant of the words' meanings a profound finality. Arthur Forester, it will be recalled, tricked the bluestocking into thinking that the brain is inverted by saying that what is called the vertex is actually the base, and what is called the base is actually the vertex. He concluded by declaring that it is all merely "a question of *nomenclature*". And, as Carroll remarks in the voice of the narrator, "This last polysyllable settled the matter. 'How truly delightful!' the fair Scientist exclaimed with enthusiasm" (*Works*, p. 417). The operation of word magic is greatly reinforced in this instance by Arthur's speaking "with all the gravity of ten professors rolled into one".

The Professor in "The Vision of the Three T's" whom we met a moment ago talking on the subject of German scholarship speaks with the inflated diction which almost invariably impresses the unlearned with a conviction of the speaker's profound erudition. In this instance, Piscator is overawed by the Professor's language and "taken in"; Venator is not. The subject of the conversation is the New Belfry at Christ Church.

PISC.   But, Sir, I will by your favour ask you one other thing, as to that unseemly box that blots the fair heavens above. Wherefore, in this grand old City, and in so conspicuous a place, do men set so hideous a thing?

PROF.   Be you mad, Sir? Why this is the very climacteric and coronal of all our architectural aspirations! In all Oxford there is naught like it!

PISC.   It joys me much to hear you say so.

PROF.   And, trust me, to an earnest mind, the categorical evolution of the Abstract, ideologically considered, must infallibly develop itself in the parallelepipedisation of the Concrete! And so farewell.

Exit PROFESSOR

PISC.   He is a learned man, and methinks there is much that is sound in his reasoning.

VEN.   It is *all* sound, as it seems to me.

(*Works*, p. 1155)

Venator is perceptive enough to pierce the veil of words and see that the Professor's utterance has little if any sense. It is noise merely, but the kind of noise which men generally respond to in an uncritical and credulous manner.[3] Listeners such as Venator and the Eaglet in *Wonderland* who challenged the Dodo's pompous use of "big words" are relatively rare; too often the general tendency of men is to allow the affective power of words to dominate their minds and to condition their responses to reality.

---

[3] All too frequently, when persons are faced with a level of discourse which is "beyond them", they react in a manner similar to that of the character in "The Three Voices" who was baffled by the metaphysical "arguments" of the woman he met on the beach:

10.4.4 *The Tendency of Men to Grant Autonomy to Words*

Judging from their responses to words, people often seem to regard them as
sovereign agents with inherent, predestined, and unalterable meanings; as "living,
conscious Entities, capable of declaring for themselves what they choose to mean";
as beings capable of acting forcefully in their own right, independent of human
control, so domineering that "poor human creatures" can only "ascertain their
sovereign will and pleasure and submit to it".

When he was thirteen, Lewis Carroll in his "Quotation from Shakespeare with
slight improvements" had Prince Hal say of the word *rigol*, "it hath passed my lips,
and all the powers upon this earth can not unsay it". This statement is literally
true; but it implies in context a willingness on the part of both Prince Hal and
King Henry to grant the word an autonomous existence and an almost divinely-
appointed independence of action. Once uttered, it could not be recalled. It was,
presumably, from the moment of its utterance, a concrete entity free to circulate
in the world of men.

In *Through the Looking-Glass,* published twenty-six years after King Henry's
admission of helplessness in the presence of the almighty word, there is another
example of the notion that words are free agents, independent of men's control.
During Alice's examination for queenhood, the White Queen asks her to explain
the cause of lightning.

"The cause of lightning," Alice said very decidedly, for she felt quite certain about this,
"is the thunder – no, no!" she hastily corrected herself. "I meant the other way."
   "It's too late to correct it," said the Red Queen: "when you've once said a thing, that
fixes it, and you must take the consequences."

(Works, p. 255)

There is both truth and falsity in the Red Queen's statement. It is true that in a
given context, such as an examination or a published book, one must take the
consequences of making a careless assertion. But it is false that once something is
said, it is "fixed" in any absolute sense: such a belief would be granting to words
a free-wheeling autonomy and the power of producing positive results in the material
world which they do not and cannot have. The only consequence that could possibly
follow from Alice's false statement is that her wrong answer might contribute to
her failing the examination. Her saying that thunder is the cause of lightning does
not necessitate that henceforward thunder will be the cause of lightning. For a man

---

"Her style was anything but clear,
And most unpleasantly severe;
Her epithets were very queer.

"And yet, so grand were her replies,
I could not choose but deem her wise;
I did not dare to criticise ..."
(Works, p. 875)

to say that he died last week cannot result in his doing so; for him to say that he
will die tomorrow does not insure that he will. Words in themselves do not have a
direct influence upon natural forces or events. It was long believed and frequently
stated that men could not sail beyond the Pillars of Hercules: in spite of the words,
men did.

Lewis Carroll knew that the only concrete influence which words have on natural
events is that which men empower them to have: men do this by subordinating
themselves to words as to a magic spell, allowing the language they use to discuss
reality to condition their own actions, responses, and attitudes towards reality.
Through the affective connotations which words possess, and through men's willingness to endow their words with "supernatural" powers, men allow themselves to
be mastered by the tools which should be their servants.

11

POSTSCRIPT

> "How far have you come, dear?" the young lady persisted.
>
> Sylvie looked puzzled. "A mile or two, I *think*," she said doubtfully.
>
> "A mile or *three*," said Bruno.
>
> "You shouldn't say 'a mile or *three*,'" Sylvie corrected him.
>
> The young lady nodded approval. "Sylvie's quite right. It isn't usual to say 'a mile or *three*.'"
>
> "It would be usual – if we said it often enough," said Bruno.
>
> *Sylvie and Bruno Concluded*, Chapter X

We, too, have come a mile or three, and during the journey have unearthed many of the linguistic bones which Carroll left embedded in the matrix of his works. Some of the bones are able to be viewed intact, some are merely fragments. Although there undoubtedly are others which we did not uncover, those which have been extracted are sufficient to provide a clear notion of both the nature and scope of his interest in language, and many of the theoretical assumptions he held with regard to the nature and functions of language.

In analyzing the patterns of Carroll's interest and the character of his linguistic insights, I have tried to avoid giving the impression that a formal system underlies his views. As a student of language, Carroll was unsystematic and non-scientific. It would be a mistake to try to discover an internally consistent philosophy of language, for none is present.

It is apparent, however, that he did spend much time thinking about language in a serious fashion; the linguistic matter presented humorously in his works is undergirded by implicit theoretical principles which are in many cases identical to those subscribed to by many twentieth-century students of language who, though more scientific in their methods than Carroll, and more systematic in their approach to linguistic problems, see fit to quote his writings illustratively in their own works. The ultimate seriousness of his linguistic concerns is seen in the few explicit statements about the nature of language which he recorded; these, serving as premises, attest the validity of our assuming that Carroll subscribed, whether consciously or not, to the principles which this study has derived by inference from the linguistic matter contained in his works. They, as statements, and the implications that they entail as statements, affirm that our inferences are legitimate. While many of Carroll's notions about language were undoubtedly intuitive, others were derived from his study and professional work. His choosing to embody the fruits of his linguistic speculation in humorous illustrations is simply a function of his peculiar personality, and of his literary aims. The fact remains that, in their implications, his whimsical illustrations reveal a serious concern with theoretical principles.

The topics discussed in this study reveal that the various aspects of Carroll's speculative interest in language are subsumed in three broad categories. The first is language conceived as a vehicle for play. In this category, two separate fields must be distinguished: manipulatory play, in which linguistic symbols, phonic and graphic, are used as counters in a game; and functional play, in which humor is derived from language's operational characteristics in situational contexts. It is this latter field which has provided the data sufficient for determining the scope of the remaining two categories: (a) Carroll's interest in the nature of meaning, best exemplified by his speculations into the nature and function of signs and symbols; and (b) his preoccupation with the process of communication, particularly with the linguistic phenomena that create obstacles to its success.

The conclusion to be drawn from isolating these categories of concern is simply this: in addition to his regarding language as a vehicle for play, he was interested in it both as an instrument of thought and as an instrument for communicating thought. This double concern caused him to ponder the nature and function of signs, their modes of signifying, and their frequently exhibited failure to produce intended responses in interpreters. In his writings, these speculations on the theory of meaning are often embodied in contexts of communication-failure. Although the breakdowns in communication he depicts may be traced to a variety of causes, he was particularly concerned with the ability of language itself to prevent the interpreter from apprehending the speaker's intended sense.

In Carroll's illustrations, communication attempts fail for two reasons: either (1) the interpreter is unable to interpret the utterance (i.e., it fails to convey any meaning at all and thus functionally remains non-sense), or (2) he misinterprets the utterance, taking it to signify something other than what the speaker intended. These two types of failure in communication attempts may be termed 'non-under-standing' and 'misunderstanding', respectively.

Illustrations of non-understanding and misunderstanding occur throughout Carroll's literary works. By filling his narratives with hypothetical speech situations ("What is the use of a book?" thought Alice, "without pictures and conversations?"), he in a sense set up a laboratory for carrying out controlled experiments. The individual dialogues form a series of self-contained episodes whose capsule form enables the reader to study each communication attempt in isolation, without distraction. Carroll's intense interest in problems of communication is attested in these narrative situations by the frequency with which his characters fail to understand one another. Often the failure is explicitly pointed out, either by authorial comment, or by one character's saying, in effect, to another: "I don't understand what you mean." It is interesting to note how frequently this statement, or an equivalent, occurs in Carroll's fiction.

Implicit in many of his illustrations of unsuccessful attempts at communication are the remedies, or aids, which would have prevented the obstacles from arising and would have made understanding possible. Many of these implied precautionary measures are linguistic in nature. It is possible that he was trying to make his young readers aware of the hidden traps which language provides for the unwary. Language is man's servant, he seems to be saying on frequent occasions, but man cannot take for granted that it will always do his bidding. Yet one must keep in mind Carroll's literary aims. Failures in communication are potentially a rich source of humor. If there is any educational aim in Carroll's treatment of language, it is subordinated to his desire to amuse and entertain.

APPENDIX A

CHRONOLOGICAL LIST OF CARROLL'S MAJOR WORKS

There follows a selective list of Carroll's publications, both technical and literary, in short titles, as described in *The Lewis Carroll Handbook* (Oxford, 1962), edited by Roger Lancelyn Green; this book is a revision of *A Handbook of the Literature of the Rev. C. L. Dodgson*, by Sidney H. Williams and Falconer Madan (Oxford, 1931). The bracketed numbers refer to Green's system of cataloguing; those in parentheses to Williams and Madan's.

1845   [1](—) *Useful and Instructive Poetry* [first published, 1954; edited by Derek Hudson]

1850   [5](—) *The Rectory Umbrella* (c. 1850-1853)

1853   [6](—) *Mischmasch* (1853-1862) [*The Rectory Umbrella* and *Mischmasch* are two family magazines containing miscellaneous juvenilia; first published (together in one volume), 1932; edited by Florence Milner]

1860   [24](14) *A Syllabus of Plane Algebraical Geometry*
        [25](15) *Notes on the First Two Books of Euclid*

1861   [27](17) *The Formulae of Plane Trigonometry*

1863   [34](25) *The Enunciations of Euclid, Books I and II*

1864   [38](27) *A Guide to the Mathematical Student in Reading, Reviewing, and Working Examples*

1865   [40](35) *The New Method of Evaluation, as Applied to* π
        A humorous skit, mathematically conceived, on Jowett's salary.

        [41](36) *The Dynamics of a Parti-cle*
        A brilliant parody of the Definitions, Postulates, and Axioms of Euclid, and a humorous comment on the contest between Gladstone and Gathorne Hardy to represent Oxford in Parliament.

        [42](30) *Alice's Adventures in Wonderland*

1866   [52](39) *Condensation of Determinants, being a New and Brief Method for Computing Their Arithmetical Values*

1867   [57](44) *An Elementary Treatise on Determinants*

1868   [64](49) *The Fifth Book of Euclid Treated Algebraically*

1869   [68](54) *Phantasmagoria and Other Poems*
1870   [76](58) *Algebraical Formulae and Rules*
        [77](59) *Arithmetical Formulae and Rules*
1872   [84](67) *Through the Looking-Glass and What Alice Found There*
        Published at the end of 1871; title page bears '1872' as date.
        [88](71a) *The New Belfry of Christ Church, Oxford*
        A humorous pamphlet on the wooden box erected to house the Cathedral
        bells during Dean Liddell's architectural renovation of Christ Church.
        One of Carroll's funniest pieces.
1873   [92](78) *The Enunciations of Euclid I-VI*
        [94](74) *The Vision of the Three T's*
        Further spoofing of Dean Liddell's architectural "improvements".
1874   [98](80) *Notes by an Oxford Chiel*
        A collection of six pamphlets dealing with Oxford topics; all are satirical
        and were independently published during the period 1865-1874. Con-
        tains: "Evaluation of π", "Dynamics", "Facts, Figures, and Fancies"
        (1866-1868), "New Belfry", "Three T's", and "The Blank Cheque"
        (1874).
        [102](84) *Euclid, Book V. Proved Algebraically*
1875   [107](88) *Euclid, Books I, II*
1876   [110-112](95-97) *Professorship of Comparative Philology*
        Three papers objecting to the half-pay salary of the deputy who took
        over Max Müller's duties as Professor of Comparative Philology.
        [115] (89) *The Hunting of the Snark*
1878   [125](102) *Word-Links: A Game for Two Players*
        An early version of the game called "Doublets".
1879   [128](103) *Euclid and His Modern Rivals*
        ["One of the outstanding examples of serious argument cast in an amusing
        style, designed to prove that for elementary geometry a revised Euclid
        is better than any proposed modern substitute." – Williams and Madan]
        A second edition, with a supplement, was published in 1885.
        [130](105) *Doublets. A Word-Puzzle*
        This game became quite popular and reached a third edition in 1880.
1881   [142](117) *'Lanrick', a Game for Two Players*
1882   [155](124) *Mischmasch*
        A word-game too elaborate to become popular.
        [156](130) *Euclid, Books I and II*
1883   [160](131) *Rhyme? and Reason?*
        A collection of Carroll's poems, containing *The Hunting of the Snark*,
        the light verse from *Phantasmagoria*, and several new poems.
1885   [182](144) *A Tangled Tale*
        A fantasy in ten 'knots' which originally appeared in serial form in *The*

Monthly Packet from April, 1880 to March, 1885. Each 'knot' contains at least one mathematical problem to be solved by the reader.

1886 [194](158) *Alice's Adventures Under Ground*
A facsimile of the original manuscript book "Alice's Adventures under Ground" (written in 1862) which was developed into *Alice's Adventures in Wonderland.*

1887 [196](170a) *The Game of Logic*

1888 [210](182) *Curiosa Mathematica, Part I: A New Theory of Parallels*

1889 [215](185a) *The Nursery 'Alice'*
An abridgement and simplification of *Alice's Adventures in Wonderland* (with colored pictures) for very young readers.

[217](187) *Sylvie and Bruno*

1890 [223](193) *Eight or Nine Wise Words about Letter-Writing*

1891 [231](204) *Syzygies: A Word-Puzzle*
Achieved a small measure of popularity.

1893 [246](220) *Curiosa Mathematica, Part II: Pillow-Problems*
A set of seventy-two problems, involving operations in algebra, geometry, and trigonometry, which Carroll worked out in his head during sleepless nights before committing the problems and their solutions to paper.

[250](216) *Sylvie and Bruno Concluded*

1894 [261](232) *A Logical Paradox*
A problem involving hypotheticals, printed in *Mind,* N.S. III (July, 1894), 436-438. It has proved interesting to many subsequent logicians.

[263](234) *What the Tortoise Said to Achilles*
A humorous dialogue involving hypotheticals.
Printed in *Mind,* N.S. IV (1895), 278-280.

1896 [270](240) *Symbolic Logic, Part I: Elementary*
Reached a fourth edition in 1897.

The above is a chronological listing of Carroll's publications which have particular significance for this study. The omitted catalogue numbers represent a large body of heterogeneous material: minor mathematical pamphlets, odds and ends of occasional verse, circulars to hospitals and booksellers, letters and articles appearing in the popular press on a variety of topics, individual mathematical and logical problems, descriptions and rules of original games, and isolated bits of educational writing for children.

APPENDIX B

CRITIQUE OF A FRAGMENT OF SCHOOLBOY LATIN

One fragment of Dodgson's schoolboy Latin, a poem on "Evening", has been preserved in Stuart Dodgson Collingwood's *The Life and Letters of Lewis Carroll* (New York, 1898), p. 23. The poem is dated, evidently from Richmond Grammar School, November 25, 1844, and is contemporaneous with the letter from the headmaster which states that Dodgson is "marvelously ingenious in replacing the ordinary inflexions of nouns and verbs, as detailed in our grammars, by more exact analogies, or convenient forms of his own devising".

Professor Roger A. Hornsby of the Classics Department of the University of Iowa has kindly supplied me with a critique of Dodgson's poem, including in it an analysis of the numerous errors which the fragment contains. Professor Hornsby's comments immediately follow my quotation of the poem.

> Phoebus aqua splendet descendens, aequora tingens
>   Splendore aurato. Pervenit umbra solo.
> Mortales lectos quaerunt, et membra relaxant
>   Fessa labore dies; cuncta per orbe silet.
> Imperium placidum nunc sumit Phoebe corusca.
>
>   Antris procedunt sanguine ore ferae.

"1.   aquā – apparently Dodgson wants an ablative of means. But this is not possible here. In Latin one cannot shine by means of water.

tingens – rather metaphorical for Latin, but not impossible, I suppose.

2.   Splendore aurato – *s.* means 'brightness', 'brilliance'.

Horace uses it of silver; Ovid of flames. Usually the connotation is of outward sheen. With *aurato* the phrase is not Latin. *a.* means 'golden, gilded, covered with gold'. But in Latin the phrase is nonsense. To convey what Dodgson wants to, one would use *a.* alone

umbra – means 'shade' as of a tree or ghost. It does not mean 'shadows' as of evening.

solo – 'land' or 'soil' is possible in the sense of 'earth'.

But not in this case (dative) with *pervenit*: *p.* means 'reach', 'come', 'fall' – but only in literal significance. Shadows can't fall in Latin.
The whole of line 2 should be rejected.

3. The line is all right.

4. If the semi-colon is correct the entire first phrase '*Fessa ... dies*' is nonsense. It is nominative and one would expect an ablative absolute or a *cum* clause. If he wants *est* to be understood, then some mark of punctuation should appear after *relaxant*. But even so the phrase is metaphorical in a way that Latin never is. A day can be spent in, but it can't be worn out (*fessa*) with work. Ovid has an example of years being worn out; perhaps this is Dodgson's source.

   cuncta – in sense of *tota* (all) not usually possible. The word is usually followed by some sort of phrase such as *terrarum* when it means everything on earth. As a substantive the verb has to make clear what noun would be supplied. *Omnia* would be possible syntactically, but not metrically.
   per orbe – not possible; but *in orbem* is.

5. Phoebe – quantity of final vowel is wrong; it should be long.
   The use of *sumo* is odd, but not impossible, I suppose.

6. Antris – wrong case; it is dative or possibly ablative.
   Either is wrong. It should be *in antros*, or better, *in antrem*.
   sanguine ore – possible, but too bloodthirsty. Reveals Dodgson, not Latin."

The poem shows little marvelous ingenuity. In fact it betrays the kind of cliches one would expect from a beginner and the kind of 'made Latin' which one would also expect from one conversant with English and with a smattering of Latin. I find no 'more exact analogies' here and only in the places mentioned in the notes above 'forms of his own devising,' but there are enough of them.

"Were the syntax and grammar correct it might not be a bad metrical trial for a young Latinist. He allows hiatus only in Verse 6 between *sanguine ore*. Elision should have occurred there. He manages the quantities of the syllables well and tries rather successfully to avoid diaeresis where a Latin poet would avoid it. Line 3 is the best where he avoids it altogether. His use of caesura is not so good, however. In Verses 1, 3, 5, it should fall after the first long of the third foot, e.g., *splendet//*, but it doesn't. It comes after *descendens* and is in collision with the diaeresis, making for too strong a pause. Verse 3 has it after *quaerunt*, i.e., after the first long of the fourth foot. This is possible and perhaps admissible. Verse 5 has it after *placidum* and it is awkward. It may have been Dodgson's intention though to put it after *sumit,* but in any event it is awkwardly managed. Verses 2, 4, 6, manage it well, for in those it has to fall in conjunction with the diaeresis, and thus tends, properly, to break the verse in two.

"For a schoolboy the exercise is not bad. I'd rate it about 'B'. If he had been composing verse for any length of time I might give him a 'C'. He should be accurate in his grammar, syntax, and metrics (in that order)."

APPENDIX C

ANGLO-SAXON LETTERS: TOOKE AND CARROLL

Reproduced from John Horne Tooke's *The Diversions of Purley* (London, 1840), p. 51. Lewis Carroll was reading this book in 1855.

Facsimile reprint of "Stanza of Anglo-Saxon Poetry" by Lewis Carroll (dated 1855), contained in the family magazine *Mischmasch*. Reproduced from Harry Morgan Ayres's *Carroll's Alice* (Columbia University Press, 1936), p. [16].

Note in particular the similarity between the 'A's' and 'T's' in Tooke's and Carroll's representations of Anglo-Saxon characters.

BIBLIOGRAPHY OF WORKS CITED

Alexander, Peter, "Logic and the Humour of Lewis Carroll", *Proceedings of the Leeds Philosophical and Literary Society*, VI (May, 1951), 551-566.

Atherton, J. S., "Lewis Carroll and *Finnegan's Wake*", *English Studies*, XXXIII (1952), 1-15.

Ayres, Harry Morgan, *Carroll's Alice* (Columbia University Press, 1936).

Boole, George, *An Investigation of the Laws of Thought* (1854) (New York, Dover Publications, n.d.).

Braithwaite, R. B., "Lewis Carroll as Logician", *Mathematical Gazette*, XVI (July, 1932), 174-178.

Carroll, Lewis [*see* Dodgson, Charles Lutwidge].

Collingwood, Stuart Dodgson, *The Lewis Carroll Picture Book* (London, T. Fisher Unwin, 1899). Reprinted by Dover Publications (New York, 1961) as *Diversions and Digressions of Lewis Carroll*.

—, *The Life and Letters of Lewis Carroll* (New York, Century, 1898).

Copi, Irving M., *Symbolic Logic* (New York, Macmillan, 1954).

Dodgson, Charles Lutwidge [Lewis Carroll], *Alice's Adventures Under Ground* (London, Macmillan, 1886).

—, *An Elementary Treatise on Determinants* (London, Macmillan, 1867).

—, *Euclid and His Modern Rivals*, 2nd ed. (London, Macmillan, 1885).

—— [Lewis Carroll], *Pillow Problems and A Tangled Tale* [4th ed.] (New York, Dover Publications, 1958).

—— [Lewis Carroll], *Symbolic Logic, Part I: Elementary*, 4th ed. (London, Macmillan, 1897).

—— [Lewis Carroll], *Symbolic Logic and The Game of Logic* (New York, Dover Publications, 1958).

—— [Lewis Carroll], *The Complete Works of Lewis Carroll* (New York, Random House [The Modern Library], 1939).

—— [Lewis Carroll], *The Diaries of Lewis Carroll*, 2 vols., ed. Roger Lancelyn Green (New York, Oxford University Press, 1954).

—— [Lewis Carroll], *The Rectory Umbrella and Mischmasch*, ed. Florence Milner (London, Cassell, 1932).

—— [Lewis Carroll], *The Russian Journal and Other Selections*, ed. John Francis McDermott (New York, E. P. Dutton, 1935).

—— [Lewis Carroll], *Useful and Instructive Poetry*, ed. Derek Hudson (New York, Macmillan, 1954).

Eperson, D. B., "Lewis Carroll – Mathematician", *Mathematical Gazette*, XVII (May, 1933), 92-100.

Fries, Charles C., *The Structure of English* (New York, Harcourt, Brace, 1952).

Gardiner, Sir Alan, *The Theory of Proper Names*, 2nd ed. (Oxford University Press, 1954).

Gardner, Martin, ed., *The Annotated Alice* (New York, Clarkson N. Potter, 1960).

Gardner, Martin, "The Games and Puzzles of Lewis Carroll", *Scientific American*, CCII (March, 1960), 172-176.

Green, Roger Lancelyn, *Lewis Carroll* (New York, Henry Z. Walck, 1962). Originally published as A Bodley Head Monograph by Roger Lancelyn Green (London, The Bodley Head, 1960).

Green, Roger Lancelyn, *The Lewis Carroll Handbook* (London, Oxford University Press, 1962).

Green, Roger Lancelyn, *The Story of Lewis Carroll* (New York, Henry Schuman, 1951).

Greenacre, Phyllis, *Swift and Carroll: A Psychoanalytic Study of Two Lives* (New York, International Universities Press, 1955).

Hargreaves, Caryl, "The Lewis Carroll that Alice Recalls", *The New York Times Magazine* (May 1, 1932), pp. 7, 15.

Hatch, Evelyn M., ed., *A Selection from the Letters of Lewis Carroll to his Child-friends* (London, Macmillan, 1933).

Hayakawa, S. I., *Language in Thought and Action* (New York, Harcourt, Brace, 1949).

Hockett, Charles F., *A Course in Modern Linguistics* (New York, Macmillan, 1958).

Holmes, Roger W., "The Philosopher's *Alice in Wonderland*", *The Antioch Review*, XIX (1959), 133-149.

Hudson, Derek, *Lewis Carroll* (London, Constable, 1954).

——, *Lewis Carroll* (= *Writers and their Work Series*, No. 96) (London, Longmans, Green, 1958).

Joyce, James, *Letters of James Joyce*, ed. Stuart Gilbert (New York, Viking Press, 1957).

Kennedy, Arthur G., "Odium Philologicum, or, A Century of Progress in English Philology", *Stanford Studies in Language and Literature*, ed. Hardin Craig (Stanford University Press, 1941), pp. 11-27.

Kirk, Daniel F., *Charles Dodgson, Semeiotician* (= *University of Florida Monographs, Humanities, No. 11* [Fall, 1962]) (Gainesville, Florida, University of Florida Press, 1963).

Lennon, Florence Becker, *The Life of Lewis Carroll* (New York, Collier Books, 1962). Second, revised edition of *Victoria Through the Looking-Glass* (New York, Simon and Schuster, 1945).

Lewis, M. M., *Language in Society* (London, Thomas Nelson and Sons, 1947).

Macdonnell, A. A., "Max Müller", article in *The Dictionary of National Biography, Supplement*, Vol. III (London, Smith, Elder, 1901), pp. 151-157.

Maynard, Theodore, "Lewis Carroll: Mathematician and Magician", *Catholic World*, CXXXV (1932), 193-201.

Mill, John Stuart, *A System of Logic, Ratiocinative and Inductive* (New York, Harper and Brothers, 1852).

Morris, Charles, *Signs, Language, and Behavior* (New York, George Braziller, 1955).

Nagel, Ernest, "Symbolic Notation, Haddocks' Eyes and the Dog-Walking Ordinance", in *The World of Mathematics*, Vol. III, ed. James R. Newman (New York, Simon and Schuster, 1956), pp. 1878-1900.

Partridge, Eric, "The Nonsense Words of Edward Lear and Lewis Carroll", in *Here, There and Everywhere* (London, Hamish Hamilton, 1950), pp. 162-188.

Reed, Langford, *The Life of Lewis Carroll* (London, W. and G. Foyle, 1932).

Robinson, Richard, *Definition* (Oxford University Press, 1950).

Ryle, Gilbert, "The Theory of Meaning", in *Philosophy and Ordinary Language*, ed. Charles E. Caton (University of Illinois Press, 1963), pp. 128-153.

Sewell, Elizabeth, *The Field of Nonsense* (London, Chatto and Windus, 1952).

Spacks, Patricia Meyer, "Logic and Language in *Through the Looking Glass*", *ETC.*, XVIII (April, 1961), 91-100.

Stewart, Dugald, *The Collected Works of Dugald Stewart*, Vol. V, ed. Sir William Hamilton (Edinburgh, Thomas Constable, 1855).

Strong, Thomas Banks, Article in *The London Times* (January 27, 1932), pp. 11, 12, 14.

——, "Lewis Carroll", *Cornhill Magazine* (March, 1898), pp. 303-310.

Taylor, Alexander L., *The White Knight* (Philadelphia, Dufour Editions, 1963). First printed 1952.

Tooke, John Horne, *The Diversions of Purley*, 3rd ed. (London, Thomas Tegg, 1840).

Van Doren, Mark, with Katherine Anne Porter and Bertrand Russell, "Lewis Carroll: *Alice in Wonderland*", in *The New Invitation to Learning* (New York, Random House, 1942), pp. 206-220.

Weaver, Warren, *Alice in Many Tongues* (University of Wisconsin Press, 1964).

——, "Lewis Carroll: Mathematician", *Scientific American*, CXCIV (April, 1956), 116-128.

Williams, Sidney H. and Falconer Madan, *A Handbook of the Literature of the Rev. C. L. Dodgson (Lewis Carroll)* (Oxford University Press, 1931). Superseded by R. L. Green, *The Lewis Carroll Handbook* (Oxford, 1962).

INDEX

abbreviation, 153, 156, 205

abstract terms, 92-93, 124-126, 160-163, 178

Alexander, Peter, 14, 105n.-106n., 137, 138, 167, 183, 184, 191, 196, 199

Alford, Henry, 47, 48

Alfred the Great, 35

ambiguity, 28, 65, 68, 85, 88, 92, 94-95, 98, 145, 146, 152, 158;
defined, 164; *contextual,* 92-94, 179-182; *homophonic,* 175-176, 197-198; *lexical,* 92; defined, 164-165; nature and functional cause, 164-166, 211; multiple definition, 166-174, 186; effect on communication-attempts, 174-175, 211; *syntactic,* 93-94, 164, 173, 175, 184, 186; 'equivocal' statements, 179-182, 211; 'equivocal' words, 164-165, 169, 170, 173, 176, 179, 184, 200, 201, 211; safeguards against, 85, 182-184; of abstract terms, 93; of comparative terms, 92-93; of function words, 92, 94, 169; of pronouns, 93-94

analogy, grammatical errors by, 54, 203-204

Anglo-Saxon Attitudes, 36

Anglo-Saxon culture, 34-38, 43, 46

Anglo-Saxon language (*see* Old English)

Arabic, 43, 44

Atherton, J. S., 152n.

baby talk, 48, 53-54, 203-204

Bacon, Sir Francis, 145

Bell, Eric Temple, 61

blends (*see* Lewis Carroll: *Language in his works*: Blends)

Boole, George, 57, 62, 64, 66, 97n.-98n., 184

Bopp, Franz, 46

Bowles, Sydney, 199

Braithwaite, R. B., 63

Butler, Olive, Ruth, and Violet, 23

Bywater, Ingram, 41

Calverley, C. S., 21

charms, verbal, 218-220

Chataway, Gertrude, 22

classification, 76-77, 78, 79, 82, 215; defined, 101-102; causes of difficulty in, 82, 106-111, 112; causes of error in, 79, 82, 102-106, 112

Collingwood, Stuart D., 16, 30, 31, 35, 36, 43, 49n., 60, 232

communication, 13, 96, 98, 111-112, 155-158, 163, 186, 188, 212, 227;
failure of: through divergent connotations between speaker and hearer, 176-177, 215-216; through divergent dialects, 55-56; through external interference, 27; through misunderstanding, 165-166, 174-178, 204-207, 211, 227; through non-understanding, 123-126, 159-163, 174, 207, 211, 227-228; through pronunciation, 204-207, 211 (*See also* Ambiguity, Conventions, linguistic (need for), Definition, Misunderstanding, Non-understanding)

comparative terms, 92-93, 176-178, 193

Compton, Henry (Bishop), as equivocator, 180, 181, 182

connotation, 118; *affective,* 72-73, 76, 90, 96, 98, 117-118, 135, 186-187, 190, 194, 210, 211, 213, 214-218; *informative,* 72-73, 76, 90, 96, 98, 115, 117, 118, 124, 135, 177-178, 190, 192, 194, 213, 214-215 (*See also* Denotation, Names, Sign, Sign-process, Signification)

content words, 91, 169, 208-210, 211, 215

context, 91-95, 144; *physical,* 93, 95, 98, 176, 179; *psychological,* 92-93, 95, 98, 176-177, 179, 181, 215-216; *situatinal,* 26-28, 145; *verbal,* 92, 95, 96, 98, 144, 165-166, 179 (*See also* Sign situation: *context of association*)

conventions, linguistic (need for), 68-69, 96, 98, 131-132, 144, 155-158, 163, 188 (*See also* Usage, conventional)
co-occurrence relations, 91, 209
Copi, Irving, 184

definition: *idiosyncratic,* defined, 146; 155, 188; *lexical,* defined, 146, 152; 146-152, 186, 190; *multiple,* 50, 57, 166-174, 175, 177; *nominal,* defined, 145-146; *stipulative,* defined, 146, 152; a safeguard against misunderstanding, 163, 183, 197; a safeguard against non-understanding, 159-163; of "Jabberwocky" words, 148-150; of words in "Stanza of Anglo-Saxon Poetry", 50-51; of 'classification' (Carroll), 101-102, 153; of 'name' (Carroll), 113-115, 117, 118, 153; of technical terms, 60, 152-154, 202
denotation, 73, 75-76, 77-78, 80-81, 82, 90, 96, 116, 118 (*See also* Connotation, Names, Sign, Sign-process, Sign situation, Signification)
derivational affixes, 84
dialects, 18, 19, 48, 53-56, 68, 169, 203, 205
Disraeli, Benjamin, 23
Diversions of Purley, The (Horne Tooke), 34, 45, 50, 145, 235
Dodgson, Charles L. (*See* Lewis Carroll)
Donne, John, 21

Earle, Beatrice, 43
Earle, John, 43, 44, 46
Early English Text Society, 48
Ellis, Henry, 36
Eperson, D. B., 59, 60, 153-154
equivocal words (*See under* Ambiguity)
equivocation, 179-182, 218
etymology, 33-34, 36, 38, 43, 45, 48, 50-52, 66, 68, 149-151
euphemism, 190, 216-218

Finnegan's Wake (Joyce), 152, 204
Fries, Charles C., 208
function words, 91, 93-94, 169, 209-210, 215

Gaisford, Thomas, 41-42
Gandell, Robert, 43, 44
Gardiner, Sir Alan, 130, 141
Gardner, Martin, 59n., 119, 134, 137n.
General Semanticists, 98, 118, 123
Gilbert, W. S., 21
Gladstone, William E., 23, 229
Goldsmith, Oliver, 162n.
Green, Roger Lancelyn, 16-17, 30n., 53, 57, 58, 229

Greenacre, Phyllis, 16n.
Gulliver's Travels (Swift), 112n.

Haigh, Daniel Henry, 37, 46
Hargreaves, Caryl, 97
Harris, James, 45, 46
Hatch, Ethel, 179
Hatch, Evelyn M., 16, 179, 182
Hayakawa, S. I., 123
Hobbes, Thomas, 46, 56
Hockett, Charles F., 208-209
Holmes, Roger W., 120n., 155n.
homophones, 22, 165, 175-176, 179, 197-198
Hood, Thomas, 21, 49
Horne Tooke (*See* Tooke, John Horne)
Hornsby, Roger A., 30, 232-234
Hudson, Derek, 16, 54, 183, 229
Hull, Agnes, 22

idiom, 184, 186, 193, 195, 196-197, 201, 211-212
import: defined, 90, 185; *idiomatic,* defined, 186; 187, 188, 193; *intended,* defined, 186; 187, 188-189, 192, 201, 208, 211; *literal,* defined, 186; 187, 188-189, 191-194, 210-211; of names, 142-143; of statements, 181, 184; *logical,* 179, 189, 193, 212; equivalence in statements of divergent literal imports, 189-191, 212; *potential,* 187, 201, 210, 211; *received,* defined, 186; 187, 188, 211; divergence of intended and received import, 66, 92, 171-172, 175-176, 186, 187, 201, 215-216; divergence of intended and literal import, 66, 184, 191-201, 215-216; divergence of literal and idiomatic import, 186, 187, 193, 194-198, 201 (*See also* Signification)
Indo-European philology, 43, 44, 45, 48, 66
inflection markers, 37, 84, 91, 209-210
Ingram, James, 47
intonation contour, 84, 86, 91, 94, 169-170, 206

"Jabberwocky" words (*See* Lewis Carroll: *Language in his works:* Blends)
jargon, 153
Jelf, W. E., 41
Johnson, Samuel, 46
Jones, Sir William, 45-46
Jowett, Benjamin, 24, 42-43, 45, 229
Joyce, James, 152, 204
juncture, 84, 85, 91, 197, 205-206, 211
Junius Manuscript, 36

Kemble, John Mitchell, 47
Kenealy, Edward V., 23

Kennedy, Arthur G., 47
Kirk, Daniel F., 14, 17, 49, 59n., 105, 106, 123-124
Korzybski, Alfred, 123

Lamb, Charles, 21
Lear, Edward, 21, 22, 25, 150, 151n.-152n.
Lennon, Florence Becker, 16n., 31, 40, 57n., 59n., 61
levels of interpretation, 83, 84, 88, 95, 185
Lewis, M. M., 219
Lewis Carroll

Life:

acquaintance with linguistic scholars, 41-46, 66; antiquarian interest, 34-35, 36, 48-50; as logician, 26, 56, 58, 61-66, 68, 100, 153-154, 179, 184; as mathematician, 26, 58-61, 66, 68, 152-154; biographies, 16, 41; competence in Greek and Latin, 32-33, 52, 232-234; concern with people's grammar, 19, 47, 202-203; conservatism, 14, 42, 47, 61, 64, 66; correspondence with child-friends, 19, 25, 55; diaries, 16-17, 32, 33-34, 41, 57-58; difficulties with Classics, 30, 31, 32-33, 232-234; family magazines, 18, 26, 35, 48, 103-104, 206; Gothic language, 33, 34, 38; Hebrew language, 38; his father, 29, 30, 31; literary works, 18-19, 48, 229-231; logic in his literary works, 13, 27, 65; Mathematical Lecturer, 31, 57, 58; non-systematic as linguist, 19-20, 26, 69-70, 226; Old English language, 33, 34, 35-38, 43; Oxford satires, 19, 25, 32, 42, 230; play with language: 18-19, 69, 227; *manipulatory,* 21-26, 227; *functional,* 26-28, 227; pseudonyms, 23, 26, 48; publications, 17-19, 26, 48, 58-60, 62-63, 229-231; reading in books concerned with language, 50, 56-58, 66; reading of J. S. Mill's *Logic,* 33, 56, 66; Richmond Grammar School, 29-30, 202, 232; Rugby, 30; Russian trip, 31-32, 38-39, 40, 216-217; study and competence in modern languages: *French,* 33, 38-40, 52, 66, 216; *German,* 33, 38-40, 52, 66; *Italian,* 33, 38, 40; *Russian,* 39, 40; Sub-Librarian at Christ Church, 31, 58; technical works, 14, 18, 59-60, 64, 100, 152-154, 202, 229-231; undergraduate years (Oxford), 17, 31, 34, 58

Language in his works:

acrostics, 23-24; alliteration, 24; alphabet games, 23, 25; anagrams, 23, 24; arbitrary nature of word-meanings, 13, 57, 97-98, 154-158, 163; blends, 13, 149-152, 204, 205, 209-210; changes between *Under Ground* and *Wonderland,* 25, 55, 109, 172-174, 180, 217; communication-failure, 13, 19, 27, 55, 212, 227-228; cryptograms, 23; definition of 'classification', 100-102, 153; definition of 'name', 113-115, 117, 118, 153; depiction of baby talk, 48, 53-54, 203-204; depiction of dialects, 18, 19, 24, 47-48, 49, 53-56, 203, 205; dialogues (fictional), 27, 55, 212, 227-228; emblematic verse, 25, 176; equivocation to deceive, 179-182, 218; etymology, 33-34, 36, 38, 43, 50-52, 66, 68, 149-151, 200, 202, 206; explicit statements on language, 15, 19, 96-99, 100-102, 113-115, 141, 154, 155, 157, 177, 202, 206, 210, 214, 219, 226-227; his monitoring translations of his works, 39-40, 40n.; imitation of archaic writings, 18, 48-49; "import of propositions", 66, 154, 157; innovations in spelling, 202; "Jabberwocky" words (*See above,* Blends); letters (personal), 16, 19, 25, 55; lexical definition, 146-152; mirror-image writing, 25; "most words ambiguous", 97-98, 164, 166, 177; neologisms, 14, 24-25, 47, 50-51, 148-152, 153, 202-204, 208-210; parodies, 19, 24, 49, 125-126, 146-147; picture-writing, 21; portmanteau words (*See above,* Blends); precision in defining technical terms, 18, 60, 100, 152-154, 202; precision in usage, 19, 47, 54, 60, 65, 202-203; proper names, 115-117, 130-132, 136-142; puns, 13, 18-19, 22, 24-25, 36-37, 39, 52n., 166, 170-172, 194; relation of words to things, 65, 96, 132-136; reticence in making linguistic statements, 5, 15, 70, 73, 96; reversed word-order writing, 24-25; style in writing, 47-48, 55, 172; verse disguised as prose, 25; word magic, 19, 28, 66, 147, 157, 213-225

Works:

Alice's Adventures in Wonderland, 18, 26, 39, 40, 55, 64, 65, 100, 105, 109, 133n., 172-174, 180, 211-212, 217, 229, 231
Alice's Adventures under Ground, 18, 25, 26, 35, 55, 109, 133n., 172-173, 180, 217, 231
"Alice's Evidence", 39
"Alphabet Cipher, The", 23
"Angler's Adventure, The", 103-104
"Blank Cheque, The", 19, 230
"Deserted Parks, The", 19

Diaries of Lewis Carroll, The (ed. R. L. Green), 16-17, 30n., 32, 57

Doublets, 23, 43, 44, 230

"Dynamics of a Parti-cle, The", 19, 25, 33, 52n., 229, 230

Eight or Nine Wise Words about Letter-Writing, 19, 177, 182-183, 231

"Elections to the Hebdomadal Council, The", 19

Elementary Treatise on Determinants, An, 59, 153, 229

"Eternal Punishment", 52

Euclid and His Modern Rivals, 34n., 59-60, 154, 200-201, 230

"Examination Statute", 23-24

Formulae of Plane Trigonometry, The, 59, 153, 229

Game of Logic, The, 62, 96, 97, 231

"Hiawatha's Photographing", 25

Hunting of the Snark, The, 18, 43, 77, 104-105, 130-132, 133n., 149, 151, 219-220, 230

"Jabberwocky", 13, 24, 25, 30, 35-36, 43, 148-152, 208-210, 211

"Lang Coortin', The", 54

Legend of Scotland, The, 48

Letters to Child-friends (ed. Evelyn M. Hatch), 16, 22, 23, 25, 27

"Mischmasch" (family magazine), 35, 149, 229, 235

Mischmasch (game), 23, 230

"Mouse's Tale, The", 25, 39, 175-176

"New Belfry, The", 19, 25, 51, 230

"New Method of Evaluation as Applied to π, The", 19, 25, 42, 229, 230

Notes by an Oxford Chiel, 25, 230

Notes on Euclid, 153, 229

"Novelty and Romancement", 55, 217

"Offer of the Clarendon Trustees, The", 19

Phantasmagoria, 24, 221, 230

"Photographer's Day Out, A", 55

Pillow-Problems, 60, 231

"Professorship of Comparative Philology, The", 44-45, 230

"Quotation from Shakespeare with slight improvements", 146-147, 224

"Rectory Umbrella, The", 35, 206, 229

Russian Journal, The (ed. John F. McDermott), 16, 31-32, 39, 55, 216-217

"Stage and the Spirit of Reverence, The", 97, 155

"Stanza of Anglo-Saxon Poetry", 35, 49, 50-51, 57, 149, 150, 235

Syllabus of Plane Algebraical Geometry, A., 59, 229

Sylvie and Bruno, 18, 22, 26, 53, 54, 55, 133n., 151, 168, 171, 231; puns in, 18-19, 170-172, 212

Sylvie and Bruno Concluded, 18, 24, 55, 202, 231

Symbolic Logic, Part I: Elementary, 62-64, 96, 97, 98, 100-101, 113-115, 117, 139, 153, 157, 219, 231

Syzygies, 23, 231

Tangled Tale, A, 19, 24, 55, 151, 164, 202, 205, 206, 222, 230-231

"Telegraph Cipher, The", 23

"Three Voices, The", 125-126, 162-163, 223n.

Through the Looking-Glass, 18, 25, 35, 50, 55, 65, 97, 133n., 149, 151, 154, 171, 211-212, 230; names in, 137-138; definition of "Jabberwocky" words, 50, 148-149

"Two Brothers, The", 49

Useful and Instructive Poetry (ed. Derek Hudson), 103-104, 146-147, 229

"Vision of the Three T's, The", 19, 25, 33, 48, 54, 222, 223, 230

"Walking-Stick of Destiny, The", 206

"Wandering Burgess, The", 54-55

"What the Tortoise Said to Achilles", 62, 231

"Wilhelm Von Schmitz", 24, 55, 205

"Ye Carpette Knyghte", 49

"Ye Fatalle Cheyse", 49, 52

Fictional characters: 37, 48, 137-138

Alice, 24, 37, 54, 68, 76-77, 78, 79-82, 87-88, 89, 100, 102, 103, 105, 106-111, 112, 119-122, 123-124, 126-128, 129, 130, 132-144, 145, 148-149, 154-156, 158, 159-160, 166-167, 168, 168-170, 172-173, 175-176, 177, 180, 185, 188-189, 191-193, 195-197, 199, 202-203, 207, 208-210, 211-212, 215, 217-218, 220-221, 224

Anglo-Saxon Messengers, 36-38, 137-138, 197, 199

Arthur Forester, 124, 127, 151, 161-162, 178, 223

Baker, The, 130-132, 133n., 219-220

Baron Muggzwig ("Walking-Stick of Destiny"), 206-207, 211

Bellman, The, 77-78, 81, 104, 219, 220

Boojum, The, 105, 111, 219

Bruno, 24, 48, 53, 54, 103, 133n., 152, 167-169, 171n., 179, 189-190, 193, 197-198, 211, 218, 226; grammatical errors by analogy, 54, 203-204

Caterpillar, The, 105, 109, 133n.

Cheshire Cat, The, 87-88, 127

Dodo, The, 159, 223

Dormouse, The, 24, 192-193
Duchess, The, 13, 108, 185, 187-190, 206-207, 210-212
Duck, The, 172-174, 179
Eaglet, The, 159, 223
Fawn, The, 133-136, 138, 215
Fish-Footman, The, 78, 81, 102, 106, 112
Gnat, The, 129, 130, 132, 133n., 138, 143, 145
Gryphon, The, 24, 25, 55, 199
Haigha, 36-38, 137-138
Hatta, 36-38, 137-138
Humpty Dumpty, 13, 50, 76-77, 81, 89. 97, 107-108, 110, 112, 136-141, 169-170, 187, 196-197, 209-210, 221; definitions of Jabberwocky" words, 148-149, 150; arbitrary nature of word-meanings, 154-158
King of Hearts, The, 78, 81, 102, 105-106, 112, 127-128, 145, 175-176, 199
Live Flowers, The, 103, 143
Looking-Glass Insects, 143-144
Lord Chancellor, The (Sylvie and Bruno), 167, 171-172, 194, 216
Mad Hatter, The, 36, 37, 105-106, 112, 168, 175-176, 192-193, 203, 211
Mad Mathesis (Tangled Tale), 164, 205
March Hare, The, 36, 168, 192-193
Mock Turtle, The, 25, 199
Mouse, The, 35, 172-174, 175-176, 179, 217-218
My Lady (Sylvie and Bruno), 94, 169, 170, 171, 216
Nobody, 199-201
Pig-Baby, The, 108-109, 110
Pigeon, The, 105, 106, 106n.
Professor, The, 103, 133n., 170-171, 189-190, 193-194, 204, 207, 211
Pudding, The, 137
Queen of Hearts, The, 74-76, 78, 81, 102, 107, 111, 123, 126, 180, 181
Red Queen, The, 103, 128, 133n., 137, 139, 177-178, 195-196, 224
Sheep, The, 13, 16, 109-110, 138, 159-160
Sylvie, 53, 54, 133n., 167, 171n., 189-190, 193, 197-198, 202-203, 204, 226
Tiger-lily, The, 103, 138
Tweedledum (-dee), 79-81, 82, 120-121, 122, 127, 128, 137-138, 190-191
Vice-Warden, The (Sylvie and Bruno), 94, 122, 169, 170, 171
White King, The, 36, 54, 127-128, 137, 196, 197, 199
White Knight, The, 119-120, 138, 166-167, 172, 187, 196
White Queen, The, 50, 54, 133n., 195, 224
White Rabbit, The, 55, 126, 127

Lewis Carroll Handbook, The (ed. R. L. Green), 17, 58, 229
Liddell, Alice, 24, 26, 42, 96-97
Liddell, Henry George (Dean), 24, 42, 43, 46, 52, 230
Liddon, H. P., 31, 38, 40
Life and Letters of Lewis Carroll, The (S. D. Collingwood), 16, 29-30, 232
linguistic code, 69, 82, 83-85, 88, 90, 95; functional contrast of elements in, 85-86, 87, 95
Locke, John, 46, 56
logical discourse, 65, 68-69, 183-184, 194-195
Longfellow, Henry W., 25, 49
Lowrie Children, the, 97

Macauley, Thomas B., 49, 180
Macdonnell, A. A., 45
Madan, Falconer, 229, 230
maps, 77-78, 122-123
"maps without territories", 123, 124, 160
Maynard, Theodore, 59n.
McDermott, John Francis, 16, 32n., 39
meaning: contextual, 85, 87, 91-95, 144; differential, 85-89, 90, 95, 170; referential, 85, 87, 89-90, 92, 95-96, 117, 169, 208-210, 216; structural, 85, 87, 90-91, 92, 94, 95, 169, 208-210 (See also Import)
message (of utterance) (See Import)
metalanguage, 119-120
metaphor, 65, 69, 184, 195-198, 211-212
Mill, John Stuart, 33, 56-57, 62, 64, 65, 66, 100, 115-117, 118, 124n.-125n., 139, 141, 165
Milner, Florence, 206n., 229
minimal pair, 87
misunderstanding, 85, 98, 158, 160, 192, 196-198, 210-212, 213; through ambiguity, 165-166, 174-178, 179
modal auxiliaries, 91
Monboddo, Lord, 45, 46
Monier-Williams, Ella, 44, 180-182
Monier-Williams, Sir Monier, 43, 44, 46
Moon, George Washington, 47, 48
Moore, Thomas, 49
morph, 84, 85, 87, 89
morpheme, 84, 85, 87, 89, 90-91
Morris, Charles, 73n.
Müller, Friedrich Max, 43, 44-46, 230

Nagel, Ernest, 119, 120n.
names, 56, 65, 100, 106, 110; defined, 113-115; as indexical signs, 118, 133; as labels, 118-121, 122-123, 126, 131, 141, 145; as linguistic signs, 117; act of naming, 78-79, 102, 112, 113; denotation, 116, 118,

136; designative function, 96, 116-118, 119-121, 135, 212; identifying function, 115, 117, 118-121, 128-132, 135; informative function, 90, 115, 117-118, 121-122, 132-144; symbolic status, 114, 117, 118-119, 120, 214, 215, 216; inaccurate in designation, 122-123, 126-128; without designative signification, 123-126, 147, 220, 222; usefulness of, 111-112, 113, 129, 132-133, 135, 145; relationship to thing named, 132-136, 178, 215, 218; loss of name, 117, 130, 133n., 130-136; types: *"connotative"*, 116, 116n., 118; *general*: 115, 116, 132ff, 215; as indexical signs, 128-129, 130, 132, 137-138; descriptive, 142-144; meaning conveyed by, 90, 142-144; *proper* (personal): 96, 115, 116-117, 129, 130-132, 133ff; in *Through the Looking-Glass,* 137-142; meaning conveyed by, 136-142; *provisional,* 113, 121 (*See also* Classification)

Nightingale, Florence, 23

Nonsense (literary), 13, 14, 22

non-understanding,   123-126,   210-212; through ambiguity, 174; through unfamiliarity with terms used, 159-160, 161-162, 211; through vagueness, 160-163, 227

null class: defined, 198; existential treatment of, 198-201

Odyssey (Homer), 201

Old English, 33, 34-38, 41, 43, 44

"one word-one meaning fallacy", 98

ordinary discourse, 65, 68-69, 183-184, 188, 194-195

Orwell, George, 123

Oxford (New) English Dictionary, 48, 50, 152

Partridge, Eric, 25, 150, 151 (notes 2 and 4)

Pattison, Mark, 41

phone, 83-84, 85, 86, 89, 212

phoneme, 84, 85, 86-89

phone-type (*See* Phoneme)

pitch, 85

portmanteau words (*See* Lewis Carroll: *Language in his works:* Blends)

Positivism, Logical, 191

pronouns, 39, 91, 93-94, 173-174, 179

pronunciation: Bruno's deviations from standard usage, 54, 203-204; as a hindrance to communication, 204-207, 211

puns, 39, 166 (*See also* Lewis Carroll: *Language in his works:* Puns)

Pusey, E. B., 29, 31

"Queen's English" controversy, 47-48

recognition value (of linguistic sign-vehicles) (*See* Sign situation: *sign-vehicle*)

Reed, Langford, 16n.

Rix, Edith, 97, 154, 157

Robinson, Richard, 14, 156, 157-158

Russell, Bertrand, 64-65

Ryle, Gilbert, 64

Sanskrit, 41, 43, 44, 46

Scott, Robert, 42, 43, 45, 46

Scott, Sir Walter, 48, 49, 50, 56

Sewell, Elizabeth, 14, 21-22, 25, 151n.-152n.

Shakespeare, William, 21, 113, 146-147, 224

sign: defined, 71, 73n., 102; *indexical,* 79-80, 82, 96, 112, 118, 132; *linguistic,* 13, 83-96; *non-linguistic,* 122-123 (*See also* Sign-process, Sign situation, Signification)

sign-process, 73n.; linguistic, 73, 82, 83-85, 88, 113, 187; non-linguistic, 73, 79, 81, 113 (*See also* Sign, Sign situation, Signification)

sign situation: components of: 71-72, 73n., 82; *act of interpretation,* 71-72, 77; linguistic, 84, 187; *association object,* 72, 82, 86, 89, 95-96, 115, 117, 118, 160; *context of association,* 72, 85, 90, 91-95, 142, 169, 210; *conventions of interpretation,* 96, 98, 163; *interpreter,* 71-72, 82; of linguistic signs, 84-85, 187, 210-212; *sign,* 71-72, 77, 78, 82, 88-89, 185, 187; *sign-vehicle,* 71-72, 74-75, 77, 78, 82, 187; linguistic, 83-84, 88-89, 92, 96, 185; recognition value of, 85-86, 88-89, 95; functional contrast of, 85, 88, 95 (*See also* Sign, Sign-process, Signification)

signification: defined, 72-73, 76, 78, 80-81, 82; linguistic, 34, 83-85, 89-90; designative, 66, 90, 117-118, 212; denotation, 73, 75-76, 77-78, 80-81, 82, 90, 96, 116, 118 (*See also* Connotation, Definition, Denotation, Import, Names, Sign, Sign-process, Sign situation)

Spacks, Patricia Meyer, 14, 155n.

Spencer, Herbert, 161-162

Standen, Maud, 40, 150

Sterne, Laurence, 21

Stewart, Dugald, 33, 56-57, 66

stress, 85, 169-170, 202

Strong, Thomas Banks, 63-64, 96

Swift, Jonathan, 21, 112n.

Swinburne, Algernon, 21, 24, 49

symbols, 21, 28, 89, 97n.-98n., 114, 116, 117, 118, 165, 227

syntactic structures, 13, 69, 84, 85, 87-88, 89-90, 91, 94-95, 172-174, 179, 186, 188-189, 206-207, 208-210, 211-212

Tasso, Torquato, 38

Tate, Headmaster of Richmond Grammar School, 29-30, 202, 232

Taylor, Alexander L., 16n., 151n.

Tenniel, Sir John, 17, 36, 108, 112, 139, 143

Tennyson, Alfred, 49, 125

Thackeray, William M., 21

Thorpe, Benamin, 47

Tooke, John Horne, 33, 34, 45, 46, 48, 50, 56-57, 66, 145, 235

Trench, Richard C., 33, 50, 56-57, 66

Tristram, Thomas, 41

Turner, Sharon, 37

usage, conventional, 13, 28, 47-48, 65, 68-69, 146, 152, 157, 158, 163, 187-188, 192, 193, 195, 198, 203, 210-212

vagueness, 65, 68, 124-126, 146, 152, 158, 160-163, 179, 184, 186, 201, 211

Van Doren, Mark, 64, 65

Vicar of Wakefield, The (Goldsmith), 162n.

Walton, Isaak, 48

Watts, Isaac, 49

Weaver, Warren, 40n., 59n., 61, 64

Webster's Third New International Dictionary, 152

Wilde, Oscar, 21

William the Conqueror, 35, 172-173

Williams, Sidney H., 229, 230

Williams, Ella Monier (See Monier-Williams, Ella)

Williams, Sir Monier Monier (See Monier-Williams, Sir Monier)

word magic, 19, 147, 157; charms, 218, 219-220; euphemism, 216-218; foreign words and phrases, 222-223; ritual repetition, 219-221; sound, 213, 218, 220-221, 222-223; sovereignty of the word, 28, 66, 147-148, 157, 213-214, 218-225; supernatural powers of words, 213, 218, 225; therapeutic powers of words, 214, 220; unusual or long words, 127, 161, 213, 221, 222-223 (See also Connotation: affective)

word order, 24, 91, 208-210 (See also Syntactic structures)

Wordsworth, William, 49

Wright, Thomas, 47

Yates, Edmund, 23

Yonge, Charlotte, 180, 181, 182

Zimmerman, Antoine, 39

JANUA LINGUARUM

STUDIA MEMORIAE NICOLAI VAN WIJK DEDICATA

Edited by C. H. van Schooneveld

SERIES MAIOR

2. Dean Stoddard Worth, *Kamchadal Texts Collceted by W. Jochelson*. 1961. 284 pp.
f 75,—/$ 21.40

3. Peter Hartmann, *Theory der Grammatik*. 1963. 552 pp.   f 108,—/$ 30.90

8. Thomas A. Sebeok and Valdis Zep, *Concordance and Thesaurus of Cheremic Poetic Language*. 1961. 259 pp.   f 75,—/$ 21.40

9. Gustav Herdan, *The Calculus of Linguistic Observations*. 1962. 271 pp., 6 figs., 43 tables.   f 54,—/$ 15.45

11. Werner Winter (ed), *Evidence for Laryngeals*. 1965. 271 pp.   f 50,—/$ 14.30

12. Horace G. Lunt (ed.), *Proceedings of the Ninth International Congress of Linguists. Cambridge. Mass., August 27-31, 1962*. 1964. 1196 pp., plate.   f 150,—/$ 42.00

13. N. I. Žinkin, *Mechanism of Speech*. Translated from the Russian. 1968. 475 pp., many figs.   f 96,—/$ 27.50

14. Ruth Hirsch Weir, *Language in the Crib*. 1970. Second printing, 216 pp.
f 38,—/$ 10.75

15. Thomas A. Sebeok et al. (eds.), *Approaches to Semiotics: Cultural Anthropology, Education, Linguistics, Psychiatry, Psychology*. 1964. 294 pp.   f 40,—/$ 11.45

16. A. Rosetti, *Linguistica*. 1965. 268 pp.   f 65,—/$ 18.60

17. D. P. Blok (ed.), *Proceedings of the Eight International Congress of Onomastic Sciences, Amsterdam, 1963*. 1966. 667 pp., 23 figs., 2 plates   f 120,—/$ 34.30

18. Pierre Delattre, *Studies in French and Comparative Phonetics: Selected Papers in*

French and English. 1966. 286 pp., 2 tables, 35 figs.   f 53,—/$ 15.25

19. Jesse Levitt, *The "Grammaire des Grammaires" of Girault-Duvivier*. 1968. 338 pp.

                                                              f 64,—/$ 18.30

20. William Bright (ed), *Sociolinguistics: Papers of the UCLA conference on Sociolinguistics*. 1966. 324 pp., figs.   f 57,—/$ 16.30

21. Joshua A. Fishman et al. (eds.), *Language Loyalty in the United States: The Maintenance and Perpetuation of Non-English Mother Tongues by American Ethnic and*

Religious Groups. 1966. 478 pp., figs, tables.   f 69,—/$ 19.75

22. Allan H. Orrick, *Nordica et Anglica: Studies in Honor of Stefán Einarsson*. 1968. 196

pp. 8 ills.   f 50,—/$ 14.30

23. Ruth Crymes, *Some Systems of Substitution Correlations in Modern American English*. 1968. 187 pp.   f 34,—/$ 9.75

24. Kenneth L. Pike, *Language in Relation to a Unified Theory of the Structure of Human Behavior*. Second, revised edition. 1967. 762 pp.   f 72,—/$ 20.60

25. William Austin (ed.), *Papers in Linguistics in Honor of Léon Dostert*. 1967. 180 pp.   f 34,—/$ 9.75

30. Jitka Štindlova, *Les machines dans la linguistique: colloque international sur la mécanisation et l'automation des recherches linguistiques*. 1968. 336 pp.   f 66,—/$ 18.90

29. Victor Egon Hanzeli, *Missionary Linguistics in New France: A Study of Seventeenth- and Eighteenth-Century Descriptions of American Indian Languages*. 1969. 141 pp. Ilustrations.   f 42,—/$ 12.00

31-33. *To Honor Roman Jakobson: Essays on the Occasion of his 70th Birthday, 11 October 1966*. 3 vols. 1967. 2464 pp.   f 450,—/$ 125.00

34. J. C. Heesterman *et al.* (eds.), *Pratidānam: Indian, Iranian, and Indo-European Studies Presented to Franciscus Bernardus Jacobus Kuipers on his 60th Birthday*. 1968. 654 pp., plates   f 160,—/$ 45.45

36. Herbert E. Brekle und Leonhard Lipka, *Wortbildung, Syntax und Morphologie: Festschrift zum 60. Geburtstag von Haus Marchand*. 1968. 250 pp.   f 75,—/$ 21.40

37. Rudolf P. Botha, *The Function of the Lexicon in Transformational Generative Grammar*. 1968. 368 pp.   f 52,—/$ 14.85

MOUTON · PUBLISHERS · THE HAGUE